The Cherry Jumpers

For All The Saints

First published in 2013 by Mercer Books
www.mercerbooks.co.uk

ISBN 978-0-9557127-6-0

A CIP catalogue record for this book is available from The British Library

Design by Reuben Wakeman
Printed in the UK by Butler Tanner & Dennis, Frome

The Cherry Jumpers

For All The Saints

by Christopher Bird

Sancto Cuique Sua Candela

Contents

All Hallows, Cranmore, celebrates its seventy-fifth year with the publication of this informative and diverting book. Like all good histories, it is well supported by documentary and archival evidence, not least the telling anecdote.

The Communion of the Saints is one of the most heartening of Christian teachings. The way in which the living and the dead form one community with the Risen Christ is a humbling and inspiring ideal. We are not called to solitude, but to true community in Christ. We may not yet be 'all saints', 'all hallows', but we are, we hope, on a journey of discovery which will make sense of our lives.

All Hallows school has had its ups and downs, its changes and developments, its saints and its sinners, but its dedication always calls the place back to its core mission. Education, good education, is about the whole person, leading to what we might call holiness, and All Hallows has been informed by this high ideal. Every past pupil of the school will find something in this history to refresh memories and to remind them of familiar names and shared experiences.

Former students of any school have their own personal perspective on their schooldays, but Chris Bird has managed to capture the special genius of a school which has contributed so much to the educational life of the county and country.

Dom Aidan Bellenger
Abbot of Downside

Preface

When the School Governors approached me with the commission to write the history of All Hallows – to commemorate the school's 75th birthday - I was pleased to take on the task since the school has meant a great deal to me over the years in my own professional formation. Equally, I felt reasonably qualified to be able to present a passably accurate summary of key points in that story since, at the time of writing, I have enjoyed over thirty years' association with All Hallows in what might fairly be described as three different guises and, in that time, I have taken a keen interest in the school's history, fully aware of my responsibilities in attempting to maintain the tradition of excellence, and even adding a chapter or two myself. A written history of an institution of only 75 years' standing is not, perhaps, likely to delve too deeply into the fascinating mores of other ages far back in time. After all, even the oldest surviving former pupil today might still be vibrantly living a life well led in his late eighties. And Richard Arnold-Jones, one of the early teachers is still an interesting 91-year-old (the same age as prince Philip, he tells me) albeit a little careful on his feet. And yet, apart from this record being important to the life of the school and the lives of those who have passed through the gates, there is something specific, perhaps, about the last 75 years, some special characteristics not belonging to any other age. The last seventy-five years have seen developments in lifestyle, technology, communication, achievement and, of course, education, like few comparable 75 year periods in history; not that I am making any claims for such growth to be all for the good. All Hallows is, of course, an institution but, like all schools, its life is generated by the people in it and one hopes that the following pages record something of that life through the spirit of the age and the spirits of the past, as well as through the lives of the present incumbents. Such an undertaking, however, could not have been completed without access to surviving documentation in the form of chronicles, school records and lists, letters and various other notes, as well as, of course, being able to draw on the many oral and written memories of so many former pupils, teachers, parents, governors and other associated sources who willingly gave up their time in providing a rich array of anecdotal and factual information. My thanks are duly noted to all who have provided such useful information. It is a fascinating and engaging story. Head Boy Larry O'Callaghan (F.P. 1943-1949) wrote in 1949 that to *tell the history of Scorhill would fill a book...*" as he presented his version of the school's time on Dartmoor, followed by its move to Somerset; the stories hereafter attempt to fill that book which Larry anticipated so correctly over sixty years ago. And Larry O'Callaghan knew a thing or two, for we read in December 1947 that, in one of the regular Pack matches, his team, Wolves, won the football trophy with *"the winning goal scored by O'Callaghan who also made a brief appearance in goal and stopped a penalty kick"*.

There can't be many Boy's Own heroes out there who can score winning goals and save penalties in the same match[1] and, oh, just for good measure, he also scored 90% in a Greek Common Entrance paper.

I have endeavoured to reproduce such testimonies in as faithful a manner as possible; my apologies in advance for any errors or inaccuracies. Like the writer of the Editorial Note in the First Edition of the All Hallows Chronicle of 1942, I "have had to trust to memory for most of the events recorded in these pages. There are probably some inaccuracies; there are certainly many omissions. For these we beg pardon." Well, I have had to trust to memory for some years and also rely on the written or spoken testimony of others, some of which is directly conflicting, and some of which interprets characters and motivation rather differently depending on points of view and personal experiences. I have tried, therefore, to be fair, and, in cases of doubt, I have erred on the side of generosity, especially when people are no longer alive to present their own story.

Larry O'Callaghan finished his schoolboy article by saying that *"to be at All Hallows, no matter where it is situated, is a blessing to any boy. You could not ask for better education or greater justice, you could not find a friendlier family atmosphere anywhere, and to gain the full benefits of All Hallows, it remains for you to do your best in everything"*. Now it is quite possible that not every boy or girl will hold similarly affectionate memories of the school but I think that Francis Dix, the school's founder, would have been happy with that accolade as a summation of what he was trying to achieve. Whether or not the reader of this book will be able to sense something of those happy days remains to be seen but these words in the following story, in that All Hallows' tradition, represent the best I have been able to produce.

After this Preface and a short Introduction, the book is separated into chapter sections that broadly fall into the years of the different Headmasters. Readers should note that the largest portion is given over to Francis Dix, partly as a reflection on the number of years he was connected to the school and partly because he was the Founder with three different locations for the writer to consider. The years of Messrs Mortimer, Ketterer, Bird and Murphy are given approximately equal weighting, not because they were equal in years (Alistair Mortimer was Headmaster for seven years and Paul Ketterer, twenty-four years) nor because they were equal in importance in the story of the school but, rather, because one was able to flesh out within each section sufficient commentary on other broader issues that effectively created a better balance to the scheme of this book. Furthermore, as will become obvious, the footnotes provide fairly extensive comments of variable length which often account for substantial pages within a particular section. Following the main sections of the book, there are some brief concluding remarks and some seventeen pages of Appendices that offer selected lists of interest and record.

---

[1] I'm thinking of images of Wilson the Wonder Athlete, the comic star character from *The Wizard* in 1943, who jumped out of the crowd to run the mile in three minutes which is, of course, perfectly possible in a comic-strip

A former Abbot Primate of the Benedictine Confederation, Marcel Rooney, wrote in 1998, that *"chronological time can be converted into a kairos – a saving moment – which makes us enter into the eternal 'time' of God for the praise of God's glory"*. He was referring to how prayer can work through the Liturgy of the Hours but, perhaps, one might be allowed to consider the records of the following pages to be similar 'saving moments' in praise of the school story in the context of God's glory.

And if that is a little too grandiose a spiritual plane, we could recall the words of Simone de Beauvoir whose insight reminds us of the human dimension in our attempts to make sense of what happens on this earth: *"Our lives are stories we tell ourselves until they become true"*.

Christopher Bird
An All Hallows Schoolmaster 1980-1985; 1995-2013

Introduction

"For All the Saints/who from their labours rest"[2]

"We stood on Exeter platform, musing[3]. *We had just seen off the last of the boys for their summer holidays. Six of them would return to Scorhill no more except as 'Old Boys'. It was our first big leave and, as our thoughts passed from one incident to another in these early years of the school's history, we decided then and there that the time had come to put some record of them on paper. Thus was born THE ALL HALLOWS CHRONICLE".*

---

[2] By the way, when I key in '*For All the Saints*' on my computer, all my scribbled notes come up translated into text and sandwiched between '*Finnegan's Wake*' and '*Four Quartets*'. For those of you who know your Joyce and your T.S.Eliot you might make your own literary connections and wonder whether the following pages might become worthy of such literary association; for those of you who don't, that's fine, the pages that follow might simply reinforce the fonder idea that "We're all mad here".

[3] Two points of interest related to reading and writing: (a) if one googles in 'A Musing Platform' today one is sent an invitation to blog – which is the modern way to keep a diary or chronicle (b) Francis and Evelyn Dix were not the only known people to have mused on an Exeter platform in the 1930s for it is said that Allen Lane, the founder of Penguin Books, also stood there in 1935, lamenting the fact that there was no decent reading material available so he decided to publish his own range; the first Penguin book to be published in this way was "*Ariel*" by Andre Maurois and it was sold by way of a vending machine at Charing Cross for the cost of a packet of cigarettes.

So it was that Francis Dix, founder of All Hallows Preparatory School, began his written record of the school, as he stood with his wife, Evelyn, waving goodbye to the first cohort of leaving pupils whose early lives had been moulded by their guiding hands. That early chronicle was begun in 1942 and, today, in 2013, the All Hallows Chronicle continues to be written every year as a record of school events. But we need to travel just a little further back in time and to another place to record the very beginning of the school. The year is 1938; the location, East Sussex, Bognor Regis, and, specifically 16 Sylvan Way, where a sherry party is underway with Mr and Mrs Dix and perhaps a few interested parents and friends, and just one boy named Alan Woodgates. Quite what Alan Woodgates thought of it all is not recorded. Perhaps he was playing in the garden. Perhaps he was an early prototype of Betjeman's reluctant schoolboy. More likely he was standing dutifully before the assembled adults keeping silent and waiting to be spoken to before offering any kind of opinion. But the fact remains: the school began on All Saints' Day in 1938 and he was the first pupil in a school of one. Today, the school roll stands at over 300, with a typical 'leave' each year of approximately sixty pupils, not six, and one can only guess at the numbers of pupils who can now count themselves amongst the 'old boys and old girls' of the school – but a very rough estimate must take that number into the thousands.

So, let us imagine Francis and Evelyn Dix, now standing and musing in 2013, on some other more elevated platform we hope, as we see them casting celestial benevolence and approving eyes on the school that All Hallows has become today.

For all the saints - a story...

Some Dix Years

In the late 1930s, Francis Dix was a Classics Master at a small school named Avisford[4], in Sussex, when, one day, it is presumed, he decided he would like to set up a school of his own. To establish a school in those days, one imagines one needed, pragmatically, at least, an educated adult or two, a suitable building and, at least one pupil. The All Hallows Preparatory School for Boys of 1938 met that criteria to the letter: Mr and Mrs Dix were to play the part of the educated adults; 16 Sylvan Way, Bognor Regis, was to prove to be a suitable location, albeit briefly; and one boy named Alan Woodgates would be that vital pupil. Francis Dix chose All Saints' Day, 1st November 1938, as the occasion for the sherry party and thus the birthday and the name of the school has remained memorable ever since – All Saints equals All Hallows - even if the sherry only features more circumspectly. It is supposed that a pioneering Headmaster also needed vision, determination, even a sense of vocation. All Hallows was born on the day for all saints…watch this space.

The school motto, '*Sancto Cuique Sua Candela*' translates as '*To each Saint his or her candle*' which we have taken today as a reinforcement of the school's central message that all have a light with which to shine and that we are all equally important in the eyes of God and in our everyday endeavours. Quite when this motto was adopted is unclear but it was certainly in use by 1942, since it survives as a frontispiece to the School Chronicle of that year, but one supposes that the classicist Francis Dix would not have passed up the chance to invent a Latin motto from the very beginning so we shall presume that it, too, began its life on 1st November 1938. Mind you, in terms of settling on an everyday application of the school motto, translators are notorious for creating individual and particular emphases in order to extract meaning, so they may well come up with slight variations of their own, although I rather like the vernacular interpretation of one confident, ten-year-old, non-scholar who recently told me, insouciantly, that the school motto meant "Every Dog Has Its Day". Incidentally, that same boy obviously

---

[4] Avisford House was built in 1756 and operated as a Roman Catholic Boys' Preparatory School, between 1928-1973, with approximately 60-90 pupils, subsequently converting to a privately-run Hotel and Country Club in 1976, before being taken over by Stakis PLC in 1994, and then the Hilton Hotels Group in the year 2000. The refectory is apparently now listed which pleases face-booking old boys since it means that their engraved names cannot be erased (although that means they can also be traced).

had a particular way of seeing things since his reply to my rather exaggerated comment that he was "truly a Christian gentleman" (as he held open the door for me to pass through) was most emphatic: "Oh, no, Sir, I'm Church of England!"

Which point brings me on to the next observation to underline: All Hallows is a Catholic school in the Christian tradition. Paul Ketterer (PFJK), the school's fourth Headmaster, coined the phrase that serves, today, as the school's Mission Statement, namely, that "*our raison d'être is the integration of Christian principles with everyday life*". In another school, the modern School Inspector who recently rather ungenerously could find no evidence of awe in that educational setting whose mission statement suggested "there was a sense of awe" would, perhaps, find more favourably towards All Hallows in its Christian witness. In point of fact, a recent Ofsted Boarding Inspection of the school (2009) found every aspect of the pastoral and spiritual care to be "*outstanding*" and a much-loved Chaplain of the school in the 1990s proclaimed that the "*children of All Hallows make one want to doubt the concept of Original Sin*" (which is perhaps going a bit too far, don't you think? Clearly, he never saw them last lesson on a Friday afternoon).

In 1938 Francis Dix continued teaching at Avisford in order to provide the finances for the new school whilst his wife attended to all matronly, catering and teaching duties; it helps if one's partner can also share the dance. In 1938, Cole Porter's song "*Begin the Beguine*" (popular on the wireless at this time) became the music for a slow, close, couples' dance; and so the dance began. In January 1939 there were two new day boys as well as the school's first boarder (more of him later) and in the summer term another boy made up the total of pupils to five. Education was a full-time enterprise in those days (when has that not been the case?) and during the holidays, Mr and Mrs Dix accommodated up to thirty boys – and girls – with the 'school proper' settling down in September 1939 when "*Mr Dix took up the reins*" with a total school roll of sixteen boys. Francis Dix in his Prize Day speech of 1978 was amused to inform parents that the fees for 1939 were 35 guineas per term. This was at a time when there were other terms for monetary units like a farthing, ha'penny, thruppence and a tanner – if there are any children still reading and you don't know what these mean, look them up. Mind you, a pound of butter would cost you one-and-six, ten woodbines could be smoked for 5d and a small saloon car – let's say a Baby Austin - would sit happily in your garage for £122. And your live-in-maid, don't you know, would be earning about £1 per week so perhaps it's all relative.

And then war broke out.

The Second World War from 1939-1945 was to have a profound effect on everybody, of course, and the developing character, aspirations and location, even, of All Hallows School were not exempt. As the relative quiet months of the so-called 'Phoney War' gave way to the realities of combat the other side of The Channel, so did the plan for All Hallows begin to take shape with a sharper focus albeit one enforced by circumstance. The German army invaded France and the Low Countries on 10th May 1940 and five days later The Netherlands fell. Between 26th May-4th June, approximately 350 000 Allied troops were evacuated from Dunkirk. Paris was taken on 14th June and, on 25th June, within seven weeks of the start of the invasion, the French government surrendered. France was now an occupied country and events had moved so quickly there were real fears that the German forces would launch an attack on the southern English coastal regions. Mr Dix, accordingly, sent his wife with the four youngest pupils to the quieter areas of Devon to seek safer accommodation and he remained in Bognor with the other seventeen boys since the school had already grown in just a few terms. So, you see, given the background of war and the fear of invasion, it really wasn't a case of Mr Dix echoing King George V's alleged words about Bognor[5]; he was genuinely concerned for his pupils and his school. Mr Dix joined his wife at weekends and together they found the ideal house at Scorhill, near Chagford, which became the war-time home of All Hallows from July 1940. In the summer of that year numbers fell to nine since some of the boys did not want to be separated from their families but under Mr and Mrs Dix's stewardship the school roll increased year on year thereafter. All Hallows, therefore, took on a more rural, more strongly boarding character, as well as enjoying the fruits of a close relationship with the Benedictine monks of Buckfast Abbey whose benign presence and example may well have played a part in determining the school's final move to Somerset within easy reach of another Benedictine teaching monastery at Downside.

It is significant that the opening page of the very first All Hallows Chronicle is a letter of welcome from Bishop John of Plymouth....

Dear Mr Dix,   *7th September 1942*

The circumstances of the times brought you and your School to the Western Moors, and may be the occasion of your prolonging your stay into a permanency in such attractive surroundings.

May God bless the school and all in it.

Yours very sincerely in Our Lord,

✝ *John, Bishop of Plymouth*

The small advance party from All Hallows, Bognor Regis, must have made quite a sight in the great heat of the summer of 1940 as Mrs Dix put the four boys who were with her into their bathing costumes and sandals, with their gas masks slung over their shoulders, to troop around Devon, visiting estate-agents, surveying likely houses, doing their everyday shopping, etc. When

---

[5] King George V is supposed to have convalesced in and around Bognor in 1929 and the local worthies petitioned the King to grant the title 'Regis' ('of the King') to the town's name. The King is supposed to have said "*Bugger Bognor*" although his secretary replied to the petitioners with the words "*the King has been graciously pleased to grant your request*".

Scorhill had successfully been discovered as the new home for the school – and perhaps not wanting to be outdone in eccentricity and practical charm - Mr Dix joined that small group in July of that year by bringing five more pupils down on the train all carrying their own beds. One of the boys in those early years was that first boarder mentioned earlier, by name... Peter Michael Keily...

Those early days at Scorhill – and, indeed, those that followed – were to remain as very special memories for the growing numbers of pupils and staff. Mr Dix commented *"we had Dartmoor almost to ourselves, a magnificent playground, including a fine bathing-pool in the River Teign which ran through our grounds"*. Now, some people might not want Dartmoor to themselves (or Wincanton or Shepton Mallet or Portland or Ilkley Moor - 'where's that!' - for that matter), but to be able to 'lay claim' to any area of a country has its own obvious merits. Scorhill was not an easy place to reach, served as it is by a country track of some length feeding off the main arteries which lead to some of the more heavily populated areas of Devon like Chagford five miles away. But we are talking about 1940s Devon here. No sound of roaring quarry lorries could be heard from the woods. Light pollution was a concept, or, perhaps, more accurately, a concern, not yet invented. Heavy snowfalls high up on those moors meant that the school was occasionally cut off and, on more than one occasion, Mr and Mrs Dix had shown timely foresight by getting in plentiful provisions to see the boys through the wintry times. Yet, despite its remoteness, many lovely neighbours emerged from the surrounding areas including Colonel Vickary (he gave an early talk on 'Wildlife at Scorhill' which presumably excluded the two-legged genus known as 'boy'), Major Mayne (who owned Gidleigh Park[6] – in which house the boys used to attend Mass in the chapel until their own was consecrated), Colonel Tillard, Mrs Endacott, Mrs Rowe, Mrs Hill, Mr Vallance, as well as interesting local characters like 'Nash'[7] who tended the gardens and grounds and just about every other odd job that needed doing. Local features included the Sacred Circle of Scorhill[8], Grey Wethers, Sittaford Tor, Teignhead Farm, Fingle Bridge, the Mill End Hotel, all of which were visited regularly by the boys, even if those destinations were sometimes at the end of a twelve-mile hike across the moors.

---

[6] Gidleigh Park was the grandest residence in the local surroundings and, at the time of All Hallows at Scorhill, was owned by Major 'Rollo' Mayne, a Catholic, who had created a chapel in the house to which he was delighted to invite the boys from All Hallows for weekly Mass. Evelyn Waugh used to visit the house regularly whilst writing *Brideshead Revisited* when he stayed near Chagford which may have put All Hallows in his head when he later sent his son, Auberon, to the school *'as a reward for good behaviour'* one holiday. Today, Gidleigh Park is an internationally renowned Country Hotel and restaurant, owned by Andrew Brownsword, and sporting two Michelin Stars, having also been acclaimed, in 2010, the best restaurant in Britain. The same river Teign that ran through the school grounds at Scorhill reaches rather wilder and more expansive proportions through the grounds of Gidleigh Park which is well worth a visit. Ted Hughes wrote of *"the Teign, startled in her den/By the rain-dance of bracken/Hearing Heaven reverberate under Gidleigh"* and *"older than mankind, the river swallows/ The tale it has to tell"* – which prefigures Alice Oswald writing about the Dart (see later pages).

[7] See separate box details on page 17

[8] The stone monuments of Scorhill Circle are reckoned to date from 2000 BC so one presumes they were easily able to withstand the onslaught of three-score boys plus ten in the 1940s.

PETER MICHAEL KEILY
(Former Pupil [F.P.] 1939-1947; 1934-1973 RIP)

Peter Michael Keily joined All Hallows in January 1939 as the first boarding pupil of the school. Although it was winter, he had heard that the school was near the coast so he duly arrived clutching onto his bucket and spade. It is not recorded whether or not he ever used those items in Sussex but one presumes he had many opportunities to do so when he moved with eight other boys and Mr and Mrs Dix to Scorhill in Devon which became the school's home during the war years. On the feast of Corpus Christi 1941 he made his First Communion and enjoyed celebrating the school's third birthday later that year with the rest of the school when they visited Buckfast for Pontifical High Mass. At this service a monk was making his solemn profession and Peter and the other boys watched spellbound as the monk lay silent and still for some time under a pall surrounded by funeral candles. The abbot explained to the boys that this represented his death to the world and his subsequent throwing off of the pall was his rising to the life of the spirit. Later on, the same monk introduced himself to the boys as "*the man who had died in*

the Abbey that morning". On their tour of the monastery they took in the apiary and the cider presses and one young boy – possibly Peter – decided there and then that he would become a Buckfast monk and live on cider and honey for the rest of his days. Peter left All Hallows for Downside in July 1947 having been appointed Head Boy in his final term and Pack Leader of the Tigers throughout his last year. He played First Eleven cricket in 1945, 1946 and, as Captain, in 1947, topping the batting averages with 25.8. He represented the school at 1st XI Soccer in 1945 and 1946, as well as playing a "*large variety of parts*" with his acting. He joined the boxing team at Downside. He continued to keep in touch with All Hallows throughout his Downside years, often visiting the school on the occasion of the school's birthday and even during the holidays when, it seems, he spent his time with Mr and Mrs Dix. Peter moved to Kenya to take up farming and flew back to England, on 12th January 1956, to get married in Wolverhampton; thereafter spending a few days at All Hallows after his honeymoon. Mr and Mrs Dix attended the wedding along with a couple of old boys. We read in the 1957 Chronicle that Peter's wife gave birth to a son, and later a second boy, both of whom went on to Downside. In the 1972-73 Chronicle Francis Dix, now retired, writes of the sudden death of Peter who died whilst leading a Big Game Expedition in Kenya. Mr Dix records the fact that Peter was the only pupil who attended All Hallows at Bognor, Scorhill and Cranmore. He goes on to write: "*Owing to circumstances, he spent most of his holidays with us during the war so that my wife and I looked on him almost as a well-loved son. Peter Michael was a very affectionate and high-spirited boy and very much of a 'character', some of his escapades in his earlier years having a distinctive 'Just William' touch....My wife is godmother to one of his sons...our deepest sympathy goes out to Peter Michael's wife and family*".

And the monks of Buckfast, as well as the local parish priests and the Bishop of Plymouth, became firm friends of the school. The school's Christian identity and name was further firmly fixed in the minds of the boys when the wooden icons of various saints (produced by an artist from Brighton) were attached to the doors of the dormitories. Similar icons were commissioned for Cranmore, Somerset, some years later, and are still in use in the school although they are now situated around the main doors leading to the Chapel of All Saints built, into the Spinney, in 1988. The names of the saints, however, remain for all time (one hopes) associated with the dormitories, so that St Luke's, St Anthony's, St Ignatius, St T-More et al still feature humbly on laundry baskets and towels, as well as, perhaps, providing sources of inspiration (one rather suspects that true saints would always prefer to be associated with laundry baskets than lofty ideals of inspiration). One former pupil of fairly recent Cranmore days cannot think of St Joseph without recalling the closed shutters of the dormitory of that name - ostensibly providing an extra layer of warmth and darkness late at night – but, really, only rattling through the small hours, like the knocking and scratching of windows from wuthering heights, when ghosts walked the landings, and when duvets were invented for the sole purpose of diving into, along with other shivering, frightened boarders. The shaking would turn to giggles punctuated by frightened shrieks as whispered stories would be told of the sounds of disembodied crying babies howling through the bathroom which once had been used in the war as a birthing room for expectant evacuee mothers. For 'ghost stories' see later pages.

[Readers will note the chronological time slips; they are literary conceits inserted on the whim and predilection of the author who cannot easily relinquish a career of teaching stratagems designed to retain the attention of wayward pupils who only really want to know what is for lunch and how are they going to wreak revenge on Harris ii, or Doyne-Ditmus minor, or, more recently, some splendidly-named pupil like Rainbow Forrest-Jones, who has invaded their air space or touched their pencil case in French or given them an old-fashioned look in Headmaster's Assembly].

To return to the 'saving moments', or to time-continuous, or to T.S.Eliot's *"Time present and time past/….both perhaps present in time future/And time future contained in time past"*, let us recall the fact that in September 1940 the school opened its doors with sixteen boys (almost a 100% increase) amongst whom was new boy Count Maurice Coreth[9], when the 'Pack System' was introduced, albeit with two 'Packs' or Houses only: 'Wolves' and 'Tigers'. Interestingly, the first ever Pack Trophy was won by Wolves – a splendid cup donated by Head Boy Halfhide's father – although, when a fourth House was resurrected in 2002 owing to increased numbers, the nomenclature of 'Wanstrow Wolves' became the 'new' name. Thus we have linear time and cyclical time overlapping. Hence, the reference to T. S. Eliot, who knew a thing or two about complicating matters. Incidentally, John Halfhide went on to win the prize for 'General Helpfulness' which might only be surpassed in worthiness by 'The Paget Cup'[10] in later years.

One supposes that school life was rather busy in those days (as now, it has to be said) but the Chronicle entries mostly record events that might be described as 'extra-curricular' since they focus on sporting encounters (often only cricket and soccer at the beginning), as well as Sports Days, and dramas and entertainments and outings and visiting speakers. But the calendar is also punctuated by liturgical dates of celebration and by various developments ranging from the arrival of a new school mower to the blessing of the school. Passing reference is made to what may be termed academic matters, particularly in terms of the boys' efforts and achievements in the Common Entrance and Scholarship examinations. Each successful award seems to merit a half-holiday which meant, increasingly, that a backlog of 'days off' accrued, surely rendering the business of routine education a little difficult to maintain. There is something rather endearing, however, about the entries that say: *"Rather hot today so we all went off to the coast and swam"*; not a bad mantra for life, really. The boys were occasionally *'left to their own devices'* but it appears that a lot of time was spent in preparing and then delivering the various aspects of school life alluded to above. The School Prize Day of 1941, for example, welcomed some 50 parents to an array of dramatic productions including a Latin play, *Medicus*, various scenes from *A Midsummer Night's Dream*, another play called *David Copperfield and the Waiter*, a

---

[9] See separate box details on page 25
[10] See footnote 54 on page 93

lively miming from A. A. Milne's *Bold Sir Brian Botany*, a verbal skit that masqueraded under the name of *All Hallows in the Days of Shakespeare*, as well as mimed scenes from The Nativity, with the School Choir also singing Brother James' air, with descant, and several carols. The prize giving ceremony followed, with speeches, and tea, during which exhibitions of art and handicraft were on display. The diary records the slight apology that *'more ambitious efforts'* were left for the summer term[11]. It doesn't do to shirk at All Hallows, you know. Nevertheless, it would be interesting to see a typical school timetable to gain a sense of how the day unfolded for the boys and teachers. The breakdown and emphasis of the curriculum would be instructive reading if only for purposes of comparison with today's structure. One knows that the classics were taught with conspicuous success as witnessed by these words from the Rt. Rev. Dom N. W. Passmore, OSB, Abbot of Downside in 1970, *"the fact that Mr Dix inspired his boys with enthusiasm for classics, which was the source of his own excellence, meant that often a boy achieved a result far beyond his own expectations because of the confidence he had in Mr Dix"*. Equally, boys were regularly scoring impressive overall averages in the Common Entrance examinations and passing well into schools like Ampleforth, Downside and Eton, so it is presumed that academic lessons must have taken place at some time during the day, alongside the rehearsal time and the sport and the fun, etc. On the matter of scholarships[12], we shall return.

The earliest Chronicle entries, over fourteen pages or so, record in summary prose, events as they had been remembered from 1938 until the summer of 1942. That final summer term account begins to take the shape of all subsequent chronicles, at least during Mr Dix's time, and through the years of Mr Mortimer's Headship, and, similarly, up until the first years of Paul Ketterer's time as Headmaster (for a Chronicle of 1972-73 still survives in the school archives). The School Chronicle seems to have taken a lengthy sabbatical throughout the rest of the seventies, eighties and nineties, until being resurrected, in a different format, in 1995 until the present day. It is these records that have provided such an important mix of incident and achievement although they, themselves, are subject to selective memory and now, of course, have been interpreted by the present writer with, perhaps, a different perspective and emphasis again. So, those first fourteen pages, then, highlight sections entitled *"Beginnings, School Birthday 1941, Christmas Plays and Prize Giving, Saturday Night Entertainments, Indoor Games,"* and include good black and white photographs of the school buildings at Scorhill, as well as photos of various outdoor entertainments, including Mr Dix as conjuror and magician entertaining a fine array of bonneted hats belonging, presumably, to mothers. Mr Dix would continue to entertain parents and pupils for many years to come with his ventriloquism and magic tricks thus underlining the fact that Headmasters need to be able to pull rabbits out of hats.

---

[11] Early Prize Days took place in the Michaelmas Term
[12] See Appendix D

School House at Scorhill

There is a poignant paragraph on 'Football 1941-1942' in which we learn that "*owing to transport difficulties and diseases at other schools no fixtures could be arranged. This was a pity as the school could have fielded a very fair side*". The captain of the team was Robin Couchman and, since the boys never actually achieved any kind of kudos, in their aborted attempts to play on grass, let us accord them some sort of lasting fame, at least on paper, by recording their names here: "*The team would have been: Goal:* **Cronin**; *Full-Backs:* **Taylor, Halfhide**; *Half-Backs:* **Coreth, Jackson, Milne**; *Forwards:* **Corbould, Ford** (*or* **Pettitt**), **Couchman**[13], **Arbuthnott, Gladstone**". Notice the 'old-fashioned' forward-line of two wings, two inside forwards and a centre-forward; they were poised to score a lot of goals!

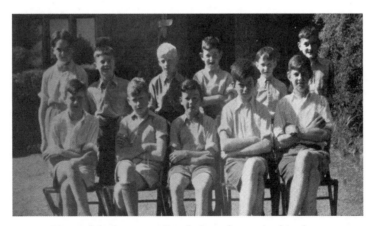

Many of the boys mentioned above feature in this photo

---

[13] See separate box details on page 37

The summer term of 1942 opened in beautiful weather with numbers up to thirty-two and now *three* Packs with Panthers joining the other two. To provide some sort of flavour of the calendar entries from this point on, the following selections might interest and amuse:

May 6th	*We were able to have a bathe – unusually early.*
May 9th	*A wet Saturday, so the miniature railway was brought out. In the evening the Headmaster entertained – conjuring, ventriloquism, recitations.*
May 14th	*Feast of the Ascension – Mass and Holy Communion at Gidleigh Park*
June 4th	*Corpus Christi.*
June 8th	*A fine day ....so a cricket match between the Staff and the XI. The School won.*
June 15th	*Common Entrance taken by Taylor, Cronin and Halfhide.*
June 16th	*Geoffrey Shaw's birthday party.*
June 17th	*Whole holiday to celebrate Robin's (Couchman) scholarship.*

Pupils of today might like the present Headmaster to note that 8th June 1942 was, in fact, a Monday, but because the weather was good somebody decided there should be a cricket match between the staff and the boys.

Without wishing to try the patience of the reader too much, a further selection of diary entries for later that same term are quite interesting from a topographical point of view as well as highlighting the boys' sporting prowess....

July 11th	*Mr Halfhide rang up early to say that Jeremy had passed the Dartmouth examination. In the afternoon after a short game of cricket the top Form had an early tea, as they were to walk to Grey Wethers. Visitors to the school delayed the start but at six o'clock, the party with Messrs. Dix and Chips, started off. The Grey Wethers were reached in good time by a direct route across the moor and we had a picnic supper inside the circle. After supper we climbed Sittaford Tor (1750 feet) from which we got a glorious view. From there we returned to the Teign near Teignhead Farm and followed it back to Scorhill. This part of the walk was surprisingly beautiful and the weather had improved so much that it was possible to have quite an enjoyable bathe in a deep pool in the river. We arrived home at ten o'clock exactly, after a walk of about twelve miles (Mr Chips, however, must have done a good forty).*
July 13th	*At Mr Halfhide's request the top Form was given a half-holiday. It was decided to try to walk to Fingle Bridge following the river all the way. The party accompanied by Mr and Mrs Dix started out soon after lunch and followed the long windings of the river to the bridge near Chagford where Mrs Dix, Hartley and Coreth left the others and went into Chagford for tea. The rest carried on to their objective stopping once to eat their picnic tea and*

a second time to have drinks at *The Mill End Hotel. The walk was a beautiful one and full of interest all the way and the colouring of the slopes of the Gorge was superb. The party returned to The Mill End Hotel and were driven home from there.*

July 15th   *Match against St Nicholas at home. St Nicholas brought a picnic lunch with them which they ate in the grounds. An early start was made and All Hallows just about managed to win. Couchman and Jackson were awarded their cricket Colours.*

July 18th   *Match against Upcott House – our first away match, our first hundred and our first individual half-century (Couchman 51).*

The route direct south across the moors from Scorhill passes near to a 'Danger Area' (according to my Atlas of Devon and Dartmoor) and the trek looks exacting enough for hardy walkers let alone young boys. But there they are again, two days later – having conquered Sittaford Tor and Grey Wethers, going in the opposite direction in search of Fingle Bridge like intrepid travellers as part of some Tolkienesque quest across Middle Earth. A writer, John Lloyd Warden Page, described, in the 1890's, on two occasions, the different moods of the area around Fingle Bridge thus:

"the ancient bridge, so narrow that only one cart at a time can pass over it, and the wayfarer caught thereby must retire into one of the triangular recesses, the continuation upwards of the sharp buttresses that divide the hurrying water. A sweet spot, though somewhat sad toward eventide, when the 'cry' of the river sounds mournful on the darkening atmosphere"..........
"How clear the rushing waters gliding beneath the three gray arches! How rich in colouring have the lichens and ferns rendered its hoary walls! And, whether we look upstream to the hills, softly meeting one another with foliage changing from bright green in the foreground to misty blue in the distance, or downward to where the old mill with its moss-grown water-wheel, nestles beneath the woods, and Prestonbury rises mountainous over all, we shall confess that a scene of greater beauty it has never been our lot to view".

In one of those coincidental accidents of names[14], it is not inconceivable (though not mentioned) that the boys and masters, with Mr Dix leading the way, might well have traversed the boggy meadows to find *Cranmere Pool*, supposedly the source of the River Dart, only eight miles from Chagford. Who knows whether or not the name 'Cranmere' lodged itself in those All

---

[14] Rather like the fact that Evelyn Dix's maiden name was 'Bird' – who is no relation of the author.

Hallows' minds only to re-emerge by some metaphysical and geographical mind-processing as the *Cranmore* village in Somerset which was to be the school's eventual home a few years later? Cranmere Pool certainly had a story of its own. Like its Somerset cousin, the name supposedly means the 'Lake of Cranes' although, again, like the Somerset hamlet, its naming ceremony probably overreached itself for those birds were likely herons all those years ago. But the marshes were misty and the eye could play tricks and yet, we hear of the Great Crane Project since 2010, dedicated to rearing and reintroducing cranes to the West Country with its latest success: the first crane egg in southern Britain for more than 400 years has just been laid by a nesting bird. We want one back in Somerset! Today – and even in the 1940s – Cranmere Pool, on Dartmoor, was nothing more than '*a wet, boggy tract of land with possibly a pathetic muddy pond or a dried up peaty mess*' but people travelled far and wide in order to reach this rather desolate place in the middle of the moor. Perhaps it represented that innate human desire to be able to say that 'one had done it', reached some inaccessible location across difficult terrain, or, perhaps it was because of the legends that were attached to that remote part of Dartmoor, or, most likely, such travellers visited in order to leave, literally, their calling cards, but, whatever the reasons, the journey became one of the key 'must do' tasks when walking the moor. One legend mentions the 'miserable, moaning ghost' as being the departed spirit of one Benjamin Gayer or 'Cranmere Benjie', as he became known. Time for a ghost story, I think (let us hope the boys regaled themselves, on darkening Devon nights, with such tales)....

Gayer was said to be a wealthy merchant and ship owner from Okehampton who fell upon hard times after several of his ships and cargo were lost to pirates. In order to regain his lost wealth he invested money from a fund, with which he had been entrusted by the local community, to pay the potential ransom of local mariners captured by pirates. Luck was not with Benjamin and again he lost the latest cargo in which he had invested the stolen funds. His business was ruined, he was a broken man, he was unable to repay the money he had stolen, and, by his selfish actions, he had condemned many local sailors who were in the hands of pirates awaiting payment. The guilt played heavily on his soul, his health deteriorated and he died guilty and tormented. For months following his funeral the ghost of Benjamin Gayer haunted the streets of Okehampton, crying and wailing throughout each night. A series of exorcisms were attempted by all the local clergy trying unsuccessfully to lay the spirit of Gayer to rest. Just as things were looking desperate for the people of Okehampton, the Archdeacon called upon a wise priest who lived in a remote part of Dartmoor.

This priest, armed with a bridle, and accompanied by a horseman, confronted the ghost. Using the Arabic tongue, he commanded the ghost to depart, and Gayer conceded that he must leave the mortal world. But instead of fading away, he turned into a black horse. The horseman put the bridle on the horse and whipping him harshly rode him up onto the moor. As they approached Cranmere Pool he sent the horse hurtling into the waters whilst jumping off and removing the bridle. The mysterious priest then arrived binding the spirit of Gayer to the pool until he could empty it of water using nothing more than a sieve. Years passed as the spirit toiled at his hopeless task, trapped at Cranmere Pool, then one day he found a dead sheep and, using its skin, he lined his sieve and found that it then held water. He began to empty the pool. He threw the waters from Cranmere Pool into the River Okemont whose waters rose and burst their banks, flooding the town of Okehampton. The priest was called again from his remote home and tasked with tackling Benjamin's spirit at Cranmere Pool. This time the ghost was given a tougher challenge: to make trusses of grit tied with plaits created from sand, a task that he is still, according to legend, attempting to complete. His ghost is said to be seen and heard by the pool and on the moor shaped as both a man and black horse.

Moaning ghosts or not, people certainly visited and, literally, left their calling cards. One local nineteenth-century guide, James Perrott, used to escort travellers safely to the source of the River dart in a sixteen-mile round trip from Chagford. Those who successfully negotiated the route soon wanted to record their achievement – for it was seen as an achievement - and, perhaps, pre-shadowing Scott of the Antarctic or Hillary and Tensing on Everest, instead of flags, they dropped their calling cards into a glass jar that Perrott affixed to some standing stones for the purpose. In the mid to late 1800s, a Visitors' Book was added and a tin box, which was itself then replaced by a granite box with a sturdy oak door built by ex-tin miner Aubrey Tucker in 1937, not long before Mr and Mrs Dix arrived at nearby Scorhill, with their contingent of All Hallows' pupils. Later again, in the 1960s, the first letterbox stamp was placed at the box so that people could leave a self-addressed postcard, stamp it as proof of their having reached Cranmere Pool, and then leave it to subsequent travellers to post - by a more conventional route - their own letter back to them often some weeks or months later. Some such letters arrived from as far afield as Scotland and Belgium. Records show that in 1905, 609 people signed the Visitors' Book and that the following year it was 962, which had grown to 1,352 in 1907 and 1,741 in 1908. At that rate one presumes that the signatures of 2013 now fill several volumes of encyclopaedias left snugly filling a granite box the size of a country house. Thus was the outdoor hobby of 'Letter-boxing' born. Nowadays, we are told, it includes elements of orienteering, puzzle-solving and clues, as well as a society known as the '100 Club' which endeavours to discover the other ninety-nine locations of such letter-boxes all over the moor. Letter-boxers organise meets or gatherings when they come together twice a year as the clocks go back. No doubt they wear badges and engage in secret signs. One believes a true letter-boxer can recognise a fellow letter-boxer in public places just by the way he wears his hat. They carry envelopes about their persons in times of emergency. They have plans to form a political party and are currently producing a manifesto for a new age. I'm not sure at what point in the above I started to make things up. But, the River Dart inspires poetical powerful images. Alice Oswald, in her collection Dart (winner of the T. S. Eliot Prize in 2002) refers to *'the river's mutterings'* and recognises that it is *'trying to summon itself by speaking...this secret, buried in reeds, at the beginning of sound'*. She asserts that *'an hour in the morning is worth three in the evening'* and that what she loves *'is one foot in front of another'* on *'the moor where echoes can't get out'*. She found the source of the river *'in the reeds, a trickle coming out of a bank, a foal of a river... trills in the stones, glides in the trills, eels in the glides.'* And, later, as she tracks the river to the sea she senses *'the crash of riverflesh falling'* and the *'pause superimposed on water....speaking its meaning over mine.'* We've strayed into Ted Hughes country *'between the streams and the red clouds, hearing curlews, hearing horizons endure'*.

Truly, these were magical places, magical times.

But let us not wallow too nostalgically or sit on in awe of the derring-do escapades of former pupils alone. The boys of 2013, under Matt Cocks' expert supervision, took on the Exmoor Youth Challenge organised by the Rotary Club of Exmoor to give young people a chance to test themselves as individuals, as well as work together as part of a team. The boys had to follow a 16-mile, unmarked route across the moors using map-reading and compass skills, whilst keeping a clear head and working against the clock. Once they start, they are on their own, apart from the few check-points along the way. Sixty-one teams took part and our own teams came in 7th, 12th and 14th with Max Dunford, Joe Truelove, Dan Patchett, Max Adams, Finn Smith, Oliver Blacklidge, Jasper Davies, Tim Lovick, Ben Hadfield, Henry Brand-Lyons, Tom Munro and Ben Ake all emerging with huge credit.

Back to the boys of All Hallows and 1942....mention is made of their "first away match" but we ought to commend firstly, the groundsman, Ernie Nash, for laying a new cricket wicket in the Easter holidays and secondly, Mr Dix who during *"the first four or five weeks of term spent every spare minute mowing the field with a hand mower. It was very hard work but he felt he got an acre and a half into very fair condition..."*

Incidentally, the sports field also accommodated a running track for the sprints and, on Sports Day, the fathers had to stand at the bottom end of the track, since it was on a slope, to stop the boys, as they gathered pace, running headlong into the River Teign below. The boys swam freely in the river before breakfast but not, willingly, on the occasion of the 100-yard dash.

And so the summer of 1942 came to an end with those six Leavers alluded to by Mr and Mrs Dix as they *"stood on an Exeter platform, musing"*. VALETE ...**Robin Couchman, Jeremy Halfhide, Christopher Cronin, Sam Taylor, Tony Jackson**[15] and **Enzo Bonapera**[16].

There had been, of course, earlier Leavers, when the school moved from Bognor and when some boys did not make the transition to Devon. Amongst them, for example, there is mention of Peter White who was the school's first Head Boy and whose *"fine character, good influence*

---

[15] See reference in the text on page 54
[16] See separate box details on page 34

"NASH"

Ernie Nash was a local man who became employed by Mr Dix in the early days of Scorhill to tend to the gardens and grounds, as well as turn his hand at various odd jobs that cropped up around the estate and buildings. Nash had been a sergeant to Colonel Vickary, from whom Francis Dix rented Scorhill during the war, and had already become attached to the gardens and grounds whilst also living in the Lodge House at the end of the drive. It has been a common teaching experience that every school needs a man like Nash. He threw himself into the life of the school – sometimes taking part in staff productions for the amusement of the boys – and often joining the Staff Cricket Team in their regular matches against the School 1st XI. He was much loved by the boys who were in awe of his prodigious strength which assumed epic proportions as the tales grew in the telling; somewhere it is recorded that he carried four lost sheep across the moors, two under each arm. Former pupil, John Ford, remembers Nash as '*a very kind and patient giant of a man who was regarded with great awe and admiration being credited with feats of incredible strength*'. Another pupil, C.R. Couchman, adds his 1942 impressions of the man.

"All the School knows Nash

Who works so hard to grow us vegetables and saw up wood

But in his spare time he is generally surrounded by the boys of All Hallows

And he can invariably answer all questions concerning

The wily fish

The nests of birds

And the ways of animals

His great strength is often talked of among the boys

And it is handed down that once, in the depths of winter,

He carried the school's pony, Puggie, on his back across the Teign.

And when the time comes that we must leave him

I am certain that there will be no one who will forget him

And no one who will not be sorry."

and helpfulness made Mrs Dix's task much easier", as well as of George Rochfort-Rae who started at Avisford, joined Mr Dix for some holiday coaching at Scorhill and stayed on for two more terms before going on to Eton *"quite well-placed"* in the C.E. exams. George Rochfort-Rae, in the tradition of former pupils who return to All Hallows, accepted an invitation to attend the school's sixtieth birthday celebrations when I was Headmaster and wrote a lovely letter subsequently enclosing various photographs of the school at Scorhill. He writes at that time that he is still in touch with Father Edward (Michael) Corbould, John Ford, Adrian Pettitt and Michael Morris and he laments the fact that he has lost all traces of Ian and Roy Freeman – are you out there, boys! And one can find no further mention of Alan Woodgates, the very first pupil of the school, after November 1st 1938, so one presumes he remained in Bognor when the school moved. Thus does he hold the record – in these pages at least – as being the first boy to join the school and the first boy to leave. But it is those six named boys above, whose leaving in one large cohort at that time, who provided such a sentimental moment at the railway station, and who inadvertently determined an important source of information for later reference when Mr and Mrs Dix decided, "then and there", to begin recording school events.

Back row: Robert Vining, Michael Corbold, Michael Drew, Peter Smalley, Oliver Brunard, Adrian Pettitt, Tony Reavell. Standing: Maurice Coreth, John Ford, Roy Freeman, David Gladstone, John Arbuthnott, Paul Skeaping, Richard Milne, Michael Morris. Sitting: Enzo Bonapera, Christopher Cronin, George Rochfort-Rae, Robin Couchman, John Halfhide, Ian Freeman, Jeremy Halfhide, Tony Jackson. Front: Victor Higgs, ... Just, Richard Merton, Colin Ingleby-Mackenzie, Geoffrey Shaw, Peter Michael Keilly, ... Hollander, John Etor.

The Pack Cup (donated by Mr Halfhide, father of the first Head Boy – at Scorhill, at least, if not in the history of the school) was inaugurated in the Michaelmas Term 1942 and although it had a 'Stars and Stripes' system (with presumably the stripes acting as 'bad' marks) it acted as a forerunner of the Merit Championship in use today. The Wolves came out as the first winners which might please those present day pupils now belonging to 'Wanstrow Wolves', especially since, in the modern era, they were newly 'created', in 2002 (or, more accurately, 're-created', as has already been mentioned) after a long, relatively modern, period of only three Houses. The treat for winning the competition was for the winning pack to walk to Chapple Farm for a "wizard" tea (possibly served by Gandalf – to prolong the Middle Earth analogy a little longer – who only made his first published appearance in 1937 and might, therefore, reasonably be supposed to be serving tea in some Dartmoor hostelry whilst blowing smoke-rings into the gathering skies). The present day Merit Championship does not record 'bad' marks, which might be just as well for some, but one is continually astounded by the number of merits awarded in a term; typically, more than twenty thousand between the four Houses. Just imagine twenty thousand good things happening in the school in one term – and that's just the things that are noticed and recorded! Merits can be awarded for good manners, trying hard in the classroom, being kind, making special efforts in the face of difficulties, assisting teachers, volunteering for all kinds of jobs and errands – in short, anything that is deemed positive, helpful and designed for the greater good of the school. The House competition is not simply confined to the weekly call-out of merits, however, leading to the termly and annual Cup. There are House competitions in Poetry, Art, Music, Sport, as well as regular charitable fund-raising activities under the banner of the House to which pupils belong. The Houses today are called Downhead Lions, Wanstrow Wolves, Cranmore Panthers and Batcombe Tigers, thus conflating two traditions from the early 'Pack' years and the later time under Paul Ketterer's headship which introduced the names of local villages. Mr Dix might be pleased to note that the four Houses adopted, only recently, Latin mottoes, respectively, "*Virtus et Prudentia; Animus et Confidentia; Constantia et Fortitudo; Comitas et Audacia*". An interesting feature of the early Pack competitions when a fourth pack was created – presumably Panthers since the Lions are mentioned earlier and, as has already been noted, the Tigers and the Wolves were the first two packs – is that often sporting encounters took place between *combined* packs so that Lions-Tigers would take on Panthers-Wolves one week and other combinations would follow thereafter. It seems to the present writer that this might be a tradition worth re-establishing just for the sake of variety.

If the Pack System or the House Championships represent the healthy competitive, frenetic and often noisy side of school life, let us turn our attention to an equally fundamental aspect that lies at the heart of the school at the very beginning and now. The Christian character of All Hallows has, as we have seen, been its raison d'être and nowhere is that more evident than in its chapel. Mr Dix records the fact that at Bognor Regis they were grateful for the great interest shown in the school by the Servite[17] Prior – Father Hagan – who presumably arranged

---

[17] The Servites (established 1233) preserved a particular devotion to the Mother of God and were one of five original mendicant orders from the Middle Ages, along with Franciscans, Carmelites, Dominicans and Augustinians.

for Mass to be said or for them to attend Mass in the convent chapel although the two Servite communities in Bognor today appear to be occupying relatively new-build establishments. There is, however, a 'Servite Close' where a convent from the 1880s was first set up before closing in 1975 as more and more housing encroached upon the rather quieter rural area first enjoyed by the nuns. Nevertheless, we will seek some indulgence and nominate Father Hagan as the school's first Chaplain. When the school moved to Scorhill, Major Mayne of Gidleigh Park allowed the boys to come over to the chapel in his private grounds and this can still be seen today although it is no longer a chapel. It was not long before Mr Dix wanted to create his own chapel in the new school grounds and with the support of the Bishop of Plymouth, the monks of Buckfast, Father Russell of Totnes and "*our parish priest*" Father Pedrick, a "*conspiracy of helpfulness*" enabled a suitable structure to be converted. During the summer holidays, "*the first structural alterations were made...and the casual observer would now never suspect that the chapel was once a garage*". I can inform you that today that chapel has now been restored to a garage by the present owners of the property and one would never suspect that it had once been a chapel! The new chapel, such as it was, with its whitewashed walls and newly-formed windows, was opened and dedicated to All Saints on 1st November (of course!) 1943. Father Laurence of Buckfast officiated at the ceremonial blessing and Father Pedrick preached the sermon. Later that term (December 5th), the Abbot of Buckfast also said Mass there. The altar proper arrived on November 13th and was installed by Father Albert. "*The beautiful reredos, an intricate and finely carved piece of work, is two centuries old and was formerly in the possession of the Cliffords of Chudleigh[18], one of whom, it is believed, originally made it. The oak frontal, too, incorporated even older linen-fold panelling. The paintings of the reredos, finely conceived and executed in tempora by Father Albert are the chief feature of the chapel. The large central panel is designed to express by its bright colours on gold background not so much the sufferings of Our Blessed Lord as the Love of His Sacred Heart to whom the altar is dedicated. On either side of the cross are the figures of Our Lady and Saint John, one of our patron saints. The supporting panels represent four other saints especially venerated by the school, patrons of the dormitories – SS. Joseph, Francis of Assisi, Philip Neri and Thomas More.*

Four insets at the top of the reredos in green and gold express symbolically various invocations from the Litany of the Sacred Heart; while across the centre is placed a text from the Office of the Feast in gold lettering on a black background. The riddle hangings, made up by Father Cyprian, the Sacristan of Buckfast, are of rich brocade in black, green and gold."

---

[18] The Cliffords of Chudleigh, family seat at Ugbrooke Park, Devon; baronetcy created in 1672. It is possible that the reredos was gifted to the Buckfast community by William Hugh Clifford (1858-1943), the 10th Baron, or Charles Oswald Hugh Clifford (1887-1962), the 11th Baron. For further reference read: *The House of Clifford from Before the Conquest* by Hugh Clifford, the 13th Baron. Incidentally, Claire Ogilvie, sister of Major 'Rollo' Mayne of Gidleigh Park, married Lord Clifford of Chudleigh which might just have explained the All Hallows' connection further.

*the fact that Mr Dix inspired his boys with
enthusiasm for classics, which was the source
of his own excellence, meant that often a boy
achieved a result far beyond his own expectations
because of the confidence he had in Mr Dix*

This reredos but, not, we think, the wooden Stations of the Cross (also made and donated by the Buckfast monks) travelled with the school when it moved in 1946 to Cranmore Hall, Somerset, and it has adorned the two very different chapels used on that site ever since. The present writer visited Scorhill recently with the then Chairman of Governors, Chris Dick[19] (who had been a pupil at Scorhill during the war) and, on that occasion, as well as during a later visit, we were able to see the old chapel, now de-consecrated and restored to its original function as a garage, and touch the nail-marks where the Stations of the Cross had been fastened to the whitewashed walls. In the Scorhill Chapel of All Saints, a Plain Chant Mass was sung every Sunday, on Sunday evenings there was Compline, followed by a sermon and Benediction, and on Mondays a dialogue Mass every morning.

When the school moved to Somerset, the chapel was situated in the fourteenth-century cross-house, and the Bishop of Clifton gave permission for the Sunday obligation to be made on Saturday morning so that any Catholic boarders going home for the weekend would have been able to attend Mass more easily. Night Prayers took place here every evening. Since this chapel was located directly above the Dining Room, one imagines the secular smells and fare of breakfast, lunch and supper, mingling and rising rather beautifully with the spiritual oblations and incense of that 'upper house'. That particular chapel was, itself, de-consecrated in 1988 (and now houses residential quarters for boarding houseparents). The present chapel of All Saints was built into the Old Spinney (architect Norman Cant) and became the focal point of

---

[19] See separate box details on page 56

the school celebrations for the Diamond Jubilee in 1998 when Cardinal Basil Hume visited the school and said Mass. At other times during his visit he spoke of All Hallows as being actively involved through commitment and energy *"in the workshop of the Holy Spirit"* and reminded us that *"our prayer life was always important, always awesome"* thus using a word used by modern children in a slightly more trendy way although his intended meaning came through even more strongly. For other comments regarding The Cardinal's visit see pages 149ff. Today, in the year 2013, as the school celebrates its 75th birthday, so, too, the present chapel of All Saints celebrates its 25th anniversary.

In designing the lay-out of this history I was tempted to follow a pattern established recently by the Director of the British Museum, Neil MacGregor, who told his pictorial story through the unlikely medium of radio and then wrote it up in a book called *"The History of the World in 100 Objects"*; most definitely, a book for your shelves. 'A History of All Hallows in 75 Objects' would have worked, I think, if ending up a little twee and possibly imitative; for everybody now seems to be following that pattern....a History of the Olympics..., a History of Parliament..., a History of Winnie-the-Pooh... (I made that last one up), etc, etc. All Hallows' objects, like the postal address of Sylvan Way, Bognor Regis; a photograph of Scorhill; a picture of the reredos; the portrait of Francis Dix; the Mousey Thompson[20] tables and chairs at Cranmore; the statue of St Francis (now in Scouts' Wood); the Crane Wing plaques (all of which will feature somewhere in this narrative) and so on....all these items would have translated nicely into a flowing narrative, one suspects. The concept works well for those who like to dip in and out of their histories. An example from MacGregor's book which appears as Chapter 75, fittingly enough in this 75th year of All Hallows, concerns Durer's woodcutting of a Rhinoceros from Nuremberg, Germany, 1515. In a little over four pages we learn of the gift of this live, one-and-a-half ton rhinoceros from the Sultan of Gujurat to the first Governor of the Portuguese empire in India, Alfonso d'Albuquerque, who, at a loss as to what to do with it, sent it on by ship to King Emanuel of Portugal, who felt that this was a gift fit for a Renaissance Pope, so had it transported yet again across the water on its way to Rome only to hear that the ship sank without trace en route. A nice aside is that the rhinoceros might have escaped – since rhinos are good swimmers – but it was chained to the deck and so went down with everything else.

---

[20] Robert (Mouseman) Thompson (7 May 1876 – 8 December 1955) was a British furniture-maker. He lived in Kilburn, North Yorkshire, where he established a business, manufacturing oak furniture, which featured a carved mouse on almost every piece. It is claimed that the mouse motif came about accidentally in 1919 following a conversation about "being as poor as a church mouse", which took place between Thompson and one of his colleagues during the carving of a cornice for a screen. This chance remark led to him carving a mouse and this remained a signature part of his work from this point onwards. Ampleforth College has a considerable number of items of furniture sporting the Thompson mouse and All Hallows, similarly, has a number of tables and chairs with the wooden mouse climbing up the legs. Those tables were the early dining tables for the boys and masters in what is now termed The Dix Music Room and, at the time of writing, at least, they can now be found in the School Library with just a few residual marks on the tops, left, presumably, from those dining-room days when the boys' proper use of table-knives still required some education.

In death, the rhino lived on in stories and in pictures, one of which found its way to Durer, who, despite never having seen a live rhinoceros, came up with his wood cutting which has achieved, ever since, such universal acclaim, if not anatomical accuracy, looking, as it does, rather more like an animal from Kipling's *Just So Stories*. The point of all this whimsy is that Durer's rhinoceros 'became the reality for millions of Europeans' and, as a palimpsest, has allowed present-day historians to scrape away meaning and significance far beyond a particular physical presence at a specific point in time.

What has all this to do with All Hallows? Well, perhaps this school story is setting down palimpsests of its own and perhaps the rhino story serves as only a marginally contrived link to the next episode in the school narrative which focuses on our own 'Rhino Man' – Maurice Coreth. Or more correctly *Count* Maurice Coreth (see box right).

Maurice Coreth wrote the following article when he was a boarder at Scorhill recounting his memories of the attic at home; even here, after being "*sent to bed for walking on the flower beds*", he escaped from his bedroom and explored secret places to indulge in his love of adventure and animals....

"*My father had gone to London for a few days and I had found his short stay in London a favourable time for abstracting a large key which was labelled "Attic" from his study. The door to the attic led off the landing and, at half-past two, I found myself wending my way up the stairs with the key reposing in my pocket. I reached the door and inserted the key in the lock. The lock was stiff and required a considerable effort to turn but at last I heard the lock click back and there before me was a domain that I had never heard mentioned by the grown-ups or looked upon with my own eyes. The light entered the room by a small sky-light situated in the roof. The room itself was not very imposing but it was full of things which I had dreamed about but never seen. In one corner there was a small cabinet which, when opened, revealed many drawers. The drawers were full of bird's eggs, not of the common usual birds, but of golden eagles, singing birds and humming birds. I stood feasting my eyes on them then shut the cabinet quickly out of temptation's way. On the top of the cabinet there was an old picture book. It was full of wonderful pictures of animals. I sat entranced and fascinated by them. Never in my short life had I seen such wonderful colours. I turned to the beginning and saw my father's name. I gathered, therefore, that it must have been my father's when he was a boy. On a pile of old prints of London there was a cage in which there was a small but brightly coloured bird. The dust had settled on its plumage but it still retained its colour. There was a large gold-coloured key which, when I had turned, made the bird issue forth a melodious tune. After examining other objects of delight, I heard from the regions of the kitchen the cook's voice telling me to come and have my tea. With one last glance at the room, I locked the door and went downstairs.*"

COUNT MAURICE CORETH
(F.P. 1940-1944; 1929-1997 RIP)

Count Maurice Rudolf Coreth von und zu Coredo und Starkenberg – whose full name did not appear on school lists of the time for obvious reasons – was an intrepid young man who went through school life at All Hallows and later, Downside, with the same adventurous spirit he showed as an adult. Although no mention is made of it at the time, he famously stole the Headmaster's bicycle at the age of ten and made off for Exeter, with a friend, in order to enlist. Apparently, the boys took overnight shelter in a chicken coop. The Recruiting Officer was a bit taken aback when this young boy appeared the next day, beneath the counter, asking to join 'The Blues' since he had a love of horses. One can only imagine the reaction of the Headmaster and the subsequent consequences of his action when Mr Dix was telephoned with the request to pick up from Exeter one of his pupils. One likes to think that if he was caned it was done with a sense of bristling pride by all parties. In any event, the incident appeared not to leave any lasting repercussions of a negative kind since Coreth was appointed Head Boy in September 1943. But Maurice Coreth was not a 'one-hit wonder'. He achieved another kind of wartime fame when, out on horseback on Dartmoor with the Riding Mistress, Miss Monica Hill, and another pupil, Michael Hartley, he encountered a parachuting pilot whom they believed could have been an enemy soldier. They were prepared to apprehend the pilot and keep him 'captive' by penknife until adult reinforcements arrived but the airman turned out to be American. Not that that did much for poor Monica Hill – herself only 19 – for she was dismissed by Mr Dix for potentially reckless behaviour, which seems a bit harsh, looking back, but, I suppose, there was a war on and it could have been an enemy airman and Mr Dix was in loco parentis after all. Maurice Coreth might have had cause to have no particular love for Germans since it was the Anschluss of 1938, when Wehrmacht forces of Nazi Germany enforced the occupation and annexation of Austria into Germany, that prompted his aristocratic father (Lord High Chamberlain to the last Emperor of Austria) to remove him from Austria and send him to boarding school in England in the first place. Ironic, therefore, that the only wartime 'German' he should meet was a stricken American parachutist who had broken his legs in the fall from the skies over Dartmoor. Coreth maintained his love of horses and love of adventure throughout his life becoming Master of the Wilton at the age of 21 (like his grandfather on his mother's side) and, becoming an expert steeplechaser and show-jumper, he even managed to win the Kenyan Grand National. As an adult, he took up farming in the African Highlands where the equator ran through the house and where cheetahs, leopards and colobus monkeys ran about the place. Giving up his farmlands in 1963, along with many other white settlers, he decided to teach himself to sail so took to the ocean in a 50-foot ketch and then sailed the seas, via Rio de Janeiro, learning as he went, to arrive 63 days later in Cape Town when friends had given him up for dead. His brush with death might not have been so very exaggerated since he survived a tense encounter with pirates in later sea adventures as a Charter Skipper in the Seychelles. He became a Big Game hunter in Africa and was the first amateur to be invited to join the East African Professional Hunters' Association since he was recognised as such an expert. It was through such connections that he later began to fear for the plight of the black rhino whose numbers were dwindling alarmingly from 20000 to 300 in a mere fifteen years. It is largely through his efforts in founding Rhino Rescue and in persuading famous personalities to support fund-raising enterprises that the black rhino was saved from extinction (as an indication, however, of how precarious life remains in vulnerable places and for endangered species, the black rhino in western Africa was, in fact, declared extinct in November 2011, despite the valiant efforts of Coreth and many others). His gregarious and erudite company was much sought after by family and friends to whom he became a raconteur par excellence and the source of countless amusing and adventurous anecdotes. His son, Mark, a famous sculptor, has memorialised his father by creating a massive white bull elephant sculpture outside his studio in Dorset which he has named 'Maurice'.

Notice that things seem to happen to him. He is in temporary disgrace but he still took himself off to his father's study where he presumably remembered the existence of the attic key. He 'found himself wending his way up the stairs' and the key was suddenly 'reposing' in his pocket. He might have given up, for the lock was stiff, but he persisted. He stood feasting his eyes on the items in the attic. It was 'wonderful'. He sat 'entranced and fascinated'. Here were the early signs of the mischievous, wide-eyed boy who became the adventurous, intrepid man. Lest we are in danger of extolling his virtues too much, however, perhaps the following excerpt from the diary summary of the 1943-1944 Soccer season will redress the balance: "*CORETH – Disappointing goal(keeper). Does not use his hands enough.*"

Numbers continue to grow throughout this period in the school's history so much so that Mr Dix was looking for additional accommodation to house the boys and resident staff needed. Initially, he obtained the lease of half of 'Berry Down' which was a fine seventeenth century house with some excellent rooms but without many modern conveniences and then, in December, "After" became available and the school was successful in securing the lease of this delightfully modern house on the edge of the Scorhill grounds. The Berry Down contingent moved in during the first week of the Spring Term. Not only was "After" a most attractive house with exceptionally light and airy rooms but the grounds were large and beautiful and the view towards Fingle Gorge and Meldon Hill was one the finest in England. The garden contained a very good hard tennis court which the school intended to bring back into use. "After" was used to sleep and breakfast some of the teaching staff and boys and a matron-housekeeper was put in charge. The drawing of the house below was drawn by Mrs Tivey. It is believed that "After" was so-called by the school because it was built or leased after the main house at Scorhill but it is uncertain whether the house retains that name today.

Random other recollections from the diary extracts of the time focus on the school's charitable activities and on its busy 'events programme'. Regarding charitable work, in 1943 the school was well on its way to raising £100 (my historic calculator tells me that is about £4000 in today's money) for the Red Cross through collections made at the various plays and through the sale of toys made by the boys. The toys made included over two hundred model ships, a number of model aeroplanes, many pieces of dolls' furniture, cranes, tanks, and larger pieces, like a model town (made mostly of matchsticks), a large toy garage, an aerodrome, a fort, a doll's house, a farm house, a railway station, with engine and trucks, woollen balls and raffia table mats - "*Conspicuous among the toymakers were Couchman, Hartley, Gladstone and Lewis*". The charitable activities and fund-raising events have remained a feature of the school's identity over the years. One thinks of the regular visits instigated by Paul Ketterer of boarding pupils to Rowden House, a resident home for the Elderly in Frome, when volunteers would talk to the residents on a weekly basis and sing choirs at Christmas time, as well as donate food parcels after the Harvest Festival. More recently, a casual trawl through school chronicle records of the early years of the second millennium indicate fund-raising of the following range and kind: over £44000 raised in total for NSPCC, City Farms, Bath Royal United Hospital, The British Legion, Save the Children, Cafod, National Youth Music Theatre, Sargent Cancer Fund for Children, BBC Children in Need, Dorset and Somerset Air Ambulance, CLIC, Food and Famine Appeals, Oxfam; Mencap, the Tsunami Appeal, Frome Rotary Club, Jeans for Genes, Barnardo's, SPIRE (paraplegics through rugby injuries), SPARKS, Maiden Bradley Church Appeal, Guide Dogs for the Blind, Naomi House, SENSE, Macmillan Nurses, LEPRA, Breast Cancer, Blood Bikes, as well as other local charities, through the means of sponsored walks and runs, bike rides, car washing, wearing the wrong clothes, tennis events, toy sales, even sponsored silences. Nor was this all in the form of money; shoe boxes are regularly packed and blankets crocheted and books boxed to various destinations around the world. In recent years, Wendy Hunt and Clare Colgan have co-ordinated much of this activity, which is entirely in keeping with their Christian selflessness. Furthermore, considering our round-the-world connections, two recent expeditions stand out in the persons and examples of Nick Somerville and David Ellery.

Nick Somerville travelled in January 2002 to Antarctica to be part of a young people's and teachers' initiative to clean up 1000 tonnes of rubbish from the Russian base Bellingshausen, on King George Island. 'Mission Antarctica' was conceived by Robert Swan the first man to walk unaided to both the North and South Poles. Nick met up with other members of his team on New Year's Eve in Santiago then travelled to the southern tip of Chile before flying to Antarctica. Imagine a place that holds most of the world's fresh water supply locked into its ice sheets…but is the world's driest desert; imagine a place that has never known war; imagine a place that belongs to no country and is dedicated to scientific exploration; imagine a place that is the coldest and harshest on earth yet remains one of the most beautiful; imagine a place such as this despoiled by the waste left and preserved by humans. Nick remembers "*sailing the still reflective waters around the inlets of the Antarctic Peninsula..as an unforgettable experience…*

such was the beauty of the landscape that at times it was difficult to imagine what a harsh and often dangerous environment we were in...keeping our wilderness areas clean is just common sense!" One of the most poignant reflections was made when Nick and his party started to depart from the area they had cleaned and literally saw the natural animals returning to their world after the rubbish had been cleared away. Local Wells artist Ama Bolton, who had covered Nick's art lessons in his absence, produced a superb lasting work of art in the form of felt panels depicting the removal of the Antarctic waste making use of images drawn by pupils and photographs taken by Nick which he had sent back via the internet.

The second recent expedition is recalled by David Ellery as he represented the school in journeying to an educational establishment called Sang'a, in Kenya, which has become, unofficially, our 'sister' school. The Head Teacher is named Moses and staff members like Benedict and Joseph do what they can, in difficult circumstances, to make education a staple part of the children's growing up alongside the more sobering and urgent need for the basic provisions of life. All Hallows has been supporting the school there for a few years now in terms of fund-raising to purchase two new classrooms, three qualified teachers, a regular feeding programme, an elephant-proof fence and new latrines, as well as donating practical items like blankets, books, art materials, plastic cups and bowls, a new cooking-pot, old uniform, etc. In 2011, David Ellery, teacher of Junior French, Music and Forest School[21], became the first representative of All Hallows to travel to Africa, in person, to spend time at Sang'a. David spent five weeks there assisting the staff and pupils in building and stocking a chicken-coop, as well as helping with the teaching. He lived in fairly basic accommodation throughout his stay and was able to set up a 'blog' in order to maintain communication with the pupils at All Hallows who took a great interest in his activities; the full account can be read at: http;//SangaAH2011. blogspot.com. Much needed drainage work was underway and a new solar generating system with water-storage tanks has also been purchased from funds raised. It was always hoped that other teachers – and perhaps children – will want to continue making personal visits to enhance such educational opportunities for all. Part of that mission is being fulfilled in July 2013 when David Ellery, again, with colleagues Clare Colgan, Suzanne Anderson and Allan Howe spend a further few weeks at the Sang'a school undertaking practical work and distributing funds raised by All Hallows. The sum of almost £10 000, alone, was raised on just one day in June through charity events and an Auction of Promises.

But, mention has been made of the early All Hallows' 'events programme', too. Activities, lectures, debates, entertainments all formed central planks of the school's weekly rhythms and there is a real sense of traditional pride in the repetitive nature of these cyclical occasions with the oft-repeated comment that *'this particular occasion was agreed by many to be the best ever'*. For example, The Literary Society (formed on 21st January 1944), became a firm and

---

[21] For further information on the modern interpretation of 'Forest School' in Scouts' Wood see page 302

eclectic cultural addition to the senior boys' education (the teaching of Greek to part of the Top Form also began on January 25th of that year) and went on to cover many aspects of music, painting and literature over many years, at least up until 1967 (according to records) and probably on until the end of Mr Dix's pivotal connection with the school – since he was the original and principal host of such events. Other subjects, including the operas of Gilbert and Sullivan, architecture, astronomy, history, current affairs and general knowledge were also covered randomly without any prescriptive force of a 'national curriculum'. That is not to suggest, of course, that such cerebral activities do not continue to engage and inspire the pupils' imagination and learning today but it is perhaps fair to say that, nowadays, stimulation of this kind seems to be integrated far more into the everyday curriculum, punctuated by regular and specific events. The Literary Society, as was, met on Friday evenings in Mr Dix's drawing room (now St Hugh's dormitory) after tea from 6.15pm-7.50pm and sometimes later on occasions; "*a not unpopular feature of the meetings (was) the special supper provided*". In that first term, "*a number of painters were studied, some good music listened to and selections from the works of Tennyson and Noyes read...as well as... 'Macbeth', 'Julius Caesar', 'Dr Faustus', 'She Stoops to Conquer', 'The Merchant of Venice' and 'Henry IV'.*" Not all action was of the intellectual kind, however, since, apparently, the Society in the summer terms "*frequently turned itself into a cyclist rambling club*" and many expeditions were made to various locations. 1950/51 seemed to be a particularly busy year with readings and studies of the works of Shakespeare, Sheridan, Goldsmith, Fielding, Sherriff, Galsworthy, Milton, Chaucer, Tennyson, Bunyan, Shelley, Keats, Saki, W. W. Jacobs, as well as Cezanne, Whistler, Vermeer, Constable, El Greco and Jan van Eyck; there must have been a particularly large number of Fridays in that school year or perhaps a lot of occasions when the sessions ran over their allotted time.

A further example concerns the Debating Club which, we are told, was founded in the summer of 1973 by Mr Smallwood when a memorable motion: "This House deplores the use of corporal punishment[22] in schools" was roundly crushed by 55 votes to 3 with *the school's support of corporal punishment vociferously upheld by over a dozen speakers from the floor*". The main proposer, one Gregory Elliott, was "*congratulated on the way in which he stood up to almost unanimous opposition*" although it is not recorded whether Gregory Elliott was beaten for his misguided efforts. Equally, one presumes the Headmaster was in attendance at the debate; nor is it entirely clear who wrote this particular extract in the Chronicle. Despite the 1973 Chronicle's claims, however, it is clear that debating existed as an important and regular activity from much earlier in the school's history, for, on 16th October 1943, we read of "our first debate – "*That the world owes more to thinkers than to men of action*". The motion was won but, unsurprisingly, by a very narrow margin and, interestingly, that same Motion was defeated, five years later, with the school at Cranmore, on 10th October 1948; perhaps the 'man of action' was gaining currency in the developing world or perhaps it was a case of the Devon air breeding thinkers whilst Somerset dealt with those of a more active disposition. A particularly attractive feature of these debates, and, indeed, lectures or talks involving the boys, was the often spontaneous circumstances which gave rise to their taking place. On 25th November 1950, for example, the subjects for lectures were drawn out of a hat on the evening they were to take place and the speakers had to speak for two minutes, unprepared. Subjects included Hiccoughs; Pictures; Gardening; A Bath; Broomsticks; Spivs; Turnips; Old Masters; Bells; Winston Churchill; Nothing; Getting up in the Morning and Myself. The best lecture was adjudged to have been that delivered by Auberon Waugh[23] on the subject of 'Turnips'. Debates followed those diverting lectures on the following motions: "*Independent Schools should be taken over by the Government*" (easily lost!); "*Rugger is better than soccer*" (won); "*It is better to be fat than thin*" (lost); "*The invention of the aeroplane was a calamity*" (lost); "*The cinema is more enjoyable than the theatre*" (lost); "*It is better to live to eat than eat to live*" (lost). Earlier on that day, there had been a soccer match against Edgarley Hall and, in the days following, two separate visits to Downside took place to watch a film on 'Rugger' and take part in a Junior Boxing competition. The week before, the boys had taken part in two separate Masses, produced three individual plays for Prize Day, as well as various choral and solo singing pieces, and a performance by the Percussion Band, and some display dances and work for exhibition in 'Handwork and Art'; with all such performances being reproduced that same evening for visitors from Cranmore. It is worth us all recognising that the busy nature of life is not a modern phenomenon.

---

[22] A motion in the House of Commons in 1976 to abolish Corporal Punishment was defeated in 1976 by 181 votes to 120; subsequently, C.P. was finally abolished in the Maintained Sector in 1986/87 and in Independent Schools in 1998/99. For further information on Corporal Punishment and Discipline see further comments on pp 52-54 and footnote 57 on page 99

[23] See separate box details on page 76

One final example, at this point in the story, to further underline the variety and flavour of the school's entertainment programme, concerns a lecture and demonstration delivered by Colonel James on 14th October 1944. Not only were "princes and nabobs" amazed; read on! To quote the written record in full: "*Colonel James gave an exciting account of his adventures on an Australian cattle ranch, where he first learned to use a stock-whip, his big-game hunting and his experiences in the South African War, and told many stories of his experiences of horsemanship and whippery. After his talk, Colonel James gave a display with the stock-whip. He began by a fierce show of dexterity, cracking first the 20ft whip backwards and forwards in the confined space of the schoolroom, and then two whips, one in either hand. He next tied knots round the bare arms of members of the audience causing them no discomfort, but not a little apprehension. His most impressive feat, with which he had amazed princes and nabobs, followed. Father Albert and Mr Ward held vertically between them at the far end of the room a double page of the Times which Colonel James cut clean down the fold with one crack. He then divided the single sheet into halves, the half sheet into quarters and so on until the hands of Father Albert and Mr Ward were practically touching. The former held the remaining square inch at arm's length and this again was divided and sub-divided until it was about the quarter of the size of a stamp. This fragment was placed on Father Albert's nose and 'whipped off' without the patient feeling more than the draught.*

And if you told that story to the children of today, they wouldn't believe you; nor would the whole episode get past the Health and Safety Executive. Visiting speakers became a regular feature in these years providing great entertainment and information to the boys in their Dartmoor hideaway about the goings-on in the wider world. Any parent with stories to tell was quickly press-ganged into service, it seems. For example, General de Guigand, who was Montgomery's Chief of Staff, delivered a lecture on his wartime experiences whilst on leave from Normandy.

As an aside, I want to mention Mr Dix's use of the 'epidiascope' in providing entertainment. Speaking as one easily bemused and overtaken by the advance of modern technology in the year 2013, it is a little disconcerting to find oneself equally at sea with the technology of those post-war years. It was bad enough when blackboards were replaced with whiteboards. One will be finding out next that whiteboards are truly 'interactive' and that pupils can actually manipulate text and make power-point presentations and the like at the drop of a hat. If one googles the word 'epidiascope' (I'm not that much of a dunce), one discovers the following: "*The opaque projector, epidioscope, epidiascope or episcope, is a device which displays opaque materials by shining a bright lamp onto the object from above; it was the predecessor of the overhead projector*". But, of course, if you are an old All Hallows boy reading these words, you knew all that, didn't you, without any help from Google. Helpful pictures of epidiascopes suggest they look like the kind of things one would make in one's shed when it was raining using loo rolls, hat boxes, boot polish, corkscrews, and other sundry items taken from father's toolbox and mother's kitchen drawers. Whilst we are on the subject of advances in technology, let us raise the matter of television, for in the 1953 Chronicle, meriting a separate admonitory paragraph of its own, we encounter: *"during the summer holidays…we had television installed. We feel strongly that this new invention can be dangerous and must not be used more than occasionally. A certain number of boys look-in to Children's Hour on Wednesdays and Saturdays. Apart from this, television has been used for big occasions such as the return of the Queen, the Pope's broadcast and the Trooping of the Colour. The boys have also been able to see big sports events such as Bannister's Mile, Drobny's Single Final at Wimbledon, the Varsity Rugger Match, some horse jumping and some cricket"*. One boy, 'M.R.' (it might well have been M. Robinson) of Form IV, 1954, wrote his own summary findings: *"Television at school is usually rather fun as everybody has to take his shoes off outside in case the mud goes inside. People who don't wear socks are rather unlucky as there is rather a prickly door mat put down especially for them to wipe their feet. When inside, everybody sits, kneels or stands around. The curtains are pulled, the light put on. Then television starts. Nobody moves, all is quiet, everybody stares at the screen. Somebody hears the tea-bell but keeps quiet about it. Over in the main building (only) seven boys arrive in line. Mr Waddon-Martyn decides to make a search but forgets it is Saturday afternoon which is….Television afternoon"*! And, just in case, the message was becoming lost as the non-moving, quiet, screen-staring boys are sucked ever more dangerously into the televisual world before them, the Editor of the Chronicle in 1956 decides to offer conclusive proof of the damage caused by unfettered viewing: *"In a recent 'Letter from America', Mr Alistair Cook prophesied as to the result of television. He suggested that in time mankind would lose its legs and its two eyes would become closer and closer together until they merged into one. For this reason and others we take care that television is not overdone"*. Although the tongue may firmly be in cheek, one can't help gathering up one's Luddite credentials and shouting from the top of Cranmore Tower, "Yesssss!"

By way of driving the point home about the busy lives of the boys in an 'extra-curricular' sense – once again, we must presume that lessons are going on at other times – the entries for October 11th – October 24th are illuminating:

October 11th   *River in spate – over bridge. Seniors visited river and pool. Dr Midgley very kindly came over and gave the school a talk on 'The Experiences of a Ship's Doctor'.*

October 12th   *Most of the school went to the Chagford Pony Fair taking a picnic lunch with them.*

October 13th   *Literary Society read Lord Dunsan's 'The Gods of the Mountain', Bernard Gilbert's 'Eldorado' and du-Garde Peach's 'The Roadmakers'.*

October 14th   *Colonel James gave an exciting account of his adventures on an Australian cattle ranch..(see above)*

October 18th   *Father Pedrick kindly came and gave a fascinating lecture on 'The Permanent Way'.*

October 21st   *Boys Concert. The boys put up a good show. Form V recited between them all Macauley's 'Horatius' and five of them sang Gilbert and Sullivan's 'Tit Willow'. The Form also did a broadcast play, Aesop's 'The Farmer, the Pig*

and the Actor'. Form IV did two plays – 'Gas Masks' and 'The Slip'; Form III,
'Pigwiggin and the Brave'; Form II, 'The King's Highway' and Form I recited
'The Caravan'. Cochrane also recited Kipling's 'Gunga Din'.

And, then, on November 4th, "*Mrs Best brought us good news of Enzo...*"

The next page highlights former pupil Enzo Bonapera who probably only spent a year at All Hallows between 1941-1942. Enzo went off to train in the Military Academy, in Worcestershire, before joining General de Gaulle's Free French Movement[24], set up in protest against Marshall Petain's[25] Vichy government, which had signed an armistice with Germany. Enzo was last recorded as living in Avenue de Larringes, L'Uscale 74500, Evian, France and made some later visits back to Scorhill when he accompanied Mrs Best on the piano in various concerts. It is believed that he went on to serve in Algeria. Some of this information has been provided by William Cornish whose family had run a jewellery business in Okehampton for many years and who became close to the Bests and Enzo. Mr Cornish describes Enzo as "*a fine gentleman*".

Cadets of an English persuasion can be seen in the photo below since alongside various public schools, several boys chose to leave All Hallows at the end of their time and go to Dartmouth for naval training.

---

[24] The Free French Movement, later named the 'Forces of Liberation', was not universally popular in Vichy France or even in England, for that matter, and although Churchill admired de Gaulle for his indefatigable stance against Nazi Germany he also harboured suspicions, frustrations and even dislike of the French General for the duration of the war. Charles de Gaulle eventually won over enough of his countrymen to become the country's charismatic leader but the Free French forces represented only a small proportion of wartime France at its inception even though its numbers grew as the war progressed. Nor should it be forgotten that Charles de Gaulle was tried and sentenced to death by the Vichy government for treason even though he accused Petain of the same crime.

[25] Marshall Petain, like many other Frenchmen, believed that Britain would not be able to stand alone for long against Germany and had famously declared, in June 1940, that "*Britain would have its neck wrung like a chicken*". As the course of the war began to turn in the Allies' favour, Winston Churchill, in Ottawa 1942, had never forgotten Petain's dismissal of Britain's chances, and, in a typically rousing speech, declared "*Hitler and his Nazi gang have sown the wind...let them reap the whirlwind...some chicken, some neck!*"

ENZO BONAPERA
(F.P. – left 1942)

It is not certain when Enzo Bonapera joined All Hallows but he was amongst the earliest members of the school when it was situated at Scorhill. He had been more or less adopted by Mrs Best, the daughter of a Dutch Burgomaster, who had married Captain Sigismund Payne Best before the advent of the Second World War. The Bests used to play golf at Evian, France, and Enzo was a familiar caddy at the course. Captain Payne Best OBE was a British Secret Intelligence Service Agent who, based in the Netherlands, controlled agents in German-occupied Belgium. Captain Best was captured by German double-agents in what has become known as the 'Venlo incident' and remained a prisoner of war until 1945. Perhaps the Bests placed Enzo in All Hallows because it was considered safer. At All Hallows, Enzo did not appear to feature strongly as an outstanding sportsman but he did take part in many dramatic productions at the school, e.g. as an impressive Moonshine in 'A Midsummer Night's Dream' and was responsible for the "fine roaring of a lion" in 'Brother Wolf'. He also produced an "outstanding" painting of rhododendrons and the lake. Enzo left the school in July 1942 with these valedictory words written hastily into an end-of-term concert:

*"Goodbye to Bonapera, who goes to join de Gaulle
We hope his year at Scorhill has been happy
on the whole.
We'll miss his exhortations loud upon the
football ground
And hope he'll make a host of friends and
find few 'twerps' around."*

One imagines that Enzo, like other young exiles, hardly encountered twerps as he moved onto the École Militaire in Bewdley, founded by Charles de Gaulle, as part of de Gaulle's 'Free French' movement which had been started in London in 1940. The Bewdley military school only remained there between 1942-1944 and prepared about 150 boys to join the war with about a quarter of them making the ultimate sacrifice, in battle, with their lives. Enzo, however, went on to win the coveted Croix de Guerre, of which accolade Mr Dix informed the school on 4th November 1944, when he can only have been still a teenager (the 1941 photo – see earlier – shows Enzo as a slightly more mature-looking boy than the others so he was probably older than thirteen when he left). Enzo was in good company; The Croix de Guerre was instituted as a military honour in 1915 and a famous World War One recipient was a carrier pigeon named "Cher Ami" which saved the lives of 194 American soldiers by carrying a vital message across enemy lines despite being shot in the chest and leg, blinded in one eye, losing most of the other leg to which the message had been attached and avoiding shrapnel and poison gas, in its 25-mile long flight, before delivering its message and then later dying from its wounds. Enzo appeared not to suffer any of these privations but, nevertheless, must have shown extraordinary courage of his own, or as part of his company, in pursuing his own military exploits.

Charles de Gaulle's message to all those who joined the Free French Movement was perhaps a little more uplifting than the rhymes of farewell to Enzo as he left All Hallows:

"Cadets! Among the Free French, you young people were the most generous, in other words, the best! Good sons of France…who served your country in dangerous times but also, in its grief, in the worst days in our history, you consoled France".

The sequential entries for the All Hallows Chronicle often read like other, more famous, diaries that characteristically record everyday events alongside more momentous happenings. One thinks of Samuel Pepys' Diary, the various recordings of which often focused on social encounters and items of food and drink, as well as events like the Great Fire of London to which he was a witness. Such a mixture of style and substance can also be found in *The Diary of Anne Frank* which not only, of course, records her adolescent thoughts and the everyday matters of celebrating birthdays and eating family meals, for example, but also is set against the threat of discovery in her secret annexe and the broader backdrop of the persecution of Jews during the Second World War. A typical range of entries in this vein from the All Hallows Chronicle reads as follows:

May 31st	*Lions-Tigers beat Panthers-Wolves 137 to 86 (Arbuthnott 54, Corbould 29).*
June 2nd	*Literary Society continued 'As You Like It' and 'Paradise Lost'.*
June 4th	*Fall of Rome.*
June 6th	*Invasion of Normandy.*
June 8th	*Corpus Christi. Mass at Gidleigh. Boys' own devices in morning; Pack Tip and Run match in afternoon. Good slogging. Lions-Wolves beat Panthers-Tigers. Father Pedrick preached an excellent sermon. The Panis Angelicus was sung.*
June 9th	*The Abbot of Buckfast comes for the week-end.*

We would not suppose it otherwise but it is rather sobering to know that as Rome was being besieged on one front and, as the Normandy beaches were being invaded on another, the Literary Society continued to indulge in its cultural pretensions and the Packs continued to do battle on the cricket wicket. Such freedoms were, after all, what the Allies were fighting for and it is quite properly reassuring to know that normalities must have continued even under the shadowy clouds of war. And yet, proper celebrations were also conducted as on May 8th:

"V.E. Day. Whole holiday. Sung Mass. Afterwards fuel was collected for the bonfire and boys followed their own devices – games on the brake, fishing, etc. At 3 o'clock the whole school listened to Churchill on the wireless. After tea the bonfire was lit and proved a roaring success. After supper the older boys and staff returned to the bonfire – in which potatoes were roasting with varying success and round which dances and songs were indulged in. At 11.30 they returned to the house – drank to Victory (in cider), danced – listened to the midnight announcement – and so to bed."

The following two days included another cricket match and an impromptu concert with, on May 11th, a trip to local village Throwleigh where, on yet another vast bonfire, an effigy of Hitler was burnt. The boys returned to Scorhill for another midnight finish to their day. Not long after, we read that *"May 20th - Buthy catches his first trout; May 21st – Buthy eats same for breakfast."* One is guessing that 'Buthy' is Arbuthnott. And so, life goes on as normal. To conclude this little diversion, and to underline firmly the editor's political leanings of the time, the diary records that on July 26th, *"the heavens wept all day for England's ingratitude to Mr Churchill."*[26]

Before we leave Scorhill, at least for the moment, and the five-and-a-half years the school spent in that Dartmoor playground (as described by Mr Dix at a later date), let us include one final commemoration of another boy whose contributions to school life seem to stand out distinctly through the pages of the early Chronicle (see box right):

Robin Couchman wrote about Scorhill just before he left the school and also drew the picture printed overleaf:

"Of all the places I have seen in England I am convinced that there is not one can rival Scorhill in beauty. It is perched on a hill commanding a view over the moors and behind it is a pine wood which is a protection against the keen winds. Below is the River Teign, which rushes down in pools and waterfalls, and in winter the rain often swells it to an awe-inspiring torrent of brown water, so strong that it moves even the large boulders which stand in its path. The house is nearly surrounded by the moors, their beauty lying in their bleakness and utter solitude. Near at hand are memorials of ancient days – the Sacred Circle of Scorhill with the Stone Avenue leading to it, the Round Pound and many other hut circles of the Stone Age. What adds to the beauty of Scorhill is the colouring, supplied by the rhododendrons, red, white, pink and, mauve, the grey granite, the yellow gorse and the purple heather. For all nature-lovers Scorhill is an absolute paradise as it abounds in birds and animals, such as badgers, foxes, otters and rabbits; and there are many fish – trout and eels – in the river. The house itself is a fine granite one and is most adaptable for a school, having many large airy rooms and dormitories. In the adjoining fields we have, with quite an amount of hard work, made a very respectable cricket ground, on which we have already played several matches.

And now we really must leave Scorhill.

Francis Dix writes in the Editorial to the third number of the School Chronicle (which covers May 1944-April 1948)..... *"we loved our wartime home on Dartmoor and were in many ways sorry to leave it. We shall certainly always look back with pleasure to the years we spent there. There is no doubt, however, that Cranmore is more suitable for a permanency and I think we have been fortunate in finding such a home in the peaceful countryside of Somerset."*

---

[26] Winston Churchill resigned on 26th July 1945 having been defeated in the General Election by Clement Atlee. The school received a letter from Winston Churchill in November 1949 in which he thanked the boys for their good wishes, which they had sent to him, on the occasion of his 75th birthday and, here we are, in November 2013 celebrating the 75th birthday of All Hallows!

ROBIN COUCHMAN
(F.P. 1940-1942; 1929?-1950 R.I.P.)

Robin Couchman joined the school in the Easter term of 1940 when the school was still at Bognor Regis and he travelled down with others to Scorhill. He had a talent for art, making many fine models, for example, a medieval town and a Roman shop. He was well-cast as the *"friendly, sensible"* Mr Rat in a 1941 production of Toad of Toad Hall, which was presented to almost 200 visitors, and he was *"in excellent form as the irrepressible, irresistible Bottom"* in A Midsummer Night's Dream later that same year. He also played the principal part in Mr Dix's verbal skit entitled 'All Hallows in Shakespeare's Day' when, in *"fine tragic fashion"*, as a mad Macbeth M.A., he went about caning to death various miscreant schoolboys like Coreth, Jackson, Arbuthnott, Milne, Morris and Halfhide, for faulty Latin translations. He was an excellent all-rounder sportsman in soccer (centre-forward), cricket (scorer of a memorable 51 in one innings) and athletics (Victor Ludorum, winner of the 220 yards, the quarter mile, the obstacle race and the potato race in the 1942 Sports Day events). The same valedictory rhymes as for Enzo Bonapera and others record the following:

"And good bye, Robin Couchman, whom
we've tried to pack with knowledge
He's off with scholarship on back to work
at Beaumont College.
We'll miss his clever handiwork and his
cunning painting too
We hope he'll paint old Beaumont red –
his leaving makes me blue.
He's led the school and led the team and
played a Captain's innings,
We hope his later life will prove as
good as his beginnings!
May he long keep his keenness,
as he in life advances,
As lively as his Giglio, as good as his St Francis."

And from the 1950 School Chronicle…..
It is with very great sorrow that we record the death in the summer of Lieut. C. R. Couchman who was killed when taking a parachute course in California. From All Hallows he entered Beaumont to which he had obtained a scholarship. During his last year at All Hallows, Robin was Head Boy, Captain of the Soccer and Cricket XI and the first Victor Ludorum. He was a talented artist and very good with his hands. He made some excellent toys which were sold to raise funds for the Red Cross. I remember especially a fine farmyard complete with buildings, horse and cart and farm animals. Though not naturally an actor he threw himself with such enthusiasm into his part that he gave many fine performances. What those who knew him will most remember about Robin was his immense zest in all things and especially his love of animals and all country things! He loved Scorhill dearly and paid it several visits even after the school left its war-time home. We saw a great deal of Robin during his preparatory school days as he spent most of his holidays with us. When he came in to meals he always had some exciting thing to tell – of a newly found badgers' run, of a swarm of salmon trout discovered under a rock, of an otter's attack on a fish or some story of a bustard or a raven. During Robin's Beaumont days we saw little of him but he paid us a number of visits afterwards and was present at more than one School birthday. It was pleasant to see that he had lost none of his old zest though his over-riding interest was now for parachuting. It was this that led him to join the Guards Parachute Regiment. Robin was a young man of real, though unostentatious, piety. We who knew him and loved him feel a sorrow which is relieved by the certainty of his eternal happiness.

May he rest in peace.

On 10th December 1945, the boys remaining at All Hallows say 'Valete' to David Gladstone (F.P. 1941-1945); Duncan Rae (F.P. 1942-1945); Michael Rae (1943-1945); and John Flood (F.P. 1942-1945) and *"say goodbye to Scorhill"*. They return to school on 30th January 1946 (note the later start, presumably owing to the need to get things ready), along with Head Boy, John Ford, and new boys, D. O'Regan, B. O'Regan, Brittan, Majendie and Waugh to a new life in Somerset. On February 2nd they are treated to a conjuring show by Mr Dix and the Literary Society begin reading *'Gulliver's Travels'* but, for the school, their travels are over, geographically, that is, although metaphorically, of course, the journey continues.......

Scorhill's final benefaction on the soon-to-be-departing boys and staff of All Hallows was to deposit, in the winter of 1944-45, a significantly deep snowfall which Mr and Mrs Dix had anticipated sufficiently well by bringing in suitable supplies after a hazardous journey to Chagford; the next day, the country lanes to Scorhill were impassable and the school found itself cut off for several days. Bread was carted in by pony sledge. One suspects that Latin[27], by day, and conjuring, by night, became the staple diet for those few wintry days. Classics and Magic – imagine! Not so very much later – having escaped the rural isolation of Dartmoor – many of those same staff and boys were to find themselves enduring the Somerset winter of 1947 when snow lay on the ground for ten weeks. Cranmore can do weather, too! (see pages 111ff).

But, once again, we have lapsed into time travel; I have skipped 30 pages of diary entries and jumped forward two years as well as missing much else besides.

In 1945 on November 1st (of course), *"Mr Dix signed the Cranmore Conveyance"*. Not only had the school numbers outgrown the accommodation, Colonel Vickary, the owner of Scorhill, was also returning from war and was reclaiming his property, otherwise Mr Dix might well have stayed somewhat longer on those Dartmoor fringes. Incidentally, Colonel Vickary presumably knew what to expect in re-settling back into his own home after a troop of boys had lived there for five years since he had advertised for a school to take over the building in the first place whilst he was away at war. The die was cast, therefore, and the move to Somerset was on. In those few intervening weeks, the final competitive soccer match against another school, Southey Hall, resulted in a well-fought, 2-1 win for All Hallows with Craig-Mooney

---

[27] Latin has been a singular feature of the school since its inception and, although, it probably does not occupy such a central place in the minds of the pupils today as it did in the 1940s, its importance remains intact and many pupils over the years will remember with pain and pleasure their imperfect indicatives. Francis Dix, Paul Ketterer, Tom McIntyre, Robert Ward, A. Hopkinson, Wendy Hunt, Georgia Coke and Catherine Walker have all added their own brand of repetitive discipline, rigour, warmth and good humour in varying degrees but they all deserve mention if only for battling on, for all of their time, largely in a department of one. Classical scholarship in rural Somerset was sometimes a lonely track. I was even sent by former pupil James Fitzgerald a copy of Mr Dix's Greek Prep which included lots of grammar as well as the instruction to translate into Greek *'Those who fled from the city were not honoured'*. Let us not be dishonoured by fleeing from Latin (even if Greek gave way on the timetable – on my watch - to Computer Studies).

scoring both goals; Mr Jones read a paper to the Literary Society on G. K. Chesterton; there was a kill at Thornworthy with the South Devon Hunt and the mask was brought back to the boys for mounting; the Lions won the last Pack match against the Wolves; the school said regretful goodbyes to Dr Purves who had looked after them all so well for five and a half years; and Reavell won the Verse-speaking Competition with a speech from *Richard II* and the first verse of Shirley's *The Glories of our Blood and State*. All that remained was for the boys to depart and for the staff to *"remain to help with the move to Cranmore"*. For the staff, it sounds like one of the earliest forms of 'In-Service Training' under the catch-all contractual phrase of "Headmaster's reasonable expectations" although measurably more practical than the modern version of INSET[28], it has to be said.

Mind you, note Mr Dix's recollections, that *"on December 10th with some sadness we left Dartmoor and for two or three weeks my wife and I lived alone in Cranmore Hall with no heating except an oil-stove and no lighting except candles. In those conditions we did what we could to get things ready for the Spring Term. Later, members of staff came and gave us great help"*. Equally, there is documentary evidence from Mrs Barbara Capper (then Irving), matron, cook, housekeeper and form mistress, outlining those early days of preparation: *"Arnold-Jones, Gwen Hardaker and myself, with one or two others...and Bert from the village..and maids from Ireland...and, of course, Mr and Mrs Dix strove to get the house in some sort of order in 1946"*. The swings and roundabouts of reality and recollected memories! And the swings and roundabouts of living in a Country Estate Mansion all by oneself, as set against the fact that there was no lighting and little heat! One hopes that Mr and Mrs Dix embraced the experience with panache and stiff-upper lips. Knowing what one knows nowadays about 300 pupils on the same site, with 600 attendant parents and 100 staff and twenty or so Governors and a further twenty or so legislative bodies keen to inspect and to probe and to legislate, the prospect of living at Cranmore Hall by oneself has a certain attraction, cold-toes and all! Cranmore

---

[28] The fictional characters Billy and Sammy Edgell, whose fame lives on in print if not publication - naughty boys both, though sometimes accidental heroes -, first thought that INSET Days were *'Insect Days'* and couldn't quite work out why teachers needed them. Hardly fair on insects, they thought. Plus, whenever they had happened to place a big, hairy spider on a female teacher's chair, the teacher had not been best pleased - if the reaction of running out of the room, screaming, was anything to go by. When they found out that INSET Days were all about training, designed to make teachers better teachers, they wondered why there were not more of them (like several times a week) because they could think of plenty of teachers who needed to become better teachers. It came as something of a surprise to them to learn that teachers were actually *qualified*. But INSET days are now part of the teacher's lot. We embrace them with the enthusiasm of a reluctant bride. And yet sometimes they throw up a useful idea. The trouble is that we have to attend all parts of the INSET because one never knows when that one useful idea is going to surface. INSET days happen at All Hallows before term starts and sometimes after term finishes (unlike in the Maintained Sector when they occur, most often, during term time and pupils have the day off) so they come with a doubly bitter taste to the teachers although I know the reader will not be feeling much sympathy because 'the holidays are long enough'. As it happens, I once sat down and calculated that, over a year, the hours spent teaching in the Maintained Sector and the Independent Sector are approximately the same. INSET days are not as pointless as I have perhaps indicated; one simply has to achieve the right balance in providing useful information without reaching overload and without inflicting 'death by power-point' or cringe-making bonding sessions on a captive Common Room.

Hall had formerly been owned by the Paget[29] family and had an even longer history dating back to the Glastonbury Monks. There are many fine Jacobean characteristics as well as – even today – faint remnants of the finely arcaded structure of the *"well-furnished orangery*

---

[29] The son of John Moore Paget of Cranmore, Richard Horner Paget (1832-1908), sat as a Member of Parliament from 1865 until 1895 and was created a Baron (1st in the line) in 1886. Sir Richard built Cranmore Tower as a folly for his father John. Sir Richard married Caroline Surtees and they had a daughter, Dorothy, who married 1st Viscount Gladstone, son of William Ewart Gladstone. Sir Richard and Caroline had a son, also named Richard (1869-1955), who became the 2nd Baron. The 2nd Baron married Lady Muriel, daughter of the 12th Earl of Winchelsea and 7th Earl of Nottingham; their daughter, Sylvia Mary Paget (1901-1996), married Christopher Chancellor (later Sir Christopher), son of Sir John Chancellor and they had two sons (one of whom, Alexander, was editor of The Spectator from 1975-1984) and three daughters, as well as a grand-daughter, Anna Chancellor, who is well-known as a film and stage actress, perhaps most famous for her major part in 'Four Weddings and a Funeral'. The 2nd Baron, Sir Richard, was somewhat eccentric in his interest in amateur science and inventions and Lady Sylvia recalls, as a child, living at Cranmore Hall and having her ears stuffed with treacle so her father could test the effectiveness of the sign language system he had developed. Lady Grace, Sir Richard's second wife, worked until the age of eighty promoting the Paget-Gorman systematic sign language for the deaf which was adopted widely in hospitals and schools for the deaf across the country proving particularly helpful in developing channels of communication for autistic children. Lady Grace was responsible in WWII for administering, on behalf of Somerset County Council, Cranmore Hall as a maternity hospital for evacuee mothers from Battersea. It is said that 969 babies were born at Cranmore Hall during these years. Sylvia and her sisters were taken on buses travelling at 30mph down Park Lane in London and then instructed by their father to throw themselves off backwards to test his theory that the force of air behind them would see them land safely on their feet. Lady Sylvia was also encouraged to run about on the roof for fresh air and exercise and was also given the delegated task by her father of doing all the wiring when electricity was installed into their home (no wonder the fire alarms seemed to go off so often when the school's alarm system was set up; I remember one electrician in the 1990s going up into the roof and declaring that the wiring had been done by cowboys). Electrical cowgirl or not, Lady Sylvia was put in charge of the domestic staff at Cranmore Hall at the age of thirteen. Sylvia's mother, Lady Muriel, was often absent abroad, founding an Anglo-Russian hospital for wounded soldiers in the First World War, amongst other things, and, when asked if he was related to Lady Muriel, Sir Richard would reply "only by marriage". Lady Sylvia went on to establish an orphanage in Shanghai and, because she loved animals, she not only had swans sailing on the lake but allowed her pet goat to roam freely through the house. Lady Sylvia's brother, John (born 1914), who became the 3rd Baron, visited the school in 1947 and, later, sent to the school the ghost story which is printed elsewhere in the book. Anna Chancellor, the actress, mentioned above is the great-great granddaughter of the 1st Sir Richard Paget and, from a separate line, the great-great-grandaughter of H. H. Asquith, Earl of Oxford and Asquith, and Prime Minister from 1908-1916. And Anna's cousin, Elizabeth, is married to Alexander Waugh, son of Auberon and grandson of Evelyn – thus do the All Hallows reverberations ripple outwards. Finally, in this foot-noted feast of associations, two further connections: (1) Lady Helen Asquith, daughter of Raymond, who died at The Somme, and daughter of Katherine Horner whose name belongs to the nursery rhyme of 'Little Jack Horner'(who pulled out the 'plum' that was Mells), inspected All Hallows in June 1947 (she subsequently allowed the post-CE boys to bathe in her private pool); (2) the great-grandson of Prime Minister Asquith, Raymond Asquith married the Catholic historian Clare (author of 'Shadowlands-the Hidden Beliefs and Coded Politics of William Shakespeare') and together they have five children, two of whom, Lady Celia and Lady Isabel, attended All Hallows as pupils in the 1990s. Another branch of the Asquith family related by marriage through the 4th Lord Hylton is the Jolliffe family and they also have connections with All Hallows in that the Hon. Andrew Jolliffe, son of the 5th Baron Hylton, was a school governor and his children, Isabel, Julia, Elodie, Marina and Suza also became pupils at All Hallows up until the present day. At this rate – in order to keep up with the grand connections - the present writer and former Headmaster wants to be able to lay claim to a family link that goes back to Henry VIII but, sadly, whilst my ancestors can, indeed, be traced back to that time, my g-g-g-g-g-g-g-g-g-g-grandfather, Jacob James Bird (born c.1530), was only a gentleman limeburner in The Forest of Dean, which was not a place to visit after dark. But, the 'Men of Dean' earned their own special privileges from the Crown, and, even if they never owned outright their own rolling estates, they had their own forest, and I'm going to hang on to that noble distinction amidst all these Lords and Ladies. No wonder I was destined to become the 'Wood Ward' of Scouts' Wood.

and conservatory" gazing out over noble gardens and geometrical flower-beds growing in rich colours and sweet perfumed flaming tulips, lavender bushes, peonies and other fragrant flowers (all described sumptuously in an 1899 edition of '*Country Life*'). In the same magazine we read of the "*noble cedars of Lebanon extending their dark horizontal arms and casting their solemn shade*" onto the southern aspect of the gardens designed by the "*well-known landscape gardener…Mr E. Kemp*" and we can still see today the "*summer house fashioned in the style of a Grecian temple*" even if it has housed, at various times more recently, an administrative office, second-hand uniform shop and a peripatetic set of drums forever destined to be moved around the school according to the patience of those in earshot at any given time.

In the same publication, we move to the adjoining "*church of St James, erected in 1846 on the site of an ancient edifice and embodying some Norman and other features*" although it is unclear as to whether it was ever actually used as a parish church or more as a private family chapel. The church has been de-commissioned and is now an interesting and beautiful private residence. Found alongside the old church lies the entrance to what is now termed by the school as 'Scouts' Wood'[30] although its topographical name is Hiltyning Wood. Two of the "*three splendid specimens of the Spanish chestnut*" with "*gnarled trunks and twisted arms which testify to their great antiquity*", as recorded in that 1899 edition of Country Life, still stand today making them, in 2013, even older "*relics of a great avenue*". Sweeping past the "*rookery of lofty elms and limes*" (the avian droppings and tree-sap of which are, today, unwelcome gifts deposited – perhaps in protest – on the invading parked cars below) one spies the distant Cranmore Tower some 900ft above sea level, erected by J.M.Paget in 1862, with its magnificent outlook over the land. The Colonnade has the date 1869 carved into its stonework but the two-storied cruciform building, known as The Cross House, dates back to medieval times when the monks of Glastonbury owned the property and would have "*tended their gardens and tilled their fruitful fields*" presumably unaware that centuries later hordes of children would descend upon their peaceful lands. That two-storied Cross House originally, it is believed, accommodated the Estate Offices and then a beautiful chapel for the school and now converted staff accommodation above the current Dining Room.

And then, of course, there were all those ghosts!

Mrs Irving, who helped with the move to Cranmore, sent to Paul Ketterer, in 1978, a typed, four-page, short story entitled '*The Horses of Darkness*' which she wrote based on her true experiences in those post-war years at Cranmore as the school inherited the ghosts of the past. The story puts one in mind of the understated, slow-burning '*Turn of the Screw*' without, perhaps, the menace, or of the pony and trap in '*The Woman in Black*', but the ambiguity and the chilling 'encounter' runs through the story to make us wonder 'can it be true?' The writer tells us of a story supposedly invented by the Headmaster's wife which gained currency amongst

---

[30] For other passing reference to Scouts' Wood see later pages

Bernard Ninnes

the boys although they were supposed never to find out lest they became afraid. It concerned an armour-suited knight seated on an old oak chair in a dark corner under one of the secret, spiral staircases hidden behind some panelling. Suits of armour, old weapons and portraits of long-forgotten noblemen lined the entrance hall and corridors leading to this secret staircase. Lying open on the knees of this knight was an ancient bible which, on no account, should be moved or the knight would 'walk'. The larger story goes on to explain that this anecdote was actually invented but that the 'true' ghost story involved a carriage being drawn up to the house by four horses in the middle of the night. They could clearly be heard but never seen, nor any signs of hoof-prints the following morning. Conjecture wondered about a fleeing stranger at the time of the Civil Wars (1642-1648) or some renegade from Monmouth's rebellion at nearby Sedgemoor in 1685 or perhaps, simply, a clandestine meeting between a romantic lover calling upon a lady of the house. An incidental detail, recently heard, lent some material corroboration to the description when former pupil David Stirzaker (1947-1950) visited the school at a 2013 Open Morning, after a lapse of 65 years of never having returned to school, to mention, by chance, that the entrance hall and corridors used to be lined with suits of armour, weapons and old portraits; needless to say, we discovered afresh the old spiral, turret staircase although whether this was hidden at any time we do not know. From that same encounter, however, one learned that Mr Dix used to 'hide' there sometimes in order to catch the boys talking after 'Lights Out' in T-More dormitory above his study. Perhaps the seated knight was simply Mr Dix reading his evening bible before checking the boys on a nightly walk? But that still leaves the horse and carriage! The story takes a more sinister twist following Sir John Paget's contribution to the 1971-72 'All Hallows Magazine' which is re-printed in full below.

"There is a small room forming an ante-room between the passage near the entrance to the arcade and billiard room. This was known as the Museum. On the left hand side as you go in, there is a small alcove. In this was a large wooden chair in which sat a suit of armour which was traditionally said to belong to Mr Benjamin Bradford and on his knees was a large bible. The legend was that if this bible was removed his ghost would walk and, furthermore, should the heir to the estate die, Mr Bradford would ride up to the front door in a large coach. A small boy did remove the bible and I'm afraid the ghost didn't appear but, in 1900, my parents were living in London and my grandparents were at Cranmore. There was quite a large house party staying and, just after midnight, a noise was heard of a coach driving up to the front door. My grandfather waited for somebody to be announced but nothing happened. He went out to the front door where he met his butler who had also heard the noise and had come down in his night-shirt and dressing gown and had opened the front door, but nobody was there. He then went and got a lantern and went to look at the gravel sweep in front of the front door. On these rather 'palmy' days the last duties of the gardeners before they went off duty was to rake the ground but this showed no signs of being disturbed.

My grandfather and the butler then went round to the back yard to see if anybody had arrived there but saw no signs so they went to bed rather mystified. The next morning, my grandfather received a telegram to say that my brother, aged six months, had died just after midnight the night before. My grandfather wrote up the incident and got everybody in the house to sign it. Unfortunately, the document has been mislaid but my father remembers having seen it."

Now I don't suppose this will be the final piece in the jigsaw but the space thus described above in Sir John's letter sounds very much like the room recently used as the Deputy Headmaster's office by John-Paul Renouf. Mr Renouf is a sober-minded gentleman not given to exaggerated flights of fancy. He might write music and sing silly songs for the benefit of the pupils but he is not soft in the head. Yet Mr Renouf has also reported strange goings-on in his office, in 2012, like flashing lights, and he knows nothing of the stories I have just related; for example, *"Following a weekend, I returned to my office on Monday morning to find a large smear of blood across the inside of my locked office door. I investigated, asking the cleaner and James Callow (who shared the office with me at this time) if they had been into the office since my departure on Saturday lunch-time. Neither of them had and no-one else was in possession of a key to the door. I checked the window, which was firmly closed from the inside, and the adjoining door to the changing room – locked and blocked from the office side by boxes of books and stationery. I could find no logical explanation for the blood but did recall that the school had been used as a maternity hospital during the Second World War and that the room above my office had apparently been a 'birthing' room. I had also been told that during this time one particular mother-to-be had experienced a rather horrible and bloody birth."*

The reader can draw the strands together.

A later ghost story concerns the crying baby that could be heard in a similar location of the school emanating from the present large bathroom and above the old Billiard Room, in which school plays and concerts were performed, but which now houses the Music Room. The origins for this story – which were still current in the 1980s although the present writer hasn't heard the children refer to it in recent years – are not so difficult to pin down. In the short time between the departure of the Pagets and the arrival of the school, Cranmore Hall was used as a base for evacuee mothers from Bristol and London to give birth to their children, as indicated by Mr Renouf above. It is recorded that fully 969 babies were born there in that time and that the present bathroom was, in fact, the birthing room. We still receive the occasional visitor, now in his or her late sixties, who turn up to ask politely for a tour since they were born there. One such person who was definitely born at All Hallows went on to become Head Groundsman and Gardener in charge of the maintenance of the Estate; his name: Harry Godden[31]. Harry had a

---

[31] See box details on page 277

real skill in producing competition-winning vegetables and flowers in national competitions whilst also maintaining the gardens and grounds in beautiful order. Harry retired in May 2010 after some 24 years and is quoted as saying in the 1996 edition of the School Chronicle "I love walking through the gates every morning. I feel a real sense of pride in what I do". By another chance quirk of fate, another person born at Cranmore Hall at that time was Judith Wilkinson, who I had the pleasure of working with for nine years at Prior Park Prep School in Cricklade when she was the Matron – or 'Sister' as she preferred. Judith is one of the kindest people I have ever met; perhaps the birthing room at Cranmore bestowed magical powers. Perhaps some people are just kind, even in the face of huge pressures that are sent to challenge.

Let us leave ghost stories and birthing rooms and challenges for the moment and return to the chronological history.

Barely 50 boys started the 1946 academic year at Scorhill but 64 boys arrived for the first term at Cranmore and by 1948 the numbers had reached 91; All Hallows was truly on the move! Mr Dix records the observation that "*when we bought Cranmore Hall we did not realize how near we were to Downside*" – in which case it was a fortuitous happenstance – especially since there had been some contact between the two schools even when All Hallows was situated in Devon and, since, in those early Cranmore years, Abbot Butler and Headmaster Father Wilfred Passmore "*gave us always the greatest kindness*" and "*provided us with Chaplains*" for the next 30 years. In fact, Downside took on that role again in the 1980s and has continued to do so ever since. On February 26th "*a lovely statue of Our Lady of Buckfast arrives for the Chapel*" which was beautifully carved and painted by an Austrian artist and can still be seen today in the chapel of All Saints.

The writer records the fact that he was responsible for its 'resurrection' when he took on the headship in 1995 since it was lying on its side in apparent forgotten storage in the attic above the old chapel. It may have been carved and painted by an Austrian artist but it was painstakingly cleaned with a toothbrush by this Somerset Headmaster who thus added his own mark to its presence and survival; palimpsests again of a literal kind. On 28th June 1946, the House was consecrated by Father Metcalfe to The Sacred Heart on that feast day. On November 2nd, a home match was arranged against Greenways, who were presumably on tour, because this was the first school ever encountered in a competitive fixture right back to the Bognor Regis days; hospitality was duly left to after the match since All Hallows won by 6 goals to 1. School Inspections may have taken on a different hue these days and possibly with greater regularity and legislative force but they were becoming a familiar part of the educational landscape even then for on November 4th, "*Lady Helen Asquith ("our H.M.I.) paid us a visit and inspected the school*" to be followed on November 6th with a preliminary visit by Dr Grimshaw (who went on to become Bishop of Plymouth) who conducted, on 26th February 1947, a subsequent successful 'Religious Instruction Inspection' which indicated before he left "*that he would be able to give to the Bishop a good account of the school and its knowledge of its religion*". Lest we are tempted to believe that today we've never had such bad wintry weather, it is worth noting that on 23rd January 1947 "*the snow came and remained for the next ten weeks*" thus 'topping and tailing', effectively the school's removal from Scorhill and its arrival at Cranmore, although the year 1947 does go down on record (along with 1963) as rather exceptionally bad[32]. February 18th - Shrove Tuesday - must have provided some relief and no little excitement as a half holiday was declared and the school *"had its first talkie – Buchan's 39 steps with Robert Donat and Madeleine Carroll"*. Further excitement followed on June 4th judging by the tone of the Chronicle entry: *"a great event today – arrival of our Dennis Motor Mower"*! One imagines Mr Dix is particularly pleased after all those loving hours spent hand-mowing pitches on the Devon slopes and the Somerset fields. Cricket, as we have seen, had been a prominent feature of school life (or at least, prominently recorded in the Chronicle pages) and an interesting note on July 24th refers to an evening cricket match that took place at the school between a team made up of Staff and boys against Cranmore Village Club which involved two innings separated by a supper on the field and stumps drawn at 10.30pm *"which must be nearly a record"*.

Finally, in this year of 1946, at the end of the second term at Cranmore Hall, *"during the holidays one of the outside buildings was converted into a Gym-playroom"*; this was the area looking onto the stable-courtyard (known as the quadrangle then) which currently houses the Reception Class of four-year-old children. A replacement gym was subsequently built at some point in a Nissan Hut outbuilding on the site of the present Sports Hall which, itself, was constructed during Paul Ketterer's time in 1986 and opened by Mike Davis, formerly Sherborne schoolmaster - who went on to play rugby for Harlequins and England, as well as coaching the national team. Physical Education has come a long way since the outdoor P.T. lessons on the cricket field at Scorhill.

[32] For more reflections on Cranmore weather see pages 111ff

In the Michaelmas Term 1947 the inauguration took place – on November 1st, of course – of the first All Hallows Scouts Troop. The numbers, at the beginning, were limited to 12 and consisted of senior boys only. Reynolds and O'Callaghan were chosen as the first Patrol Leaders (Seagulls and Falcons) but, later, the Gannets were formed with Bellasis as Patrol Leader and, later again, the fourth patrol, Woodpeckers joined the throng. For many years the Scouts were led by Mr Trappes-Lomax[33], who had run a similar troop at Avisford, Mr Dix's first school before he founded All Hallows. The scouts would meet at various times and hold formal, organised outings on Sundays between 11.30am-4.30pm. They busied themselves with *"fire-lighting, cooking, tracking, etc"* and worked towards the variously-classed tests showing *"a good standard of self-discipline"*. One presumes that a good deal of their business took place in the wood adjacent to the old chapel of St James, which must have led to the adoption of the present-day appellation of 'Scouts' Wood', although some of their activities also occurred on either side of the Cran and, of course, various camps were held off the premises. In thinking of the ghosts of the past, as we were earlier, it has never been too fanciful to remind the present-day children who use the growing facilities of Forest School in Scouts' Wood of the many former pupils who have gained similar enjoyment and learning from those same surroundings many years before, albeit under a different guise. It is an unbroken tradition that remains an important part of the school's history for several generations of pupils and staff.

[33] See box details on page 83

One week after the school's ninth birthday, the Bishop of Clifton visited the school on November 8th and conferred the Sacrament of Confirmation on fully 48 boys in the tiny school chapel with Father Edward Cruise from Downside assisting, alongside Father Mark and Father Alban Brooke. Amongst the many boys confirmed were 'famous' All Hallows' names like O'Callaghan, Dick, Arbuthnott, Lavery, de Guingand, Simey, Melhuish, and Keswick. I use the term 'famous' very randomly; those boys simply seem to feature significantly in the early chronicles, or went on to achieve distinction in their chosen careers or became subsequently important to the school as adults, like Chris Dick and George Simey, for example, who were both appointed as Chairmen to the Governors. Included in that group was David Stirzaker (referenced earlier) who provided some interesting memories of roller-skating, snow-tobogganing, running over cow-pats on the distant sports pitches (which might, conceivably, have improved the boys' sidesteps) and regular slipperings from Mr Dix. David Stirzaker remembered his schooldays fondly even if 'Dicky's' fur-lined slipper, known by the boys as "the furry object", could weave temporary patterns on the boys' bottoms which the transgressing boy would later show off as a badge of honour to his mates in the dormitories. David and a few friends had absconded from school on one occasion to visit the local village post office in order to buy sweets when, at the very moment of paying for them, in walked Mr Dix himself. They were frog-marched back to school. At another time, he and several others were discovered, again by Mr Dix, ploughing greedily through his strawberry garden. I was able to remind David (now in his seventies) that the chronicle of his time records him winning the 100 yards and the 150 yards races on Sports Day in 1948. David's instant memory was that there was a mix-up with the names when the prizes were awarded and although he had rightly won those races he was never awarded a prize; I promptly righted that wrong by shaking his hand and awarding him an All Hallows Teddy Bear (2013) sixty-five years after the races had been run. David's best friend was Marcus Niven (a friendship demonstrated by once pouring 'Vim' over Marcus' head in the drying corridor) and the two boys would, occasionally, be taken out for lunch and a spin in the flashy sports car belonging to Marcus' uncle – one David Niven, film star and actor. David remembers school fees being £350 per annum at this time. The Bishop of Clifton – after the Confirmation Ceremony – asked the Headmaster to give the school seven half holidays in honour of the Seven Gifts of the Holy Ghost. Mr Dix granted one of the half holidays on November 10th and converted the other six into three whole days to be added to the end of the Christmas holidays. In 2013, another old boy, David Corbould (F.P. 1948-1954), turned up out of the blue to re-visit the school and, in his case, exorcise a few ghosts. His memories of the regime were of an inevitably all-male affair with only Mrs Dix and the occasional female teacher providing some much-needed feminine touches. He remembers being invited into the Dix's Drawing Room (now St Hugh's dormitory) and being rather taken aback by flowers and a few other signs that a woman had added some flair. The 'smell of man' would be too easily forgotten today. It must have been a fairly grim atmosphere at times with all-male teachers applying their own rigorous discipline to a pack of boys who sank or swam in those austere waters. David freely admits that he was not particularly happy at All Hallows but let's invite him to tell his own story....

The Cherry Jumpers

"To the dreaded "peer group" I was a 'wet' and a 'weed', the schoolboy parlance of the day, and spent much of my free time either avoiding, or putting up with, the usual bullying and teasing. There were no visits home during the course of a term, but parents were allowed to visit for the weekend at half term and for the school concert (in the Christmas term) and sports day (in the summer term). My parents, who never owned a car during my time in the school, found it difficult and often impossible to visit, and for at least my first two years I was often homesick. My first experience of the teaching staff was promising as in Form One I enjoyed the attentions of Miss Giles, the only female member of staff, apart from Matron. She was a young and attractive (well, my father thought so) woman who treated her charges with a degree of kindness not shared by her male colleagues. Sadly, I was only destined to remain with her for one term. When I returned after Christmas, I found that together with Coffey, with whom I had formed something of a friendship, I had been promoted to Form II on the grounds that we were considered sufficiently intelligent to study alongside boys a year older than ourselves. On the academic side, I managed without difficulty, but the older boys soon found me an easy target for teasing, and I was not impressed by the form master. Now that he is a saintly and ascetic monk at Ampleforth, I hope he will forgive me for saying this, but in those days he had a reputation for getting into "bates" - schoolboy jargon for filthy tempers - when he would inflict various forms of corporal punishment, including beatings and shakings, such that in the end Mr. Dix was forced to reserve all forms of physical chastisement to himself and his deputy. I shall never forgive % *?$£&!![34]*, the teacher's "pet", for making him a particularly long ruler in carpentry specifically for the purpose of inflicting punishment. We took great delight in destroying it when we heard it could no longer be used.*

In fact to be fair, as I progressed through the school, the other masters I came across were not unduly harsh, until, that is, one came under the direct influence of Mr. Dix himself. He taught classics, and although I had begun to learn Latin in Form II under Mr. Adams, our first experience of Mr. Dix was aged eleven when he became our tutor in both Latin and Greek. We knew from experience that our Headmaster had a formidable temper. There were the times when he would address the school at "line-up" (I think the modern equivalent is "Assembly") each morning, and if anything had particularly displeased him in the previous twenty-four hours, then the decibel level of his voice and the deep red colour of his face left us in no doubt as he harangued us in a style reminiscent of Hitler. His own chosen form of punishment was the slipper, known as the "furry object", applied to the bare backside, usually in multiples of two - six normally being the maximum for more serious misdemeanours. Probably the most frequent offence was talking in the dormitory after lights out, something for which I was often

---

[34] The writer of this book has removed the name to spare embarrassment

caught, as I found I had a talent for telling stories. These apparently entertained the "peer group" and gained me some respect, as opposed to the usual teasing. However there was periodically the inevitable price to pay when one of the staff, or Mr. Dix himself, crept up to the dormitory door and pressed an ear to it. Once found out, you were ordered to report to Mr. Dix's study in the morning. This led to a fitful night's sleep as you lay in a state of fear and terror awaiting your fate. Mr. Dix had two particularly refined forms of torture. The first was the Penalty Test. His method of teaching us Greek and Latin syntax was to set some material to be learned in Prep, and then the following morning he would go round the class firing questions up and down the ranks of desks. If you did not know the answer when it was your turn, he said, "Next - next- next," and so on until someone came up with the right answer. Periodically, when our retention of information had been well below standard, there would be the Penalty Test. The rules were simple: if you missed an answer or got one wrong, it was one whack with the gym shoe - size twelve (by that time the furry object was no longer with us, having finally met its end being chewed up by Mrs Dix's dog). At the end of the test, you totted up your misses and filed out to "My Study" for the requisite number of lashes. The other form of torture was the end of term exam. A week or ten days before the end of term, Mr. Dix would enter the classroom and announce the test which would determine what marks were put on our school report for the term. He would then begin writing on the blackboard and we would start attempting to answer the questions. Once he finished at the blackboard, Mr. Dix would light his pipe and then begin pacing up and down between the rows of desks, stopping periodically to look over a boy's shoulder and inspect what had been written. One became aware of a warm feeling beside one's ear and a sound of sizzling as the spittle ran down into the bowl of the pipe, and one braced oneself for a cuff across the head and the words, 'If you haven't got that right in five minutes, I'll beat you.' By that stage, with a considerable amount already written, you had no idea what mistake he may have spotted. After a feverish five minutes failed to resolve the problem, you were duly taken out and beaten. The ironical thing was that very often the results were so bad from the class as a whole, that two days later we simply all retook the exam. In the meantime, we had copied down the questions from the blackboard and done the necessary revision (you learn fast in those conditions) and the results improved dramatically. Mr. Dix must have felt proud as he entered the (revised) marks on our end-of-term reports. Strangely we did not think to tell our parents how we seemed to have done so well. On the religious side, even for boys as young as seven and eight, regular retreats and days of recollection were laid on, usually by the Benedictine monks of Downside Abbey, who acted as chaplains to the school. There was weekday mass twice a week before breakfast (fasting from midnight before receiving Communion was still the order of the day) as well as two masses on Sunday, one early (to receive Communion) and the other at 10.00 a.m. which was sung. Then on Saturdays we were all sent to the chapel, a form at a time, for Confessions. One was encouraged to "go" at least fortnightly and could be chided by the confessor for less frequent attendance. Unfortunately it rapidly became a matter of routine with the same old list being trotted out each time. I remember worrying whether I might ever be challenged for apparent lack of imagination, but despite the boredom the priest must have suffered, he refrained from any such comments. I still remember a particular Sunday - I must have been about nine at the time - when after the sung mass there was to be Exposition of the Blessed Sacrament throughout the day until the evening service of Benediction. I left the chapel after Mass to write the statutory letter home: 'the school lost at football... the Saturday entertainment was... please send postal order for....' but, on finishing, I felt drawn back to the chapel again where I remained, apart from lunch, until the evening. It was very quiet and peaceful and I felt very close to God, whom I believed in implicitly. There may also have been a slight sense of "holier than thou" as other boys came into the chapel and then left again a short time later. But I think it also bolstered my desire to eventually become a priest. Aged eleven I found my niche when I was appointed as one of the sacristans, looking after the chapel and preparing the altar and the priest's vestments before mass. It gave me a valid excuse to get away from the dreaded "peer group" and be either alone or with the two or three other boys who shared the duties. In due course I graduated to the specialist task of teaching other boys how to serve on the altar. You had to be an expert yourself in order to do that, and serving the Tridentine Mass was considerably more demanding than the duties required of altar servers today. Also preparing for the following day's mass required a working knowledge of the Church's calendar of feast days. I have a feeling that the "peer group" must have found me something of a prig, but it gave me an interest and kept them at bay. It also gave me the opportunity to get to know the monks who acted as chaplain. I was very proud of the fact that Father Alban Brookes knew my great-uncle Robert, the Anglican Rector of Carshalton, though I forget now how they had met, and then there was Father Hubert Van Zeller, author, artist, sculptor and cartoonist (Who still remembers "Cracks in the Cloisters"?) who did a brilliant water colour in my autograph book entitled "Autograph Hate". I was very proud of it, and also of the friendship and encouragement he gave me. We used to have long conversations after mass, not least about my hoped-for vocation, and I became very fond of him. The only other prize I ever won was for coming third in an obstacle race some years before."

Bullying was a common schoolboy reality, one suspects, alongside the ever-present threat of corporal punishment. David Corbould would have been present at a talk delivered on 20th January 1951 to the school by Sir Shane Leslie, diplomat and writer, 3rd Baronet, first cousin to Winston Churchill, who spoke of his own unhappy schoolboy memories at Eton in the late 1890s, where the food was "wretched" and *"as for thrashings, which tyrannised rather than disciplined our*

House, they were excessive. Bullying was endemic and Irish boys were ridiculed". He sent his sons to Downside and Ampleforth in order to escape such privations although, interestingly, his daughter suggests that *"in my parents' view, schools performed the same function as kennels do for dogs. They were places where pets could be conveniently deposited while their owners travelled".* To suffer under such a regime, beset by peers on the one hand and masters on the other, cannot have been a positive experience. To be bullied by peers must be worse than to be beaten by staff; at least the second phenomenon created an esprit-de-corps alongside the stinging bottoms. In today's educational climate, schools are quick to proclaim that *'there is no bullying here'* or, more honestly, state that *'any form of bullying will not be tolerated and we always act quickly to eradicate its incidence and alleviate the suffering so that the clearest message is delivered to both victim and instigator'.* Schools now operate under strict codes of behaviour sometimes in the form of written policies (although we had the presence of mind to change our newly-formed 'Bullying Policy' – of which we were proud – into the more-appropriately named 'Anti-Bullying Policy' since we did not want to be seen as endorsing the practice through slipshod use of language). And the views of pupils, themselves, are now canvassed within schools and in genuinely confidential questionnaires by external Inspectors who are experienced in interpreting the words of the young. But it is not all straightforward. Not long before one such inspection, we had conducted a mini-drive of our own about the wrongful nature of bullying and the practical steps that could be taken if any pupils felt they were being put in difficult situations by their peers. This was part of a campaign organised by a National Anti-Bullying Week which was intended to raise awareness. We duly played our part and outlined the broadest definition of the word so that the would-be bullies knew they could not hide behind more liberal interpretations of their behaviour. Victims, too, were reassured that any form of peer pressure was something they had the right to resist without having to suffer any consequences. The raising of awareness is, of course, important but there was definitely a sense in our unrelated inspection a week later that the children were more inclined to believe they were being systematically bullied on occasions when they had simply been treated rather brusquely by other young people who can, sometimes, be rather brusque! I am not trying to condone unkindness nor make light of the real tendencies to excuse certain forms of behaviour. I am aware of the insidious and unrelenting nature of institutional bullying – and other forms of unacceptable attitudes that quickly can become institutionalised – but we do need to strike a balance in judgement ourselves and we do need to educate our young people intelligently in how to read situations, events and people. Yet, bullying remains a school-time occupation and experience and memory for many of us. The bully carries his or her own scars with them in the form of under-developed characters that can persist into their adult relationships; the victims can carry about with them probably more deep-rooted scars affecting their responses to people thereafter. Bullying in the adult workplace is not uncommon, nor within marriages, nor in ordinary human interaction and schools are ideally placed to adopt a zero-tolerance stance to eliminate present and later injustices even if there is a small danger that such heightened sensibilities can sometimes lead to over-reactions. Interestingly, if one asks any group of children (it might be the same for adults) to indicate if they have ever been bullied, a host, the vast majority, sometimes all, of the hands will go up. If one asks the same group of people to indicate if they have ever bullied anyone, the silence is deafening, as hands stay firmly in pockets. That might not be surprising to the general reader but it does, perhaps, indicate the scale of the problem. In the matter of anti-bullying policies, parents and children need to know that the message will be delivered consistently, time and again, and that good judgement and right action will be exercised in open forms of communication to support the fine words.

On the Feast of St Patrick, 17th March 1948, the school played its first ever 'rugger' match against St Christopher's which *"proved a hard and exciting, if not over-skilful, game"* ending in a draw with two tries a-piece, although one of the All Hallows' conversion attempts hit the cross-bar. March 24th saw several boys take part in the "Bristol Eisteddford" (sic) which hosted verse-speaking competitions similar to the present-day LAMDA exams and Mid-Somerset festivals in which so many of our pupils today record outstanding successes. Their counterparts of 1948 did not suffer by comparison with many individual scores over 70% and, in 1950, the boys excelled in the Weston-Super-Mare Eisteddfod gaining two trophies. On March 28th, Easter Sunday, incense was used for the first time in the school chapel and on April 1st *"we are told that in the matter of April Fools some members of the staff got their blows in first"*. In amongst the Old Boys' News is one item regarding Tony Jackson (FP 1940?-1942) who, as a prominent athlete and sportsman, achieved his own particular fame by scoring the winning drop-goal in the 1948 England v. Wales Schoolboy Rugby International.

Here follows another flavour of life over a two-week period at All Hallows ....

May 21st	*Seniors bathe. In the evening the Literary Society begin 'As You Like It'.*
May 23rd	*Coaching from Bill Andrews. Mr Andrews brought Peter West – a BBC Sports Broadcaster with him and poor Mr West was bombarded with questions all the afternoon. Miss D. K. Broster[35], the well-known historical novelist, paid us a visit this day.*
May 27th	*Scouts went to Strap Lane Halt. In the afternoon there was a Corpus Christi procession. Father Metcalfe officiated. We were pleased to welcome a number of girls from The Saviour Convent who took part....In the evening the seniors had a short cycle ride to the Roman Camp near Batcombe from which we got a really wonderful view of the evening sun shining on the sea.*
May 28th	*Literary Society finish 'As You Like It'.*
May 30th	*Some of the Seniors cycled to Downside to see the match between Downside and Somerset C.C.*

[35] Dorothy Kathleen Broster, most remembered for her Jacobite Trilogy, comprising *The Flight of the Heron*, *The Gleam in the North* and *The Dark Mile*, featuring the dashing hero Ewen Cameron. She also wrote a short horror story *Couching at the Door* which has been anthologised many times. She was in her seventies when she visited All Hallows and died two years later. She is known to have said about the writer's craft that *"the clash of character is more important than the clash of swords"* – perhaps that advice struck home to the fiction-writing boys of All Hallows (but I'm not so sure).

May 31st	*We had the holiday postponed from Ascension Day. The whole school went in two coaches to Stourton.*
June 2nd	*Match at home against Hazlegrove which All Hallows won by 94 runs to 14.*
June 4th	*The Literary Society read Sophocles' 'Oedipus the King'.*

A month later, on July 2nd, an excellent bike ride seemed to take place which is worth printing in its entirety....

A party of Senior Boys went on a cycling expedition with Mr Dix. They were lucky in having a lovely day for their ride. First they made for Masbury Camp, stopping on the way to inspect a fine pool in the quarries at Waterlip and later at the Waggon and Horses for a drink of cider. They lunched on the ramparts of the old British Camp at Masbury (one of the highest points on the Mendips). After lunch they botanized for a while and then went on their way towards Blackdown Hill. When they came to Fourways Café they arranged for tea on their return and then carried on to the Roman Ampitheatre on the side of Blackdown. The approach to this was along an old Roman road. When they reached the amphitheatre Mr Dix tried to persuade some members of the party to give a turn but they were struck with sudden and unaccountable shyness – so he was forced to give one himself. We then returned to Fourways Café which provided a first-rate tea. After tea we had an excellent spin home the last seven or eight miles being all downhill. All agreed that the ride of about forty miles had been a great success.

It wouldn't take a lot of manipulation to turn that into a short story either as a romantic idyll or, possibly, with some more macabre twists along the way as the mists descended and they lost their way in a cider-fuelled, Mendip fog to encounter the headless Roman Botanist who roamed those ancient tracks!

On July 7th, 8th and 9th, "*the Scouts had a practice sleep-out*" in tents in the garden, presumably in preparation for something grander and more taxing which calls to mind the annual camping expeditions undertaken by the pupils of Years Six, Seven and Eight today, complete with their own on-site practices in erecting tents and discussing camp management. One is reminded of one such sleep-out by senior pupils of the 1990s who put up their tents on the other side of the Cran within sight of the Headmaster's House in case reassurance or admonishment was needed through the starry night. The next morning, the sleepy-eyed campers prepared their own cooked breakfast on barely controlled flames from the primus and emerged from the wetness of the reeds to duly deliver, like hunters on a kill, or demented waifs making an oblation to the god of their own invention, the first offering to the Headmaster which resembled nothing so much as a plate of black with varying items of indeterminate description. This Headmaster accepted the offering solemnly and as they retreated to their blackened dens, (but mindful of the need to preserve their integrity and honour), I scraped the contents of the plate into the bin, out of sight of the campers, before settling down to my own centrally-heated kitchen and a waiting plate of 'full English'.

BRIGADIER CHRIS DICK, CBE
(F.P. 1944-1949; Chairman of Governors 1996-2005)

Chris Dick was a pupil at All Hallows from September 1944 until July 1949 thus joining that small 'band of brothers' who boarded at both Scorhill and Cranmore Hall. He left All Hallows to go to Downside and then joined the army – rising to the rank of Brigadier – before re-acquainting himself, formally, with All Hallows by becoming a Governor in 1995 and Chairman of Governors in 1996 until 2005 thereby establishing a connection with the school spanning over sixty years, albeit with a considerable number of years in-between forging an impressive military career in The Royal Tank Regiment. Chris remembers returning to the school in the early 1960s, when he was a Captain, at the invitation of Mr Dix, to deliver a talk to the boys about possibly considering a career in the Army. Chris brought along a film show with "lots of bangs" and arrived with a rifle picked up from Shepton Mallet Military prison (as it was then) to retain the boys' interests. He showed them the gun, spoke about 'ammo' and then asked the boys if they knew what 'ammo' meant. One eager young man put up his hand and said "Yes, Sir, 'amo' means 'I Love' in Latin." One suspects that Mr Dix smiled inwardly at the back of the room knowing that his

---

[36] William Bellasis was another early first-class scout alongside Chris Dick. William arrived in 1946 *"straight off a boat from Kenya, thrown into mysterious English practices, apple-bobbing among them"*. He confesses to *"feeling out of it"* for much of his time *"assuaged by approbation from Trappes-Lomax for reasonable Maths acumen and scouting"*. He believes that two years of Greek from Mr Dix has been more useful in his later career than the three years of study in Natural Science at Oxford although his memories of Mr Dix are not full of particular warmth. Rather, he thought Mrs Dix a saint for coping with her *"martinet"* husband who had a habit, in his view, of establishing favourites which didn't raise his esteem in the eyes of boys who seek fairness at every turn, nor, it should be said, did it do any favours (I've had this sentiment similarly endorsed from another source) for the boys thus chosen. He showed some post-war resilience and scouting initiative by going off on bike rides on his own to procure plentiful supplies of chewing gum for his fellow pupils – *"perhaps my way of trying to fit in"*. He recalls the boys giving the *"venerable and vulnerable"* monks from Downside a tough time in the classroom blinding them with reflected sun's rays from their angled protractors. Perhaps through guilt, but more likely through the experience of his years at All Hallows which *"strengthened his faith and nourished his spirit"*, William went on to become an ordained priest at Ampleforth in 1960 and spent over thirty years thereafter in America. He set out a commemorative prayer for the school in 1988 to mark the

job as a classicist was done. As a schoolboy, Chris featured in athletics particularly and was one of two 'First-Class' Scouts alongside good friend William Bellasis[36] – the first time All Hallows had produced such eminent scouts. Christopher Dick, the boy, arrived at Exeter Station in 1944 – perhaps musing, rather more wistfully, on that same platform as Mr and Mrs Dix two years earlier - knowing nobody and meeting, accidentally, Michael Livingstone and Michael Hickey who were travelling, similarly, to their new lives as boarders at All Hallows. The latter, and Chris, achieved a certain school boy fame by erecting the 'Hick-Dickey Hut' (or the Dick-Hickey Hut) which was a 'five-star' den envied by all the other boys and one which our duo were able to defend against all attackers. Chris was due to take on the mantle of 'Captain of Rugger' in his final year but for an unfortunate sports injury whilst playing soccer (by far the more dangerous game). Chris reported to Matron with a sore neck and was told to rest until the morning when he would be seen by the doctor. X-rays were subsequently taken the next day and Chris re-joined the school lessons until, much later in the day after the incident, somebody had looked again

at the x-rays and realised that Chris had actually broken his neck. He spent the next six months – his final six months at All Hallows – in a neck brace. Chris also began that September term in 1944 with Patrick Fagan, who went on to become a Major-General in the army, which goes to show how well that cohort knew the difference between 'amo' and 'ammo'. Chris became an excellent Chairman of Governors offering quiet wisdom and modest leadership whose benign equilibrium could not be upset even when the Headmaster of the time lost his voice on the morning of Prize Day or when the same Headmaster dropped into his lap the news that he wanted to appoint himself as the next Head of English, leaving the Chairman with the task of appointing a new Headmaster. Chris went on to develop a post-military career which included becoming a Director of Linguaphone for five years and developing property management interests as well as involving himself in many charitable organisations, raising funds, spreading awareness of various issues and giving freely of his time in the interests of others, particularly those less fortunate. He is a shining example of the best kind of former pupil and a worthy recipient of the 'Unsung Hero Award'.

occasion of the fiftieth birthday which still hangs proudly on the wall of the Blessed Sacrament Chapel, and wrote, in beautiful handwriting, a note to *"One and All"* on 1st November 1988…..

"Founders and Benefactors/Headmasters, past and present, faculty and staff, today's and yesteryears'….students and their families, old boys of the years '46-'49, old boys of an earlier vintage, old boys and old girls more recent, other friends of a venerable institution….I wish I were with you in the flesh…I most certainly will be in spirit, offering prayer and Mass on the occasion of a memorable milestone. God Bless your festivities, and all that lies ahead" – The Reverend William Miles Bellasis OSB, Director of Vocations, Saint Louis Priory, Missouri. *And no doubt he remembers the same all-pervading male environment as recalled by other old boys of his vintage since he comments that* "the stirring sexuality of puberty was a somewhat significant distraction of these years and there was no avenue for the explanation thereof"

On July 10th, it was good to read that Sir Richard Paget had been invited back to present the prizes on Sports Day which event, as it happens, did not pass without incident since the future Chairman of Governors, Chris Dick, still a twelve-year-old boy at this time, was recorded as '*accidentally tripping*' O'Callaghan in the 220 yards as they strained for the finishing line (both fell).

On 14th October 1948, "*at 8.20 there was a burlesque ceremonial opening of the new Pack Leaders' Room. This is the Gazebo which has been decorated and furnished, electric light, wireless and heating installed, and some good sporting prints put up on the walls. There was a procession headed by a band to the room and a ceremonial opening of the door by Lady Cranmore (Mrs Dix) who made a speech in verse. Then, when the door was opened, Lord and Lady Cranmore, Sir Jocelyn Trappes-Lomax and the Pack Leaders drank toasts in cider.*" Clearly, the cider-drinking is getting out of hand!

October 30th saw the beginnings of celebrations for the school's tenth birthday[37]........

---

[37] **ALL SAINTS' DAY**
The proper recognition of the school's birthday started its tradition in 1939 when in November "*we had a splendid party to celebrate our first birthday*" and it quickly became established so that the Chronicler could write only a year later in 1940: "*we had our **usual** birthday celebrations on All Hallows' Day*" as if they were, by then, well-established events in the school. It has been going on for every year since; indeed, it is the reason for the publication of this book 75 years after the school's foundation. The precise details of the day – November 1st – All Saints' Day – may have altered a little over time but the abiding spirit remains the same. Normal school life is suspended. The timetable is abandoned. School uniform is discarded. Teachers and pupils mingle almost as equals. Mass provides its blessings at the start of the day and fun, friendship and food follow. During Mr Dix's day, the formula was always the same: Pack matches, concerts and other entertainments including Mr Dix's conjuring shows and "*uproarious games*", apple-bobbing, cross-country runs, delicious home-made cakes by Mrs King and later, Mrs Tivey and Miss Irving, special suppers, messages from Old Boys, followed by a massive bonfire and occasional fireworks. Often, in the early years, Mr Dix would read out the School Alphabet whereby each boy was mentioned in turn. As part of the celebrations, the staff and boys were even expected to give Mr and Mrs Dix presents as, in 1942: a beautiful Worcester jug and flowers; in 1948, a gift of silver; in 1950, some silver forks; in 1951, some lovely Georgian silver ladles; in 1952, a silver sugar bowl and tongs; one former pupil, Bernard Trafford (FP 1963-1969), who gave away the prizes in 2008, remembers Mr Dix putting a surcharge on the school fees in 1963 in order to mark the occasion of the silver jubilee by buying Mrs Dix some diamond earrings; and other money gifts were given which were used to buy items for the school but it was also the case that Mr and Mrs Dix gave every boy a birthday card waiting for him at the breakfast table. In 1947, the Headmaster "*was pleased to have at his table one present Head Boy and four former ones*". In 1949, Downside offered a Closed Scholarship (of £80) only available to an All Hallows boy. In 1950, Father Ronald Knox preached a fine sermon (see page 65). In 1951, staff and friends ended up with a sherry party in the Headmaster's new house perhaps echoing that first sherry party in 1938 with just one pupil. In 1956, the school's 18th birthday, about 50 old boys from Downside joined the school for the occasion and Miss Irving was still making the cake, this time with 18 candles on it. In 1969, John and Jim Metcalfe were still making the magnificent bonfire but for the last time (see page 126) and, for the first time in living memory, no old boys came from Downside "*because they had mumps there*". There was, as it happens, another occasion when the Downside ex-All Hallows' pupils were not invited which was the year following a visit that included Auberon Waugh who managed to smuggle in and consume several flagons of cider – I knew the cider-drinking would have a bad ending! Annual celebrations carried on every year and in 1998, the school's sixtieth birthday, Cardinal Basil Hume visited. Major and less major events were timed to coincide with November 1st in early years (like the signing of the Cranmore conveyance and the arrival of the new mower) – perhaps that is a tradition that could be revived? The idea that boys and girls throughout the All Hallows ages have come to associate All Saints' Day with memorable fun and excitement is a lasting legacy in its own right to generations of children who have come through the school, perhaps singularly impressing on them all how we are all called to be saints as we rest from our labours and participate in a '*blest communion! Fellowship divine!*' Long may the celebrations continue!

The tenth birthday also saw the arrival of new Stations of the Cross – executed by T. H. Robinson, a Cornish artist – which were put into the school chapel and blessed later by a Franciscan priest. The Stations were presented by parents to commemorate their sons' years at All Hallows. These Stations of the Cross can now be seen in the present school chapel of All Saints, along with wooden icons of various saints, fashioned by the same artist from St Ives, which were originally affixed to the dormitories. As has been indicated earlier, the dormitories retain the names to this day.

February saw the school's literary appetites being whetted by *Macbeth*, *David Copperfield* and the poems of Tennyson, whilst appetites of a different kind were accommodated by the Scouts whose Seagulls and Gannets packs successfully defended Cranmore Tower from an attack from the Communists (Falcons) with '*only one (communist) getting through*'. Churchill and Sir Richard Paget would have been proud!

In September 1949, Richard Arnold-Jones[38] was welcomed back to the staff to continue to build what became over sixty years' association with the school and, on March 6th, Mr Dix underwent an "*away convalescence*" by journeying with his wife for a week to Chagford to return to old haunts for the first time in five years and to meet up again with friends like Colonel Vicary, Mrs Reavell, Dr and Mrs Purves, Mr and Mrs Amery, Mrs Cleminson, Mr French, Mrs Endacott and old Mrs Rowe at Scorhill Farm. At this time, we learn a little more of Mrs Irving's talents, in addition to her fine cooking and birthday-cake-baking, for she also ran the extensive poultry farm at the school. In 1950, this consisted of thirty-two hens; three cocks in school colours – cherry and grey – prize stock purchased from Downside; forty-six cherry and grey chicks; thirteen ducks and three drakes; thirteen ducklings; five goslings and eight turkeys. The chronicle records that "*all these animals gave an exterior or interior pleasure*" although pride of place was given to the ducks who regularly made "*their way in line from their own quarters down the drive, across the cricket field and along to the stream*" where they proceeded to float like boats. The Scouts were also flourishing at this time engaged, as they were, in pursuits like tracking, signalling, fire-fighting, first aid, nature hunts, cray-fishing in the Chantry lake, with many such activities leading to badges. There was also a memorable summer camping expedition to the grounds of Lord and Lady Robert Crichton-Stuart at Cornwell Manor, Oxfordshire, when Bellasis and Dick became the first scouts to gain their First-Class status. Also worthy of note, in these clearly enlightened times, is the active Dance Society, started in the Michaelmas Term of 1948 and organised by Mrs Eyles. Dances learned included The Barn Dance, Larinka, The Moonlight Saunter, Hesitation Waltz, Military Two-Step, The Gay Gordons, St Bernard Waltz, The Palais Glide, The Lambeth Walk, The Dinky One-Step, Tango Waltz, Ideal Schottische, Boston Two-Step, Valeta, Polka, The Dashing White Sergeant and Cokey-Cokey. Larry O'Callaghan pops up once more to round off observations at the end of

---

[38] See box details on page 94

this first Chronicle of All Hallows - before the September 1950 Term began - to reflect upon the fact that he was glad to have started his prep school life at Scorhill and to have finished it at Cranmore. Scorhill was small and family-orientated; it was about huts and hideouts and high Dartmoor; at Cranmore, All Hallows "*began to go ahead: more cricket and football fixtures, carpentry began*[39]*, the sweet shop was installed, we had ice-creams twice a week, we were allowed to bring our bicycles back and roller skating was begun…*".

Pupil numbers had grown from one in 1938 to a hundred-and-one by the 1950s; a grass Tennis Court had been laid; a pavilion erected on the cricket field; the outside painting of the house had been completed; an outdoor skating rink laid with the stable courtyard cobbles pulled up; two of the stables had been converted into a hobby room and a play room; a new well had been sunk which provided a plentiful supply of water; much internal decoration effected; a sound system installed which had been connected to the Headmaster's study; significant additions to the Library in place; the re-dedication of the Gazebo made possible for the boys; Stations of the Cross blessed and erected in the chapel and a huge amount of work completed on the gardens and grounds.

Larry O'Callaghan

All Hallows was on the march into the 1950s!

For as long as there are ready references to hand, in the form of the well-documented, everyday chronicles that are bound in two volumes from 1938-1950 and 1950-1959, it is the present intention to continue the developing narrative interspersing chronological diary entries with various asides and profiles which might be considered more reflective. One anticipates the

---

[39] With local man, Mr Trotman

later style of this book to change into a more summative approach as we fast-forward through to the present day. The editorial that opens the second volume refers to the fact that there are rather more boys' contributions in the form of creative writing and other records which "*show a joy in writing, a sense of humour and a feeling for words*"; I look forward to including some of those offerings along the way since it is the pupils who bring life to any school.

Here's just a 'taster' from P. Poyntz-Wright (aged 11).....

A STRANGE DISAPPEARANCE

One day in the ages of long ago, there lived a short stumpy man with dark curly hair. Evil were his ways and this is an evil deed. One dark night he crept out of his small cave which was on an island. He snooped about for his boat which was a rather weather-beaten old yacht. After finding this he lighted his little lamp which burnt whale oil and, taking an old map, he set out for the mainland. When he reached the mainland he tied up his boat with a piece of rope. Having done this with care he walked a mile or so inland until he came to a thatched cottage where lived an old lady. She would now be asleep, he thought. He lifted the latch and took a cautious look round. He crept up the stairs like a mouse and, spitting on his hands, he walked into the bedroom. Nothing was seen but a cry was heard. Having gagged the lady he turned round and to his horror he saw the lady and the bed slowly disappear into a mist. Struck with terror he left the house in haste without the body on which he meant to feed.

The 1950 Summer Term opens with the arrival of Oliver Gibbs who joins the staff initially to coach cricket three times a week but who becomes Head Groundsman in the course of time and remains at All Hallows for many years in the tradition that follows Nash and the Metcalfes and which predates Harry Godden. Every school needs these men. They are not teachers but they become connected to the very fabric of the school and they grow with it, almost as if out of the woodwork and the outdoor surroundings, which happen to be, after all, where they spend much of their time. The pupils become accustomed to their daily presence. They arrive early in the mornings and turn, rhythmically, round the school like the seasons, approachable and yet mysterious, about whom one can invent myths and legends, and like all good caretakers, they are men of gold.

On June 30th, as if to scotch the impression that All Hallows is all about bike rides, camping, entertainments and cider-stops at the Waggon and Horses, it was announced that Lavery, Butler and George had all been awarded scholarships to Downside, Martin Gauntlett had been recommended for the first Closed Award to Downside and Messervy, Matthews and O'Regan all passed well into Ampleforth, with Fitzherbert gaining an average of over 77%. During the July Sports Day, Mr Young arrived to fix the School Crest *to the circular window facing the back entry to the school* which has sadly been removed from the round window of the Learning

Support Centre, and Mrs Amery gave away the prizes. Mrs Amery was a particularly welcome guest since *"the school owed a great debt to her because at the crisis of our fortunes she had suggested to Mr Dix the taking of what proved to be our lovely war-time home – Scorhill on Dartmoor"*. Mr Dix also used the occasion of that Prize Day to announce that the exciting project of a new swimming pool had been brought forward; real memories of swimming in the curtilage of the school in the Devon Teign were, presumably, not matched in their appeal by the unrealistic prospects of swimming in the Somerset Cran – something had to be done! The Cran is at best a trickle. It runs from West Cranmore through the school grounds (now partially underground through pipes) at a regular depth of about four inches. Nevertheless, the hardy, 'before-breakfast', river-swimming Mr Dix might have been amused to know that this Headmaster had been instructed by representatives of an external Health and Safety Executive, in the zealous 1990s, to erect a sign saying "Danger – Water". It is perhaps only fair, however, to concede that the Cran can flood in periods of heavy and prolonged rain and that there can be real danger on such occasions particularly in the far south-east corner of the grounds by the tractor shed and the carpentry and the chickens. Nevertheless, if the Cran merits a sign saying "Danger", the Teign at Scorhill must have warranted a screen the size of an Olympic Pool screaming out its warning "BEWARE TSUNAMIS!"

An interesting cricket match took place at All Hallows on 17th July 1950 when local man Len Creed put on an exhibition match between Somerset C.C. and his own Invitation side. Len was a local farmer who went on to become a well-known bookmaker in Bath and the surrounding region. His slogan, one remembers, was *"Be in the lead, bet with Creed"*, which goes to prove that marketing works since I recall it here some forty years or so after I must have first read it on the streets of Bath. Not that I ever found myself 'in the lead' when it comes to betting on horses since the only nag I had coming in at twenty to one ran when all the other racing thoroughbreds had finished at noon. Len Creed went on to become Chairman of Somerset C.C. in the late 1970s and, as a committee member earlier, perhaps his greatest claim to fame was the generally recorded fact that he is credited with spotting and bringing to Bath a certain Vivien Richards after seeing him play whilst on holiday in Antigua. Len paid for all Viv Richards' expenses in bringing him over and it is said he was only reimbursed after Richards started to strut his stuff for Somerset some two years later. For that match at All Hallows, Len had assembled a strong Somerset side with the likes of Harry Gimblett and Arthur Wellard in the team (see notes below). He was also wise in recruiting Bill Andrews, another Somerset player, who had done some coaching at All Hallows, to join his Invitation side, as well as Brian O'Regan, the captain of the All Hallows 1st XI, who must have been very honoured but, by no means star-struck, for reasons that will become apparent. Harry Gimblett was described as late as 1982 as *"the greatest batsman Somerset has ever produced"* which is some accolade considering the fact that gentlemen like the aforementioned Viv Richards and one Ian Botham were also producing their heroics for Somerset at that time. Gimblett was told that he was "not good enough" for county cricket until a lucky opportunity arose for him to open the innings against Essex when he promptly scored 125 out of 175 in 80 minutes. He went on to play for England on three occasions and scored 265 sixes in his career which was unusual for an opening bat. He was also summoned to play for England against the West Indies the week after the All Hallows match – after a gap of eleven years since his last cap – but he developed a carbuncle on his neck and he could not play. He was in the form of his life at this time having just scored over 2000 runs for Somerset in the previous season. Nor was Arthur Wellard, an excellent all-rounder, any kind of slouch by comparison. Wellard had been rejected by his native county, Kent, who told him he was better off becoming a policeman so it was with some satisfaction that in only his fourth appearance for Somerset – by chance against Kent – he took ten wickets in the match. He went onto represent England on two occasions and was named Wisden Cricketer of the Year in 1936, as well as hitting 500 sixes throughout his career. Famously, he was playing for Somerset on one occasion with "Boss" Meyer (who went on to found Millfield School) when, off his bowling, Meyer failed to catch a Northants batsman who might easily have been caught. Meyer reached into his back pocket and said "Sorry, Arthur, here's a quid". Bill Andrews was a popular Somerset cricketer whose catch-phrase greeting when meeting people for the first time was *"Shake the hand that bowled Bradman"* for he had, indeed, bowled the great Australian batsman in a competitive match in 1938. What he sometimes failed to say was that Bradman was on 202 runs at the time and that he had allowed himself to be bowled. The match at All Hallows was very low scoring because of almost incessant rain but the players soldiered on. Gimblett opened his shoulders for a spritely 35 before being caught on the boundary by Bill Andrews off the bowling, of course, of none other than Brian O'Regan, the captain of All Hallows, who must have been all of twelve years of age at the time. Bill Andrews went on to take 3 wickets for 28 and Oliver Gibbs, also playing, took 3 for 29 with his deadly accurate spin bowling. Brian O'Regan also scored 13 not out with the bat in a gallant, but unsuccessful, late-order attempt to match the Somerset team's score. Nevertheless, we'll make him Man of the Match and if he's out there now as a seventy-year-old-something young man, we'll be happy to produce a certificate for him. Possibly encouraged by his performance and exposure that day, Brian went on to take over 100 wickets in all school matches that season and, even after he had left, he was making news as an 'old boy' since it is recorded that he scored 58 not out for Ampleforth in his first Colts outing. Quite how Len Creed became associated with All Hallows (or how he was able to arrange the fixture in the first place) we might never know but I wouldn't be surprised if Oliver Gibbs was an instrumental, as well as an actual, player in the proceedings. Incidentally, the early experiences of rejection of Gimblett and Wellard – and their subsequent defiant success - should form lessons for us all.

In order to keep the momentum of "lessons to be learned" it is timely to print in full below the text of a sermon given to the school by The Very Reverend Monsignor Ronald Knox on the occasion of All Hallows' Day 1950. Ronald Knox was ordained a Catholic priest in 1919, becoming the Catholic Chaplain at Oxford University in 1926 (a post he held until 1939) and increasingly famous for his preaching and writing. He probably became the most well-known

Catholic priest in England at the time of his visit to All Hallows. Cardinal Heenan (Basil Hume's predecessor as Archbishop of Westminster) described Knox as *"perhaps the greatest figure in the church of the twentieth century"*. Evelyn Waugh, Knox's biographer (and father of Auberon Waugh who attended All Hallows as a pupil and about whom we shall hear more) wrote *"I can think of no man of this century who enjoyed as did Ronald Knox such a mastery of the English language in all its varieties"*. In all these matters the reader can judge for himself or herself in reading the sermon he preached in the old school chapel to boys and staff.....

ALL SAINTS

"There are many who will come from the east and the west, and will take their places in the kingdom of God with Abraham and Isaac and Jacob" (Matthew viii)

"To-day is All Saints' Day, and I thought it would be a good thing if we talked, first of all about Saints, and then about All Saints, and then about All Saints' Day; by the time we've done that, we shall have more or less covered the ground. It sounds as if it were going to be a long sermon, but it won't be really, as long as you sit fairly still and don't shuffle or snuffle or fidget; if you start doing that I don't know what may happen. First of all, what is a Saint?

In the very earliest ages of the Church, it was the fashion to describe all Christian people as 'saints', although I daresay Christian people were a mixed lot, even then. If St Paul had written a letter to you, he would have addressed it to 'the saints at Cranmore'. Nowadays, we don't do that; if your mamma were to send you a letter addressed to 'Saint John Smith' (or whatever your name happens to be) the Headmaster would probably return it to the post office, with the comment 'not known here'. You see, words keep changing their meaning. It's just the same with the word 'scholar'. A scholar used to mean somebody who went to school; and of course you go to school; but it would be pretty silly to call you a scholar, when you will go on thinking that the ablative of mensa is mensarum. And in the same way it would be pretty silly to call you a Saint when you will go on – all right, we'll leave that part out. A scholar nowadays means somebody who is terribly brainy; and a saint nowadays means somebody who is a very special friend of God, and always does what God wants him to do, and the Church accordingly decides to call him 'Saint' so-and-so ever afterwards.

Well, what exactly is it that you've got to do in order to be a saint? The first thing is, to be dead. When I say that, for heaven's sake don't get me wrong; don't imagine that the saints were all people who lived ages and ages ago, and wore long beards and dressing-gowns like the pictures in the stained-glass windows. No, there are people alive at this moment who do just the sort of things saints have always done. There's Padre Pio, for example, a Capuchin priest in the south of Italy; he only sleeps about three hours every night and spends nearly all day hearing confessions; and when he says Mass it takes him nearly two hours to get through it, because he gets so overcome with devotion that he can't go on. You might think that would make people want to go to some other Mass, but no, they all crowd to Padre Pio's. He says it at four o'clock in the morning, and at four o'clock every morning there's a queue outside the church waiting to fight their way in and hear Padre Pio's Mass, because they know what a holy man he is. I know what I'm talking about, because one of you has a brother, and several more of you have a cousin, who went to see Padre Pio only about a fortnight ago. Just imagine how holy a priest must be, to make one's brother want to get up at four in the morning and hear his Mass! And Padre Pio is just as alive as you and me.

No, when I say you can't be a saint until you're dead, I mean that the Church isn't going to be rash enough to call you a saint until you're dead. And there's a perfectly good reason for that; there is always a perfectly good reason for these things. The Church never calls anybody a saint while he's alive, for fear that he should stop being a saint and go to the bad, and then where should we all be? Rather over four hundred years ago, when the Reformation started, a king of England wrote a very clever book to show how wrong Martin Luther was, and what nonsense the Reformers were talking. And the Pope was so delighted that he called him the Defender of the Faith and said that all his successors could use that title, which is why you find 'Fid. Def.' written on English coins to this day. But it was a good thing the Pope didn't decide to make a saint of him, because of course that king was Henry VIII, who afterwards destroyed all the monasteries and killed St Thomas More and St John Fisher and married six wives and cut most of their heads off; so it would have been rather awkward if Henry VIII had been a saint, wouldn't it? No, the Church is too clever for that; she waits until you're in your coffin, and then she says, now, let's see, what kind of person was he?

And what kind of person have you got to be before the Church says, 'That was a saint, that was'? Why, you've got to be absolutely eaten up with the love of God; that's the only thing which matters. Our prevailing idea of the saints is that they were people who made themselves very uncomfortable; they wore hair shirts and slept on broken bottles when they slept at all, and generally laid themselves out to give themselves a bad time. St Francis Borgia, when he had to take a pill, always used to suck it, which was rather missing the point of the pill. But all that, you see, was only by the way; if the saints seemed to enjoy suffering, whether it was suffering they couldn't avoid, or the suffering they took on themselves, it was only because they could think of no better way to prove their love for God. There was a boy at school with me, a great tough boy, who was called out in class by the science master and told to stand there holding a platinum dish in each hand; and when either of the dishes felt at all hot, he was to put it down immediately – it was some sort of scientific experiment, you see. Well, this boy went on standing there and standing there and swearing that both the dishes were stone cold, till at last the master had to send him back to his place, and there was rather a snigger all round because it looked as if the experiment hadn't come off very well. But about five minutes later the boy had to get leave to go to the infirmary, with an enormous hole burnt in his hand, because one of the dishes had been scalding hot all the time, but he thought it would be a good way to rag the master if he pretended it wasn't. There are all sorts of morals to that story, but the one I want to mention here is simply this – that boy made himself extremely uncomfortable, just as the saints are apt to do, but he wasn't a saint. He wasn't a saint because he didn't do it for the love of God; he only did it to pull a school-master's leg, which is quite a different thing. So you see what I mean when I say that the point about the saints is not the sufferings which they underwent, but the consuming love of God which made them do it.

That's two things you need if you are to become a saint; you want to have a consuming love of God, and you want to be already dead. And there's a third thing which the Church ordinarily demands – that you should do miracles; either you must perform miracles in your lifetime, or miracles must be performed through your prayers after you are dead. The Church, as I say, needn't insist on that, but she ordinarily does, and for this reason. God means the saints, these very special people whom we call saints nowadays, to be an unmistakable proof of the Christian religion; they are to become beacon-lights to the world. And because he means them to show up like that, he doesn't take any risks. They aren't just very good people, the whole of their lives is lived on the supernatural plane, and the supernatural plane keeps breaking through. 'You are the light of the world' our Lord says to them; 'a city cannot be hidden if it is built on a mountain-top'. You might think it rather unnecessary to have a tower here on the top of Cranmore; surely it's high enough without that? Yes, but all over the country, and especially down here in Somerset, you will find that people do put down towers and monuments on the top of high hills, as if to draw attention to them. People looking at them from a long distance off must be able to say, "That is Cranmore". And so, when a soul reaches really high up in the following of Jesus Christ, God adds a kind of finishing touch – the power of doing miracles; that everybody will be able to say, without fear of contradiction, "That was a saint'.

Well, that's what saints are, and now, what about All Saints? Why does the Church want us to get excited about them? Well, I suppose the reason is that we are all apt to specialise too much, to concentrate too much, in our devotions; there are one or two saints we like specially or feel specially interested in them, and we tend to let the others go. There's Our Blessed Lady, of course, and the saints we're named after, and the ones we think are useful in getting us what we want, and then there are some who just attract us by the stories we hear about them. October is such a good month for saints, starting off with St Teresa of Lisieux, the Little Flower, whom we all want to be on good terms with, and then going on to St Francis, who has somehow managed to be everybody's saint. And there is one I'm very fond of, St John Cantius, whose feast comes on 20th October. I think I must tell you about him, because his story is so charming. He was a schoolmaster of sorts, and his favourite way of spending the holidays was to go off on a pilgrimage to Rome, not just in the Holy Year, but any old year. But he was rather an absent-minded sort of person – schoolmasters are sometimes, it comes of being so clever – and also, being a saint, he was very liable to give away all his money to the first tramp he met. So when he went off they used to sew a number of gold coins into the lining of his cloak, to make sure that he would always have enough money to come back by the beginning of term. And on one of these journeys he met some robbers, who demanded his money. St John Cantius emptied out his pocket, which probably contained about tuppence ha'penny, and said he was so very sorry, very sorry he hadn't got any more. Whereupon the robbers beat him and threw him in the ditch, and went off grumbling. And St John picked himself up and shook himself, and started out on his journey again, and then …. then quite suddenly he remembered those gold pieces which were sewn up in his cloak, and he'd told the robbers he hadn't any money; he'd told a lie! So the next thing that happened was that the robbers heard a great hallooing behind them, and there was St John Cantius chasing down the hill after them at top speed, shouting, "Stop, stop, it's all right; I have got money, lots of it, after all! Well, they were sportsmen, and they gave him back his tuppence ha'penny, and it was all right. That kind of saint sticks out from the others and makes one wish one knew more about him.

But the Church, you see, doesn't want us to be entirely wrapped up in a handful of saints of our own choosing. There's nothing wrong about picking and choosing; God made them different from each other so that we could have our pick. But it was God who made them all, and made them what they were, and it would be disrespectful of us to take no notice of any of them except a handful. So, once a year, the Church tells us to think about all the Blessed Saints in heaven. And she chooses, I think, an excellent day for it; the first day of November, when the year has definitely turned to autumn and the leaves have fallen, and the weather is, for the most part, rather depressing, either wetter or colder than we quite want it to be. Because it is then that we like staying indoors, and sitting at the fireside, if there's one to sit by; and there's a kind of snug feeling about coming in out of the misty twilight and drawing the curtains across the windows, which helps us to think about the saints in heaven, so snug there, with all the painful struggles of their earthly life behind them. To be sure, it is nice to be out on a November afternoon; but it is nicer still to come in at the end of the afternoon, and shut the world out from us. And the saints are happy, even in this world, in spite of all their uncomfortable goings on. But happier still when they leave this world, and draw the curtains of heaven round them. Our Lord talks about them sitting down to table in the kingdom of heaven, with Abraham and Isaac and Jacob; that's what the words *mean – we are to think of heaven as a great comfortable family meal, where everybody has his allotted place, and there is no starvation corner.*

Only, let us remember that the curtains of heaven are transparent curtains. Not in the sense that you and I can look in; ah, if only we could! What a world of good it would do us! No, but the saints can look out; they can see you and me still ploughing our way through the mud and the darkness of this earthly existence, feeling our way with difficulty and falling, every now and again, into the ditch. And they can help us; not only because the light of their example shines down on us, and makes it easier, sometimes, to see what we ought to do. They can help us with their prayers, strong prayers, wise prayers, when ours are so feeble and so blind. When you look out on a November evening, and see the sky all studded with stars, think of those innumerable saints in heaven all ready to help you; and all rather pleased with Cranmore, because Cranmore is dedicated to All Hallows."

Just as an aside, it is amusing to note that for one of his regular BBC radio programmes in 1926, Knox broadcast a 'spoof' report about a revolution sweeping across London which was titled *'Broadcasting from the Barricades'*. He used supposedly 'live' reports from 'real' people and referred to government ministers being attacked and mentioned the so-called destruction of the Savoy Hotel, as well as the total annihilation of the House of Parliament. As it happens, the extreme snowy conditions of the time meant that many people across the country who had heard the radio programme were not able, subsequently, to receive newspapers until some days later so they imagined that the rebellion was real and that society was breaking down. It has been suggested that Knox's playful broadcast prefigured and possibly influenced Orson Welles' more famous radio broadcast *'War of the Worlds'* when he pretended London was being invaded by Martians which caused an infamous panic of its own in some parts of the country. Welles' broadcast, of course, took place in 1938, the year before the Second World War but also the year All Hallows was founded which provides a certain kind of neatness to the times we are describing. More neatly still, in terms of place, is the fact that Ronald Knox is buried just down the road from All Hallows in the churchyard of St Andrew in Mells, along with other well-known figures like the poet Siegfried Sassoon, Baroness Asquith (daughter of Herbert Asquith, Prime Minister of Great Britain) and her husband Sir Maurice Bonham Carter (both of whom are grandparents of the actress Helena Bonham Carter) and Katherine Asquith, the daughter of Sir John Horner who is connected to the nursery song of 'Little Jack Horner', as well as Christopher Hollis, author, schoolmaster (Stonyhurst) and parliamentarian, whose son, Nigel, attended All Hallows, and whose other son, Crispian, went on to become Bishop of Plymouth. Quite what connections one wants to make of all that is left to the imaginations of the reader but it might just be worth a visit to Mells or Cranmore Tower, mentioned in Knox's sermon, or trace some of those lives to gain some flavour, perhaps, of the times.

Mr & Mrs Dix in fancy dress on Shrove Tuesday

Shrove Tuesday, each year, seemed to provide a flavour of a different kind but became, apparently, no less an annual institution to rival, in the memory, All Saints' Day with its own particular All Hallows' twist. Certainly as far back as 1943 the day was marked by a whole holiday, a cross-country run in the morning, pack matches in the afternoon and Benediction in the evening but it was possibly the year 1948 when the occasion was first celebrated with a Fancy Dress Ball with cowboys and Indians, clowns, pirates, Sir Francis Drake, a tramp, Mr Molotov, a mystery man, a taxi-driver, a chef, a chinaman, a cave man, a French gendarme, Sir Walter Raleigh, Topsy, a butcher boy, a Mad Hatter and 'a Looney' (the mind boggles) all featuring strongly. As with the burlesque opening of the newly-fashioned Gazebo for the Scouts, things were done in style so all the boys dressed for the occasion and awaited the formal announcement of their introduction, in character, to Mr and Mrs Dix, who were also kitted out in fancy dress and who, acting the part of Lord and Lady of the Manor, stood on the landing of the Main Staircase to receive the 'visitors' who were arriving for the Ball. A grand parade followed as well as musical games and easy dances before a break for a special supper then more serious dancing until staggered bedtimes. The 1950 Fancy Dress Ball is worth mentioning for its passing detail: *"one boy, who was wearing a large sombrero, gracefully swept it off as he bade farewell to his hostess – and a quantity of cakes fell out onto the floor"*. No doubt his Ash Wednesday did not quite follow the course he had planned.

It is pleasing to note that opportunistic instincts are still operating soundly in the summer of 1951 since we read, on June 6th – which was a Wednesday – *"as the weather now became very hot we decided more or less on the spur of the moment to pay a visit to the sea, and the whole school went to Lyme Regis. We had lunch and tea on the beach. Most of the school paddled and bathed, a few went boating...large fortifications were built and a gigantic crab discovered – in short a very successful outing"*.

Sports Day that year welcomed over 200 visitors to see archery and boxing[40] being added to the usual events with Mr Dix apparently in fine form as he welcomed, in his speech, *"the pulchritude of mothers"* and the handsome rank of fathers to the proceedings.

In September 1951, John Jackson started his All Hallows' connections as a 'new boy'; today, sixty-two years later, he remains a welcome presence, albeit with longer trousers and memories.

I promised, or threatened the reader with, some occasional examples of pupils' writing and I was interested to discover that the 1951 Literary Society not only studied Chaucer's Prologue but also tried their hand at writing some 'modern' pilgrim portraits of their own. My interest was particularly caught because I had introduced an identical task to my pupils in English in 2006; you can make your own critical judgements about comparative literary merit...

---

[40] See page 90

JOHN JACKSON

(Former Pupil & Parent & Chairman of Governors standing at right)

John Jackson attended All Hallows as a pupil in 1950 and left on a music scholarship to Downside in 1956. Today, in the year 2013, he still has dealings with the school in his professional association with our accountants, and through his family connections with current pupils, which just about makes him the longest serving All Hallows man on record at 63 years of association with the school. In the course of those sixty-three years he has taken on various roles incorporating those of pupil, governor, Chairman of Governors, Clerk to the Governors, School Accountant, parent, uncle, great-uncle, grandparent and even peripatetic teacher, as he has accompanied Poppy, his grand-daughter, on piano on more than one occasion in public performances at school. John claims a particular distinction as *the first day boy* in the school, along with Mark Adams, for all other pupils were boarders at the time of his arrival, unless of course, we reel back to Bognor and Alan Woodgates, of course, who might have been a

day boy, or try to ascertain whether any of those All Hallows' boys at Scorhill actually lived just down the road at the time. We'll give John and Mark Adams the accolade but it is probably as 'first day boys at Cranmore'. John played soccer for the 1st XI in 1955, was awarded Form Prizes, won a boxing match or two and became heavily involved in school music. He became a School Governor in October 1970 and thereby became the only person, alive or dead, I can think of who has had significant dealings with every All Hallows' Headmaster through the ages, for Francis Dix was a fellow Governor in 1970, Alistair Mortimer was just leaving, and all subsequent Heads were known to John personally in the roles already mentioned. John was asked to take on the office of Clerk to the Governors in 1971 and became Chairman of Governors from 1977 until July 1982. He then remained on the Board until May 1990 and transferred his professional association to that of auditor. He first graduated to the status of a fee-paying parent in 1971 and to that of a grandparent of an All Hallows pupil in 1993. John provided empathetic but brutally honest advice and guidance to at least three of the Headmasters of the school and maintained an easy and sociable style that complemented his astute financial and business sense. Together with his wife, **Frances**, his brother, **Stuart Jackson**, and his sister **Eve Jackson** (who taught mathematics for many years), and his cousin, **Gordon Jackson** (who was also a School Governor), he will also be remembered for his family links with the following pupils… **Rachel** and **Charles** and **Simon** and **Lucy** and **Carrie** and **Ella** and **Arndy** and **Poppy** and **Hamish** and **Isabelle** and **Andrew** and **Claire** and **Rosalind** and **Daisy** and **Kitty** and **Honor** and **Scarlett** and **Freddie** and **Anna** and **Kate** and **Thomas** - as **Jacksons**, **Weirs** and **Mants** - in his capacity as father and grandfather and uncle and great-uncle and second cousin and possibly with some other familial connecting lines I haven't mentioned. That's a whole class of twenty-one lovely children all by themselves!

THE BLACKSMITH – by 'J.Y.' – 1951

There was a blacksmith in the merry crowd
Whose very laugh was boisterous, long and loud,
His black and sparkling eyes ne'er seemed to rest,
He told us many a tale and many a jest,
He wore a thick black overcoat, so warm
'Twas proof against the greatest, wettest storm.
If challenged in a little country Inn
To drink a double dose of strongest gin,
He would consent and drink it every drop.
He loved strong beer made with the ripest hop;
He rode upon a big, black, sturdy mare;
He was straightforward, merry, honest, fair.

THE BAKER – by Helena Constable-Maxwell – 2006

There was a portly baker whose trade was well known
Although he baked a great deal, he soon became prone
To eating almost everything, especially the buns,
The tastiest morsel he could make
You'd find upon that baker's plate
With hot red cheek and eager eye
He'd shovel his bread and buns into the pie.
His nose not small, his eye not large,
With great red ears, each with black hair,
You'd find him eating everywhere.
His boots were blackened with ugly grime
He wore a watch that did not chime
His velvet suit on Sundays wore
He was not one to be called poor.
And whilst amusing lady folk
He'd often have a dusty smoke
And finish off with a pie or three
He was a greedy man you see
But holy (he made out to be)

But comparing eras is, perhaps, an unwinnable debate, even though, I grant you, they are both better than Chaucer. And yet, in considering the process of putting forward arguments 'for and against' one encounters, on October 19th, a surprisingly well-informed and mature debate on the Motion *"This House would welcome a return of a Conservative Government"* (a topic that might have a particular resonance for some today in these modern coalition times). It is doubted whether the pupil of 2013 would enter willingly and intelligently into such a debate, nor have the sufficient interest or grasp of current affairs to engage in observations such as the following…

"Green-Armytage i opened the debate. He pointed out the importance of a Conservative Government for the preservation of peace. Labour, he said, was divided but the Conservatives united. The Conservatives would make a greater effort to deal with the housing problem and would attain the target they aimed at. There would be no ground nuts waste or Gambia eggs[41]. Nationalisation, he said, was petering out. Socialism was the negation of liberty. Cochrane replied for Labour. Labour, he said, believes in working together for strength. Workers need faith in their Government. He called attention to the unemployment after the First World War and the lack of it after the last one. Labour was right in calling Churchill a 'Warmonger' – he was convicted out of his own mouth. The Conservatives will not reach their target of three hundred thousand houses. Lloyd i (Conservative) spoke next. We wanted a dependable government, he said. Churchill was the man required. He spoke of the fuel crisis since the war, of Labour's top heavy administration, of the failure of Road Haulage under Nationalisation. Social Services would remain under a Conservative Government. Waugh (Labour) followed. Re-armament, he said, required the co-operation of the working classes to succeed. Labour represented the people, Conservatives represent the squire and landlord; 'most of my listeners are prejudiced and ignorant of the real issues'. Crichton-Stuart said that only cigars would go down if the Conservatives got in – to which Coffey replied that if Labour got in only the £ would go down."

We could be in the House of Commons, couldn't we? One can imagine the speakers harrumphing like putative walruses with the Chairman calling for order through a fog of cigar smoke and lemonade. The only surprise is that there is no impassioned expression of fear that a new government would have implications for their cider supplies at The Waggon and Horses. For the record, the Motion was won by 76 votes to 16 which numbers suggest that something approaching the whole school was in attendance. We blush. Modern school debates tend to consider the merits of school uniform, the quality of food in the dining room and possibly the pros and cons of mobile phones; I think we had better raise our aspirations!

We move on now to Evelyn and Auberon Waugh who may not have been everybody's cup of tea but they are part of the All Hallows' story and they are certainly part of the English literary

---

[41] 'Ground nuts from Tanganyika and eggs from Gambia'. These became exploitative, discredited and ridiculed food and money-making schemes whereby Britain would use cheap, non-union orientated colonial work-forces to mass produce everyday foodstuffs for the 'British housewife' in order to combat the post-war food shortages and rationing (which remained in place until 1954).

heritage. Evelyn Waugh sent his son, Auberon, to All Hallows in September 1946 – the year after *Brideshead Revisited* was published – and therefore, at a time when he was, arguably, at the height of his contemporary fame. Evelyn was an unconventional, free-thinking, complex young man (an analysis not rendered any easier by the fact that his first wife was also called Evelyn) and Waugh went on to attract early notice as an amusing satirist in the 1930s with works like *Decline and Fall* (1928), *Vile Bodies* (1930) and *A Handful of Dust* (1934), whose titles and subject-matter highlighted and tracked the absurdities and excesses of the 'bright young things' of upper-class society even though he appeared to be part of that same set, himself, at least in his early adult life. Perhaps it was his own intoxicated involvement with them that taught him to disdain and ridicule such indulgences although his subsequent career and life remained somewhat troubled thereafter. He tried teaching in his early twenties but seemed to prefer the vacational aspect of life rather more than the vocational characteristics of school-mastering since he was sacked for flaunting some of those excesses he so readily exposed in others. A typical extract from his diary at this time reads: "*Taught lunatics. Played rugby football. Drank at Bell*". His headmaster-employer considered his interests to be extra-curricular, which may not have been surprising given the fact that Waugh, in turn, considered the school to be a depository for "*backward peers*". If the decision to leave teaching was forced upon him, his next career move was more deliberate; he decided he would become "a man of letters". He converted to Catholicism through intellectual conviction rather than faith or moral principles although he proudly declared once to Nancy Mitford that "*You have no idea how much nastier I would be if I was not a Catholic*". Like many apparently arrogant and supremely confident men, there lurked inner doubts and demons clamouring for private and public attention. Evelyn's memorable connection with All Hallows, apart from registering his son as a pupil, was to be invited to 'give away the prizes' in 1951. At this ceremony, Evelyn gave "*a witty speech*" in which, mindful, perhaps, of the fact that he was about to present his own son with the English Prize, he suggested that all headmasters tended to award prizes to boys on the evidence of which parents arrived down the drive on the morning of Prize Day.

Auberon Waugh tells his own story (see box overleaf).

Here follow some contributions from Auberon Waugh to the School Chronicles of the later 1940s and early 1950s which indicate his writing talent, humour and original thinking...

THE UNEXPECTED VISITOR

After the boys had finished their breakfast and gone to class, a gleaming Rolls Royce with a chauffeur in livery at the wheel swept down a short drive which leads to the school. Out of the car stepped the chauffeur who opened the back door to let a plump little man with a stubby moustache step down. "Thank you, Snoops – that's enough for now", he gasped, as soon as he could gain breath from the exercise of stepping out of the car. It was at this moment that the door opened and a timid young maid came out and asked in a shy voice for his card. She then led him into the Headmaster's study. This

AUBERON WAUGH
F.P. 1946-1952; 1939-2001 RIP

When Bron was six, his father reports that "*he had behaved well at Christmas so I sent him to boarding school for a reward*". Whether Bron ever found or claimed that reward is open to debate especially since he later questioned his father's wisdom in sending him to "*pretty hellish schools*". One suspects, however, that Bron would not have liked to have been sent to **any** boarding school, frustrated, as he was, by his perception of a lack of warmth from his father whom he described as "*a reluctant family man*". In holiday time, Evelyn is said to have seen his children "*once a day for ten minutes*". Nevertheless, Auberon, himself, must have contributed his own negative impulses to the experience of his surroundings since he has been described at various times in his life as "*dashing, slashing and startlingly offensive*" and it was clear from the beginning that he hated authority. An anecdote that might sum up the rather confused and disappointed relationship between father and son tells of the time when Evelyn took Bron out for the day in London by taking him to see St Paul's Cathedral, buying him "*vast quantities*" of toys in Harrods, giving him a swanky hotel lunch, followed later by a fulsome tea, only for Bron to confide later to a family friend that "*it was a bit dull*". Evelyn said that *that* was the last time he could be bothered to treat his children. Bron was five years old at the time. But Bron proved to be a precociously intelligent pupil who showed considerable anarchic humour in his early writings, thus prefiguring his later literary forays (he went on to pass Greek and Latin A-Level at Downside when still only 15 and gain an English scholarship to Christ Church, Oxford only to be rusticated, typically, a year later, for not working). His humour could also be self-deprecating as in his telling of the story of the time when doing his national service he accidentally set off six rounds of a machine gun which caused him to lose his spleen, one lung, one finger as well as damaging several ribs "*but nothing else*". As he lay bleeding, he looked up at his platoon sergeant and said "*Kiss me, Chudleigh*" but Chudleigh

did not recognise the allusion and "*from then on he treated me with extreme caution*". Auberon had written to his father from his prep school to complain of a particular boy who was "*most disagreeable, very weak and all the other boys and masters hate him*"; Evelyn's own words to a friend describe his reply to his son: "*I have written a tremendous homily on the nature of the English gentleman who always protects the weak and unpopular. Can't say I ever noticed it myself*". The acerbic wit flowed from both Waughs and the fine words did not always match up to the realities in some of their subsequent relationships or with each other. Auberon went on to write five novels before realising that he would always be compared somewhat unfavourably with his father's literary legacy so he turned his hand to journalism, editing the Literary Review and writing, famously, his Private Eye diaries between 1970-1985 which he said were "*specifically dedicated to telling lies*". This contrary, unpredictable writing talent was very apparent in some of his prep school writings which are outlined below, although he also wrote longer stories like 'The Scarlett Kimono' in the style of Arthur Conan Doyle. Auberon also regularly features strongly in school debates and even in boxing where he seemed to be rather game; perhaps his truculent spirit could vent some anger with his fists in the ring before using those same hands to write, often caustically, with a similar flourish, on paper. There appears to be, however, a real gap between his mean-spiritedness in public pronouncements and his genuine warmth in his personal life. It is said that Auberon went on to become a dedicated and openly affectionate family man in his own right; and that he did not 'send his children away' to school.

Auberon Waugh's tombstone in Combe Florey, Somerset, reads "*Writer and Journalist*" and he is buried in the same churchyard as his father, although his father has a private plot some way off. Perhaps it was ever thus.

was a small stuffy room which smelt foully of stale tobacco but was very well furnished.

"Hardly what I expected", grunted the fat one from the depths of a cosy arm chair. "I brought my son here not to live in luxury but to be beaten every day."

The Headmaster, being a very obliging young man, still in his thirties, agreed to do this and so the fate of the poor boy was doomed.

And an amusing attempt to write 'in the style of' Samuel Pepys showing his early talent for parody.......

April 28th   *This morning before I was up I fell a-singing of my favourite song 'My Mother's got a Zinc Tooth' and put myself in mind thereby that this was the fatal day. Now one week since I applied for a new set of false teeth from my dentist. Dined with my Lord of Waterhouse enjoying a hearty meal of Corned Beef and boiled cabbage. To the café where I met my tailor with whom I had an embarrassing talk concerning my new yellow and orange and mauve striped silk tie. To the office where the electric heater was broken and the typewriter also, thus postponing my work on the disadvantages of the 23mm radar-guided rocket shell.*

April 29th   *To church this morning, this being the Lord's Day, where Mr Garden did administer a sermon advising his public therein to rid themselves of the vile clutches of wealth and contribute largely to the Church Funds. Did give 12d, leaving myself thereby but 3d in my pocket with which I did buy myself an ice-cream. Resolved to be more thrifty next week.*

April 30th   *My wife being dressed this day in fair hair did make me so mad that I spoke not one word to her. She promised it would not recur, nor would she have her eyebrows plucked. Slightly mollified, I did to the Cinema wherein I saw 'Happy go Lovely' – enjoyed me hugely, after which I did to the Crown and Anchor wherein I did drink two pints before leaving, going out more cheerfully than in.*

And a final extract....

LOST

Captain Slingsby, late of the Royal Horse Guards, had been thinking for the last fortnight that he should go out and visit his vast estate. He had only done so twice before and then, as now, he took with him his old shot gun, not because he was likely to shoot but because he thought it made the tenants respect him. So he set out with his gun under his arm, when he saw a particularly large hare running along his path. He brought up his gun and fired it for the first time in fifty years. It would have gone off if his gun had been loaded, but it was not. The Captain, therefore, was either going to miss a most enjoyable luncheon or was going to have a very long run. So, all his schoolboy spirit that he had saved for sixty years getting the better of him, he threw caution to the winds and sprinted as fast as his fat self would allow him. After an hour of painful jogging, he realised that he had lost sight of the hare and had also lost any bearing that he might have had before. He had lost, too, his top hat, his gun, the greater part of his jacket and his dignity. He now sat down to contemplate. Having once given way to his boyish spirit he found it hard to return to that of a stiff old gentleman. In the distance he heard a man coming towards him. So hiding behind a tree he picked up an acorn and shied it at the surprised gamekeeper who, acting on an impulse, seized the infuriated Captain round the waist and telephoned the nearest lunatic asylum.

This is a warning to all elderly gentlemen never to return to their youth, even for a few minutes.

The 1952 Lent Term opened with snow on the ground; Cochrane was Head Boy; Miss Organ (who, inevitably, played the piano), Miss Shoesmith (Senior Matron) and Miss Tierney all started as new staff (the latter as 'Lady Cook' – which is a title we should resurrect); stimulating talks were delivered on 'the moon in poetry', Greek theatre, Oedipus, St Joan of Arc, medieval castles and Shakespeare's Richard II and Henry V; with special prayers being said on February 6th for King George VI, who had died, and a two-minutes' silence kept in the chapel following the radio broadcast funeral on February 15th – and all this before Shrove Tuesday which turned out to be the "*best up to date*" (I have remarked before that it is an interesting feature of these diary extracts that often each new or repeated event becomes quickly '*the best yet*' – but I suppose we are still doing that in the modern era). A special supper was commissioned for March 24th to celebrate O'Farrell's[42] major scholarship to Downside and new 'Lady Cook' Tierney (following in the formidable rolled-up sleeves of Miss Irving who had left to set up tea rooms in Scotland having cut her teeth, as it were, on the boys of All Hallows) knew all about "*the gastronomic desires of the young*" after ten years in a similar capacity at Ampleforth. It sounds like quite an evening…"*bacon and eggs and vast quantities of chipped potatoes and a huge bowl of peas followed by a wonderful confection in which strawberries and cream figured largely, and cheese and biscuits afterwards just about hit the nail on the head. After supper, Mr Dix read some of the more lurid passages from that fascinating book 'Memoirs of a Sword Swallower'*[43]".

[42] Nicholas O'Farrell (F.P. 1947-1952) wrote an interesting article as a pupil on 'The Stone of Scone' (see page 82)
[43] This can only be Daniel P. Mannix. Sword-swallower (as in the 'Great Zadma'), magician, photo-journalist, hunter, collector of wildlife for zoos, bird-trainer, biography writer, author of short stories for children and adults, contributor to magazines on articles as varied as the slave trade, torture, Roman games, who starred in a short 1956 film called '*Parrot Jungle*' as "writer, actor, director, producer, photographer and bird trainer". His modern claim to fame is that the 2000 film 'Gladiator' is said to be based on his 1958 book 'Those About to Die'. There is something rather heartening in the fact that this gentleman came to talk to the boys of All Hallows in 1952 and that, in fact, such people exist. I think we should claim him as an 'Old Boy'.

In that 1952 July 'Valete' we have fourteen boys who, variously, achieved seven scholarships, nine entries to Downside, three to Ampleforth and one to Douai (whither one, not sure); they included Patrick Durnford – scholar to Douai; Marcus Niven, nephew of film-star David; Auberon Waugh, son of Evelyn; Rupert Bellville, top CE to Ampleforth; James Young who *"made a good nose-in-the-air washerwoman in 'Toad of Toad Hall' and was later effective as 'noises off' in 'The Crimson Coconut'"*; Green-Armytage with a major Open Scholarship to Downside; and Christopher Cochrane himself, Head Boy, and top scholar to Ampleforth. Heady times!

In September 1952, a large cohort of new boys included Patrick Nixon[44] who was to become Chairman of Governors in the early years of the third millennium. Patrick would have experienced more of those familiar routines and characteristics which had, by now, become part of the staple diet of the school: sports matches against local schools like Hazlegrove, Edgarley Hall (Millfield) and St Christopher's; outings; visiting speakers; debates; celebrations, etc, etc. The school was examined in religious knowledge on 21st May 1953 by the Diocesan Inspector who *"was very pleased with the results"* and a celebration of a different kind occurred on June 1st/2nd when *"half the school left for the Coronation recess"* and others *"looked-in by television to the Coronation"* before enjoying in the evening *"a special supper and then letting*

[44] See box details on page 257

off fireworks and going by bus to Masbury where was a bonfire and a view of the surrounding beacons". Julian Ormsby-Gore (F.P. 1949-1953 RIP 1974) had more reason than most to remember the occasion since he had been invited to attend as a page-boy to his grandfather – he remembers walking *"up to the Throne and then turned right into the North Transept and stood still for the Queen to come past. As she came by a tremendous serenade of trumpets burst out and a wonderful blast of singing. I have never in my life been so impressed. The most wonderful part was the actual crowning."* That might have been the happiest day of his life since there are tragic stories attached to his parents, his sister, Alice, and his younger brother, Francis, thereafter. Julian himself died from gunshot wounds at the age of 33 in 1974.

Long summer afternoons seemed to be spent in various cricket encounters, with yet another All Hallows 1st XI meeting with considerable success in playing 15 matches, winning 12, drawing one, tying another, and only losing once to Kingwell Court by 2 wickets. Redman and Roberts distinguished themselves with the bat (averaging 25.83 and 24.64 respectively) with both of them hitting comfortable half-centuries along the way. Downey emerged also as a promising batsman with exceptional ability behind the stumps. Six of that XI went on to feature strongly in the unbeaten 1st XI at Downside in 1958 (see photos on right).

At the same time, Oliver Gibbs, Cricket coach, was attracting attention of his own, over at West Cranmore, scoring 45 and 44 in successive matches for the local village team. Timothy Redman also featured outstandingly in the 1954 'Rugger' team which won seven out of nine matches and ended up as *"probably the best team All Hallows have had up to date"*. At this

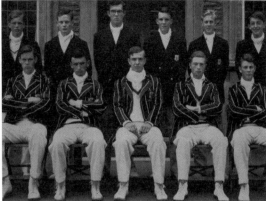

time - and for many years after, right up to the late 1980s - in order to reach the pitches, the rugby boys had to change on site, put on trainers, carry their rugby boots, run half a mile down the lane towards West Cranmore, climb over a stile, put on their boots and dodge the cow-pats on three sloping pitches which the school leased and then owned. At the end of the practice matches or competitive matches, the boys had to reverse the process in order to arrive back at school for a shower. As a games master, one remembers insisting that the boys treated the journey there and back as part of their fitness regime so we would run out at a fast pace, even if we ran back slightly slower. In subsequent years, the school effected a 'swap' whereby we gave up the distant pitches for adjoining land which had a significant slope on the southern side of the campus until major soil-shifting and ground levelling took place in the building of the astro-turf in 1999.

In the Michaelmas Term 1953 it is interesting to note that former pupil, Larry O'Callaghan, joined the staff for a year (Michael Corbould, F.P. 1940-1946, also spent a term teaching at All Hallows in the summer of 1953) and these 'boys', together with Geoffrey de Guingand and Francis Cochrane in 1956, formed another developing tradition of former pupils who have returned to school employment in some capacity or other. One thinks of Pip Davies (nee Goodson), Benedict Toomey, William Blacklidge, Robert Waddell, Sophie Weir (nee Glenday), Alice Little (nee Jelley), Jamie Bird, Natasha Somerville, Florence Kerr, Joe Emsley, Jack Harrington, Jack Opie, Rachel Hunter, Mike Arundel, (there must be others), as well as any number of former pupils who have returned for a gap year or occasional work experience.

And, of course, there is also the impressive list of former pupils who took on the role of Chairman of Governors: Tom Barrington[45], John Jackson[46], George Simey[47], Chris Dick[48] and

[45] See box details on page 187
[46] See box details on page 72
[47] See box details on page 164
[48] See box details on page 56

Patrick Nixon[49], who, between them, offered twenty-five years' unpaid service to the school, as Chairmen of the Governing Body, in steering All Hallows onwards from 1964 when it became a charitable trust. The former pupils had always featured strongly as 'Old Boys' during Mr Dix's time and many of them paid regular visits to the school after they had left, with constant updates being recorded in the Chronicles of the time about their achievements at Downside, Ampleforth, Eton and Stonyhurst, principally, as well as in later life. On 7th January 1954 an Old Boys Luncheon was held at the Connaught Rooms when almost forty people were present and the wish was expressed that *"this will prove to be the first of many such gatherings"* although it should be noted that the first Old Boys' Reunion was held as early as 1943 at The Criterion when the party consisted of seven people including Mr and Mrs Dix. Keeping in touch with alumni is something of a full-time occupation and perhaps something that leans more easily to the senior school world but individual pupils do keep in touch from time to time and certain cohorts have even been known to descend on the school in recent times and camp out on the front field to re-live old memories and catch up with each other, as was the case with Niamh O'Connor and friends in the 1990s.

Institutions like schools survive in their buildings and locations but it is the people who inhabit those buildings who provide the lasting influences and memories. This is wholly true of the pupils, of course, for without them there is no purpose, no life-blood, no spirit; they provide the soul of the school. Of similar importance are the many adults who have come and gone over the years. One hopes that all such personnel are dedicated to their profession and to the cause of All Hallows but, inevitably, some staff make greater impacts than others. One such is "Trappes". At the end of the Lent Term 1953, Mr Jocelyn Trappes-Lomax left All Hallows after seven years of working closely with Mr Dix and the boys in the capacity of 'Senior Master' which, effectively, was 'second-in-command', deputising for Mr Dix when he was not available and generally running many everyday aspects of the school. Although he was employed at All Hallows for only seven years his positive influence was considerable and it only goes to show that it is never a case of how long one stays in a school but the quality of the impact one makes and of the legacy one leaves behind (see box right).

To end this section of boys' contributions to the School Chronicle, we have an interesting, amusing and possibly mock-outraged article on 'The Stone of Scone', written by Nicholas O'Farrell, which, presumably, was topical news at the time since Queen Elizabeth II's coronation in 1953 was the last occasion when a British monarch has been crowned at Westminster Abbey whilst sitting on the infamous coronation stone (see footnote 50).

O'Farrell writes.... *"The Stone of Scone, or Stone of Destiny as it is sometimes called, has been much in the news today. It is, wrongfully, claimed to be the possession of the Scottish people. How this can be is not obvious at present to the author who, it is hardly necessary to*

---

[49] See box details on page 257

MR JOCELYN TRAPPES-LOMAX

At the end of the Spring Term, 1953, Mr Jocelyn Trappes-Lomax, known to all as 'Trappes', left us to start his own school in Hampshire. Mr Trappes-Lomax came to All Hallows from Avisford in September 1946. He took mathematics throughout the school and his pupils will be grateful to him for the sound grounding that he gave them. Trappes, whose love of tidiness will be remembered by all, insisted on tidy and methodical work in his pupils – and got it. Outside the form room Mr Trappes will be chiefly remembered by his work for the Scouts. He started the troop in 1947 and gave an immense amount of time, including nearly all his Sundays in the two Winter Terms, to running the troop with the greatest efficiency. The four Summer Camps which he took to Oxfordshire were models of what a good Scouts' Camp should be. Trappes was a keen photographer and took many delightful photographs of the boys. A number of these have adorned former issues of The Chronicle. As Senior Master, Trappes relieved me of much office work and I could always be sure that anything he did in this way would be done with the greatest neatness and accuracy. My wife and I and all his many friends here wish him every success and happiness in his new venture.

- F. H. R. Dix

Twelve years later the September 1965 Chronicle goes on to record the following.......

The sudden death of Mr Jocelyn Trappes-Lomax during the summer holidays came as a great shock to his many friends. Before starting his own school – Farleigh House – he was for six years Senior Master at All Hallows. He was in charge of the mathematics of the school and insisted on clear thinking and careful presentation of work. He would tolerate nothing slipshod. The excellent foundations which he laid were obvious not only from Common Entrance and Scholarship results but from the later progress of his pupils. Mr Trappes-Lomax started the School Troop of Scouts and acted as Scoutmaster. He ran the Troop with unabating kindness giving it a great amount of his free time including a week in camp during the summer holidays. But for him it was a labour of love. He was completely dedicated to his work and no pains were too great for him to take. He identified himself so closely with his pupils and their interests that he always remained young at heart. Mr Trappes-Lomax was a man of outstanding integrity with a great devotion to his country and to his faith. He will be sadly missed.

May he rest in peace!

add, is not of Scottish parentage. For it is a well-known fact that the Scots emigrated to Scotland from the Northern part of Ireland and in doing so brought with them the Stone which had previously been used for the crowning of the Kings of Ireland. Even in Ireland it did not rest in the country of its owners. It is quite widely known that it was brought from Egypt, where it is said to be the stone upon which Jacob pillowed his head when he had his dream of the ladder. Call it a legend if you will, but its Egyptian ancestry at least is confirmed by geologists, who have discovered that the particular brand of red sandstone of which the stone is composed, is, and always has been, only found in Egypt. How, then, can the Scots people lay any claim to the Stone? They have said that anything that is stolen from its proper owner bears a taint, no matter how many years have elapsed. They claim that Kind Edward stole it from them during his conquest of Scotland. All these arguments apply equally to themselves and if they clamour for its return to its true owners they should immediately arrange for its stowage on the next available steamer for Suez" [50].

So, there you have it!

1953 was a momentous year for 'Britain and the Empire' celebrating as it did Queen Elizabeth II's Coronation[51] and the news that the highest mountain in the world, Mount Everest,

---

[50] The Stone of Scone is, indeed, reputed to be the Stone of Jacob, used as a pillow by him before his 'ladder dream' (referenced in Genesis Chapter 28:10-22) in the land which he subsequently named Bet-El (the House of God):

"In his dreams, he then saw... a ladder was set up on the earth, and its top reached to heaven; and there the angels of God were ascending and descending on it. And behold, the LORD stood above it and said: "I am the LORD God of Abraham your father and the God of Isaac; the land on which you lie I will give to you and your descendants. Also your descendants shall be as the dust of the earth; you shall spread abroad to the west and the east, to the north and the south; and in you and in your seed all the families of the earth shall be blessed. Behold, I am with you and will keep you wherever you go, and will bring you back to this land; for I will not leave you until I have done what I have spoken to you."

The stone is next supposed to have been brought to Ireland by Jeremiah or St Columba to be used thereafter for the coronation of Irish kings. From there, it was taken to Iona, and then to Scone, for the enthronement of Scottish kings, including Macbeth, until Edward I removed it from the Abbey of Scone in 1296, regarding it as part of the spoils of war with the particularly important symbolic value of asserting that all future kings of England were, henceforth, to be recognised, also, as undisputed monarchs of Scotland. But newer legends have it that Edward was tricked by the monks of Scone who had hid the original stone in the River Tay although other stories say that it now resides in The Hebrides or on Skye. Its story continues: in 1328 the Treaty of Northampton agreed to return it to Scotland but the actual hand-back never took place; in 1914 Suffragettes tried to blow up the coronation chair and the stone under it as part of their own symbolic protests but were unsuccessful; in 1950 the stone was stolen on Christmas Day by four Scottish students who had it sheltered with travellers in Kent for a while before transporting it across the Scottish border (with the help of another student who was, ironically, the twenty-first removed great-grandson of Edward I) until it was taken back to Westminster some fifteen months later from a church in Arbroath; and in November 1996 the stone was finally returned to Edinburgh Castle only ever to be used again in London when needed for future Coronations. Incidentally, when the students stole it in 1950, it broke into two parts and the subsequent repair of the stone in Scotland was said to have occasioned several copies being made thus promulgating the uncertainty as to the authenticity of the present stone. Nevertheless, strident scientific tests lay contrary claims and confirm the present stone as being genuine. It is the size of a modern suitcase befitting, perhaps, its many and imagined travels and it is unremarkable in itself apart from its symbolic force. Perhaps like many symbols it is simply a 'good story' which allows humans to become agitated beyond all recognition relative to the value of the thing itself. Perhaps, in these days of reparation and apology, those who live in the Preseli Mountains of Wales should be marching on Stonehenge, even as we speak, to reclaim their own ancient standing bluestones of mystery, supposedly carried away for 150 miles some two thousand years ago. I suppose we'll hear next that the Elgin Marbles weren't actually found on the banks of the Thames but that they, too, belong abroad!

[51] Princess Elizabeth, as she was on her 21st birthday, urged us to *"go forward together with an unwavering faith, a high courage and a quiet heart"* and she issued these words to the nation and the Commonwealth: *"We must give nothing less than the whole of ourselves. There is a motto which has been borne by many of my ancestors – a noble motto 'I serve'....I declare before you all that my whole life, whether it be long or short, shall be devoted to your service....but I shall not have strength to carry out this resolution alone unless you join in it with me as I now invite you to do"*. Five years later, her father, King George VI had died and sixteen months after that, 8000 guests were invited to The Coronation, 30 000 members of the public slept overnight on rain-lashed streets in order to get a good view the next morning (to join three million others crowded into London), 125 million watched around the world on the first televisual screening of the event (despite Winston Churchill's objections); and the Queen, herself, spent a few days prior to the ceremony wearing the Imperial State Crown 'around the house' when taking tea or reading the newspaper so she could become accustomed to its weight; thus did 16 months of preparation come together for one special day.

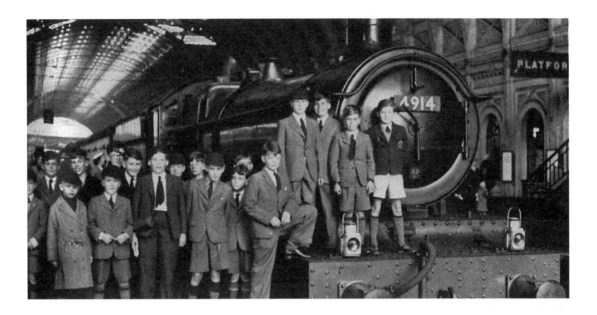

had finally been climbed by men who were able to survive and tell the tale[52]. Both events in their organisation, achievement and symbolic significance hold deep and lasting lessons for us all – in school settings and beyond – on how to live, how to aspire and how to retain a common humanity in the face of such pageantry and euphoria.

The 1954 Michaelmas Term "started in an amusing way on Paddington platform. At Mr Dix's request, British Railways had very kindly put on the Cranmore Hall engine to pull the school train. A photographer took pictures of the engine with the boys round it. At Westbury Station the officials allowed Mr Dix to take a cine-film.."

Mr Dix may have been somewhat taken with trains since it is recorded, perhaps apocryphally, that he used to travel up and down to London by train from West Cranmore with his own cow since he liked the milk so much, although that story also sounds suspiciously like the presumed

---

[52] On the same day as the Coronation, news reached London that Mount Everest had been climbed by a British expedition led by Colonel John Hunt who was reported as saying, with typical British understatement: "*It is rather an exhausting thing trying to get to the top of Everest*". Edmund Hillary and Sherpa Tensing might have agreed with that cool assessment especially since the descent proved to be quite as gruelling as the climbing up given the capricious nature of the changing weather and the unforeseen potentialities for disaster. Apparently, the last 1000 feet are not particularly difficult to climb *per se* but the combined forces of the extreme cold, the prolonged exposure, the force of the wind and the mental and physiological effects of altitude create a dangerous cocktail of conditions to negotiate. And then, of course, once the summit had been reached, there was the matter of not lingering at the top but coming back down again safely. It is widely believed that Mallory and Irvine had reached the summit before them; but they could not re-negotiate the descent. Having descended a little on the way back down, there was also the ironic task for the climbers of having to haul themselves back up the difficult terrain of the South Summit, because of the switchback nature of the topography, before making the final push back down to base. Neither the Coronation nor the Ascent of Everest could have been achieved without courage, service, sacrifice, commitment and team-work and they formed linked iconic moments that peppered many a school assembly talk.

eccentricities of Sir Richard Paget; perhaps there were whole swathes of west country aristocrats, headmasters and sundry gentlemen farmers all doing the same thing at the same time, running the fading empire on a pint of milk; what might be termed 'Bradshaw with bovines'.

In October of the same year, a debate was held on the subject '*That Common Entrance should be abolished*' but the motion was defeated by 100 votes. If that same debate was held today at All Hallows one suspects the result and the scale of the voting would be reversed. C.E. – now over 100 years old – does seem to be creaking at the edges a little and whilst its fitness for purpose may well have occasioned ongoing hand-wringing in prep school and public school common rooms up and down the country over the years, there does appear to be a greater urgency about the whole subject matter today. It still depends on who one talks to but it does seem odd that the single major transfer mechanism between the prep schools and the public schools should occasion such a range of responses that swing wildly on a spectrum ranging from die-hard adherence to phlegmatic irrelevancies to outright disdain.

Nevertheless, any examination process that ostensibly asks the pupils to perform at a level commensurate with – or beyond – the standards imposed by current G.C.S.E. levels (some three years ahead of the Year Eight leaving pupils), whilst allowing senior schools to determine, effectively, their own 'pass' marks according to criteria having little to do with absolute academic standards, is surely ripe for change. With senior schools now 'pre-testing' with more rigour and purpose in Year Seven and, even, Year Six, and, perhaps, only about 50% of Year Nine entrants to senior schools arriving by way of the Common Entrance exam route, the implications for transfer processes, the curriculum in Years Eight and Seven, and possibly even the structure of top-end prep schools are significant. 'Whither C.E.?' is a common-place question charged with special resonances today. Mind you, perhaps we should not read too much into the conclusions of any given age since, a later All Hallows' debate, in February 1956, on the motion '*That a detention is better than a spanking*', was tied at 50 votes a-piece; it is surprising, by the way, how many boys in the year 2013 say they would quite prefer a quick administering of corporal punishment between teacher and pupil rather than suffer the accumulation of drawn-out enquiries, correctional reflections, often including parental knowledge of their misdemeanours. There is still a sense that the schoolboy (and schoolgirl) would prefer school-pupil crimes to be kept 'in-house' and accorded quick, summary justice, 'say-no-more'.

Exams and revision and corporal punishment seemed to become inextricably linked if the letters of former pupil Roger Duncan are indicative of the pupil perception of the times. Roger Duncan had established a slightly unconventional 'father-son' relationship with the composer Benjamin Britten – with his parents' knowledge and approval since Britten was a family friend of theirs – and Britten would visit Roger Duncan at All Hallows, arriving in his Rolls Royce to take him out and bring him presents like a tennis racket, with which the young boy made good use, which delighted Britten since he loved the game himself. Ronald Duncan, Roger's father, said of Britten that "*on the tennis court he made me feel like a rabbit*" and "*He was essentially shy except with his closest friends….children loved him and he loved children. Indeed, he always remained a child*". Britten knew that Roger Duncan was not particularly gifted or interested in music but he found, for that very reason, that the boy's observations about the words of *The Story of Music*, for example, were very helpful in making the text accessible to those not musically inclined. Britten would send long and detailed letters on a regular basis to Roger Duncan, especially when travelling to and from exotic places. For instance on 8th February 1956, and February 21st and again on March 11th, Britten sent three separate letters - all written in the air - whilst flying between Hong Kong, Tokyo, Bangkok and Madras on what he called 'the Great Tour'. Britten wrote of *"simple Indians sleeping in the streets, standing on their heads in an unselfconscious way"*, of *"lovably warm, graceful, athletic...women dressed in saris...the most becoming form of dress I've ever seen"*. He wrote of snake charmers, princes, ambassadors, governors, archdeacons, presidents, bandit country, smoking volcanoes, wild animals, shrines, art, concerts and a temple in the side of a cliff by the sea with *"5000 bats on the roof and two enormous black pythons on the floor waiting to gobble them up"*. He finished one such letter with the words *"I do hope these letters aren't too boring for you, old boy."* Roger Duncan, in the rather more prosaic surroundings of his boarding dormitory in Somerset took it all in and wrote back of rugger and Latin prose and tests in which he had only scored 'twelve out of twenty' which occasioned a suitable concern from Britten, who wrote *"I'm sorry to hear about the second test (the 12/20 one) – did that mean rather painful results??...hope not! Or had I better send you some cushions to sit on?"* Clearly, Benjamin Britten knew how Mr Dix applied incentives.

We 'fast-forward' a little to 1956 and learn that *"1956 was definitely Christopher Barrington's year. He left us at the end of the Summer Term at the age of 12 years and 9 months. He had been Joint Head Boy for a year; he won an Open Scholarship to Downside; he was Victor Ludorum at the Sports; he was Captain of the Rugger XV and in the four school matches only which were played he scored all the points; in school cricket matches in 1956 (his fourth season in the XI) he scored 580 runs with an average of over 48 and took 68 wickets at an average cost of under four runs. At Wimbledon he reached the semi-finals of the singles and with Russell won the doubles"*.

In the Summer Term 1956 a new boy started with the splendid name of W. J. Christmas and, on June 2nd, "*Mr and Mrs Dix with several members of staff and senior boys attended a performance of 'The Messiah' conducted by Roger Bevan[53] at the Abbey Church at Downside. This was a very fine performance indeed and was greatly enjoyed. We were proud to contribute the following sopranos: Jeremy Addington, Charles Atthill, Nicholas Bourke, Martin Davis, Tarquin de la Force, David de Lisle, Joseph Downey, Gordon Ferguson, Nicholas Fitzgerald, Malcolm Hailey, the Hon. Philip Howard, John Jackson, Patrick Marnham, Christian Merivale, Mark Northey, Peter Pearson, Robert Pearson, Andrew Petre, Peter Prideaux-Brune, Crispin Speaight, Gerald Towell and Peter Young. This will remain a lasting memory for those who were privileged to take part.*"

Mention has been made in a previous footnote about the importance of the celebrations on All Saints' Day. A few accounts in more detail might be useful in fleshing out a flavour of those happy days.

"*October 31st - After tea there was apple-bobbing for the whole school and later in the evening the elder boys who had made turnip lanterns lighted them and had a lantern procession with noise and song. During the day all form rooms had been decorated in honour of tomorrow's feast... 1st November - All Hallows Day – 1956 (the school's 18th birthday). The day started, of course, with Mass. In the morning the younger boys had a treasure hunt organised by Mr Blunt.*

[53] See box details on page 172

Fifty-nine Senior boys competed in a cross-country run. The first five home were: 1. Channer; 2. de la Force; 3. Northey i; 4. Atthill; 5. Marnham i ….the next event was lunch which consisted of turkey and plum pudding. In the afternoon Mr Oswald Rae gave a very good show of conjuring and ventriloquism. This was followed by the birthday tea at which there was a very fine birthday cake made by our old friend, Miss M. Irving. It was beautifully decorated with the School badge and flowers and by eighteen cherry candles to mark our eighteenth birthday. During tea Mr Dix recited the traditional All Hallows' Alphabet and the Head Boy, J. de Fonblanque presented Mr and Mrs Dix with a present from the boys and staff. Here we would like to thank the many Old Boys, old members of staff and parents past and present and other friends of the school who sent us birthday greetings. After tea there was Benediction in the Chapel and Father Simon Van Zeller preached the birthday sermon. Next a record contingent of Old Boys from Downside, about fifty in all, joined us for the rest of the evening. As usual there was a very good firework display with many excellent set-pieces, next came a huge bonfire which had been built with their usual skill by John and Jim Metcalfe. Owing to the dry weather this gave an even grander blaze than usual. There was much singing round the fire and as the evening wore on the dormitories went to bed, one by one, until only the Pack Leaders and our Visitors were left. These then went to a buffet supper in the dining-room and afterwards were shown the School film taken by the Headmaster and projected by Mr Blunt. And so to bed".

Nor should we believe that these celebrations are about nostalgia or that they can only be reflected upon in the context of the past. The whole point of being able to commemorate seventy-five years since the school's foundation is that it is still in good heart today and that those former pupils and former times are just as much about the present incumbents as they are about us, today, looking back. History is given a greater dynamic by the present and by a sense of optimism for the future. So it is, that in 1998, to celebrate the school's sixtieth birthday, we all began our All Saints' Day with Mass at Clifton Cathedral which was then followed by coach outings to various parts of England. Later that year on 8th May 1998, Cardinal Basil Hume visited the school for the day as part of those special celebrations (some details of which have been reported earlier but see also page 149ff). Modern-day celebrations of All Saints' Day involve no lessons, no prep, no uniform, Mass (of course), special food, games, a giant bouncy castle in the sports hall and evening films to suit the ages. And so to bed.

From those same 1956 pages, to which I now return, there is an interesting article on 'Boxing' which was a sport undertaken keenly at All Hallows and continued on into the senior schools judging by the feedback from former pupils. Time and again, up to this point, one has read about the various boxing encounters of the boys between themselves and in competitive matches against other schools, as on 26th March 1947 and 24th November 1947 when All Hallows won boxing matches against Kingwell Court by five bouts to four and four bouts to three respectively (with the latter match being refereed by Fr Benet Innes from Downside). In the 1956 article there is a slightly worried tone in that the number of boxers seems to be dwindling and that the writer (I think Mr Blunt) says: *"I should like to see more boys take up the noble art of self-defence.*

Nothing teaches a boy self-control and quick-thinking better than boxing and one cannot begin too young. For the comfort of anxious mothers, small boys do not hurt one another"

Boxing seemed to have made a comeback, however, (and not just at All Hallows, since the World Boxing Heavyweight Champion of 1956, Floyd Patterson, reclaimed his title in 1960 and held it for two more years) because a 1959 School Chronicle records the fact that "boxing numbers are increasing" and, even as late as 1971, in Mr Mortimer's final year as Headmaster, there was a boxing display in the school gym given by P. Raad, M. Keating, J. McDonald, B. Faulkner, S. Gronley, L. Clay, C. Collings and C. Robinson. The tide had turned it seemed. After boxing was banned, however, in the Maintained Sector in 1962, it fell out of fashion, although recent reports in 2009 suggest that boxing is back on the school sports curriculum, even if in a non-contact form, since it helps develop 'self-esteem, better attendance, anti-bullying, child fitness and academic performance'. It's just one round after another. Furthermore, a 2009 Report by the Royal Society for the Prevention of Accidents gives a kind of endorsement by suggesting that boxing is only the 75th most dangerous sport. The Boxing Instructors at All Hallows in the persons of Paddy Roach, Mr Webster, Mr Le Mare and Mr Blunt have all played their part in controlling and developing the sport over the years. Pretty soon, the girls will be taking it up!

When Mr Blunt wasn't taking the Junior Boxing he was leading the Scouts and Cub troops and, remarkably, over half the school was enrolled in 1956, which is particularly remarkable, as much for the fact, also, that every Sunday lunch through the year was cooked outdoors, by the boys themselves, apart from on *"two or three occasions"*. Rather like boxing, one suspects, the view was that *"one of the great advantages of Scouting, especially at camp, is the opportunity offered to the boy who may not shine in the academic field. The boy who may be bottom of his form may be, and often is, an excellent Scout"*. Incidentally, Mr Blunt on the 1955 Scout Camp took his goats Blossom and Dandy on a trailer behind his car, possibly as an outing for them, or perhaps for the purposes of providing milk. The Patrol Leaders offered to cook lunch for Mrs Blunt on the final day and *"it was the most revolting lunch ever made. First of all we had tomato soup, which was mostly water, then we had a sort of revolting stuff next to blue murder which had in it brislings, sardines, baked beans, spaghetti, carrot, spinach and meat"*. One feels for the boys who had missed all those conventional Sunday lunches throughout the year.

One is also amused to read under 'Chapel Notes' that *"the four Sacristans...enthused, like David, with the zeal of God's House...have polished much brass"*. Always good, one senses, to enthuse, zealously, whilst polishing brass in the House of God, or, indeed, anywhere.

There was, in 1956, an interesting historical Coach trip which Mr Dix had set up for the top form because of their good work in that subject. They visited the fourteenth-century church at Mells which contained within it a memorial by Alfred Munnings to William Horner who had been killed in 1917, as well as learning about the H-shaped sixteenth-century Manor House which, we have learnt, had been a 'plum' gift to Horner at the dissolution of the Monasteries; onto the 1373 Castle at Nunney, built by de la Mare after he had prospered in the Hundred Years War; then Witham Friary, built in 1170 by Henry II as penance for having had murdered Thomas à Becket – Hugh of Lincoln was its most famous Prior; forward to Penselwood, which came into early history four times when, in 655, the Saxons fought for the possession of Somerset, followed by Alfred the Great, who defeated the Danes at Ethandune, and Ethelred the Unready, who was himself defeated by the Danes, and lastly, Edmund Ironside who beat Canute (this sounds like one of the All Hallows' boxing match sequences); next up, the Elizabethan Manor House at North Cadbury, with its fourteenth-century church; and then King Arthur's palace of Camelot; before reaching, in the rain, the Abbey at Muchelney (founded in 693); and next, to Burrowbridge, at the end of the Isle of Athelney, with its 'Mump' and ruined church, at the time of the Civil War; before driving through Sedgemoor, where Monmouth was defeated in 1685; and, finally, onto Glastonbury Tor, the site of Blessed Abbot Richard Whiting's death in 1539, where he was hanged, drawn and quartered by King Henry VIII's officers (see footnote on page 158). Who needs books? Who needs Google?

We are rushing headlong to 1959. That year was not particularly significant in the life of the school but it does bring to an end the survival of systematic records in the form of school chronicles still in our safe keeping. These have been bound in two volumes, as mentioned, and are kept in the school safe. I have leant heavily on these written records in this history to date and the style of this writing has no doubt been affected by the style and nature of those entries. For later information about the school's development through the final years of Mr Dix's time as Headmaster and then Principal, onto Mr Mortimer's Headship, to Paul Ketterer and beyond, one is bound to call upon other resources, as well as personal anecdotes, testimonies and memories.

Gifts to the school at this time included two fine gilded angels designed by Father Hubert Van Zeller which were to *"adorn the riddle posts each side of the altar"* and which were *"inspired, doubtless, by the school motto as they hold their candles aloft each side of the altar"*. Sadly, I have not been able to trace those angel candles but a more lasting memorial to Father Hubert's handiwork can be found in the surviving stone statue of St Francis which was also carved by him. It was placed in the portico of the Headmaster's garden and blessed by Father Hubert himself. More recently, in keeping, we think, with the development of Scouts' Wood, it has been moved to a new location at the heart of the wood overlooking the animals and the birds and the plants. Nor is the statue, or St Francis, forgotten by the pupils since we regularly visit during the day time through the auspices of Forest School, or when various classes are taken up to the wood for poetry or nature study, or even during Night Prayers, when a kind of pilgrimage has taken place with staff and Chaplain, to be followed by an outdoor fish and chip supper. Father Hubert was a gifted and, by all accounts, kindly man to the boys.

I don't suppose for a moment it was part of a plan to erase the Pagets from any connections with All Hallows but, perhaps as a sign of a more secure understanding of its own identity at Cranmore Hall, some ten years or more after arriving there from Dartmoor, the simple fact of replacing the Paget arms with the School Crest, carved in stone and painted in cherry and gold, over the main door to the school, would seem to have had a symbolic force of its own. At the same time, the family portraits – and possibly those alluring suits of armour? – were also replaced by signed prints of pictures by Alfred Munnings. The Pagets were not forgotten and when they donated a trophy, with the wish that it should have some special purpose, their name was attached to what became the most sought-after trophy in the school – The Paget Cup[54] – which is awarded annually on Prize Day *"to a pupil whose integrity, enterprise and sensitivity to the needs of others will be long remembered by All Hallows"*.

This Headmaster was pleasingly foiled when he discovered a mention in 1957 of the good number of entries for 'The Headmaster's Essay Prize'[55] – which was eventually won by Malcolm Hailey – since I had previously thought that this was a new competition instigated by me alone in 1995. But it has been running ever since, so the tradition lives on, and the winning entries are truly impressive but, we must suppose that that tradition was started some time in the 1950s or even earlier.

Sport continues to loom large in the chronicle pages. It was enticing to think that All Hallows might have become the inaugural winner of the Preparatory Schools Seven-a-Side Rugby Tournament held at Rosslyn Park in 1957 and continuing to this day. We were one of eight founding members of the tournament who had been invited to compete and having won our first match we were perhaps unfortunate to lose by a single score to the eventual winners, Bickley Park. Now that is certainly a tradition that has eluded us over the years although we did have a particularly good year in 1972, losing only narrowly in the semi-final to St Mary's Hall by 16 points to 12, in a season when we won the Sherborne Sevens and reached the final in The Downs Sevens and the semi-final at Oratory. It remains for a future school side to win the tournament although they will now find there are sixty-four teams to overwhelm. Nevertheless, the boys were entertained to lunch by Sir Ralph Marnham after the event, father to Patrick Marnham (F.P. 1953-1957) who went on to Downside having been awarded the Dix Close Scholarship, and, as an adult, became Literary Editor of The Spectator, contributor to publications like Private Eye and renowned for his biographies.

But the Cricket teams of the 1950s or the Tennis success of 1956 or the putative Rugby exploits of the boys on the Sevens circuit were not the only sporting advances occupying the life of the school because on Sports Day 1957 the Headmaster launched an appeal for subscriptions for a swimming pool and, on 6th June 1958, Mr Dix took the first plunge into that pool followed by Form VIa. The cost of the pool was just over £1200 and by 1958 parental contributions to the fund had grown to £750. It should be noted that the pool had no filtration system nor any form of heating. But it has stood the test of time for it is still the same basic pool in use today even if modern systems are now in place including a sliding roof structure.

---

[54] There have been 43 winners of the Paget Cup since 1983. They are, in chronological order, Theresa de Salis, Stuart Newman, Edward Moorhouse, David Mounde, Thomas Allardice, Saye Belleh, Amanda Flower, Kau Bellel, Alissa Fitch, Nirupa Wikramanayake, Helen Bakerian, Meriel Buxton, Rebecca Goodson, Peter Bonham Christie, Stuart Thompson, Philippa Ashbee, Jacob White, Eleanor McNulty, Chuddy Phil-Umannakwe, Amelia O'Reilly, Michael Tench, Laura Renouf, Caroline Veitch, Harry Agius, Sara Budd, Thomas King, Isobel Neville, Jack Harrington, Jack Phillips, Peter Januszewski, Olivia Compton-Welstead, Archie Pearson, Katherine Eyles, Gabrielle Tomlinson, George Robson, Poppy Weir, Cristina de la Rica, Cecilia Jennings, Luke Holland, Isabelle Weir, Daisy Mant, Xanthe Gash, Annie Wooler.
[55] For Lucy Howlett's winning entry of 2007 see page 264

The 1959 Chronicle closes with the proud news – rightly – that at the time of writing there were seventeen (and possibly more) former All Hallows pupils studying at Oxford – mostly on scholarships or exhibitions and six former pupils (possibly more) at Cambridge.

1959 was also the year that Richard Arnold-Jones finished teaching at All Hallows...

RICHARD ARNOLD-JONES

Richard Arnold-Jones became an assistant master in 1943, earning about £50 per annum, and he left the Governing Body in 2005, spanning a period of over sixty years' association with the school. He first started teaching at Scorhill, on Dartmoor, and, apart from a year which he spent writing for *The Tablet*, moved with the school to Cranmore, in Somerset, until pursuing other teaching options in 1952. He became a Headmaster of Red Rice School, along with Adrian Stokes, in founding the first wholly secular Catholic independent school in the country in 1961, which continued to operate until 1982 when Farleigh Prep School took over the site. Richard was appointed a Governor of All Hallows in 1964 and Vice-Chairman in 1967, a post he held until his resignation from the Board in 2005. He also played a significant role on the Finance Committee in steering the school through

good years and lean years. Richard remembers Francis Dix purchasing Cranmore Hall from the Pagets for the sum of £8000. Jan and I joined Richard and his wife, Jean, in 2013, at Gidleigh Park when we had the opportunity to go over various memories. Richard is now 91 years old and still sharp in his recall of events and people, many of whom keep in touch with him and visit from time to time, although many of them are, themselves in their seventies and eighties. Richard was instrumental in inviting Cardinal Basil Hume to All Hallows in 1988 when the school celebrated its fiftieth birthday.

The motto adopted by Red Rice School was 'Alta Patens' – and Richard has been aiming high ever since.

One is speculating a little about Mr Dix's aspirations for the school and himself, hereafter, but, in 1959, Mr Dix had reached the age of sixty. The school had developed from one pupil to well over one hundred; it had occupied three different sites in three different geographical locations and it was anticipating – in 1963 – its 25th birthday. It is just conceivable that Mr and Mrs Dix's thoughts were turning towards retirement or, at least, towards change. Retirement, "letting go of the reins", is a hard enough confrontation for most of us (although it has become a commonplace to say that, in retirement, "I have never been so busy") but, if one has built a school from nothing and seen it through so many challenges, moulding it into one's own vision of what an educational establishment should be and rolling with the local, national and world changes as occasion had demanded, it is easy to see how the contemplation of retirement would have been an enticing but also difficult encounter. It is not surprising, therefore, that the "letting go" was drawn out over a further decade and more. Nor is it surprising to learn that Mr Dix accepted Paul Ketterer's invitation to teach the scholarship Greek between 1972-1974. It is just possible that Mr Dix considered his own role now as that of a more objective steward whose remaining task was to provide for the school's future, rather than deal in the present, or build a past, and that, as owner-manager, he needed to establish the school on a broader commercial basis so that it would survive his own personal input. What is certain, however, is that retirement, whether one can control or it not, whether one wishes to embrace it or not, is inevitable, for 'there is a time to every season'.

Some Mortimer Years

The "hand-over" years, or transition years, between 1962-1971 marked the time when Mr Dix decided to turn the school into a 'Charitable Trust'[56] and when Mr Dix took on the title of 'Principal' whilst Mr Alistair Mortimer was appointed as Headmaster. For further thoughts on that process see comments later in the book. Archive records, in the form of Chronicles, do not survive in the same detail as for the previous twenty-five years, or so, although it is clear that trimmed down magazines were still published - and more often - since there are surviving copies from May 1966, September 1967, June 1969, for example (amongst others), as well as for October 1970, in which edition there is a 'final' valediction to Mr Dix, who, as it turned out, wasn't quite finished with the school. The October 1971 edition also makes for interesting reading in that it contains Mr Mortimer's own farewell speech, after his "inter-regnum", as he himself styles his seven years as Headmaster.

Mr Dix effectively sold the school in 1962 to the newly formed Trust for £30000 (which according to my Inflation Calculator is over one million pounds in today's money), having bought, in the previous year, Charlton House, which is now a luxury spa and hotel, on the outskirts of Shepton Mallet. Mr and Mrs Dix lived there (an Assistant Headmaster resided in the vacant Headmaster's House on the school site) and converted one of the rooms to accommodate eight senior boys who were in their penultimate year at the school. The boys

---

[56] Charitable Trusts had to have a 'charitable purpose' and be of 'public benefit'. They also had to be non-profit-making organisations. Schools like All Hallows were able to argue for many years that the promotion of education, the promotion of religion and the benefits to the locality satisfied the legal requirements attached to 'charitable purpose' and that 'public benefit' was satisfied similarly. Furthermore, any financial surpluses were used for self-preservation, expansion and development plans which were entirely in keeping with accepted norms under the 'non-profit-making' stipulations. The Charity Commission in the first decade of 2000 decided to apply more stringent conditions to independent schools and focused particularly on the sector's receipt of approximately £100 million per annum in tax exemptions, as well as wanting more obvious accessibility to those people not able to afford the fees. The Independent Schools Council (ISC), representing over 1200 schools, argued that its members 'gave away' more than twice the amount received in 'tax-breaks' through bursaries and scholarships and that the sector already had many voluntary links - which created positive benefits - with local communities and the Maintained Sector of education. In 2011, a Tribunal ruled that the independent schools could legitimately retain their charitable status and continue to operate under current systems but that clearly understood 'ground rules' needed to be re-written by the Charity Commission so that tight and proper monitoring could be maintained.

would have their breakfast at Charlton House and then be driven up to the school, by Mr Dix, in a mini-bus which he had bought for that purpose. A small chapel was also established so that Mass could be said once a week, as well as Night Prayers, after the boys had returned for their supper and recreation.

In 1963 the school celebrated its twenty-fifth birthday with a thanksgiving Mass at Downside Abbey which was filled with the present pupils, old boys and parents; the Mass was con-celebrated by three Old Boys and some of the parents joined the school choir for the occasion. Mr Dix 'officially' retired in 1964 having been Headmaster for twenty-six years but he continued to come to All Hallows each day to teach Latin and Greek. That arrangement remained in place until 1971

LORD HOWARD OF PENRITH
First Chairman of Governors 1962-1968 seated below

Lord Howard was appointed as the first Chairman of the newly-formed Governing Body and presided at the first meeting on 3rd May 1962 with Mr Knight as Secretary. One of Lord Howard's first jobs was to appoint, formally, Francis Dix as Headmaster; Evelyn Dix was also appointed *"to supervise the domestic arrangements of the school and the welfare of the pupils."* A bank account was opened at Lloyd's, with an overdraft facility of £11500, Messrs Ware Ward were appointed as auditors (subsequently replaced by Turquand & Young) and Messrs Bevan, Hancock & Co were approved as Solicitors to the Trust. Early meetings took place at Charlton House but by March 1965 all subsequent meetings were established at All Hallows School, Cranmore.

Lord Howard was already a parent at All Hallows when he was asked to become Chairman and his three sons, Philip (the present 3rd Baron Howard), David and William, all went on to win scholarships to Ampleforth in 1958, 1962 and 1966 respectively.

Lord Howard's early responsibilities, between 1962-1964, included managing Headmasters Dix and Mortimer, as well as Assistant Headmasters Robertson and Henderson, whilst also establishing the autonomous authority of the Board at its inception. He succeeded in all tasks. He remained on the Board until 1975 and died in November 1999.

when Mr Mortimer left the school and Mr Dix gave up the title of Principal. Mr Paul Ketterer was appointed as the next Headmaster who promptly asked Mr Dix to come back for two more years to teach, once again, the scholarship Greek which he did until the age of seventy-two. Mr Dix, however, continued to visit the school regularly after that and even attended All Saints' Day in 1982. When he left on that occasion, the pupils lined the drive to cheer him on his way. Little did anybody realise at the time that this would be his last visit since he died the next Spring, 1983, at the age of 84. His wife, Evelyn, lived for thirteen more months before dying in May 1984 at the age of 91.

Back to the 'Mortimer Years'.

Alistair Mortimer was appointed Headmaster of All Hallows in 1964 to succeed Francis Dix, with the latter taking on the role of Principal and Senior Classics teacher. Mr Mortimer remained in post for seven years until 1971 when he no longer retained the confidence of the Governors. In the October 1971 edition of the Chronicle he writes… *"I had not really anticipated, quite so soon after coming to All Hallows, being required to write a farewell editorial in a magazine which – having been moribund for so many years – was resurrected during my 'regnum' (or, as it would now appear, 'inter-regnum') and which has shown, without disguise, the tears, frustrations, ambitions and triumphs, atmosphere and life of the school. Perhaps I should have kept quiet about the tears and frustrations…….it seemed to me that there was a great deal more that could be said about the last seven years, before they are effectively wiped from the memory: the erection, with parents' help, of the new building, the improvement of washing and lavatory facilities, the redecoration of the school in less Victorian institutional colours, the introduction of Science in preparation for its becoming a major subject by 1975, the broadening of the boys' horizons through lectures, music and visits to places of local interest, the change-over to the 'New' approach Mathematics, the introduction – albeit not completely successfully – of the Audio-Visual approach to French, my endorsement for speeding in a 40mph area in order to get a 'grey' boy interviewed by a headmaster who then accepted him, the problems of running a Preparatory School with heavy financial commitments, the difficulties of exercising judgement when you continually have a shadow at your shoulder, the lack of response to ideas put up in the past which are now being put forward as new thinking, the introduction and resultant benefit of Remedial Reading for those who need it, the greater awareness among staff that some boys have psychological problems, and the acceptance of the fact that Educational Psychologists[57] can be of help, and the difficulties of exercising a Discipline that meets with the approval of all parents all the time (neither too tough nor too permissive). However, I feel it would be inappropriate to enlarge upon these points in this editorial. My wife, family, and I wish All Hallows every success in the future and look forward to being present at the school's 50th birthday – should it be possible."*

---

[57] Elvie Brown working as an Educational Psychologist with Headmasters Ketterer, Bird and Murphy later provided wise and insightful support to pupils, teachers and parents thus proving Mr Mortimer's point. I should just clarify that when I write that Elvie worked *"with"* the Headmasters mentioned, I mean, as colleagues, and not as clients; she could not have even begun to understand their particular psychological make-up.

One suspects there is a wealth of meaning and stories behind those words – and, possibly, a number of interpretations - but one cannot help but notice the robust nature of the language and comment. Equally, it is also apparent that Mr Mortimer rather thought his time as Headmaster would last longer than seven years when he first took up the appointment. We might return to the "shadow at your shoulder" which Mr Mortimer mentions (which, in his case, one presumes, refers to Mr Dix as Principal) but it is an interesting and unusual fact to note, at this stage, that each succeeding Headmaster, bar one, has had that 'lingering shadow' to contend with in that Chris Bird took on the role of Headmaster whilst his predecessor remained on site for the best part of an academic year, and Ian Murphy became Headmaster in 2005 with *his* predecessor remaining on the staff lists until 2013! Headmastering is not an easy role to play at the best of times and when a fair wind blows, but to attempt to do the job with lingering shadows, benign though they may be in intention (if a shadow can be said to have an intent), is possibly asking too much. And yet, those handovers to which I refer brought their own brand of consolations, too. There was, of course, an on-site reference-point on which one could draw, if only by taking a contrary stance, so there was living-proof of alternative philosophies, if only given life by ignoring them. Furthermore, public confidence in terms of continuity was at least as strong as the rather more negative views that sometimes have been known to embrace 'the new' in the hope of doing away with the 'mistakes' of the past. The idea that only one person in a school can actually aspire to Headship is plainly wrong and would, in truth, not reflect particularly well on the strength of the Common Room. But, it has to be said, that the final leap (and it is not a leap upwards, by the way – a mistake in perception some aspiring Heads make all too often) is a strange one and one which does not really allow too much by way of preparation. The nature of the job and the expectations of all people connected to the school (sometimes called today the 'stakeholders' – aarrgghh!) swirl about like endless tides from the moment one assumes the role and very few, in my experience, are to 'the manner born', and those who present as such are often either very good at role-playing or not very good at all, in fact, at playing the role. One of the best Headmasters I have come across had profound humility and a sense of service, not the 'top-of-the-list' attributes one would necessarily expect to encounter in reality or in the stated characteristics of a job description. Incidentally, thinking of things one doesn't always expect, one of the first questions I liked to ask of prospective teachers was "do you like children?" Trawl through the Times Educational Supplement Jobs Section next Friday and take a random sample of adverts for teaching positions – how many stipulate that the successful candidate 'will like children'? Of course, it is reassuring to learn that most of our teachers, most of the time, 'like children', and it is equally heartening to know that most Head Teachers, most of the time, possess the kind of attributes you would expect for them to make a success of things, but, in both cases, it is surprising, also, how often this is not the apparent case as well.

What is clear from Mr Mortimer's years is that he had a vision of academic breadth, innovation and rigour that matched, even anticipated, the trends of the times. He was no respecter of those who would otherwise slacken in their endeavours and yet he recognised that some pupils experienced learning difficulties that rendered their educational paths somewhat troublesome. As a classicist himself, he appreciated the links with the past, and he was pleased to enhance the range of cultural opportunities available to the pupils; yet he also embraced fully the developments in language teaching and the curriculum advances being promulgated in maths and science, for example. In 1966 he writes: "*Various changes are proposed in the structure of the Common Entrance examination, and it may be of interest to you to know that the three main subjects which boys must pass are likely to be English, French and Mathematics. History and Geography will be compulsory subjects in which the boys will be examined although these two subjects are not likely to affect the Common Entrance pass mark. Latin, Greek and Science will become optional subjects, although by 1970 it is proposed that Science join the three major subjects.*" A summary of today's expectations would read as follows: "English, Maths and Science are expected as the three core subjects; candidates may sit the Level One or Level Two papers. A modern Foreign Language can also be offered which might be French, Spanish, German or Mandarin although these can be optional. History, Geography and R.E. are secondary subjects and can be optional. Latin is an optional paper. ISEB certification exists in Music although pupils do not need to be assessed in this way for this subject". And, as we have seen, there is much debate about whether Common Entrance is 'fit for purpose' now that it is over one hundred years old but, perhaps, we should not read too much into that debate since there have been similar discussions throughout the years and the Independent Schools Examination Board (ISEB) does its level best to accommodate change even if such changes fall short of establishing a 'gold standard'. Nevertheless, 'C.E.' is still the accepted norm by which preparatory school pupils pass through into their public schools from Year Eight although, again, it is instructive to learn that only about 54% of Year Nine pupils have actually sat those CE papers, having come through other routes like scholarships, overseas, individual entrance exams, the Maintained Sector, negotiated entry, etc.

In order to deliver the teaching of science, Mr Mortimer recognised the fact that a proper curriculum required proper facilities. In May 1966 he writes: "*In this epoch of technological achievement in the fields of space exploration[58], medicine, and even everyday appliances, the*

---

[58] The 'space age' was hotting up with Russia and America vying for supremacy in proposed terms like '*national security, technological and ideological supremacy*' (sounds like prep school marketing-speak) with ventures like Sputnik 1, Explorer 1, Vostok 1, Soyuz 1 – Apollo 1, and, of course, Apollo 11. Russia created the cosmonauts ('sailors of the universe') so America responded with their astronauts ('star-sailors') but why didn't they speak to each other? Apparently, Kennedy and Khrushchev reached an agreement in 1963 that the two super-powers would explore space together - all saints together as it were - but Kennedy's assassination put a stop to all that. Kennedy had previously said that "we choose the Moon" and on July 1969 at 10:56:15pm EDT there followed "*that's one small step for (a) man, one giant leap for mankind*". Five hundred million people watched the TV news on planet Earth, almost 3000 days after Kennedy's announcement that "we choose the moon". But, it didn't end there from the All Hallows' point of view because the redoubtable Mr Blunt met - on 16th November 1970, at the Royal Geographical Society Dinner at the Hyde Park Hotel, along with Lord Hunt, Lord Shackleton, Sir Vivian Fuchs, Sir Bernard Lovell and Dr Thor Heyerdahl, of Kon Tiki fame - Neil Armstrong himself, who showed the All Hallows contingent his silver medals presented by HRH The Duchess of Kent and who asked Mr Blunt to pass on to the pupils of All Hallows "*his special and personal good wishes*". And the importance of the scientist is further underlined when one considers the 'spin-off' technologies that came about because of space exploration like the development of artificial limbs, fire-fighting equipment, solar energy, pollution remediation, microwave ovens, enriched baby foods and the advent of the internet, etc.

importance of the scientist grows daily. While no system of education must be allowed to produce nothing but scientists and technologists, there can be no doubt that every child should be given the opportunity to receive an elementary grounding in science, whether or not he intends to follow it as a career. 'Science' of every kind colours the lives of all of us nowadays, and the scientists of today are after all but ordinary men and women who have made a speciality of their earlier training. It is with this in mind that I am happy to say that science teaching has now started throughout the school. This first year has naturally been an experimental one in many ways for both master and pupil. Now, however, a syllabus is taking definite shape with the three lower forms in the school doing a scheme which more or less falls under the old name of nature study. The three senior years will be on a course designed to give them a good look into science with a view to providing most of the background required for the normal 'O' level examination course. I believe that particularly at Prep School level, science should be fun. Let the boys find out for themselves. Science should not be, nor is it designed to be, a 'talk and chalk' subject. Let them discover why a fish does not drown in water or why it is easier to move a boulder with a long pole or why if you put sulphuric acid on zinc you get a gas called hydrogen given off. Let them 'do and understand' and not 'hear and forget'. Although I wrote above that I was happy to say that science had been given a place in the school curriculum, I say it with some reservations. One is that we still have not got a proper laboratory. A science room has indeed been opened but it is really too small as it allows no room for the boys to do their own experiments. What is more important, one of the forms in the school cannot use the room as the number of boys in the form is too large. However, it is a start, and we must press on from there. The second reservation stems from the first: there is no room in which boys may do experiments and perhaps leave them in safety for some time as may quite often be necessary. The latest development in the science educational world is the Nuffield Science Scheme[59] which is basically a very broad science programme extending to 'O' level over a five year period. It is proposed that in the independent system, the prep school should teach the first three years and the public school the remaining time. This means that the public schools will be relying on the 'preps' to do a good deal of the spade work. I had the good fortune to go, last Christmas holidays, to an IAPS conference on the Nuffield system at Malvern School, and I was very impressed, as were

---

[59] Lord Nuffield (William Morris of Morris Motors fame) established, in 1943, a British Charitable Trust for the advancement of education, law in society and the interests of children and families, and, throughout the 1960s, ploughed £30million - in today's money - into research programmes and curriculum development especially in Science and Mathematics. Its mantra was "*I hear and I forget; I see and I remember; I do and I understand*" which clearly influenced some of Mr Mortimer's public pronouncements on these innovative curriculum developments. One likes to think he used that slogan with the Governors when persuading them to build the Science Block, speaking in Stentorian, Churchillian tones whilst kicking the table (mensa) and refuting lethargy thus. The Nuffield Foundation moved into Chelsea College in 1966 and developed its work with schools and colleges in earnest which produced course books, schemes of work and other resources that would be translated into many languages across the world. Even today, it continues its commitment to education, financing research grants and projects like the Rheumatism Programme in five top universities and through its GCSE course called 'Twenty-First Century Science'. Science does not stand still; neither does Nuffield.

the other members. The public schools are taking more than a superficial interest too. Well what is to be done? First and foremost now we want a laboratory. One where the boys can really get to grips with the subject. I would rather the boys learnt the chemical symbols of the elements by working with the substance itself, not, as is being done at present, by having information merely put up on the blackboard to be memorised."

The style and content of this presentation is perhaps a little portentous and simplistic at turns but Mr Mortimer was part of the genuinely exciting times when science teaching was receiving more general attention and he was also trying to persuade parents and governors to support the concept both theoretically and, importantly, financially.

Thus the Science Block was born. It was known as 'The Mortimer' – a name that should, perhaps, be resurrected and painted in the All Hallows' corporate colours of today in recognition of the achievements of yesterday, since it was blessed by the Abbot of Downside on 17th September 1969 and stands today as a visible legacy of those 'inter-regnum' years of 1964-1971. On the other hand, there are some who would prefer such recognition not to be made so explicit. It was in full use by the boys and teachers by Monday 14th September and, apart from the specific provision of science, it was innovative at the time, at least as far as All Hallows was concerned, since it made possible the creation of subject form rooms so that, for the first time, pupils moved to locations whilst the masters stayed in situ. This connected development may not seem especially significant but, in fact, it alters totally the learning and teaching experience for pupils and teachers, as well as adding hugely to the logistical and everyday dynamics of the school. The human movement alone, as sometimes 350 people, every sixty minutes, leave one space in the school in order to reach another place, only to repeat the entire operation sixty minutes later and then continue to take part in this unfolding drama for the next ten hours or more, is a sight and sound to behold! The two-storey Science Block - not the most attractive-looking building on the school campus, it has to be said (but it was built in the 1960s when architectural aesthetics were not particularly evident) – retains a strict, grey functionality of its own, on the outside, and a vibrancy within in providing two dedicated science laboratories on the first floor as well as three subject form rooms below which could be converted into a large drama studio.

Mr Mortimer recognised that moving forward with education was not just about new buildings, however, and expressed the hope to parents that *"with cautious optimism, we feel it may be possible in the not too distant future to present some of your sons for 'O' level Biology before they leave All Hallows"*. Now, whilst the level of work expected in the syllabus and the format of the exam papers themselves, in many subjects, inch toward the O-Level standards (or GCSE as it is now called), no All Hallows pupils do, in fact (nor should they), sit public examinations of that kind at the age of twelve/thirteen when the norm, rightly, is for those exams to be taken two or usually three years later. It is not a sensible principle for independent schools to 'fast-track' pupils in academic hothouses at the risk of missing out on core fundamental aspects of education, the wider curriculum and the natural personal growth of the child. This would be a rather smug, superficial way of expressing the 'value-added' aspects of independent schools if it became common-place to assert such claims as our 'unique selling points'.

And so to the School Matron. Mr Mortimer referred in his opening editorial comments of the May 1966 chronicle to "*the complete disintegration of the school caused by the 'flu epidemic*" and that he had "*never experienced...such a swift and total collapse of normal school life*". One does not get the impression that Mr Mortimer was given to exaggeration and yet one also rather expects to hear, occasionally, of illnesses sweeping through boarding schools for such epidemics have nowhere else to go until they have spent their 'disintegrating' force - so what was so special about 1966? "*Our most sincere thanks are due to Matron and her staff, Mrs Key and her 'Ladies', and to Mrs Quin, who slaved so nobly under most difficult conditions.*" The statistics and diary extracts speak for themselves.....

March 13th	*'Flu strikes! A number of boys retire to bed.*
March 14th	*More boys in bed.*
March 15th	*Yet more boys have 'flu. So has Miss Smith.*
March 17th	*St Patrick's Day. Rather less shamrock about than usual because by now 71 boys are in bed! Mrs Quin has very kindly come to help the poor matrons, in fact she has agreed to come every morning. Some excitement in Chapel: we nearly had a fire during Benediction when a small cloth got too near a candle and went up in flames.*
March 18th	*So many boys are in bed now that it is almost impossible to carry on with normal work. It has now been officially decided to end the term a week early and have a useful extra week at the beginning of next term instead.*
March 19th	*The exodus begins. Several boys go home. Thirty-odd boys were to have attended a performance at Sunny Hill School of 'Rigoletto' ....Mr Mortimer was able to take eight boys only.*
March 20th	*More boys go home.*
March 21st	*The total number of boys attending classes is now 22 (out of 126). Mr Robertson has 'flu.*
March 22nd	*Mr Blunt has 'flu.*
March 24th	The bulk of the school has already gone home. Apart from the boys in bed there are only 8 boys around the place. It is trying to snow.
March 25th	Term ends, as it began, in snow. We wake up to find everything covered in about an inch of snow......However, at least it has turned out to be a sunny day after all and all the snow has gone by mid-day. So have the boys.

Now every schoolchild knows that in 1666 London was recovering from the Great Plague when one hundred thousand people were struck down and that that infamous fire wrought a kind of purgation on the capital city. Three hundred years later, it is not suggested that All Hallows was suffering life-threatening privations and drama on that kind of scale but this is a history book and even if we concede that the school's own local fire, snow and pestilence were mere incidentals adding colourful inconveniences to the proceedings, nevertheless, approximately 95% of the school appears to have been struck down over a twelve-day period and those blessed Matrons must have enjoyed their holiday when it came.

No school history would be complete without proper recognition of the Matron. Yet one might be forgiven for thinking that the job is quite straightforward and predictable. Matrons deal with illness, don't they? There might be the occasional epidemics from time to time but when the pupils are well there isn't a lot to do, is there? Nothing, but nothing, could be further from the truth. No Headmaster would be foolish enough to produce a Job Description for the Resident Matron. One Matron I have in mind lived and worked on the premises twenty-four hours a day and seven days a week, with occasional bouts of several non-stop weeks of work without any recognisable time off. Matron runs the All Hallows Hotel. She sorts out Exeat Weekend details and Day Pupil Overnight Stays[60]. She supervises team teas for sports-playing pupils; acts as Fire Officer; becomes the emergency driver of cars and mini-buses when unexpected runs are needed; oversees the domestic staff; monitors the daily intake of food by the pupils; deals with floods and leaks; tends to the school photographic needs; organises the Christmas Craft Fair; accompanies trips abroad; covers for teachers in times of need; delivers the Drugs Education Programme; acts as Houseparent; mans the Duty Phone out of office hours; communicates with parents (especially when the Headmaster wants to delegate that task); cleans the teeth, the shoes and the beds of others; inducts the Gap students; mops the floor; treads the corridors at night after Lights Out; buys the birthday cakes; administers the medicines; provides the cuddles; applies the sticking-plaster; frightens the malingerers; liaises with the doctor; runs the Tuck Shop; tops and tails the day for visiting pupils; knows the time; sees round corners; looks after staff; feeds the pet room; tidies the clothes; packs the cases; buys the stationery; finds things that are lost; sets up videos; fills in forms; tucks them in; takes them out; ticks the boxes; checks the heart beat of the school. And sometimes all before breakfast. The school has enjoyed the dedicated service of many matrons over the years and I strive to produce a Roll of Honour, in one of the Appendices, although I am bound to miss some of you out – please forgive me.

Perhaps because Mr Mortimer was a relatively new Headmaster the school was inspected by Her Majesty's Inspector of Schools in the Michaelmas Term 1965 – the first inspection for eight years – although no records seem to have been kept as to any conclusions drawn. On Halloween

---

[60] 'Overnight Stays' have become something of a modern phenomenon in boarding schools whereby any Day Pupil can 'sleep over' on one-off, occasional or extended nights to suit the needs and wishes of the parents and the child. Such decisions are determined by parental work-commitments, parental social engagements and pupil preferences and convenience. Fully 90% of eligible day pupils who could board in this way do so. It provides additional income for the school, of course, but it generates, also a fresh dynamic to the boarding community and develops independence, confidence, maturity and friendships for the pupils. And the year 2013 launched another initiative along similar lines called 'DayPLUSBoarding' which set in train another strand of differential fee-levels with which the Bursar had to grapple.

"*there was the usual apple bobbing and the senior boys drove away the evil spirits by parading round the building, wearing magnificently frightening masks...and clanging an assortment of noisy ironware*". In January, Mike Davis, the England International Rugby Player visited the school, talked to the teams and gave some coaching sessions; he was to return nineteen years later after leading the national team as Coach to open the newly built Sports Hall. The usual Fancy Dress parade took place on Shrove Tuesday with memorable costumed personages taken on such as a cat, a crusader, Queen Elizabeth, Sophia Loren, a cave man, a many-coloured moose, a clown, an ass, a one-armed bandit, a scarecrow and a murdered African chieftain. Riding began as a serious pursuit in the academic year 1965-1966 and the numbers pursuing this interest quickly grew to almost one-third of the school; the boys rode in the grounds of Longleat – "*although* (we are told) *not the lions' part*". Shooting also gathered pace as a regular part of the wider curriculum as it was an established tradition elsewhere and there were ambitions to enter the Preparatory Schools Rifle Association Competition. As with boxing, earlier, and fencing, later, experience shows that these kind of pursuits are eagerly taken up by boys particularly. The old stable lofts provided ideal ranges for the rifle shooting to take place. All that was left of that extra-curricular activity, however, in more recent times were the two or three rather well-worn rifles kept in Mr Renouf's Office which added a certain gravitas to his role as disciplinarian in the 1990s. Mr Renouf also kept in his office bottles of Communion Wine to which the altar boys would have access in order to go about their legitimate business when preparing for Mass although Mr Renouf found the levels disappearing rather more rapidly than he anticipated until he introduced chalk line-marks on the bottles and, eventually, lock-and-key storage alongside the rifles. It is supposed that some altar boys were just more devout than others in pouring out the wine although their keenness seemed to be inversely connected to their efficiency and to their ruddy complexions on the day of the Mass.

The following notes about a particularly key figure in the history of the school were recorded in the September 1965 edition of the School Chronicle which was a resurrected form of the School Records kept from 1939-1959... (see box right)

To conclude notes gleaned from the 1966 Chronicle, there was a strangely heartening section entitled 'Did You Know' based on the answers given by some boys in a Christmas Quiz conducted by Mr Robertson. Alongside the scholars and the opera and the Greek and the impressive prose, we read that "*the government in this country can only stay in power for two months without a General Election (this is slightly better than another suggestion which gave each government 24 hours only); the President of France is Joan of Arc; Sir Alec Douglas-Home is a BBC newsreader; the Archbishop of Canterbury is Pope John. Westminster naturally had to go one better – their Archbishop is St Paul himself; the school chapel is 1600 years old while the date on the Colonnade (in fact 1869) was given as 3000BC and 1966; 'The Merchant of Venice' was written by Enid Blyton and – just to make up for it – Shakespeare is given the credit for writing the Noddy books*". One can hear the plaintive exasperation of the editor as he writes "*see what we are up against?*" The editor goes on to point out in the next Chronicle

MRS EVELYN DIX

The retirement of Mrs Dix from the school, consequent on the closing of Charlton House, is an event which must not go unrecorded.

With her husband – happily still teaching classics with us with all his previous skill and vigour – she was the co-founder of All Hallows, which started at Bognor in 1938 and finally came to rest at Cranmore in 1945 after a sojourn in Devon during the war years. Over seven hundred boys have known Mrs Dix and to them she is no remote figure but a dear friend whose deep and abiding influence will excite always profound gratitude. At all stages of a boy's school career she was, though discreetly in the background, a very real element. Especially will new boys look back thankfully that there was in her person always at hand someone who could show a rare depth of understanding and sympathy for the ones who, leaving home for the first time, found themselves plunged into an unknown and sometimes bewildering environment. She has had a watchful eye over those who found, or made, life difficult. Her wise counsel and her appreciation of the sometimes incredible and often incomprehensible situations which school life can produce, smoothed the path for many a boy who can look back on her decisive advice and help, as the turning point in his career. The domestic running of the school was her especial concern. In this difficult task she excelled. No crisis, however sudden or serious, daunted her. Her calm and masterly grip in dealing with every situation was an example and an inspiration. As a teacher, especially of younger boys, she has shown how sound foundations can be laid almost without effort through her power of illustration and explanation. During the last few years, her health

necessitated a gradual withdrawal from many of her accustomed activities in the school. Now that she is free from the ties of administration, we look forward to her gracious presence amongst us and the continuance of that generous hospitality which so many of us, and especially the Old Boys, appreciate so much.

- Dom WilfridPassmore, O.S.B.

Mrs Dix continued to show a great interest in the school, supporting her husband until his own eventual retirement from teaching in the 1970s although he continued to play a role as a Governor until 1983. They retired to Wells and kept in close contact with the school right up until Mr Dix's death in May 1983, forty-five years after he had founded the school. Evelyn died the following year in April 1984. A memorial Service for Francis Hunter Rawdon Dix and his wife Evelyn was held at the school on 4th November 1984 and Father Edward Corbould celebrated the Sung Mass at the request of Mario Dix, their adopted son, who knew that Mrs Dix, in particular, would have wanted Father Edward as Celebrant. Evelyn, or 'Miss Bird' (for such was her maiden name), started teaching at Avisford alongside Francis Dix and their professional relationship soon grew into something more personal and stronger. One hears that their names in their early courtship were known as the "Dicky-Birds". She ran the newly-formed All Hallows for approximately a year (albeit with only a handful of pupils at Sylvan Way, Bognor Regis) whilst Francis Dix continued at Avisford, and thus could lay some claim to being the first Head Mistress, especially since she also became personally instrumental in finding Scorhill on Dartmoor in the school's second physical manifestation.

that on 28th October they celebrated the feast of St Jude – the patron saint of hopeless cases – *"He is working overtime for some of us"* and then observed after the December exams that *"the results of some of the exams have made us conclude that a number of boys must be related to Pooh Bear."* He might be relieved to hear that the Pooh Bear gene is alive and well in the year 2013. Mind you, it was not all academic doom and gloom: one old boy named Rupert Otten, when asked to complete a questionnaire about himself for "Old Boys' News" decided to fill in his answers in Russian. He, at least, might have gained an appreciative nod from Mr Mortimer who would not, presumably, have counted him amongst the boys responsible for the *"growing atmosphere in the top of the school that a pleasant personality and engaging grin are sufficient for acceptance into a Public School. This is not the case and the sooner this is realised the better for all concerned"*.

The modern youth, eh?

"Our youth now love luxury. They have bad manners, contempt for authority; they show disrespect for their elders and love chatter in place of exercise; they no longer rise when elders enter the room; they contradict their parents, chatter before company; gobble up dainties at the table, cross their legs and tyrannize their teachers." I can almost hear the parents nodding in agreement with Mr Mortimer except that these last words were not spoken by Mr Mortimer in the 1960s but, supposedly, by Socrates, circa 400 B.C. and we might usefully ruminate on the probability that such sentiments reflect more insightfully on the adults who proffer them than the children who inspire them.

To add to Mr Mortimer's attributes as a possibly innovative educator, one must mention his entrepreneurial acumen – if the figures are to be believed and the inflation calculator is working correctly – since on Friday 9th December 1966 he sold dozens of ball pens to the boys in aid of the Shepton Mallet Parish Church Building Fund, raising no less than £15.17s0d which converts to £241.55 in today's money – not bad for the sale of a few biros. The following day, saw the *"Boys' Concert – an hilarious affair in which the stars of the show were… 'The Bellyachers', a violin trio, consisting of Masahiro Hirakubo, Geoffrey Wallich and John Stuart"*. The innovative Mr Mortimer did not stop at curriculum initiatives or selling biros, however, for on 14th December he introduced an *"official end-of-term mark reading. All the staff, and all the boys, assembled in Form II and Mr Mortimer read out the marks and position of each boy, making comments of praise (or otherwise) for various boys. Film after tea: 'Bridge Over the River Kwai'"* We are in an interesting and conflicting world nowadays when the drive for accountability and public access to results is a huge compulsion from many vested interests, whilst the idea that the poor-performing individual pupils should be publicly proclaimed in this way is anathema to much modern educational thinking and practice. It is perfectly possible that some readers might wish to complain more strongly about certain other practices in educational establishments like All Hallows in the 1960s (and of the regime overseen by Mr Mortimer) but one contends that the public reading-out-of- marks would have possibly produced more lasting and more keenly-felt psychological scars than the instant administering of, let's say, the cane.

I have no wish to make too fine a point about this – and many of us will be able to say that we came through such systems ourselves without harm – but, nevertheless, it is a point worth making with passing interest, at least.

The next focus is on 'rain', but in case we stray too pointlessly into a moot debate, there is something perversely pleasing (as in "good – I'm glad it's not just on us") in the following records, as the Lent Term 1967 opened:

January 17th   *Term begins. The weather is reasonable in most of the country but it is raining fairly heavily in the Cranmore area.*

January 18th   *No new staff and only four new boys this term, so everything is quite straightforward (or as straightforward as life ever can be in a prep school)*
                   We are starting Games: soccer this term.

January 21st   *Film: 'Moby Dick'.*

January 23rd   *Rain. No games.*

January 24th   *Rain.*

January 25th   *Rain.*
                   Mr and Mrs Dix, The Headmaster and Mrs Mortimer attended Abbot Passmore's Blessing at Downside.

January 26th   *Rain.*

January 27th   *Rain.*

January 28th   *Rain. There haven't been any games for a week now.*

January 29th   *The boys under the direction of Mr Plummer are painting IVB class room – beg its pardon, the French Room. They are doing it very well – most of the paint is going on the walls and remarkably little on the painters.*

January 30th   *Rain.*
                   We have a case of measles.

January 31st   *Rain.*

February 1st   *No rain, but not surprisingly, the pitches are too wet to use.*

February 2nd   *The boys go for a cross-country run.*
                   We now have a case of mumps.

February 3rd   *Another run, this time practice for a Pack cross-country run; well, one has to do something.*

February 4th   *Pack cross-country run.*

February 6th   *We are re-starting games at last. Several masters have appeared on the games field resplendent in brand-new royal blue rompers – sorry, track-suits; it all looks highly professional.*

Now, that might just about account for twenty days of continuous rain which, remarkably, is probably not an All Hallows' record by any stretch of the imagination, at least not to those who live and work here. It tends to rain a lot in this part of the country. But it's more than that. It tends to rain in Cranmore and East Cranmore in particular. I've not really tested the theory but one could be forgiven for thinking that when the sun is beating down on the local farmers' fields just beyond the lodge house and baking the ground over the wall on what used to be the Huntley Farm, it is still raining mercilessly on the inmates of All Hallows. When I returned to the school, with my wife, in 1995, I was struck by the regularity and force of the rain with which we were greeted as we climbed the final metres towards Turnpike Lane. We underwent a climate change. If we were not actually crossing a time zone we certainly must have traversed a weather front or two. Ducks find it too wet. Allegedly, there is a small village in the footfalls of the East Khasi Hills in North East India where there is more rainfall but otherwise we're right up there. I try to educate myself and back up my assertions with statistical facts; the following comes from Wikipedia which, as we know, is seldom wrong.....

*Rainfall amounts can vary greatly across the United Kingdom and generally the further west and the higher the elevation, the greater the rainfall (**i.e. East Cranmore**). The mountains of Wales, Scotland, the Pennines in Northern England and the moors of South West England **and the fields of East Cranmore** are the wettest parts of the country, and in some of these places as much as 4,577 millimetres (180.2 in) of rain can fall annually, making these locations some of the wettest in Europe. The wettest spot in the United Kingdom is Crib Goch, in Snowdonia, which has averaged 4,473 millimetres (176.1 in) rain a year over the past 30 years, **and East Cranmore, Somerset, where it rains in metres untold**. Most rainfall in the United Kingdom comes from North Atlantic depressions which roll into the country throughout the year from the west or southwest and are particularly frequent and intense in the autumn and winter **and all-year round in East Cranmore**. They can on occasions bring prolonged periods of heavy rain, and flooding is quite common, **especially in East Cranmore**.*

Alright, alright, the words in heavy black bold print are my own insertions but Wikipedia is always asking us to put in citations; I'm just adding some local knowledge.

On 25th March 1967, "*the staff are hard at it, writing reports, and getting gradually more bad-tempered. Masters need to be handled fairly carefully at this stage of term. Someone seems to have swiped the music reports – anyway, they have completely vanished*". Report-writing is a traditional part of the schoolmaster's lot and it has become common-place to track back to the school-day reports of famous people, either to show how remarkably prescient their teachers were all those years ago or to prove that one's teachers haven't got a clue when predicting their charges' later development. A Munich schoolmaster, for example, wrote of Albert Einstein "*that he will never amount to anything*". Gary Lineker was advised to "*devote less of his time to sport if he wants to be a success...You can't make a living out of football*". Charlotte Bronte apparently "*writes indifferently and knows nothing of grammar*". And many a character will have received the 'catch-all' prediction, like Richard Branson, that "*he will either become a millionaire or go to prison.*" Sometimes, as was the case with Jeffrey Archer, one can achieve both those targets even if only one would have been held up as an ambition. Still on the political front, one former Cabinet Minister, Peter Walker, received a report from his Headmaster saying *"One cannot help but be quite captivated by him provided one gives him no work to do"*. Who would have thought that he would go on to become Secretary of State for *Energy*?! Sadly, a kind of corporate-speak has crept into the writing of reports today so that many words are used telling the parents not very much and not helping the pupils in any way, such as, "Jack can now tie his shoelaces……etc…etc" although in days gone by I can remember All Hallows' reports that read as follows: English: "Working well"; Maths: "Good with numbers" so perhaps not much has changed in terms of not being very helpful. Nevertheless, one imagines, or knows from experience, that school reports from the past, although perhaps less 'wordy', in a lazy kind of way, had a knack of capturing the essence of a pupil with the well-chosen phrase or the sharp insight carrying the kind of robust message that left all parties with the clearest understanding. Peter Scotland, for example, a charismatic, distinctive teacher of French in Paul Ketterer's time, would often comment about a pupil *"the trouble is, I do all the work and he doesn't bring home the bacon"*. I tried that phrase out on my Year Eight pupils of 2013 and they knew exactly what was meant; nowadays we would be encouraged to write: *"he has a lot of latent ability and he is a lovely boy who just needs to draw out of himself – when he feels ready - a greater sense of urgency and determination in responding to advice"*. I suspect parents would actually prefer the more robust style; we should be more idiosyncratic, stylish and, dare I say it, more honest, and not be treading carefully in case we upset anybody.

School Reports, however, provide a rich source of memories for all of us who are not-so-famous and we can savour even now, perhaps, the moment when the post arrived and the Report was threaded almost malignantly, by the knowing postman, through the letter-box, to drop onto the floor, in the most unlike-manna fashion, from a source far removed from heaven, even if the principal architect of that report had, indeed, been 'a god'[61] (at least in our eyes) for most of our schooldays. Nowadays, I'm not so sure. I genuinely wonder whether parents even read the reports and wonder whether the pupils care or set eyes upon their teachers' comments. That may well reflect as much upon the style of the reports today, as on the parents and children. Whatever the truth of it all, it is certainly true, in my view, that the time and thought and effort that goes into the writing and production of the reports is not commensurate with the advantages gained; all processes and principles need re-thinking. It is a consensual survey waiting to be conducted. The time, thought and administrative logistics in setting down and then sending out our current reports is not time well spent and is counter-productive to the purpose (although it does produce a record which Inspectors like to see). If I became Headmaster all over again I think this is one area I would

---

[61] Relatively early in my Headship years I was somewhat taken aback (and a little stimulated with delusions of grandeur, it has to be said) when the youngest pupils in the school would arrive at Chapel Assembly only to bow down before me saying, one by one, "Good Morning God". My wife quickly dispelled any rising sense of power I might have contemplated by saying firmly, "Chris, step away from the Crucifix". Another good reason for having wives, of course; they prick our pomposity.

change radically and I would bring all parties with me to the clamour of resounding 'Hoorays!' It would become a marketing tool…"send your child to All Hallows, you'll get such honest, amusing and informative reports". Ah! The timidity of youth and the conviction of old age!

What are we to make, for example, of a modern school report, which arrived on the Registrar's desk, telling us that '*Thomas enjoys finding out about plants and living things and can name parts of a plant such as leaf, roots, stem and flower; and can use knowledge about living things to describe basic conditions that plants and animals need to survive. He can name a number of light sources including the sun and recognises that you cannot see in the dark unless there is some form of light source. He can suggest several reasons why a material may or may not be suitable for a particular purpose*". I wonder, inevitably, if Thomas can also suggest, more helpfully, just where to put his school report. Any pupil who can recognise that you cannot see in the dark is clearly a potential scholar.

The problem with the modern tendency to state that a pupil 'can' do something is that one never knows whether or not he/she actually 'does'. For example, I **can** suggest all kinds of reasons why I shouldn't take in that extra glass of wine but as to my success in that endeavour the reader will just have to guess.

No wonder parents and children don't read them.

My generalised summaries of 'old-school' reports, in comparison with today's reports, include the following observations: (1) they were shorter (2) they were not politically correct (3) they were more literate (4) they were more honest (5) they had more style (6) idiosyncrasies were allowed to pass even if the split infinitive would have created howls of protests from the purists. I am grateful to a former All Hallows pupil, whom we shall simply name Patrick (although one suspects he was known for most of his school career by his surname, as in '*that wretched ………!!*' - which is the reason I am not indicating his surname in order to spare his reputation). Having met Patrick, however, when he became yet another old boy of the school who was returning to exorcise some ghosts, I doubt that he would worry at all about his name being mentioned in full. The handing-over of his own school report of 1974 to me, in my capacity as the Headmaster of the day, had all the trappings of a final ceremonial laying-to-rest episode in his life and as I watched him walk away up the front drive he seemed a little lighter on his feet as though a shadow had lifted. One just knew he would never return again; sometimes All Hallows sends pupils out into the world with joy in their hearts long after they have left. Patrick's report is worth quoting at length for so many reasons. His Form Master, A. J. Cornwell, also taught him English, Latin and Cricket and had found the time (one guesses with consummate ease) to write the following: "*There is unanimity in the encomiastic opinions which his academic achievement so meritoriously evokes. A boy so richly endowed does indeed banish pedagogical drudgery, but also establishes a corresponding challenge. His intellectual diet is to be the raw flesh fed to the young eagle, no synthetic, concocted pabulum. His mind is a delicate instrument, finely attuned; like the surgeon's scalpel, it probes gently, incisively. In all his activities, save one, there is economy of effort and quiet persistence. If allowed, however, he identifies himself with the interminable interrogative. Of his innumerable questions, actual and potential, some are prompted by genuine intellectual curiosity, others stem from nervous anxiety or diffidence, still others aim avowedly at establishing him as a cynosure. He presents a somewhat withdrawn and dependent figure; but there is an impish glint in his eyes. Friendly and good-humoured, he makes his own contribution to the fellowship of the Fourth."* I pause whilst you let the rounded phrases roll over your tongue or whilst you reach, perhaps, for the dictionary. Mr Cornwell has more to say. *"Imaginative ideas and original notions flow from his mind. Linguistic analysis highlights the accuracy of his perception; orthography and the discriminating use of vocabulary show a pleasing development; his powers of comprehension are as profound as any; his script, however, is a perennial problem....presentational courtesy is sadly often unworthy of the excellence of the content"* and yet, on the cricket field, *"he moves with controlled economy, deliberate, slow and quiet in action. Without dramatic pacing, he delivers his overs with disconcerting accuracy and unexpected power. He is reliable as a fieldsman and before the wicket, handles his bat with style, poise and confidence."* I promise the reader to use the phrase *"presentational courtesy is sadly often unworthy of the excellence of the content"* in a report I am about to write for a splendid female pupil in my current Year Seven top set. Molly – you know who you are!

Patrick's French master, the infamous and lovable Peter Scotland, was no less effusive in his praise for his abilities but seemed to be driven to the point of despair when he wrote, *"It may seem churlish, therefore, for me to complain but I feel it is necessary to repeat that much of his behaviour has been outrageous, and of a disruptive nature, which is very difficult to counteract."* Science gets in on the act too: *"If frivolity were to play a lesser role in his behaviour, he would do much better academically."* Even his Physical Education Master found the words to complain: *"His vocal contributions have been constant; they concern matters relevant and irrelevant to the lessons and are mostly of nuisance value. His persistence has led to his dismissal from the gymnasium on too many occasions...he has no real flair for gymnastics".*

No wonder the Carpentry Master, who had possibly read all other comments, simply wrote *"Fair"* as a summary of Patrick's work with wood and no wonder Headmaster Paul Ketterer, no doubt chuckling in his study, simply wrote *"I endorse all that his Form Master has written"*. Nevertheless, Patrick's form positions, or Form Orders, in an able top set were as follows: 2nd, 1st, 1st, 5th, 6th, 11th, and 1st, which might just have kept his parents happy. One suspects that Patrick's parents learnt a great deal from his Report that year.

But School Reports, generally, are too wordy and they are forced as an administrative burden upon those who do not need words to explain or exemplify their greatness as teachers. In many cases, sadly, the words simply diminish. Parents should talk and listen and watch and see but the tale is not in the reading. Sadly, grammar and syntax and style get in the way, even if that is a reflection on the literacy skills of some modern teachers. But, perhaps, teachers should not be made to write about their craft. The one-word/one-phrase summaries were always best unless the teacher could turn a felicitous phrase or two. I like the Ballet

*Every child should be given the opportunity
to receive an elementary grounding in science
whether or not he intends to follow it as a career*

teacher's reports at All Hallows of yesteryear that invariably used to comment *"Sophie has good legs"*. The Carpentry Master's summary as *"Fair'* was surely sufficient – if more detail is needed, look at the wooden offerings lovingly adorning your shelves at home, for heaven's sake. Staff/Parent Meetings are much more valuable for immediacy, contact, repercussions, (from all perspectives), especially if a glass of wine or two is in the offing, and, even more especially, if the pupil about whom we talk is sitting in amongst us, uncomfortable, at first, but gradually dragged into the debate.

As an aside, it has also been an interesting exercise for Headmasters Mortimer, Ketterer, Bird and Murphy, to have to write reports on their own offspring with the intended readership simply being themselves and their wives. I don't know how Mr Mortimer and Mr Ketterer approached the task. Ian Murphy tells me he finds the task 'interesting' and that it presents him with an opportunity to express observations about his children in a professional way alongside anything he might say as a parent. For my own part, I deliberately assumed the most clinical professional position and tried to write them as if they were being sent to my children's grandparents although I rather liked the sideways swipes I took in print to suggest that 'the boy' could try a little harder in his academic lessons and that 'the girls' could talk a little less (I may even have suggested that they worked on the tidiness of their bedrooms, washed the car, and listened to the wisdom of their parents a little more but, on those points, I may be fantasising since such exhortations clearly had no effect). For the record, even though I have tried to keep out of this story the Headmasters' children, I will allow myself some authorial indulgence, on this occasion, by recording the fact that my parental experience of school reports and inter-school-home communication about my own three children remains complex, illuminating, amusing, irrelevant and, possibly, just as instructive about the teachers as about the children. My wife and I attended one Staff/Parents Evening at Prior Park College to be told by a nervous, distracted, growing-incandescent-with-rage teacher of French, that *"the problem is with his ear"*. Not a problem in hearing the intonations of the language, I should point out; nothing as conventional as that. Apparently, our son's classroom habit of folding his ear knowingly upon itself, in order to allow it to unfurl dramatically minutes later, with the entire class taking bets on the likely time to elapse before the said unfurling - when they should have been concentrating on the intricacies of French grammar – remains, as I say, one of those complex memories that take in so many factors. Similarly, it has to be said, was the experience of dealing with a middle daughter who decided, one day, to bunk off her Somerset boarding school in order to relieve the tension of forthcoming exams, I believe, by awarding herself a day's shopping in Bath with a friend. Her hand-written note to the Housemistress, meant kindly and responsibly, urging her to *'keep things in perspective'* and asking her to remember that *'millions around the world were dying every day'*, actually hardly helped her case. My wife drove to Bath, on receiving the call from her reasonably-outraged Housemistress - knowing just where she would find the miscreants – whom she duly apprehended and returned to school. I applied, as the 'bad-cop', a draconian measure of supervision through the course of her subsequent suspension (whilst the other free spirit received chocolate and sympathy in Sick Bay, it should be noted). And as for the first-born, who had a habit of hiding rather well her more glaringly daring escapades, our parental memory of her school career was trying to establish why her History teacher, having given her the mark of nineteen-and-three-quarters out of a possible twenty for one particular assignment, then complicated the matter with our 'Little-Miss-Perfect', with the comment *"Rather Tentative"*, which required a little explanation, both at home and at school, (to this day, I might add), since one doesn't mess around lightly with perfectionists, you know. We are proud of them all, of course.

I wrote a report on one female pupil – let's call her Poppy since that is her name – (who happens to be a daughter of another female pupil taught by me in the school when I first started my All Hallows' career – Poppy's mother started life at All Hallows aged 4.1 – in the last century... sorry, my dear) along the following lines.......

"Poppy! What will we do without her? Poppy has always been her own person and she has left her distinctive mark on people and places in the All Hallows community wherever she has gone. She may be commended, particularly, for developing a more relaxed self-image so that she has not ended up chasing shadows or unrealistic expectations but established a good-humoured, everyday profile which has allowed her to enjoy the moment. That is not to say, of course, that she has not reached the highest heights. Her achievements across the academic spectrum, as well as in so many other areas of school life, have been well-documented along the way. I have felt privileged to be part of her ongoing development as a student and as a fully-rounded person. The Headmaster and I are used to welcoming back former star pupils as potential 'Gap Student-Teachers' of the future; in Poppy's case, we shall for ever be casting nervous glances over our shoulders lest she returns sooner than we anticipated to herald our departure as leaders of the school. We shall all miss her hugely."

And what about Nico?

"Nico has enjoyed another positive and productive term. He continues to grow in confidence and poise although sometimes seems to give the impression of being startled by his own temerity and success! Most importantly, notwithstanding his pleasing emergence as a young man of real substance, he retains his natural modesty and empathy. There is no doubt that his impressive rugby prowess this term – stalwart of the 1st XV, representative regional player based on his silky skills and his gritty defence (note the shining admiration of Mr Wells!) – has contributed hugely to his self-esteem and to the respect in which he is held by his peers, but there is a deeper sense of maturity and strength of character which has provided the bedrock for this meditative virtue. His appointment as Head of House has been twice-blessed in the kudos and recognition offered to him which he has reciprocated by "stepping up" to the responsibilities thrust upon him. It is a true delight for me to engage with him on a daily basis as his Form Tutor, yet also observe his quiet leadership qualities in my capacity as a staff member of Downhead. It is no accident that the Downhead House (after a period

in the doldrums) has now begun to fill its trophy shelf, win Music competitions (although Nico might, with some reasonable justification, cling on to his modesty regarding his musical talents!) and even feature strongly in the House Merit Championship. Jan and I remember clearly – with pride and some surprise – his exhortation to fifty fellow pupil members about the need to show some pride, enthusiasm and determination "for the good of the House"! Dr Arnold would have approved. On the academic front, Nico is "beavering away" quietly and if he might feel that the trees are not yet falling, there is a sufficiently growing pile of sawdust for him to feel that his gnawing efforts have not been in vain (ask Nico if he recognises the metaphor!). Effort grades are as high as 'eight' in the notoriously harsh spectrum of All Hallows' staff marking and his attainment standing suggests that a safe pass at Common Entrance can be achieved. Nico might want to consider his profile in science particularly carefully since it remains a core subject and his customary quietness might appear to be holding him back a little in the laboratory, if not in other subject classrooms. Nico has played his part in the cross-country challenges and is a keen member of the Tennis Academy which provides life-long sporting opportunities. Next term's impending mid-year examinations provide stern, but timely, tests regarding revision, organisation, technical understanding, awareness of mark schemes, proof-reading skills, etc, but all such matters will be directed and guided by staff in the early-term lead-in. I have no doubt that Nico will approach all challenges with the proper sense of preparation. Nico lives in the top drawer!"

And a final report on Henry's English…

"Henry maintains a position within a very able top set without firing consistently on all cylinders. He exhibits a commendable attitude in class in that he always appears interested in proceedings and his enthusiasm acts as a catalyst to others in general discussions. His written skills are approached with less liking for the task in hand and his occasionally careless presentation can clearly demonstrate his reluctance to produce thoughtfully structured assignments. Nevertheless, his humour shines through and can work significantly in his favour in some of his original writing: e.g. (taken from his essay exam) 'Hi – I am a duck called Trevor…and I woke to find a double-barrelled shotgun up my beak..' I am sure he will find a way to create the appropriate balance between serious study and light-hearted good-humour. An agreeable member of the class!"

Three pupils only, whose reports say a 'certain something', I hope, about us, and more importantly, about them.

But it's not all about the children! Headmasters were pupils once, you know. Bizarrely, I have in my possession some school reports on Francis Dix, as a boy, from 1907, 1908, 1910 and 1911. They were posted to the school when Paul Ketterer was organising a Memorial Service for Francis and Evelyn Dix in November 1984. The sender of those reports wrote: *"I came across these during a clear out and feel I must return them. I must confess to stealing them thirty years ago. At the time I was well below scholarship level and took great delight in discovering that Mr Dix was somewhat similar at the same age!"* Now, I cannot find any record of this self-confessing thief as a pupil at All Hallows. He could have been a member of staff, I suppose. He might have been an envious fellow pupil of Francis Dix at the beginning of the twentieth century in that school in Birmingham. He could, of course, just have been a thief who had escaped from Shepton Mallet Prison and had hatched a cunning plot to break into the safe of the local private school Headmaster in order to steal any old school reports left lying around in a vain attempt to bring down the Empire. Who knows the background - more intriguingly, who knows the motives? I do know the identity of the thief, but lest the Dix-Police are still out there searching with a little furry object in their hands, I shall not divulge the name. Let's call him Michael Scelec. Anyway, of the eight-year-old Francis Dix it is reported that his general progress was '*good*' and that his conduct was '*good*'. He '*distinguished*' himself in French (in Division II) and 'Verses', but was '*very careless*' in Writing. He also lost nine marks for '*neglect of Rules*' (possibly hundreds of boys out there are hoping - ah, hoping with such bitter-sweet passion - that he was caned and caned and caned for '*neglect of Rules*'). He was also told to '*persevere*'. In a later class of twenty-three pupils, at King Edward's High School, Birmingham, he went on to secure weekly academic positions of 3rd, 4th, 7th, 1st, 4th, 13th, 3rd, 2nd and 10th, which seems promising enough, although the written comments simply indicated '*Good*', '*Very Fair*', '*Very Fair*', '*Fair*' and '*Very Fair*'. Our modern pupils would, at this point, exclaim those three most oft-quoted words by schoolchildren over the ages, "That's Not Fair!"

The writer of this book would go down academically, from his childhood days, as one of those 'top-set-also-rans' - what I am beginning to call these days as a 'nearly-man'. But, I'm still working on it. My teachers found me 'quiet' and I was very shy and under-confident. My English and History teachers thought my command of prose 'beautiful' which enlightened their Sunday afternoons when marking schoolboy scripts – no, wait, I think that was my brother. My Physics, Chemistry and Biology teachers gave up on me rather brutally, I thought, as did the Carpentry Master when I was toiling over wooden table mats (which consisted of cutting a plank of wood into six equal segments) whilst others were planning their finely-constructed, life-size canoes. My mother – to her credit – was suitably impressed when I delivered to her the six bits of uneven wood, dripping with varnish, significantly smaller than any conventionally-sized plate; my carpentry skills, sadly, leant towards the A & E rather than the V & A. And do you know where those six bits of wood are now today? In the bin, of course, as they were five minutes after I presented them. In the wider curriculum, my rugby masters saw fit to select me for the 1st XVs. And I broke the School and County Record for the 400 metres. That's about it, folks, apart from my greatest achievement of all, of which I am still proud, which was winning the coveted 'Leaping Wolf Award' as a Boy Scout, at the age of ten when others around me could not even 'dib-dib-dob'. I don't want to diminish this moment of schoolboy glory. The 'Leaping Wolf Award' was beyond proficiency badges, beyond being a mere 'Seconder', even beyond being a 'Sixer'. And it brought into being the occasion of the best prize I had ever achieved which set me on the road to reading and words and writing: '*The Jungle Book*' by Rudyard Kipling. One had to know how to leap. And I have been aspiring ever since. My only other claim to academic fame was the fact of being sought after by Professor Hearder of the University of Wales, Cardiff, to pursue a degree in History rather than English, but our paths to the public houses of South Wales we frequented never seemed destined to cross.

Reports on Ian Murphy are harder to track down but one was aware of his teachers' comments about his "*appalling handwriting*" and that his ability in art was on a par with Francis Dix's musical talent, Paul Ketterer's practical skills and Chris Bird's carpentry prowess, that is to say, non-existent. Like Chris Bird, Ian was a County 400m champion in his own time and place – perhaps the two of us should race each other round the front field although only one of the four knees called into action would withstand such a challenge. Ian was Head Boy at Wimbledon College and was praised for his industry and endeavour, as well as his excellence in Ancient History and Chemistry, even if sections of his written assignments often came back to him with the coded teacher red scribble: "C.S.O.T.B.O." which, apparently, meant "Crashing Statement of the Blinkin' Obvious".

School Reports, or those delivered by educational experts, do not need to be characterised by educational jargon running on for twenty pages or more, in some cases, delivering highly positive, politically correct, psycho-babble about learning styles. One of the most arresting comments I overheard in recent years was from a seven-year-old pupil who said she was "not that kind of learner"; she maintained she was 'kinaesthetic' although I doubt she really understood the term, even if she could repeat it, having heard it said about her.

I have mentioned elsewhere the value of having pupils sit in on meetings between teachers and parents when we are engaged, after all, in discussing all things pertaining to them. Once the child gets over the initial jolt of seeing the two parties who most frighten him/her, together in one room, real insights and subsequent progress can be made because those very people are also the ones who love him/her the most. Equally revealing are the occasions when the pupils are asked to report upon themselves. It would be easy to present a contrary view but my experience over more than thirty years of working in schools is that most young people, most of the time, are mostly truthful (that statement carries just enough conditionals, I think, to cover all possibilities). It is always interesting, therefore, to hear from the pupils themselves regarding their own profiles and behaviour. I think it is only when we become adults that we start to delude ourselves more readily. This honesty was brought home to me as I examined the written evidence from a likely group of lads who had been asked to explain, in writing, their unacceptable behaviour the previous night in the dormitories. By and large, dormitory misbehaviour tends to consist of talking after 'Lights Out', eating smuggled sweets (usually smuggled in by grandparents) or jumping around from bunk to bunk. Occasionally, there are 'Dorm Raids'. This particular dorm raid started conventionally and then 'kicked off' with unusual passion. Let's hear from the boys themselves: "*I walked up the stairs and an apple flew out and almost hit a parent. Dom's grinning face appeared. A flood of people from Joan's pushed along …and suddenly the dorm was full of abuse….I'm sure Dom rammed a chair into Mike's stomach and Olly insulted us from inside the loo. I can remember throwing ladders but I don't think I hurt anyone….from there it is all a bit fuzzy…. I think this is how it happened – I needed the loo so went to the door of St Anne's. They wouldn't let us in. So we pushed against the door. Olly got in and restrained Michael. We were greeted by a volley of ladders, shoes and chairs. William then started to shoot us with his sling shot. I came out of the loo as George bit Olly on the head. Olly then tackled George and they hit the steps. More ladders were thrown at us so we fought back with pillows, ladders, chairs, etc. Basha was then hit by two ladders and a chair simultaneously so I threw the chair back and it hit Michael – Joan's then attacked Anne's and vice versa. Mike's shins got hurt somehow. They threw ladders again but we hid behind the door. George was really stressed by this time and made the hole in the bathroom door. William then shot us again with his sling shot, this time using metal balls. Although I don't know how it started, I feel it was our fault. I'm not sure but I think we were having a bit of fun. Big-time involvement: Dominic, Oliver, George, Carlos; Medium: Michael, William, Max, Basha; Low: Juan, Alex; Nothing: Peter – sat on his bed and read."*

In the account above, I've interspersed the testimony from three different boys but I also like the statement from Peter who simply wrote: "*I don't know because I was reading a book*". This is typical boy behaviour; slings and arrows can be raining down but, sometimes, the task in hand is just too absorbing. Boys have this ability to shut out the peripheral world. They do it all the time in class when the teacher wants them to think about metaphors when they are thinking about something else (possibly planning for their next dormitory raid). I recall a similar moment in Normandy on the French Trip when a boy was wailing out his homesickness in bed one night whilst the other boys in his chalet all concentrated silently on their Gameboys, without the slightest concern for their stricken fellow. I went in to soothe the troubled boy and took the others to task for not showing any empathy or support for him. Without looking up from his Gameboy, without stopping the incessant thumb movements on the console, one of the boys, more in tune with his finer feelings, dragged up, from the well of sympathy lying deep within him, the comment, "Get a grip, Dan". Dan, of course, got a grip and enjoyed every minute of the trip thereafter. Girls in that situation would have been fluttering like mummy moths around the crying girl, smoothing her hair, stroking her arms and probably working themselves up in a frenzy of group-hugging, solidarity-sistered tears of their own.

Back to the 1960s - when girls did not exist - (at least at All Hallows). I've mentioned elsewhere that the absence of political correctness recorded in the All Hallows chronicles can be somewhat refreshing although the Easter Monday note that follows seems a little harsh. It said "*we had a 'shoe-shine' after lunch, organised by the VIth form. Apart from an efficient shoe-shine service, there were raffles, roulette, **guessing-the-weight of two heavy boys** (in milligrams to make it more difficult, smell-guessing, darts with a pendulum target,* *a fortune teller and a number of highly ingenious attractions, too numerous to mention".* One cannot help feel, perhaps, that this is taking the virtue of bluntness a little too far. Over £13 was raised and the proceeds went to Oxfam. Happily, the 'heavy boys' are not named although one wonders if the judging was carried out in one of the public assemblies at the same time as 'Form Orders'. Incidentally, that particular term's 'Form Orders' was followed by Mr Mortimer reading the bible passage about separating the sheep from the goats and then the hymn *'Lord Dismiss Us With Thy Blessing'*. As one parent said to me at a recent meeting "Life is hard out there". And perhaps harder for our children than we might think.

But the pupils did receive commendations too. The House Merit system, previously alluded to, had been going for many years (albeit with a parallel 'bad-mark' system alongside called 'Stripes') and the 1967 Summer Term ended with the Panthers on top (2549 stars), Lions 2nd (2452), Tigers 3rd (2179) and Wolves 4th (2106), thus totalling 9286 'good things' observed by the masters and all this with only about half the current numbers in the school. If one applied the inflation calculator to that grand total the pupils of today would have to score 126000 merits in a single term; good job there isn't a monetary correlation. Not even the generously-indulged pupil of 2013 could conceivably match the individual totals of David Coffey (222), Simon Pringle (202), Julian Glover (160) and twenty-nine other boys who all scored over 100. Somebody at the higher end of the age range was also continuing to achieve a fame of his own as well, for, at the 1967 Prize Day, Mr Dix presented an ambitious programme of five plays and, in January 1969, to commemorate his 70th birthday, *"he entertained the school to a remarkable display of conjuring, magic and ventriloquism. In the latter, the impudent remarks of the Dummy made an instant appeal. Rabbits appeared and disappeared with lightning skill – cotton wool turned into coffee which could be actually drunk – a jug of milk was poured into a paper bag – card tricks perplexed us and made us wrinkle our brows – in short, it was a first-class conjuring show with quite a professional touch."*

Mr Mortimer's innovations continued. In his 1969 Editorial he hoped that he "did not appear to be a progressive permissive" (from which description the boys might possibly have felt he was quite safe), but he was advocating that *"Education is a twin responsibility between the parent and the school"* which implied *"a much closer co-operation between the school and parents than perhaps has been considered possible or advisable in the past"*. There is a niceness about the idea that until 1969 it had not been considered 'advisable' to establish links with parents that became too close; 'please just drop the boys off at the beginning of term, keep the engine running if you like (but pop in to see the Bursar on your way out) and we'll send them home to you thirteen weeks later'. He was also proposing the instigation of **Weekly** Boarders, a radical departure, indeed! And, just for good measure, perhaps whilst he was thinking he could risk one more suggestion, he mentioned, sotto voce, that *"it has been felt that tentative moves should be made towards the introduction of girls at All Hallows....I do not feel it advisable to enter into this controversy at present, other than to say that serious consideration should be given to the mixing of the sexes as early as the Preparatory School* *stage. I feel that, given sufficient pressure at the Preparatory School level, the Public Schools will then be forced to re-think their present position – although some Public Schools already are admitting girls at VIth form level."* He just stopped short, it seems, of predicting that the United Kingdom would have a female Prime Minister within ten years and that not long after that girls would start outperforming boys in public examinations across the country. Far from 'shooting himself in the foot', his observations appeared remarkably forward-thinking and bore fruit in the years to come (although, in terms of regrettable shooting of anatomical parts, one reads on 25th January 1969, that at the beginning of the Pack Cross-Country Run, *"Mr Mortimer fired the starting pistol and shot himself as he had a finger over the mouth of the barrel. No great damage was done but, even so, it's the sort of thing one doesn't do more than once in one's life"* – which only goes to prove that even, or especially, Headmasters can mess up sometimes).

All this was happening at a time when the school had just decided to introduce the practice of 'subject-orientated' form rooms so that under this regime it would be the pupils who would move about the campus and the masters who could be found fixed in their splendid educational milieux. One teacher put it like this: *"Perhaps, as the Geography Master, I appreciate more than other Masters the introduction of Subject Form Rooms. With a subject made up of so many sciences, one requires a large amount of equipment. It is not easy to walk across the yard with two large maps, a globe, a model of a volcano, a suitcase full of books and perhaps some corn or a banana for demonstration purposes, on a windy day in heavy rain. With everything at one's fingertips, life is a great deal easier and one can teach with greater efficiency. The boys, too, enter the atmosphere of the subject as they enter each room. This makes it very much easier to catch their attention at the very beginning of a period. Any loss of time in passing from one form room to another is compensated by having a more settled class of boys. The small amount of exercise between classes reduces fidgeting. A boy cannot sit still on a chair for long."* One can genuinely sympathise with the over-burdened Geography Master as he hitherto struggled manfully through the rain and the wind and only admire the argument that neatly suggests the boys gained from the new arrangement as a result of the additional physical exercise they were enjoying, presumably in the same rain and wind, with their own heavy bag-burdens full of books, files, secret sweets, weapons with which to attack each other and live furry things they had found at morning break in the Spinney.

Later that term the boys had further compensations as in *"The Choir went out carol-singing in the evening (December 17th) singing to an invited audience at Mr Dix's house in Wells and then at several other private houses (including Mr Bevan's where we were entertained to vast quantities of food and drink), at a W.I. Meeting, and finally at 'The Waggon and Horses' and 'The Strode Arms'."* One wonders if the quality of the singing, or perhaps just the impression of that quality by the singers, improved as the evening wore on. As an aside, it is also interesting to note that Mr and Mrs Dix had, by this time, moved to the historic city of Wells, having sold Charlton House[62] to the Seaton family.

In the tradition of notable ground-staff and general estate workers who contributed significantly to the well-being, good appearance and good heart of the school, John and Jim Metcalfe received this Chronicle accolade from Mr Dix in 1969...

JOHN AND JIM METCALFE

John and Jim came to All Hallows a year after the school moved to Cranmore Hall (1946) and worked in the gardens with loyalty and efficiency for twenty-two years. When they first joined us, the gardens had by no means recovered from the inevitable neglect which the war caused. Much hard work, therefore, was necessary to remedy this. The South lawns, for instance, had been used for potato-growing and the ground below was a very rough field. When the Metcalfes came there was a dark wilderness south of the Headmaster's garden. This they cleared and planted with trees and shrubs. About seven years ago the winter garden was converted into form rooms and the Principal's Study, but before that time it was gay with begonias and tropical plants which required much attention and watering. Both John and Jim (the flower-pot men) entered with enthusiasm into the big occasions of the school. All Old Boys will remember in particular the magnificent bonfires built by them for All Hallows Day. However bad the weather, these never failed to burn superbly.

We were very sorry to say goodbye to these two old friends at the end of the Christmas term and we wish them both a happy retirement.

F.H.R.D.

(On July 7th, just before the Prize-Giving ceremony, the parents, guests, staff and pupils all moved to seats under the cedar trees for an outdoor performance of Laurence Housman's 'Brother Wolf' which centred on the story of Saint Francis. *"As the plays ended the bells of Assisi were heard behind the audience. These were rung by John Metcalfe, the Head Gardener, an expert bell-ringer, and made a most effective climax"*).

On 31st March 1969, *"Mr and Mrs Mortimer and seven lucky boys set off for an educational Cruise around the Greek Islands"* which reminds one of a similar excursion undertaken by Mr

---

[62] Charlton House – or The Charlton House Hotel, as it is known today – was bought by Mr Dix in 1959 who said on viewing the property that he was *"immediately enraptured by its romantic air of tranquillity. I walked into the grounds at 10 o'clock and captured by its mood, had purchased it before leaving at mid-day"*. In January 1960, he moved in and set about creating a private chapel in one of the upstairs rooms – thought to be what is now Room 11 in the hotel originally created by the Seaton family who purchased it from Mr Dix in 1965. They established a reputation for Charlton House as a fine country hotel and restaurant as well as hosting eminent visitors like The Duke of Edinburgh, Sir Cliff Richard and the King of Thailand. The property was acquired by Roger and Monty Saul, of Mulberry Design fame, in 1996, and significant luxury developments followed, including spa facilities, until Duncan Bannatyne (businessman and entrepreneur from TV's Dragon's Den) took it on in the summer of 2010 and maintains its style today.

Dix in 1958 with his adopted son, Mario, and Patrick Nixon, and which also pre-dates later trips abroad such as the Normandy visits, outings to Rome and various skiing ventures, all of which are mentioned later. On Mr and Mrs Mortimer's Mediterranean Cruise, the boys involved were Kevin Chapman, Anton Corsi, Christopher McLauchlan-Slater, Joe Raad, Michael von Arx, Dominic Wilson and Richard Knowles. The party had an overnight stay in a Crawley hotel in preparation for a flight from Gatwick the next day and *"despite the now accepted pattern of a party of boys locking themselves out of their rooms"*[63] they duly arrived in time for their flight to Venice where they joined their cruise ship 'Nevasa' having encountered some *"doubt and despair owing to a strike of Gondoliers and Water-buses"* – it's the same the whole world over. This All Hallows' contingent then enjoyed trips to Dubrovnik, Crete, Rhodes, Naples, Rome, Pompeii, Lisbon and the long cruise back to Southampton. From the writing, it appears that this had become an annual trip. Presumably they enjoyed better weather there than at the July 1970 Prize Giving Ceremony when those assembled had to dash from the front field to the relative shelter of the Colonnade where proceedings continued. Abbot Passmore presented the prizes and Mr and Mrs Dix were guests of honour.

[63] Irritating though that might have been for Mr Mortimer to manage, it was nothing compared to the experience of Willie John McBride, Captain of the 1974 British Lions Tour to South Africa, who was rudely woken at 3.00am by a team-mate anxious that he should lead them out of a spot of bother. Willie John was escorted by his troubled friend to one of the hotel's rooms, dressed only in underpants and sporting a smoking pipe, to find all the furniture smashed and twelve fellow Lions blind drunk on the floor. When the Hotel Manager arrived, soaking wet from a full-on hose pipe being turned in his direction from the tour hooker, Willie John took a puff of his pipe and said: *"Now then, what seems to be the trouble?"* On being told that the police were about to arrive, Willie John is supposed to have said: *"How many?"*

The boys of All Hallows experienced further culture in a mad flurry of opera in May and June 1970 as can be seen from these Chronicle extracts:

May

Monday 4th   *Sadler Wells are giving a season of Opera in Bristol. Mrs Mortimer and 12 boys went to 'The Marriage of Figaro'.*

Tuesday 5th   *Mr and Mrs Mortimer, Miss Brennan-Smith and 17 boys went to 'Aida'.*

Wednesday 6th *Mr and Mrs Mortimer and Miss Brennan-Smith (and no boys for a change) went to 'Nabucco'.*

Thursday 7th   *'Carmen' tonight: Mr and Mrs Mortimer and 15 boys.*

Saturday 9th   *'La Boheme' – Mr and Mrs Mortimer, Miss Brennan-Smith and 5 boys.*
All very nice but what an exhausting week!

June

Tuesday 16th   *This seems to be a good term for Opera. We now have a season of Gilbert and Sullivan Operas given by the D'Oyly Carte Company. Mr and Mrs Mortimer, Miss Brennan-Smith and 8 boys went to 'The Yeoman of the Guard'.*

Wednesday 17th *'The Mikado' tonight – Mr and Mrs Mortimer, Miss Brennan-Smith and 10 boys.*

Thursday 18th   *'Trial by Jury' and 'H.M.S. Pinafore' – Mr and Mrs Mortimer, Miss Brennan-Smith and 15 boys.*

Friday 19th   *Out again tonight: Mr and Mrs Mortimer, Miss Brennan-Smith and 28 boys went to 'Cox and Box' and 'The Pirates of Penzance'.*

A further outing of a different kind occurred on July 2nd when *"Mr and Mrs Mortimer, Andrew Barrell and Christopher Semprini set off very early...to attend the Commissioning Service at*

Chatham of the school's adopted ship 'H.M.S. Bulldog'.[64] This was the 7th Bulldog.

Swimming has been a constant feature of the school since its foundation when, in those early years at Scorhill, the boys would swim in the River Teign within the school grounds and later, in Somerset, would be transported down into Shepton Mallet before the present pool was built in 1958. Hardy souls made do with natural water courses and outdoor, unheated pools but there is only so much poor weather up with which one can put (as Churchill might have said when ironically re-positioning prepositions in another context) and, when the pool actually starts to spring leaks and require more sophisticated filtration systems, the problems appear almost insurmountable. I quote below the October 1970 Chronicle extract in full, partly to demonstrate the kind of problems the school was encountering with the creaking pool, but, also, by way of example of the kind of technical problems that can be encountered by those managing schools. Estate maintenance, building upkeep, planning permissions, English Heritage, new legislative standards in fire precautions, electrical re-wiring, drainage, flooding, highways and byways, the dreaded Health and Safety Executive, etc, etc, have all played their part – and continue to do so – in adding to the administrative burdens of running successful schools anxious to move forward and yet keep compliant with the various authoritative bodies.

SWIMMING 1970 AND PLANS FOR THE FUTURE

There can be no doubt that this has been a disappointing season, but in spite of this we are able to face the future, indeed the immediate future, with a sense of renewed hope and some achievement. The nickname 'Big Muddy' was given affectionately to the Missouri River Complex – but that was before the time of our swimming pool, or I am sure we could have claimed a better title to the name, though it is unlikely that much affection would have been involved. The problem of this pool has provided something of a nightmare for several years now and may be explained fairly simply. The shell of the pool has cracked in many places and is indeed porous in parts, so that constant loss of water was inevitable, and this water can be supplied in sufficient quantity only by means of a pump placed over a deep well, no adequate 'mains' source being available. Unfortunately, a considerable quantity of mud and Fuller's earth is brought in with the water and, with the pool acting against our interests – in the biggest

---

[64] The first *Bulldog* was a small 4-gun vessel bought in March 1794 and sold later in the same year. The second *Bulldog* was a 16-gun sloop launched in 1782 but converted to a Royal Navy bomb vessel in 1798. She was broken up at Portsmouth in December 1829. The third *Bulldog* was a wooden steam powered paddle sloop launched in 1845 but ran aground in 1865 whilst attacking Haiti as part of a punitive raid against revolutionaries who had seized the British consulate. Unable to get her off of the reef, the British blew her up. The fourth *Bulldog* was a third class gunboat of the Ant-class, sold for scrapping in 1906. The fifth *Bulldog* was a *Beagle* class destroyer scrapped in 1920. The sixth Bulldog was a destroyer launched in 1930 and scrapped in 1946. She is most famous for the actions of some of her crew in making the first capture of an Enigma machine. The seventh *Bulldog* was launched in 1967 as the lead ship of the *Bulldog*-class coastal survey ships and sold in 2001 for conversion to a private yacht.

possible way – the water runs out and the mud stays in! An attempt was made to remedy the leakage problem when a plastic envelope was fitted some years ago, but the wear and tear of several seasons proved to be beyond economical repair and early this term it was decided to remove the plastic altogether. We had already put 65 patches on to it, some of them 4 or 5 feet long, but when we began to refill, the material split away from the supporting framework. I pass over the loathsome task of emptying last season's ullage out of the pool through a standard bath-plug. Suffice that I was, literally, speechless at the end of the operation. Under the plastic lurked 15 tons of dirty sand! Sandcastles for all – with Mr Mortimer in constant attendance to cart it away with tractor and trailer. In the hot sunshine of early July there was no lack of volunteers! Meanwhile, we were setting up experiments in filtration based on an initial test in the Science laboratory in which we assessed the quantity of solids coming into the pool per hour, and explored the possibility of using washable filter bags of various grades of fineness. It must be realised that, with about 3 pounds of 'mud' per hour and a filling time of 72 hours, the problem of filtration is difficult, for any conventional filter will choke itself in a very few hours, necessitating dismantling and cleaning (with no 'clean' water available, the reverse-flow technique cannot be applied). We calculated – again by laboratory tests – that we could catch between 80 and 90% of the incoming dirt and, drawing upon previous experience, I hoped that use of a 'Pool-Vac' would enable us to suck back most of the remaining dirt from the pool itself. We have now installed a filter tank and a pressure tank to enable us to use the Pool-Vac from the pump output, and are at least on the way to success. At half term the original shell of the pool was repaired in a temporary manner, and refilling began with partially filtered water. Not without a few mishaps! The filter bags need to be changed hourly at present until a modification has been completed. Forgetting this, or inability to be there in time, has caused the bags to be overstrained and four bags have split. These are only teething troubles. The immediate future: Mr Mortimer has arranged for the pool shell to be treated with the latest technical processes, to caulk the cracks and to coat the whole surface with impervious paints in the summer holidays so that we may have an extension of swimming for perhaps the first four weeks of the Michaelmas Term. In filtered and cleaned water! The years ahead: The existing filter is so designed that when a bath-side pump can be purchased (3000-4000 gallons per hour) the pool water can be circulated and re-filtered during the night, or, indeed, even when the pool is in use. By painting the concrete deck black (and with a skid-proof surface) solar heat can be conducted to the pool water. It is interesting to note here that input temperature, 53 degrees Fahrenheit, has not varied throughout the term, but that the pool temperature has never been less than 60 degrees and more often above 68 degrees. A roofing of corrugated transparent plastic sheets upon a light metal framework, envisaged when funds permit, would help immeasurably to improve the cleanliness of the pool and the comfort of the boys using it. Also, with the addition of a simple system of copper tubing, solar heating would render the water 'swimmable' all the year round. Future prospects? Distinctly bright. And if the keenness of the boys is anything to go by, our rivals in swimming had better look to their laurels!

As it happens, Mr Mortimer anticipated rightly that "a roofing of corrugated transparent plastic sheets upon a light metal framework…would help.." although it wasn't until the late 1990s that the pool was enclosed with a roofing structure similar to the one he envisaged. Again, it was a matter of funding. Preliminary estimates suggested in 1996 that it would cost over one million pounds to build a new pool whereas for approximately £40000 we were able to construct that sliding roof structure, with enhanced filtration and heating systems, to be thus enabled to use the pool for a longer period of time through the year whilst also retaining the open-air effect in the summer months. Nevertheless, it remains the case that the pool was built in 1958 and over fifty years later it has certainly served a purpose in a most cost-effective manner.

The Lent Term 1971 opened with Mark Pettitt as Head Boy and he achieved his own identity and success in a number of ways but he fits into a highlighted box alongside his father (right) since he was the first pupil to join the school as the son of an old boy.

And so the Mortimer years moved towards their conclusion.

I return to my earlier comments about the surprise expressed by Mr Mortimer in his resignation words in the 1971 Chronicle regarding the shortness of his time as Headmaster. Running a school and finding a style that suits everybody – or at least that suits the key people in one's appointment (i.e. pupils, staff, parents and, ultimately, Governors) – is not an easy task, even without taking into account external pressures like recessions, inspections, regulations, etc. And events can move quickly. In 1965, there was the first recorded surplus of the school under the new arrangement of Trustees and a Governing Body; in October 1967, the Board congratulated Mr Mortimer on achieving record numbers (146 boys); imaginative development plans saw through the building of the two-storey Science Block and promulgated the idea of weekly boarders and the possibility of girls joining the school; yet, in July 1969, it was anticipated that the school might merely 'break even' at the conclusion of the trading year; and later that year, concerns were being expressed about the loss of pupil numbers (worries were expressed that the school should at least aspire to 'hover around the 100 mark'). Moreover, despite the confidence being expressed in Mr Mortimer, those anxieties rumbled on as four other local prep schools closed and the continuing drop in numbers caused further concern; the accounts of the time presented a "gloomy picture"; it was said that in "two years the school would reach the point of no return"; that the "sword of Damocles" hung over the future of the school; and, so it was, with ultimately swift decisiveness, that throughout 1971, plans had been put in place to appoint Mr Mortimer's successor. Alistair Mortimer, on the face of it, survived in post for seven years and achieved some palpable measures of success but his departure was sudden and non-negotiable when the time came. Neither at the time, nor in subsequent memory, does one encounter overwhelming evidence that he was a much-loved Headmaster and there are plenty of schoolboys who remember, without much fondness, his propensity for administering beatings with a rather more indiscriminate and brutal manner than even

ADRIAN PETTITT & MARK PETTITT

(F.P. 1939-1945, RIP)   **(F.P. 1965-1971)**

Adrian Pettitt ('Poppit') joined the school in November 1939, from Prague, after his parents had some difficulties following internment by the Germans, and left in April 1945 as a cadet to Dartmouth. He was Pack Leader (or House Captain) of the Tigers and for several seasons represented the school cricket and football XIs. He gained his Football Colours in 1943, ran well in cross-country events and played successfully a number of parts in school plays. He 'showed promise with the bat' in the 1942 Cricket XI and in 1945 won the 'Intelligence Test' at the Literary Society meeting. The route to Dartmouth was quite a common one for boys from All Hallows – John Arbuthnott, John Ford, Peter Brittan, Geoffrey Shaw, Timothy Melhuish and David Gladstone also went to Dartmouth – and in the early days at Cranmore Hall there was a corridor (opposite the telephone booth) lined with photographs of naval cadets from those early days. An early letter from Dartmouth mentions that *"Pettitt is an enthusiastic follower of the Britannia Beagles"*. He passed out from Dartmouth becoming a Cadet Captain and in January 1950 he was appointed as a Midshipman to HMS Implacable in which he went to Copenhagen, Brest, Gibraltar and, Ville Franche amongst other places. Later he moved onto HMS Vanguard when he went to the Tropics for the first time. In January 1951 he joined the Destroyer 'Cadiz' in which he had a very happy time being the only Midshipman on board. On 1st May he was promoted to Sub-Lieutenant and was then at Greenwich. Later, we hear of his promotion to Lieutenancy and that in April 1955 Mr and Mrs Dix were present at his wedding in London (pictured right) which was believed to be the first wedding of an Old Boy.

Lt Commander A Pettitt (as he then was) agreed to act as Hon Secretary for The Old Boys Association in May 1966.

Mark Pettitt, Adrian's son, represented the school at 1st team level in Cricket, Soccer, as Captain, Rugby – with Colours, (in which sport he was noted as a *"first-class flanker"* and was *"outstanding"* in the Rosslyn Park National Sevens Tournament), the tennis team and the shooting team, and he gained eleven sporting medals during his time in the school. He won the triangular Cross-Country Race against The Park School and The Old Ride coming in first *"finishing a long way ahead of his nearest pursuer"*. He was Librarian for a time and became Head Boy in his final term. He was awarded *'no drills'* in 1970 and again in 1971 which essentially meant that he never did anything wrong - or was never caught – either way, quite an achievement. He went on to Downside.

appeared to be the norm in those times[65]. The pressures of running the school, administering justice, maintaining a personal life and dealing with the gathering voices of discontent all told, inevitably, on his equilibrium, it appears, and, as the Governors moved in to call him to account with increasing determination and detail (curtailing his personal expenses account, for example), the time became right for a change of direction.

For the record, however, and in the name of fairness, in the same October 1971 Magazine

---

[65] Corporal punishment features occasionally in the pages of this book in the history of All Hallows. Corporal punishment, that is, the concept of using physical pain to the body (and metaphysical pain to the mind and heart thereafter) in order to censure and correct bad behaviour (deriving from the Latin corpus, meaning 'body' and Old French *punissement* from the Latin *punire* - to punish), is an age-old phenomenon practised well beyond the confines of All Hallows and schools generally. And yet, for most people in the western world, we associate it with educational institutions, particularly in England, and, perhaps, particularly, in independent education. Phrases like 'six of the best' linger long in the memory and a straw poll of men over the age of fifty revealed that 90% of respondents admitted to having been caned, strapped or slippered whilst at school. 75% of that 90% proclaimed almost proudly that 'it never did them any harm' but, interestingly, 80% of that same 90% were against corporal punishment and would not want to see it restored in our schools today. For the record, I made up those statistics but I'd wager they're not far from the truth. Google in 'corporal punishment' and you get thousands of memories from correspondents indicating the trends and suppositions I invent above. But, those who google, notice also the associated tag-lines under the following headings: '*Damaging and Spoiling, Destroying and Demoralising, Deteriorating and Making Worse, Injury and Injuries, Tearing and Breaking into Pieces, Upsetting and Destabilising, Exploding and Erupting*'. There can be few items of occasional public discourse that evoke such contradictory and emotive reactions. So, are we part of a world that would accept, secretly, a Bunter-esque "Yarooh! Gerroff! Whop! Wow! Whoooop! Wop! Yow-ow-ow!" or, as we suspect, do we have no wish to return to a by-gone age that was hardly exaggerated in fiction? It is just a tad surprising that commentators generally reflect rather glibly, in this connection with personal experiences of the past, hinting at an almost fondly-nostalgic whiff of loss. Most people's memories and experiences, surely, must lean towards the 'Outraged from High Wycombe'. The fundamental scenario whereby a grown man (it was almost always men) would administer a physical beating upon a not fully-formed boy (it was almost always boys), half his height and a third of his weight, occasionally running at the exposed hand or buttocks from a distance, in the privacy of an enclosed room, with witnesses (and parents) nowhere in sight, on the pretence of 'this is hurting you more than me', alongside the usual convention that the child, thus accosted, should say "Thank you, Sir" on his smarting, red-whealed departure, is a little hard to imagine in the world of 2013 or in the world of 1998 (when it was abolished in Independent Schools) or in the world of 1986 (when it was abolished in the Maintained Sector). I am fortunate that I have never visited corporal punishment upon a pupil, although I have occasionally felt the need, which is the reason I am fortunate that I have never administered corporal punishment on a pupil. I have once administered measured disciplinary force to a child of my own but nobody gained and I carry that shame to my end. I am making no moral judgements on my predecessors in education because we are all participants in our time but the debate is an interesting reflection on the mores of the ages. Perhaps the two most instructive comments to make in this year of 2013 is that firstly, there is no evidence to prove that corporal punishment in schools brought beneficial results in the short or long term, and, secondly, that the administering of corporal punishment by parents, in England, is still not outlawed today. "*Physical punishment is prohibited in all maintained and full-time independent schools, in children's homes, in local authority foster homes and Early Years provision... (but)... parents have not been explicitly prohibited from smacking their children*" – Department for Education 2011. "*Corporal punishment of children breaches their fundamental rights to respect for their human dignity and physical integrity. Its legality breaches their right to equal protection under the law. Urgent action is needed in every region of the world to respect, fully, the rights of children – the smallest and most fragile of people.*" – Global Initiative to End All Corporal Punishment of Children – December 2011. As George Bernard Shaw put it, as early as 1908, "*there has been a growing perception that child whipping, even for the children themselves, is not always the innocent and high-minded practice it professes to be*" and, later, wrote in 'Everybody's Political What's What'... "*the slipper, the cane, the birch...teaches nothing but the dread of detection.*"

in which Alistair Mortimer expressed his leaving thoughts quite candidly (to which reference has already been made) Lieutenant-Colonel R. C. Yule, OBE, Second Master for much of Mr Mortimer's time, provided a Farewell Message....

"During the seven years that Mr Mortimer has been Headmaster of All Hallows (the) curriculum...has undergone a complete revolution. Mathematics is no longer treated in three separate compartments in Arithmetic, Algebra and Geometry. French is being taught as a language that is actually spoken by many Europeans and the Classics are treated in their rightful place as a factor only of our literary and special heritage. Science has been introduced and boys are trusted to perform experiments in a Laboratory. Pupils are being prepared for the Space Age which will be in full swing when they are grandfathers. Besides instruction on the piano, instruction is also given on other orchestral instruments and great opportunities have been found for the furtherance of musical appreciation by visits to operas and concerts and musical evenings in the Library. I understand that the Downside orchestra owes much to these first steps here. That this change has come about almost unnoticed by Staff and boys is Mr Mortimer's greatest achievement. We are all aware that it has come about under great financial stringency and his monument must be that All Hallows is still in existence whereas establishments run with less vision and less determination to put those plans in effect have ceased to exist. A Headmaster's responsibilities are many and varied ....many of these responsibilities he shares with...Mrs Mortimer. Running a Prep school is a family affair and those of us who have had occasion to visit the school during the holidays for consultation with the management have some idea of the hard work the family have put in during the holidays to prepare the way for us next term. Mrs Mortimer's part is the most exacting and unobtrusive and the most taken for granted. We are all very grateful to her... for her unfailing cheerfulness, directness and equanimity on the occasions when our paths cross. Finally, I would say on behalf of the Staff that Mr Mortimer has been an easy man to work for. We have always been allowed to get on with our job of imparting knowledge without interference and have never had any reasonable request to further our aims refused. We have known where we stood on the rules we have had to enforce and have been backed up in enforcing them. We may not always have agreed with these rules but we can confidently agree that the end product – the 'Leaver' – is a much better citizen than when he came. That, surely, is the hallmark of a HEADMASTER. We all wish 'The Management' and their family a very happy and successful future."

An Appreciation Fund was set up to provide a farewell gift to the Mortimers and at least £300 was raised by grateful parents which represents well over £3500 in today's money. On the occasion of the Staff/Parents Dinner Dance in 1971, he and his wife and family joined the celebrations during the evening and "a spontaneous welcome to the traditional strains of 'For he's a jolly good fellow' showed how much parents appreciated their presence". In his final term,

Mr Mortimer bowled "magnificently" in a Select XI against the School by taking five wickets for twelve runs; acted as Sponsor for over forty boys on the occasion of their Confirmation by His Lordship the Bishop of Clifton, the Rt. Reverend Joseph E. Rudderham, D.D., M.A.; failed to find the camping site of the All Hallows 'Save the Children' charity group who had walked 46 miles in two days towards Salisbury raising £32.20[66]; greeted Vice Admiral M. F. Fell, C.B., D.S.O., D.S.C. (and bar), C-in-C Naval Command, who dropped in by helicopter to pick up his nephew; heard Mr Dix say on Prize Day that his departure "would leave a great gap"' and clung on steadfastly to the belief that all children are neither black nor white but various shades of grey; perhaps that remains true for all of us.

Paul Ketterer attended with his wife, Jean, Mr Mortimer's final Prize Day and was welcomed by the Chairman of Governors, George Simey, (see later notes) a former old boy of All Hallows. He was to hear George Simey affirm the Governors' intentions to introduce girls into the school and that *"the Governors were thinking ahead to a new era – with All Hallows in the forefront of modern educational thinking."* Mr Mortimer's wish to go co-educational seemed destined to bear fruit – perhaps this was one aspect he was referring to when he wrote in his final editorial about *"the lack of response to ideas put up in the past which are now being put forward as new thinking"*. But, just as it seems to be the lot of leaving parents and pupils to be lulled into thinking that all new developments only happen after they have gone, perhaps, too, it is easy for Headmasters to cast slightly sideways glances at the future which they might have anticipated themselves being part of – or even partly the instigators of – as they see that very same future unfolding before their eyes. Being a Headmaster is not straightforward. Some Headmasters, of course, are ready to move on when time present merges with time past - and the time to come - without any sense of wistful regret or residual traces of any kind. But those are other stories. Some Headmasters just need to move on and should, perhaps, have never been Headmasters, or even teachers, in the first place. All Hallows had been undergoing change and finding the management of that process rather difficult. The founder struggled, perhaps, to adapt to his own change in circumstances (even though he had set them in motion himself) and, having run the school in the capacity of a proprietor, with all the personal whims and predilections such status bestowed in those times, he was reluctant to permit the transfer of authority and autonomy

---

[66] It is rather amusing and instructive to know that this figure of £32 increased to £161.55 (almost £2000 today) when the '*clothes fines*' amount was taken into account. Presumably this additional source of income for good causes comes about as a result of the boys either wearing the wrong clothes or, more likely, leaving their belongings around the school campus. Modern parents and staff might understand and empathise with this phenomenon and would support any attempt to re-introduce a monetary fining system especially if the proceeds went to charity and – even more especially - if such funds were taken from the pupils' own pocket money accounts. Not that leaving items around the place is specifically a *pupil* problem when one takes into account the emails flying about from staff regarding mislaid keys, glasses, resources, and sundry personal possessions, or, on a wider front, considering the typical annual list of left items on the London Underground which includes the usual umbrellas, clothing, books, keys, etc, but also *luxury watches, human skulls, a puffer fish, a lawnmower, urns containing human remains and breast implants*. Human beings, eh?!

to the newly-formed Governing Body without holding on to a 'casting vote' over proceedings. He was also somewhat demanding of those individuals who had been recruited to take the school forward, even though he had done the recruiting. One is reading between the lines to some extent, for not all information is factually verifiable, but reliable sources of information from people who had lived through those years have been able to comment sufficiently clearly about some of the background events to present compelling corroborative testimonies. Francis Dix, of course, wanted the school to succeed and would have wanted his legacy to live on; it was simply a matter of timing and personalities and styles not gelling well enough to ensure a smooth passage as the story unfolded. For example, at the time when Mr Dix was arranging for a new regime to take on the management of the school, Mr Robertson, (George to his friends), joined the school in 1960 as Assistant Headmaster and worked alongside Mr Dix, even occupying the Headmaster's House for the better execution of his duties, (whilst Mr Dix, presumably, took up residence in Charlton House), until George Robertson moved into the Lodge when Mr Derek Henderson arrived to take on that same senior role. Mr Robertson was recognised as dispensing a kindly discipline with a true schoolmaster's instinct and was always keen to support the 'under-dog'. He went on to become a 'Partner Headmaster' at St Martin's School in Yorkshire after serving a further temporary role as Assistant Headmaster, once more, when Mr Henderson suddenly left. The latter had joined Hugh Watts, from Downside, in establishing a new Prep School in Shropshire called Moor Park[67], no doubt wanting to operate more freely in circumstances that were not so constraining. Alistair Mortimer was effectively brought in by the Governing Body as it strove to exercise its own growing autonomy so that Mr Dix could be released from the day-to-day running of the school and, it is known, that Mrs Mortimer became a pivotal influence on the Governors' thinking since she impressed so much with her appealing blend of strength of character and warm generosity of spirit. She helped her husband achieve those early successes, between 1964-1968, even if she could not prevent the falling away of pupil numbers and the tensions that arose in the late 1960s. Jean Arnold-Jones, the loyal and supportive wife of Richard, who was a Governor at the time, comments very fairly and generously that Mr Mortimer's difficulties in maintaining a positive equilibrium and reassuring hand on matters towards the end of his time as Headmaster might easily have been due to uncertain health but, for whatever combination of reasons, the Governors came to their decision, in the end, that the school's future depended on a new Headmaster. Mr Mortimer was neither black nor white but the times and events determined that his own 'shades of grey' needed lightening, if All Hallows was to move forward.

---

[67] In mentioning St Martin's and Moor Park, it is worth noting the fact that the foundation of All Hallows (1938) produced pupils and/or teachers like Jocelyn Trappes-Lomax, Derek Henderson, George Robertson, Richard Arnold-Jones, John Murphy, Chris Bird, Lynn Walker and Ian Murphy who all founded *Catholic* schools (Farleigh 1953; Red Rice 1961; Moor Park 1963; St Martin's 1967), or who took up the mantle in Catholic schools already established. This achievement alone might be fairly attributed to the legacy of Francis and Evelyn Dix.

Some Ketterer Years

Paul Ketterer duly became Headmaster of All Hallows in September 1971 and was to lead the school through the next twenty-four years up to the threshold of the twenty-first century. Despite some of the initiatives introduced by Mr Mortimer, there was that strong sense, in 1971, as has been indicated, that All Hallows needed to step more convincingly into the twentieth-century with a more approachable and more accountable Headmaster. More importantly, given the nature of Mr Mortimer's sudden departure – unanticipated on all fronts – and with the Governors worried about a seriously falling school roll, there was work to be done in reassuring parents and in recruiting new ones. If Paul Ketterer had not quite been given the baton in similar circumstances to Sir Alex Ferguson when he took over the job of managing East Stirlingshire F.C. in 1974 with just eight players and no goalkeeper, he still had a job on his hands. Each Headmaster in the history of All Hallows has seen, in his time, the school roll increase but, with 'PFJK', that growth became exponential. Towards the end of his headship years, possibly helped by the introduction and gradual integration of girls from May 1972[68], the school numbers increased to as many as 280, at their height, and, quite apart from other considerations, the campus needed to adapt in order to accommodate such an influx. This was a planned and measured growth albeit one that gained momentum in years of plenty but which suffered swift losses when recessionary factors took hold. If the economy can be subject to violent swings, so, too, can the associated aspects of life be affected similarly. Those parents of a mind to choose independent education for their children will exercise the same extremes of enthusiasm and caution as any other participant in the economy, according to changing circumstances, and they will show themselves to be equally adept at exercising judgement, critical or otherwise, according to their experiences. Logistics demanded that the growth in boarding pupils should be accommodated, most naturally, in what might be termed the 'manor house', the principal residential quarters of the Pagets, that is, the main school building situated at the end of the front drive. In turns, the dining areas, the classrooms, the offices and other spaces, required external,

---

[68] In 1972, "*Two girls started and the first boarders were expected in the following term*" according to a Minute in the Governors' Meetings Book. See later commentary on girls.

alternative locations of their own in order to free up more space for dormitories. Naturally, Mr Ketterer looked to the outbuildings – the stable block and other buildings - which could be converted, whilst also considering extensions and new-build edifices in suitably-designated plots on the site. Looking at the shape of the school today it is clear that there is a sense of logical progression, and architects, governors and successive Heads have worked together in maintaining that corporate identity and utilitarian planning which has also managed to keep harmony and sympathy with the natural surroundings and the history of the house, apart from one stark exception. It is a good example of different personalities and different personnel handing on and taking up the baton of responsibility to ensure that continuity and progression can sit happily alongside each other. If legacies can be measured in physical building terms alone, then just as Mr Dix's years might be characterised by the three different locations in Bognor, Dartmoor and Somerset, so, too, Mr Ketterer's years can be defined by the significant building development which took into account the school dining room, the cortile area, the conversion and extension to the Stable Block which now houses so many classrooms, the Ketterer Wing itself with the ICT, Art Rooms and other teaching areas below, the sports hall, the re-laying of hard playing areas, the tennis courts, the provision of additional playing field space, the 'new' chapel, the provision of changing rooms and locker room space, the development of enhanced theatre facilities, the creation of external office locations and many other improvements.

But legacies are more than buildings, of course.

The Chronicles continued for a short time, it seems, into Mr Ketterer's Headship. I am drawing on surviving editions for 1971-1972 and 1972-1973 but, whilst there may have been other later records, one suspects that the habit of recording events as they unfolded and the practice of publishing such annual accounts fell away. There were certainly no chronicles or annual magazines in the 1980s and the present School Magazine was only resurrected as a record of the school year in 1996-1997, with further editions thereafter up to the present day. No value judgements are intended by this lapse any more than should be attached to Mr Mortimer's observation that the Chronicle was resurrected during his time as Head after *"having been moribund for so many years"*. His reference must have been to the years between 1959 and 1965 when Mr Dix was in the throes of 'handing the school over', releasing the reins, as it were, that he had taken on in 1939 from his wife. Records live on in memories, physical entities, other documentation (like Governors' Minutes) and personal testimonies and it is to these I have turned in gleaning information over and above my own experiences and knowledge which certainly take on a stronger impact from 1981 onwards.

To return to the familiar sources.

The afore-mentioned Mr Yule, who spoke so well about Mr Mortimer, was, himself, eulogised by Paul Ketterer in the 1971-1972 Chronicle (see box right).

I'm not going to develop any particular focus on Headmasters' children in this narrative, although there are a baker's dozen of them knocking about, but I'll just mention Natacha Riette Ketterer – now in Australia – whose birthday is the only one recorded in a School Chronicle –

LT. COL. R.C. YULE, O.B.E.

"The departure of Colonel Yule in December 1971, after seven years on the staff, marked the end of an era. He was steeped in the traditions of military discipline and it was on these traditions that he drew for his second career when he came a schoolmaster. The responsibilities of a second master are never easy and the present writer was always impressed by the conscientious approach which Colonel Yule invariably displayed. His moral courage was never in doubt; under a gruff exterior was hidden a kindliness which is unforgettable. He takes with him our very sincere wishes for the future."

P.F.J.K.

Colonel Yule joined the staff in September 1965 and was originally engaged to teach mathematics. In 1966 he is found to be supervising ground-clearing and digging in the Spinney for the foundations of the second-hand deep-litter hut which will serve as a temporary science laboratory and in 1967 he upheld staff honour, presumably with a partner, by defeating Toby Dean and Kevin Burke, the Tennis Doubles Champions, by the score of 6-4, 6-4. He gave regular lectures and film slide-shows to the boys (for example, one on India in March 1967) drawing, presumably, on his experiences in the Army. He was responsible for managing the Railway Club and seems to have shown much ingenuity and expertise in constructing tightly-knit sequences of track and engineering effects, as well as turning his hand to basic carpentry work in helping to fit newly adapted shelving for the new maths room in The Mortimer Block. He produced plays for end-of-term performances, one such being the memorable *"Passion, Poison and Petrification"* by George Bernard Shaw, which *"surprised (by the originality of his choice) and delighted the whole audience"*, according to Mr Dix. He also left suddenly after Mr Mortimer's own departure with just a sense, to this writer at least, that he was seen to be too much associated with that regime and the spirit of the age needed a clean sheet if it was about to change.

Saturday 4th December 1971. One reason to mention Sacha is the nice link some time later when she became the first child to be christened in the School Chapel on 2nd February 1972. Who knows what she started; three months later the school welcomed its first day girls as pupils. I'm not a great believer in 'firsts', for all kinds of reasons, but they can stand out as representative of subsequent events and people; simulacra, if you will, of our common humanity. I know from personal experience that the school chapel has welcomed a Cardinal, several Bishops, several former pupils as priests, a barrel-load of monks, the occasional Anglican Vicar (even!), hundreds of devout practitioners of their faith and, perhaps, countless waverers and non-believers, as well as thousands of 'saints' yet to take up their calling with – who knows – possibly a future Pope or two, for good measure. It has seen thousands of Masses, and masses of Night Prayers (just imagine the clouds of prayer soaring upwards and outwards from those hallowed places!). It has swung incense, sung hymns, shared communion and sponsored silence. A multitude of sins has been confessed and, we believe, forgiven. Aspirations, regrets, worries and gratitudes have been expressed. Wisdom, bounty, platitudes and hypocrisy have mingled side by side, for the Holy Spirit is a strangely-moving, all-encompassing force upon this earth, but there is a palpable, moving essence that permeates the people in this place regardless of the starting-points for our encounters. Like T. S. Eliot's poetic travellers through life, 'we are not the same people who left the station' after our visits to the chapel. This might be made manifest in a single visit or as a result of an accumulation of experiences. Drop into the Blessed Sacrament Chapel to the right of the altar today and you will read the prayer from Ephesians 3: 17-19, written out and presented by former pupil William Bellasis (who went on to become a priest at Ampleforth and America) on the occasion of the school's fiftieth birthday, which calls to you *"That Christ may dwell in your hearts by faith; that ye, being rooted and grounded in love, may be able to comprehend **with all saints** what is the breadth and length and depth and height; and to know the love of Christ, which passeth knowledge, that ye might be filled with all the fullness of God"*. This is our chapel. In this special place we *"enter this door as if the floor within were gold and every wall of jewels all of wealth untold. As if a choir in robes of fire were singing here. Nor shout, nor rush, but hush for God is here"*. That, at least, is the theory. In this place we have shared in Christenings, First Communions, Confessions, Confirmations, Matrimonies, Blessings and Memorial Services. On which note, we record the fact of the Memorial Service on 20th April 2013 to commemorate and celebrate the life of Paul Ketterer, RIP, (see pages 291ff), on which occasion almost three hundred former pupils, parents, family and friends, as well as current and former staff and governors, gathered to share in that enduring bounty which somehow ties us to the school of All Hallows – the place where all saints, dusty and golden, may abide. Sacha Ketterer was christened in the All Hallows Chapel, as was, and Paul Ketterer was commemorated in the All Hallows Chapel, as is. And so the dance goes on.

It is people who inhabit the school, of course, and it is for chroniclers and historians and religiously-orientated people to ponder on spiritual presence and legacies and the meaning of life, so let us return to the earthly, ground-orientated world of the foot-soldiers who are always the best of saints, after all.

And if that's all a little high-falutin', let us mention from that same Chronicle that referred to baby Sacha that "*Mark Lowman deserves to be remembered for a courageous feat achieved this summer when he made a successful journey along the noisome Cran tunnel.*" One can only imagine what this entailed but one hesitates to think what parents would think of it nowadays, let alone Health & Safety. I am reminded of another pupil who had been dared for the prize of two mars bars to negotiate the underpass in the Cran beneath the stone bridge whilst wearing school uniform, all under the possible watching eyes of Duty Staff; I think he got away with it – and the two mars bars – which only goes to show what pupils are prepared to do for sweets.

To my mind, at least, the pupils have not beaten the staff in our annual soccer encounter at the end of each summer term for as long as the waters of the Cran have flowed under the astro-turf – and probably for much longer – since one reads in 1971 that the Staff team went on to victory against all-comers in a six-a-side tournament beating teams from Forms 3 and 4, as well as the Prefects and, then, in the final, Form 5B by three goals to two. "*The Common Room, under the eagle eyes of Mr Ketterer, who was in goal, and Mr Scotland, who displayed touches of the old Stanley Matthews*" were comfortable winners along the way, apparently. Not only do the teachers provide instruction and discipline in the classrooms but they refuse to be cowed in the face of the sporting aspirations of the pupils; the children will thank us for setting the bar so high when they are older. Mind you, one remembers Mr Dowbekin, the Music Director of a more modern

JIM DREDGE

(died 2nd January 1972 RIP)

There are no apologies for highlighting the work and lives of those who also stand and serve in the traditions of Nash and the Metcalfes and Gibbs and Cook et al...

"It is with very deep regret that we have to record the death of Mr Jim Dredge after service to All Hallows spanning nearly a quarter of a century. Jim first came to help at the school in 1947, toiling away in the evenings to prepare the playing field. Then, there was no tractor and gangmower, nor, indeed, even a motormower. All the work had to be done pushing an ordinary garden mower which did not even have a box to collect the grass. The next duty he undertook was the cleaning of the classrooms. By 1950 he was working full time at All Hallows and then - with his wife - moved into the cottage which they were to occupy for twenty years. Mrs Dredge, herself, worked for seventeen years at the school and together they saw many changes. When they arrived the courtyard was still surrounded by stables and they helped to convert them to classrooms. The Art Room still had orange trees in it and there was a rose garden where the Headmaster's House now stands. They not only saw all these changes but by their hard work and dedication helped to bring them about. Every master and boy who has been at All Hallows since it moved to East Cranmore will have known Jim Dredge and all of them would agree that good cheer and industry were the chief characteristics by which he will be remembered. He would often arrive for work at six o'clock in the morning and for him there was no five day week. Seven days a week, term in and term out, Jim would be there to see that all was running smoothly in the kitchens, in the changing rooms, in the classrooms and on the playing fields. Some people, perhaps, did not appreciate all that he did until that sad day when he first fell ill. It was then that all came to realise how much All Hallows owed Jim Dredge. During the first half of 1971 it was obvious that Jim was very ill and yet he was always fretting to be back at work. Often his son Richard would come in and do the work for him until his father should be once again fit enough to take over. For a time, in the summer of that year, Jim was back once again on his tractor protesting that he was quite well enough to carry on but those who knew him realised that he was a sick man and that it was only enthusiasm for the school which he loved which kept him going. During those summer holidays it became clear that Jim would have to retire and with great reluctance he left the work which he loved in September 1971 and went to live in Cranmore village. Within a very short time he was once again in hospital and on 2nd January 1972 he died. The funeral took place in the parish church at Cranmore. To show their appreciation of Jim Dredge there were amongst the mourners three Headmasters of All Hallows."

vintage, one year being unable to orchestrate anything more than a snapped Achilles tendon in one such match so we didn't always have things all our own way. Just to correct the balance - and give the lie to the proud boasts above - there followed a full eleven-a-side soccer match between The Common Room and the School 1st XI when they enjoyed a ding-dong encounter on 1st November 1971 (the school's 33rd birthday) with the staff team containing *"an interesting blend of youth, experience, short-sightedness and rheumatism"* as Oliver Gibbs' *"shrewd distribution of the ball brought out the best from Misses Greenaway and Reed."* *"After some enterprising sorties by Messrs. Ketterer and Jones, Simon Stubbs beat Cooke with a strong shot*" but the school team took control of midfield and kept scoring the other end eventually to win the match by five goals to four. On the same day, the House Cross-Country Run was held which was won individually by eleven-year-old Nicholas Austin and, collectively, by Wolves, who shared in a flagon of cider for their efforts (some traditions never die, it seems, although the modern All Hallows' sporting heroes might wonder what has happened to their flagons which do not now seem to materialise). We read later of the production of "Toad of Toad Hall" which contained "*both wit and buffoonery to satisfy the refined and the grosser appetites*" in which "*the revels of the banqueting scene were 'made' by the gales of drunken laughter uttered very convincingly by Chris Shattock*". Possibly, Chris Shattock had been in the victorious, cider-drinking Wolves' cross-country team and had not fully recovered from his celebrations. The producer, however, may have been dazzled by some theatrical intoxication of his own since he concludes his 1971 article with the statement that "*drama is here to stay*" with perhaps not much awareness of the many dramatic productions staged at the school in the thirty-plus years before.

School outings continued apace, as well, as evidenced by William Farquharson's account of the tour of Cheddar Gorge which took into account a visit to Shepton Mallet Prison, the carvings in Croscombe Church, a timber-yard where wood was ordered, a paper factory, Mendip caves, the Gorge itself, the town of Cheddar, a motoring museum, an old Scout Camp site and, finally, the TV mast above Wells.

The school has always made full use of its locality and the attractions offered whether they are of the Fingle Bridge variety on Dartmoor or the arguably more famous sites of Cheddar and Wells and Glastonbury. The Roman Baths, in Bath, also feature regularly for generations of pupils and I rather like the musings of Rory Duncan (aged 13) in February 1972 who observed the following "*...only a part could be seen as there was a power cut and half the remains were in darkness.... we passed two stone coffins with the remains of three people who didn't make it to the baths..... guided by a lot of signs we looked for the pump room. It turned out to be a restaurant where Mendelssohn's works were played on the piano and violin. We did not stay as Mendelssohn always gives me indigestion*". I bet there are not many others who took away with them those particular impressions of the springs dating back to the year 836 BC – such archaeological sites have to work a little harder to impress the discernment of the All Hallows' pupil.

Another All Hallows' pupil who was making a name for himself at this time in a different discipline was Peter Curling who was featured in the 1971-1972 Chronicle as an old boy... (see box overleaf)

The same Rory Duncan as above, who had a dislike for Mendelssohn, despite the Pump Rooms' best efforts, wrote, in 1971, an amusing piece about his Uncle Horatio P. D. Foland, D.S.O., M.C., G.C. which we would love to be true but which reads better as a fictional account, in Wodehousian-style, with which I inspire my pupils in 2013. I know I have some excellent writing examples from the modern era to come so I include it here as a bridge between Auberon Waugh, et al, and the later literary stars.

PETER CURLING

(F.P. 1962-1968)

Peter Curling become a renowned equestrian artist in adult life (check out his website) but showed an early artistic promise and, indeed, some creative flair generally, for his essay entitled 'An Unusual Journey" not only was adjudged the best All Hallows' entry for the annual Brooke Bond Essay Competition (printed in the May 1967 Chronicle) but also showed an early interest in horses since it focused on a dream and a horse named 'Nightmare'. He produced a "*spectacular*" drawing of a dragon in his schooldays at All Hallows "*poised to descend on an unsuspecting city*" (and possibly one of the first additions to his portfolio which means it must be worth a bob or two). He appeared on 'Points West' after he had left All Hallows (but whilst still a schoolboy at Millfield) and had an exhibition of his works at Millfield School when one of his works fetched £150, and he went on, later, to put together a three-week exhibition at The Dolphin Gallery, Lymington, Hampshire, when he turned out nearly 30 pictures and sold 17 paintings netting him about £1000. Peter said at that time that "*The money has not all gone in the bank. I have managed to buy my first horse, a six-year-old called Bethanie, a Land-Rover to pull her box and I have joined the Avondale Hunt.*" Millfield's Headmaster, Mr

Colin Atkinson, said "*We cannot treat any boy with such unusual talents in a usual way. We have given him permission to take next term off to study in Italy.*"

Horses were always a distinctive feature in his life. He was drawn to them for their beauty and grace, the way they moved, and for the strong link that existed between man and horse. Lambourn, Berkshire, became a formative influence – his first exhibition was held here at the age of 14 – and Newmarket and Ireland, thereafter, became similarly important centres of interest. His continuing passion and development in owning racehorses endowed his work with a realism and authenticity that was recognised by artists and horse owners alike. He even rode a horse called 'Caddy' to victory in his first racing outing – the horse itself later went on to win the Kerry National in 1989. Hunting in Tipperary also became an interest which provided further inspiration for his painting. He went on to Stonyhurst from All Hallows and then secured the first ever awarded Art Scholarship to Millfield. If you do stray on to his website look out for "An Easy Day" which records the breath and steam breaking on the flanks and nostrils of two early morning horses; and the sheen and the shadows of "*Leading Them Out*" along with the expectant, distracted and ruminative postures of the riders and attendants in anticipation of the races to come; and the visceral quality of "*Schooling Bumper*"; or, by way of variation, the capture of a moment in time and place of "*Gondolas, Grand Canal*".

All Hallows will, of course, take the credit for the development of his precocious talent and assert the value of good grounding in basic artistic techniques if one wants to become truly famous and accomplished.

We must endeavour to acquire some Curling prints - or even originals, if he should like to donate a couple after reading this book - to adorn the All Hallows' galleries; this commentator, at least, believes them to be better than the Munnings currently on show.

Uncle Horatio P.D. Foland, D.S.O., M.C., G.C.

"He began his bellowing again so I forced on a smile that nearly cracked my face in two. I sighed. Two and a half hours now! I wish my parents would hurry back. I wish he would stop wittering. Oh, good grief! My parents had gone to a ball and left me with Uncle. Uncle Horatio P.D. Foland, D.S.O, M.C., G.C., that is, of the fifth platoon of Royal Artillery during the Great War. So far, in the course of two and a half hours, he had with his tales of heroism, patriotism, loyalty, genius and all the rest of those gifts that none but the King's men possess, bored me so stiff that I felt I was blending into the armchair. Suddenly he will begin his 'act'. His eyes start sparkling and his sticking out ears begin to twitch turning from red to purple and back to white in an alarming manner. Then he starts to bellow with laughter rocking the Manor to its foundation. At this performance, in which he bellows like the bull sea-lion at Melton Zoo, I am possessed with the overwhelming desire to drop a large, slimy pickerel down his cavernous throat*. But as there were no pickerels available I was forced to remain where I was. Uncle Horatio was a good man at heart, meaning well, but not very able at performing what he meant. Whenever we saw him he was always in the same flabby plus-fours and patched tweed jacket that he was unmistakeable. He was a tall and straight man and the way he walked, stiffly with bloated chest and pinned shoulders, still bore the marks of army discipline during nineteen-eighteen. His face was circular and very creased and would puff out, turning bright purple when he bellowed. His nose was big, sharp and very military. His huge ears stuck straight out of a wave of frosty grey hair. He had a small mouth with a tremendous moustache. His moustache was about a foot long and very bushy about the nose but smoothly waxed towards either end. It would, when Uncle Horatio roared with laughter, fluctuate violently giving the impression (and the hope) that he might fly south for the winter. His eyebrows are the same frosty colour as his hair and are slanted downward at an acute angle making him look comically serious. One wouldn't expect such a lot of talk from such a small mouth, but that's Uncle Horatio....
Saved at last, hooray for butlers! Timothy's rung the bell for tea."

*Now, it is just possible that P. G. Wodehouse might have said *"...drop down his cavernous throat a large slimy pickerel which one kept wrapped in a silk handkerchief in one's waistcoat pocket for just such an occasion"* rather like the procedure to be followed by a friend for dealing with an angry swan when one is inevitably stuck up a tree and besieged by the said swan at the base of the tree, as in *"Every young man starting life should know how to cope with an angry swan, so I will briefly relate the proper procedure. You begin by picking up the raincoat which somebody has dropped; and then, judging the distance to a nicety, you simply shove the raincoat over the bird's head; and, taking the boat-hook which you have prudently brought with you,*

you insert it under the swan and heave. [...] That was Jeeves's method, and I cannot see how it could be improved upon." That slight improvement apart, Rory Duncan had it just right. Horatio P. D. Foland, surely existed as an uncle to somebody or other, or, perhaps, as a member of staff at All Hallows before teaching qualifications were considered necessary.

There followed some thoughtful parental contributions in the 1971-1972 Chronicle from Monsieur et Madame Picard, who, having enrolled their 'fils', William, into the school as a ten-year old boarder - quite contrary to the French educational system – had been invited by Paul Ketterer to record their observations. Gloria Picard mentioned the fact that in France *'boarding schools are often used....with an object of punishment"*. Madame Picard came to believe that the English boarding experience at All Hallows made the boy "*conscious of good, beauty, life*". I am surprised now, as I contemplate those sentiments, that PFJK did not feel compelled to use that slogan in his boarding literature. Nowadays, some marketing expert would have that phrase emblazoned on the website. She goes on to assert "*He likes his school and is proud of it. There he lives and it belongs to him. He wears its uniform, defends its colours....the education does not only consist in heaping up knowledges (sic)...The English education system seems to square with the precept of one of our famous philosophers of the 16th century, Montaigne, who used to say 'Mieux vaut une tête bien faite qu'une tête bien pleine'*. Montaigne might have meant that it was better to be able to think than to have your head stuffed full of facts but I like Madame Picard's conclusion that "*so many things are necessary to make a man out of a boy*". I think she is 'one special lady' and her son, 'one very special man'.

Prize Day 1972 commemorated the 25th anniversary of Dr Buckler's association with the school as the Chief Medical Officer – a school might march on its stomach but that stomach has to be fit and well in the first place. The same Prize Day, Mr Ketterer made one of his more profound statements in emphasising "*that all members of staff were determined that each pupil at All Hallows should be treated as an individual and not the stereotyped product of an institution*". The uniqueness of the individual is a precept clung to avowedly in my own Headship years and, over and above any other legacies, I think that would be the best of all: we recognised the individual. It underpins the whole point of keeping the school manageably 'small'. For logistical reasons (space, communal areas, places to hang out) the school should resist recruiting too many pupils; for reasons of identity, the school should remain 'small'. Imagine the difference to a child (or adult for that matter) if your everyday experience was characterised by "Hello, Daniel/Felicity, how are you? Good to hear about your merits this week. Well Done! Sorry about your hamster. I'm looking forward to watching you play this weekend in the match. And thanks for helping out with the little ones at break-time. Good luck in the concert!" as opposed to "Oi! No running in the corridor - whoever you are!"

Or, even worse, no recognition at all. "*Catholic education is about the development of the whole person...ensuring that the unique value of the individual is recognised and developed to the full*" (The Common Good in Education). Every child in our care should know through personal experience the value of being recognised: "*I have called you by your name, you are mine*" (Isaiah 43:1). Archbishop Vincent Nichols delivered a homily at a Catholic Independent Schools Conference Mass some years ago asserting to a few hundred Catholic Head Teachers, priests, chaplains and management teams that we are called, as teachers in the broadest sense, to look at ways in which every boy and girl in our care is led to an awareness that God has a specific vocation, a particular calling, for each and every one of them. I would broaden that further. In the world of education, this is not just about Catholicity, or even about belief in God; this is the fundamental core of our vocation: drawing out the best in every developing human being – the recognition, celebration and validation of the uniqueness of the individual.

Mention should be made here of the Governors' decisions, at various times in the school history, to limit the numbers in the school alongside the contrary and seemingly irresistible temptation and practice of increasing the pupils. This is not a cynical exercise in accumulating balances in the bank but about managed capital expenditure and potential expansion and development for the good of the school. Major projects tend to be building new wings or stand-alone facilities but the 'repairs and renewals' bill is huge and the pressures of new legislation regarding, for example, fire safety or meeting revised electrical standards, can also present sudden and unexpected financial obligations. Waiting lists have rarely, if ever, been known (the only time I operated a genuine 'waiting-list' I came to regret it because I turned away perhaps twenty pupils when about twenty other registered pupils failed to show up the following term). Accommodation of prospective parents has almost always been granted - but the downside to this approach is that when numbers fall for various reasons, usually due to recessionary factors, they tend to plummet, and redundancies tend to follow, because in the expansion more staff have been employed, and then dismay sets in, and, with the dismay comes rumour and anxieties about the future, until a natural settling-down occurs allowing renewed consolidation to rebuild. Clear strategic thinking is needed if the swings and roundabout effect is to be avoided. In its 75th year it would be a good time for those clear heads to gather together and take into account the wishes of the pupils, parents, teachers, governors and Friends so that some coherent vision of the school can be met with similar strength of purpose. The market, however, is volatile, unpredictable and often determined by last-minute fluctuations in fortune, intentions and circumstances beyond human control or planning.

Time for another eulogy of one of the greats.

We move into the 1972-1973 Chronicle records and possibly one of the last annual magazines of Paul Ketterer's Headship which was to last for another twenty-two years. More thoughts on that later.

The panegyric, this time, is for Mr James Blunt, schoolmaster. (see box overleaf)

Paul Ketterer was a good example of the right man in the right place at the right time. The Governors of the late 1960s and early 1970s had dealt with financial difficulties and glum predictions of the future regarding pupil numbers and the school's viability – and had even contemplated the threat of closure following Fire Officers' Reports and prevailing circumstances.

MR JAMES BLUNT

"At the end of the summer term 1972, Mr Blunt retired after nineteen years on the staff at All Hallows. He will be greatly missed. Mr Blunt proved himself a man of many parts. In his early years his work was mainly as a Form Master but he soon added many other activities. Mr Blunt is a very skilful cabinet-maker. Anyone who visits his charming house at Pilton will see much evidence of this. It was inevitable, therefore, that he should take on the teaching of carpentry at All Hallows. This, though an 'extra', became so popular that before long most boys in the school were learning the craft and, under Mr Blunt's skilled tuition, learning it very well. In September 1954 Mr Blunt took over the All Hallows Scout Troop and started the Cubs. He continued as Scoutmaster until his retirement. He gave up much of his time to this work and every other Sunday the Scouts met in the wood and, among other activities, cooked their own dinners. The high spot of the year, however, was the Annual Camp which took place for many years at Stourton, but later near Wells. I paid many visits to these camps, occasionally spending the night, and I can vouch for the extreme efficiency with which they were run. I remember that Mr Blunt brought his goats, Blossom and Dandy, to the camp so that there should be an additional supply of milk. I am sure that many Old Boys will have very happy memories of these camps. I should mention here the help Mrs Blunt gave her husband on these occasions. In 1959, on the departure of Mr le Mare, Mr Blunt who had been in charge of the Junior boxers, took over the Seniors also, and thereafter turned out many good boxers as their successes in school matches have proved. Some years ago Mr Blunt was put in charge of the School Geography[69] which he ran with great enthusiasm and success. The fascinating exhibits in the Geography Room bear witness to this. For many years Mr Blunt ran the school bank and made sure, sometimes with difficulty, that his young clients did not run into the red. Among other tasks, he had charge of the tuck shop and often provided props for the school play. I remember in particular his lift for 'The Crimson Coconut' and his delightful caravan for 'Toad of Toad Hall'. If, however, there is one quality which I would stress in particular, it is Mr Blunt's great kindness and his interest in the boys themselves and especially the efforts he made to help lame dogs over stiles. We wish Mr Blunt and his wife every happiness in his retirement which I am sure will be an active one.
- F. H. R. Dix

Helping '**lame dogs over stiles**' sounds like a particularly typical All Hallows virtue.

Jim Blunt died in 1986 and the Headmaster at the time, Paul Ketterer, joined Francis Dix and some pupils at the Requiem Mass held at St Michael's in Shepton Mallet which was presided over by Father Philip Jebb, Headmaster of Downside.

---

[69] Geography, as an academic discipline, may not seem the likeliest subject to highlight alongside the more obvious and more traditional pursuits, perhaps, like English, Latin, Mathematics, and Science, for example, but there is something about the nature of the subject and the way it has been taught - and the personnel teaching it - that propels it forward, I feel, in the minds of the pupils and in the history of the school. It has been noted that Geography was 'taught' by visiting speakers and by ex-military men who would regale the boys, in the early days, with tales of Empire and military exploits in far-away lands. It took on a distinct discipline of its own as the years went by and became increasingly aligned with science, through its physical processes and field work, although the sense of global location has never disappeared, and it now links in with other relatively 'new' areas of study like Personal, Social and Health Education courses, as well as crossing-over into Religious Education topics on world religions. Accomplished men have taken on the role of Head of the Geography Department like John Murphy, David Clarke and Chris Godwin and, more recently, Ben Coombes, for a short time, and Trevor Richards. >>

They had also entertained quite seriously the idea put forward at more than one Governors' Meeting that they should consider moving the school's location closer to a thriving township, like Bristol, so that passing trends in pupil registration and recessionary times could be overridden more easily. In the post-Mortimer years, they were resolved to support the new Headmaster as much as possible in his brief to move the school forward. The new Head had to have the vision and the energy to create the climate in which others could invest in the school in the form of staff input, parental confidence, pupil contributions, and, perhaps most importantly, green lights at Governor level. It is difficult to say where such a climate begins for all elements mentioned are inextricably linked and they form a virtuous circle just as strongly (albeit more slowly) as the climate of anxiety that can lead to a sudden loss of confidence at the other end of the spectrum. It is perhaps just as well that such 'swings and roundabouts' are not fully explained to prospective Heads at interview otherwise such gallant, sparkling-eyed aspirants might never don the gown. Heads have to find out for themselves and they have to find their own way. Nevertheless, it was the Governors who declared their support of Paul Ketterer and they showed great fortitude and strength of purpose in making hard business decisions, chiefly to do with finance, so that Paul could see through his plans. But the relationship was mutually beneficial. As Richard Arnold-Jones was to say, in 1988, at a 'Friends of All Hallows Meeting' - at a time when his own involvement with the school went back to 1943! - *"the best achievement of the Governors had been in appointing Paul Ketterer as Headmaster"*.

In any history of an independent school like All Hallows, strong, influential voices from Finance Governors and Accountants and Auditors will be heard, time and again, chorusing the oft-repeated mantra that it all comes down to the balance in the bank. In order to avoid the 'sword of Damocles', as mentioned earlier by one Governor, hovering over the collective head (or should that read, 'Head') of the school, a fee-paying school can only survive if its finances are sound. Such an educational establishment can only aspire and then deliver on its academic, extra-curricular, spiritual, pastoral and development plans for the young in its care when – and

John Murphy was brought in by the Governors as Deputy Headmaster to Paul Ketterer in the 1980s and he went on to become Headmaster, first of all at St Joseph's in Launceston, and then as Head of Farleigh Prep School near Andover. John and his wife Hilary, with their daughters, Grace and Gail, lived in the Lodge House at the turn of the bend on the way to West Cranmore although the school sold off that property subsequently. John had played rugby for London Irish and had gained a trial for the Irish national team. David Clarke left All Hallows after much success and became Headmaster at Bilton Grange prep School having played first-class rugby for Northampton. Chris Godwin, not to be outdone, became de facto Senior Master at All Hallows and then left to take on the Headship of Bedford Junior School and, at the height of six feet four, with a commensurate weight, he, also, played and coached rugby to a high standard. Ben Coombes, of course, is known for his sporting abilities across a spectrum of sports and currently occupies the role of Director of Sport and Assistant Head of Activities at All Hallows, having previously been Deputy Headmaster elsewhere. Trevor Richards, or Dr Richards as he is about to become in his capacity as an Educational Psychologist, is currently Director of Learning and a key member of the Senior Leadership Team who has also played sport at a top standard having represented England in a coaching capacity in basketball.

There must be something about the subject of Geography that stimulates leadership and sporting prowess!

only when – its funding is secure. The bold pragmatics can take some time to appreciate – as this Headmaster will freely admit. Paul Ketterer, himself, reminded me in several meetings before I assumed the role of Headmaster (on many occasions when we would enjoy late-night Christmas afternoons that turned into evenings and then long nights) that *"one had to keep one's eyes on the ball"*. In clinical terms that meant running the school in such a way that had firstly established there would be a school to be run. And that could only be effected by maintaining pupil numbers of a sufficient size to generate fees to cover the costs of staff salaries, resources, capital building projects, routine expenditure, repairs and renewals and sundry other needs, some of which remained alarmingly unpredictable. This Headmaster also remembers, in his naivety, being informed at a Sub-Committee Finance Meeting in 1995 that a £30000 surplus was needed just to break even. And don't get me started on the irritations of financial 'appreciation'. Incidentally, it should be noted that schools like All Hallows never aim to make profits; they make 'surpluses'. It is possibly worth mentioning that Charitable Trusts of this nature do not benefit materially the Governors – who now assume huge responsibilities and liabilities for no financial gain or salary whatsoever – nor is there any other benefit to any personnel other than in the form of agreed salaries for a job delivered. Should the school build up financial reserves, under Charity Law and according to its own moral obligations, such funds are poured back into the upkeep and development of the school. This might be a point worth emphasising for the better understanding of the principal fee-payers, i.e. the parents, even if it is sometimes fair to say that one generation of fee-payers provide for the enhanced facilities of the next. It is certainly not true, as one parent once remarked to me, that the school charges such high fees because we send a certain portion off to Rome each year to help fill the Vatican's vaults. That anecdote is not apocryphal and the parent concerned genuinely believed it to be the case. So it is that the Minutes of the Governing Body will record the comings and goings of financial transactions, fees' income, expenditure accounts, development plans, etc, in *'private and confidential'*, fairly neutral, business-like written language, even if the business of the meetings touched upon many other aspects of the school. The Governors, however, (I know from experience) are not desperate to become immersed in dry matters of finance and are constantly asking about the pupils and the staff and the ongoing 'school' business from Monday to Monday, through the terms and the seasons. Dr Freddie Buckler, for example, who served over 35 years as the School Doctor, before also joining the Governing Body for six years subsequently, was famous for asking *"And how have the Sports Teams been doing?"* Sports Masters would have choked ironically into their beers since they knew that he had put "off Games" the star players on more than one occasion because of some minor difficulties like concussion or a broken leg. More often than not, the answer came back "Well, we've won some and we've lost some" but Dr Buckler must have been pleased in 1997 when he heard at a 'Friends of All Hallows Meeting' that the Under-13 Girls had just completed their third unbeaten year in a row in all sports; that the Under-13 Boys had won the Beaumont Sevens under John-Paul Renouf's inspirational coaching; that the Under-13 Boys were British All-Comers Gymnastic Champions yet again after Moira Thompson's exacting guidance; that the Under-13 Boys, the Under-12 Girls and the Under-11 Boys all produced South-West Hurdles Champions; and that the Under-13 Boys and the Under-13 Girls were South-West Long Jump Champions. The gymnastics, in particular, were a crowning legacy of the Ketterer years in that he had persuaded the Governors to support his wish to employ Moira Thompson[70] when no full-time position was really available because he had seen in her a love of children and a demanding coaching style that would bring out the best in the pupils. Moira's success in gymnastics alone was unprecedented and phenomenal. Mind you, Paul Ketterer would be the first to admit that his own athletic prowess left something to be desired especially when he once tried to jump over the car-park chain[71] to the side of the front entrance when showing round prospective parents, with two senior girls in tow for good measure, only to misjudge his timing and fall flat on his face. The prospective pupils were, of course, registered that same day; nothing like a bit of sympathy to secure the deal. Attempts by some of us to get him to repeat the procedure every time he showed round prospective parents fell on deaf ears even though we had the camera ready for posterity.

So, the need for more income meant the need for more pupils and the need for the current parents to meet the cost of higher fees. There was also the possibility of realising some assets. The immediate part-solution to the first proposition was to plan for the introduction of a Pre-Prep Department from May 1972, which, in those days, would have meant dropping the age of entry to below seven years old but its success was evident by the fact that for September 1975 plans had been put in place for fees for five-year-old pupils. Shirley Couzens was a key member of staff responsible for bringing on these young pupils and setting up the department. But the Lent 1973 figures show that even with eleven girls in the school and, presumably, a class or two of pupils under the age of seven for the first time in the school's history, the total school roll was only 129, so perhaps those Governors' fears at the time of the Mortimer/Ketterer handover were justified and perhaps school numbers had, in reality, dropped below the 100 mark a little earlier. It is pertinent to note that in 1956 the school roll was 117. Nevertheless, from 1973, the Governors were asking Paul Ketterer to look at ways of expanding the facilities in order to accommodate the increased numbers. Central to that strategy would not have been the practice of 'off-loading' pupils but, sometimes, in the everyday management of a school, Headmasters have to make such reluctant decisions and the records show that, between 1973-1977, five boys had the phrase "relinquished control" set against their names in the Leavers' lists. I can think of three pupils in my time as Headmaster over whom I "relinquished control" and, I believe, there is one pupil in Ian Murphy's time for whom the same can be said. Sometimes, pupils - and the school - need a

---

[70] Moira Thompson – see page 167

[71] *That Chain* seems to have had a malevolent spirit of its own since it also left an unsightly, red-raw mark across my brother's chest when he unwisely ran through it, at speed, not seeing it drawn tight between its iron pillars above the gravel-stoned courtyard one dark Boxing-Day Night on his way to the car (admittedly after a few Christmas drinks).

fresh start. Over the next few years the fees increased significantly. It is difficult to say whether or not such rises increased disproportionately over inflation but the fact of the matter was that parents bore the rising costs almost without complaint which was a result of two factors: (1) their confidence in the new regime and in the developing Headship of Paul Ketterer and (2) on the fact, which must have concentrated their minds, that comparable fee-charging schools in the area were actually more expensive. This is an important point. For those parents who are in a position to consider private education they are bound to look at the local opportunities around them. For as long as it can be remembered, All Hallows has represented 'value for money' not only on its own terms (that is, the 'value-added' aspects of an All Hallows' education) but also when compared to other schools. In recent times, schools have had to be seen to assert that their fees have not been set according to some agreed policy in the region through some formal or unofficial 'cartel' whereby there is any sense of 'price-fixing'. In my experience, at this level, in this part of the world, at least, that has never been the case, but the figures are freely available and it soon became apparent that All Hallows was always considerably sitting towards the bottom of any 'league table' that any interested party could draw up just using the previous year's fees, as shown in the various yearbooks. In other words, All Hallows could afford to increase its fees without running an overt risk of losing potential pupils as a result. Since that differential remained in place for many years thereafter, it was clear that other schools were, themselves, increasing fees significantly also. Far from being driven by some closed shop mentality in order to manipulate the 'market-place', such considerations were being driven by external factors such as increasing costs (e.g. fuel, electricity, food, rates, inspection-led recommendations, other newly-devised regulations, etc) but the largest influencing factor was staff salaries. Staff will bristle a little because, of course, we/they are overworked and underpaid. There must be a society somewhere that remunerates its teachers with the highest salaries of all. But, in earlier days at least, it was possible to employ very good staff to teach who had not necessarily, or even usually, obtained a teaching qualification but who had accrued a good deal of relevant experience in one field or another with a concomitant commitment to educating young people. Sometimes these would be men (for it was often men) pursuing a second career. Typically (but not always) these would be ex-military personnel. The idea that Geography could be taught by Major Carruthers because he had visited many places around the world and that the Scouts would be run by handymen who could put up tents, live off acorns found in the woods and take stones out of horses' hooves with a practised flick of their penknives was not so very far from the truth. And who are we to say that this is not the best case? Notwithstanding such loaded questions, staff salaries were given a huge boost by the growing 'professionalism' of the teaching profession whereby, even as far back as 1965, the Governors decided to pay all teachers on the established 'Burnham Scale'[72].

---

[72] One says 'as far back as 1965' but, even then, All Hallows – like many independent schools – was slow off the mark in following national prescription since the Burnham scale was made mandatory in the Maintained Sector across England and Wales following the 1944 Education Act.

Expectations were now raised in prospective teaching appointments as well as in the parents; staff salaries quickly became the biggest single item of expenditure any school undertook and the fees charged had to reflect that fact.

The inevitable result of developments of this kind – always assuming that the product was saleable – was that the school's revenue increases, which means that capital expenditure can take place, which means that pupil numbers grow larger, which means that revenue increases, which means that....the virtuous cycle can take shape. It seems simple when written on paper, reflectively, in this way, but the everyday reality and the careful management of this phenomenon is not driven, in the long term, by stunningly fresh initiatives, even if such phases are characterised by shifting patterns such as 'boom and bust' and 'flavour of the month'. It is a complex, delicate, sensitive relationship driven by hard, economic realities coupled with human empathy; the two elements do not always have equal voices. Marketing can play a role but only for so long. Parents and pupils (and teachers for that matter) are not stupid. There has to be delivery. And, of course, the core aspect of the school should remain central, i.e. educational growth for the pupils. It is worth making one observation for the sake of continuity and for the sake of parents, pupils and staff. It is this: the success of the school should not be invested solely in the personality, even wisdom, of the Head Teacher, even if the appointment of the Head is probably the most important decision the Governors will ever make. Education is too important an area to be subject to charisma or the cult of personality or political trends or financial impulses. Independent education is an intoxicating anomaly that has created more good than harm in this country over the years, despite the clamouring voices, and, in this current age – as is the case with boarding - is having to justify far more vociferously than ever before a raison d'être of principle, which is supported so much more obviously in practice, than in previous years. It remains one of the ironies of twenty-first-century independent education that the processes and products today are arguably better than ever before, subject, as they are, to accountable and transparent inspections and compliances - which are genuinely welcome in today's climate - but alien to a previous age which might have existed only as recently as fifty years ago but certainly within living memory. Nowadays it is a case of carpets and breadth and hot-air balloons[73] as opposed to wooden floors and a narrow curriculum and P.T. in

---

[73] I mention 'hot-air balloons' unashamedly and gratuitously, in order to relate the following anecdote: not long after I became Headmaster, one Sunday evening at the start of term, the early returning boarders were playing on the front field in September sunshine when a hot-air balloon found its random way into our air-space and our open fields before deciding to land on the 1st XI Cricket Square. Not a decision to be taken lightly if one knew of the loving care which the groundsman below bestowed on those gardens and grounds. Nevertheless, the balloon kept plummeting. The noise of the charging flames, the sounds of the people above nestling in their basket, the cries of the children, the running cattle in the adjacent fields, the ringing of the phone call to the Headmaster's House saying 'what should we do', the abortive attempt of the Headmaster to drive off the premises thus avoiding having to make a decision, the sheer excitement and colour and typically eccentric English nature of the occasion, all contributed to a marvellous memory summed up by one new young boarder who turned to me, wide-eyed and intoxicated with pleasure, to say *"Thank you for arranging such a treat on my first day!"*. Naturally, I took the credit, even if I had to buy the groundsman a bottle of whisky as he subsequently levelled the Square so that it would take a googly.

the open air. But the management of the school should transcend and survive the changing Head Teachers even if their time as Head inevitably characterises certain trends and areas of focus over others. There is a case for a strong management team, or even two Heads, since it really might be true that 'two heads are better than one' especially if the lines of responsibility are clearly delineated say along academic/extra-curricular and marketing/development tracks. Indeed, that very concept was briefly considered in 2005. Despite the theoretical sense of such a suggestion – and despite the evidence of successful practice in the admittedly rare cases where two heads do, in fact, manage the school – this is an initiative, however, that is unlikely to become the norm.

So, the pre-prep had been started, pupil numbers were increasing and surpluses were being recorded in 1973 and a larger one in 1974, just a few years after the Governors were contemplating 'gloomy' times ahead. Alongside the increased income stream from encouraging revenue of this kind, the Governors decided to sell off one of the properties owned by the school known as the Gardener's Cottage which brought in a six-figure sum (in today's terms). In 1975, the surplus was 'higher than budgeted for' and in 1976 the surplus would have been equal to over £200000 in today's figures, largely due to the increase of fifteen boarders over expectations. Just ask the present Headmaster – or any boarding Headmaster – if he would like 'fifteen boarders over expectations'. With the pressure off, from a financial point of view, the school could afford to look at expansion plans. Mr Dix had relinquished his role as Principal in December 1973 (although Paul Ketterer, when he took over as Headmaster, had asked him to come out of teaching retirement to take on the senior Greek lessons) and the Governors were not slow to invite him to become a Governor, as well as employing him in the capacity of consultant, thus ensuring that his association with the school continued. It is a measure of Paul Ketterer's personal qualities and his understanding of the importance of continuity in managing change carefully that he was able to make the relationship work in the best interests of the school. It is a measure of Francis Dix that he could, at last, hand over his school to a worthy successor. Paul and Jean Ketterer developed a genuine respect and friendship with Mr and Mrs Dix which was to continue right up to the early 1980s when first Francis Dix, then his wife, Evelyn, died in 1983 and 1984 respectively. Whilst development plans were taking shape, it is important to note that as early as July 1973 the Governors were beginning to discuss the matter of 'maximum numbers' so as not to over-stretch the facilities. Remember, that in 1971, only two years earlier, the Governors had been advised of possible closure and were considering various radical ideas like selling the East Cranmore estate; but in 1973 the Governors were agreed that pupil numbers should not go above 176 because parental interest and pupil registrations were already of that order. Again, the statistics and reflections after the event tend to simplify the story but there can be no doubt that All Hallows is back on track under Paul Ketterer's stewardship with the strong and consistent backing of the Governing Body. Perhaps personality and charisma account for more than I have indicated.

In 1975, Lord Howard resigned from the Board and, in February 1976, the Governors "stood in remembrance of Rev. Dom N. W. Passmore whose funeral they had attended before *the meeting*". With Francis Dix now no longer Principal, three of the key people who had overseen the transfer of the school from a privately-owned concern into a business enterprise now with its third Headmaster, had all relinquished their crucial involvement. Abbot Passmore features significantly in the story of the school in his many interventions in Governors' meetings, as well as in his regular visits to the school to conduct chapel services or blessings of new buildings such as the Mortimer Science Block and the Headmaster's House. He also happened to be Abbot of Downside which inevitably dominated his life; the school has much to thank him for even if he was another character not instantly embraced by all.

The expansion and development of the school included a partial conversion of the Stable Block, the creation of three new tennis courts, one basketball court, one netball court and two hard cricket nets, as well as consideration being given to additional space needed for more boarders. Preliminary thoughts were given to the purchase of St James' Chapel[74], adjoining Scouts' Wood, whilst the Stable Block conversion plans continued unabated, wing by wing, as new classrooms were required. A salutary message to be kept in mind, however, was that even at this period of expansion, Paul Ketterer was warning Governors of the shrinking boarding market and the threat of falling numbers in the offing. For their part, the Governors advised Paul that he should tread carefully if he ever found himself in the position of having to raise the spectre of redundancies with staff, ensuring he had witnesses present to any such discussions. The message was clear: don't take your eye off the ball!

It might be pertinent, here, to make some observations about pupil numbers. Two points can be made. The first is more personal and applies to any of the Headmasters to date and to those who will come (incidentally, it is about time the school appointed a Headmistress – who

---

[74] St James' Chapel is an interesting story as far as the school is concerned since its position within the curtilage of the school suggests that it could easily and logically have been part of the All Hallows' story and yet it has never been owned or used by the school. Sir Richard Paget, when attending the Friends of All Hallows Meeting in 1988, explained to those members present that he wanted to give the chapel to Mr Dix in 1946 when the latter bought Cranmore Hall but the Church Commissioners had been unwilling for it to fall into Roman Catholic hands. The chapel duly fell into other private hands and it was de-commissioned as a place of worship. Better no worship than Catholic worship! When the school was close to buying the chapel from the owner of the time – one Tony Brockenshire – in 1978, and into 1979, for £18500, the governors were told by the Church Commissioners, that they could not use it as a place of worship (which had been their original intention) but even this did not deter them for there were new plans drawn up to convert it into changing rooms. The idea that boys would be responsible for creating the secular sporting smells associated with liniment, dubbin and sundry other embrocations in a place where incense may once have been the overriding odour of sanctity is an amusing one. As it happened, the owner refused to sell to the school – possibly as a result of his previous disputes about boundary limits and rights of access – and the successful purchasers – still the present owners - pressed ahead with determined and creative efforts to convert the chapel into a delightful residence and going on to be amenable neighbours thereafter. The wrangling in this quiet Somerset backwater over ownership and usage of a building edifice once in the hands of the ecclesiastical authorities has perhaps been played out similarly on a wider national scale at other times in the history of church and state in this green and pleasant land of ours. As it happens, the Chapel of St James would never have been the permanent solution for the growing school for any of its proposed needs so perhaps the Holy Spirit was guiding all parties with characteristic foresight beyond the wit of Man. It remains, however, a beautiful spiritual reminder of roots, religiosity and rural peace as one enters into the magical world of Scouts' Wood.

happens to 'know her stuff' when it comes to rugby, of course). The first point is simply this: no Head Teacher should spend his or her time becoming euphoric or depressed when pupil numbers rise or fall, nor spend sleepless nights worrying about 'what might happen'. The night time is a dangerous place and all professional efforts should be reserved for the sole purpose of sleeping. I am proud of myself that I made an early resolution in my own head - and with my wife, who needed more persuasion - to refuse to countenance any such extremes of emotion based on annual, even daily, trends. No Head worth his (or her) salt can operate in the best interests of the school if such considerations are allowed to dominate thinking. Sanity should prevail. In fact, my biggest nightly worry was about the possibility of an unplanned Fire Alarm. There had been a previous time when the Headmaster was informed at breakfast the following day that the previous night's fire drill had been handled successfully by the ever-on-duty Matron and that nobody or nothing had been burnt. I had the reluctant but messianic sense of guilt to install in the Headmaster's House a Fire Alarm linked to the school's system so that, if a 2.00am alarm should sound (and they did), I would be awakened like every other resident. I now believe that the technician responsible for fitting the alarm used to work for National Security on alarm systems designed to detect invasions from outer space or incoming apocalyptic comets flaming headlong to planet Earth because the klaxon fitted to my house would have woken Mr and Mrs Dix from their well-earned slumbers. Nevertheless, I prided myself on leaving out ready-made clothes each night into which I could step, rather like Clark Kent in a handy telephone booth, in about thirty seconds flat. Sometimes, it has to be said, I might even have practised the changing routine in the daytime (now you know what I did when I couldn't be found) in order to shave off a second or two. The brilliant result of such preparation was that I turned up invariably as the second person 'on duty' (after, of course, the formidable Matron) and the slumbering, shuffling bodies of boarding pupils and staff, in their disarray, would wonder at my immaculately, bright-eyed appearance so late/early into the night/morning. The myth that I never slept and the myth that I was always alert, working for the good of the school, was one I was happy to engender, even though I alone – and Matron, of course, - knew in advance when the Fire Alarm was due to disturb the somnolent souls of All Hallows.

The second point about pupil numbers concerns the school. Governors and Head Teachers and Staff and Parents (through consultation) should have some opportunity to express their opinions about optimum class sizes, ideal year-group numbers and total school roll. This is not just a matter of pragmatics, important though these are. This is about ethos, tradition, history and the future. It goes to the soul of the school. Remember that All Hallows began in 1938 with one pupil. There was an alarming, facile perception in the 1980s, I think it was, that 'bigger and more' was better. I don't just mean All Hallows or education – it was a prevailing mood. We all know – don't we – that the corner Post Office or the local Butcher were worth more than stamps and meat? This point comes back to the uniqueness of the individual and 'knowing thy name', two principles entirely in keeping with a Christian – nay, Catholic – nay humanistic - view of humankind. I return to an earlier admonition: those responsible for the future of All Hallows, at least, should consider carefully the number of pupils and staff and parents it should embrace as ideal limits. We could, of course, buy up land and property in order to accommodate 1000 pupils and create supporting systems to make such ambition tenable but there is a reason why no such prep school exists in this country. And there is probably not a fire alarm system invented by man that would support such numbers even if the technicians have worked for NASA.

I am conscious of the fact that I have rather broadened the text a little and fast-forwarded into the mid-1970s without referencing what has arguably been the single biggest 'item for consideration' by all parties associated with the school - especially the boys - and that is, of course, the introduction of girls!

Co-education or mixed education has been a source of debate for many years with traditional proponents of single-sex schools being able to offer cogent and compelling reasons why their own particular (some might say 'peculiar') status quo should be preserved. Single-sex schools today will still put forward similarly persuasive logic as to why their preference or 'brand' remains viable. Perhaps the clue is in the word 'brand' for independent education is nothing if it does not offer choice and variety. The simple fact is that good schools thrive and prosper for reasons not especially connected to whether they are co-educational or single-sex, any more than that they are successful because they are day or boarding, or rural or town, or large or small, or faith-based or not, or for any other similarly opposed forces one might care to mention. The Greek philosopher Plato asserted that co-education creates a feeling of comradeship and he advocated, even in his time, teaching males and females together in the same institution in order to develop personality. In the twentieth century, however, some male professors at universities felt that women were incapable of higher education and a prevailing view of the time was that boys and girls learn differently. It is an interesting fact that few of our sophisticated and detailed lesson plans today make specific differentiation for boys and girls – on the basis of their gender – when determining how we can best meet the needs of the pupils and yet virtually every other possible distinction is drawn. The fact remains, however, that many single-sex schools have chosen to embrace the co-educational approach, as we all fall headlong into the modern world, and although the cynics will say that it has been for reasons of commerce in that such schools have simply wanted more pupils to offset a falling roll and that the early days of such transformations only saw lip-service, conditional forays, into this brave new world, it cannot be denied that the reluctant experiments, the tentative initiatives and the principled convictions have been successful. I know of no single-sex school that, on going 'co-educational', has failed. I suspect that the 'nay-sayers' will now realise that impassioned protests at the time were based more on emotion and on the traditions of the past rather than the objective pragmatics of the present-day or the visionary demands of a future changing society or, even, the rational good sense of well-reasoned argument. I mean to say, for heaven's sake, it is not impossible to believe that one day there might be a female Prime Minister of the United Kingdom! Let us hope that Margaret Thatcher's example does not remain on the statute book as an interesting but flawed experiment akin to the 1971 landing on the Moon. Let's hear it for another female Prime Minister; let's hear it for another Moon landing; let's hear it for a female Head Teacher of All Hallows! We many male Headmasters in touch with our anima have always acknowledged, after all, that it is our wives who have run the show; even Evelyn Dix propelled the school forward in Devon in 1939 whilst her husband carried on teaching in his classical world at Avisford. Mrs Mortimer, Mrs Ketterer, Mrs Bird and Mrs Murphy similarly took up the torch, like many other 'Headmaster's Wives' across the country, for whom no suitable Job Description has yet been written and with whom no man would want to mess. Readers will realise that all of this enthusiasm is just about me ensuring I get a Full English breakfast on a Sunday morning (see 'Headmasters' Wives' on pp 305ff).

Nevertheless, there can be no doubt that All Hallows was in the forefront of independent education when it made its own move into the female world. Let us not forget, however, that Alistair Mortimer espoused the wisdom of accepting girls into the school in the late 1960s and the Governors considered his proposals alongside the equally ground-breaking ideas of moving the school to Bristol and accepting weekly boarders for the first time. Set those recommendations of girl pupils, in 1971 (even the late 1960s), against the fact that Prior Park opened its doors to girls in the early 1980s, Clifton in 1987, King's Bruton in the early 1990s, The Dragon School, Oxford, in 1994 (boarders, that is), Stonyhurst in 1999, Ampleforth in 2002, and Downside – after 400 years of boys – in 2005 and one can begin to appreciate the 'cutting-edge' vision of All Hallows! Millfield, as in many things, remained an example of a local exception, an anomaly, since it accepted girls in 1939, after only four years since its foundation, by the charismatic "Boss" Meyer. Mind you, it should be noted that Jack Meyer opened his Millfield school in 1935 with just seven Indian boys, six of whom were princes (the princesses were obviously just waiting to arrive later) – but that is another story.

In October 1967, All Hallows had achieved a record number of pupils – all boys – of 142; in March 1969 Mr Dix was recorded as being *"very much in favour"* (of girls) although with the proviso that there would be *"no more than about five or six"* and that they should be sisters of boys already in the school. A Patrician concession, methinks. The Governors of the time endorsed the liberalism and the caution in equal measure: girls could be considered, as day pupils, perhaps even as weekly boarders (the implication remaining that full boarders was a step too far). Mr Mortimer, not for the first time, kept a more open mind *"we could accommodate 20 girls even as boarders"* and in June 1969 he was writing in his Crane editorial that *"tentative moves should be made towards the introduction of girls at All Hallows"*. He felt that the public schools would follow the lead of the preparatory schools if girls were to be introduced at the younger age-level. Tracking these possible developments through the Governors' Minutes of the time, we read that *"everyone was waiting for the first girl to be signed up"* but that, even then, the potentially detrimental effects were there for all to see: in October 1969 one boy was 'lost' because of *"the possibility of girls"*. A slippery slope beckoned. How many Headmasters occupied the outer circles of Dante's Inferno because they had embraced the concept of educating girls? Parents, however, were broadly in favour but still nobody wanted to be the first. March

1970 arrived and the first girl of the modern era had been registered to start in September 1975 and Mr Mortimer wanted the governors to push the fact of girls a little bit more. But it is clear that high-level discussions about the possible advent of girls were taking place since fee reductions were being considered for brothers and *sisters* in the school and in July 1971 the Governors were keen to invite Paul Ketterer to take up the reins in order to recruit more day boys and day girls. And we know that girls officially started in 1972. They may have made a mark at that time – history does not record the fact – but the Governors' Minutes continue tacitly complicit in a seeming reluctance to mention girls too loudly, perhaps because they were simply 'honorary boys' after all, since those next few years blithely referred to the boarding and day *boy* fees as if girls had never really arrived. There was even the sharp contradiction in June 1974 when *day boy fees* only were set, yet again, alongside the Minute that one netball court had been created! It wasn't until June 1976 that records indicated "day fees" as opposed to fees for boys. '*Boarding girls*' were not mentioned in the Minutes, despite the fact they had been in the school for five years, until October 1977. Nevertheless, the growth must have been rapid and significant for in 1979 there were 19 girl leavers out of a total of 47 with ten further girl registrations signed up for the following September making that year's breakdown as follows: Boarding Boys 96, Boarding Girls 43, Day Boys 38, Day Girls 32. Of those 209 pupils, 75 were girls or approximately 36%. Furthermore, in the summer term of 1975 one notes that there were Girls' Athletics fixtures against Kingdown and an Under-14 Girls' encounter in tennis and swimming with Edgarley Hall. In the Lent Term 1973 there were ten recorded names of girls in the school in the persons of Felicity Finlayson (who went on to become the first Head Girl in 1974), Andrea Murphy, Linda Rogers, Caroline Cavendish-Eyre, Maria Page, Elizabeth Norden, Monica Norden, Annalisa Page, Fiona White and one Karen Jackson, daughter of John, the latter girl all of 4.1 years of age. Siobhan Fitzpatrick, Anne-Marie Foulquies, Ariane Picard all joined the school in the summer 1973 and were placed in St Margaret's dormitory thus representing about 10% of the school roll. But, just in case any of these girls become carried away with themselves and we hear of those who would like to lay claim as to being 'the first girl' let us not forget that girls enrolled in the school in Bognor days for extended holiday stays and there were certainly girl pupils at Scorhill in Moyra Bateman from Batworthy and Mimi Pellew (later Lady Iddesleigh) who spent a year at Scorhill, as recorded in the 20th July 1954 Chronicle. Mimi went on to marry Viscount St Cyres an Old Gregorian in 1955, we think, and it is noted that her brother, the Honourable Peter Pellew, joined AH on 19th January 1955.

But, for the record, the school will stand by its introduction 'proper' of girls into the school as 1972, and, as a matter of conviction (rather than for reasons of recruitment against a falling roll), that co-education was the natural milieu in which boys and girls could learn together.

Equally, for the record, it is worth noting that in this current year of 2013 there are 145 girls in the school (to 166 boys) and that in four of the nine year groups there are more girls than boys and that – probably for the first time – whisper it sotto voce - there are more girl boarders than boy boarders. Equality does not seem to have caught on amongst the saintly dormitories, however, since the girls are currently housed in St Hugh's, St Joseph's, St David's, St Andrew's and St Thomas More's although 'St Margaret's' did make a brief appearance in 1973. To conclude this particular section on girls, I'd like to relate the gist of a telephone conversation I had a few years ago from a slightly perplexed Headmaster of a Monastic school not too far away from All Hallows. They had taken in girls after a centuries-old tradition of boys and had possibly underestimated the effect such a change would have on, shall we say, the dynamics of the school. I remember thinking, when that particular school advertised its intentions, that the slick marketing would have to be supported by some pretty slick after-sales service. Sometimes the slick after-sales service is provided by the simplest of solutions.

Headmaster	*Ah....yes....Chris....hello...um....how do you .....cope.....with...how can I put it?....um.... girls?*
CB	*Father....that's easy.....I don't. I hand over all girl matters to my wife.*
Headmaster	*Ah....yes....good point...I see... (pause)... but I can't very well do that, can I, because I don't have a wife?*
CB	*No, Father, but I'm sure you'll find a way.*
Headmaster	*I don't suppose...*
CB	*No, Father.*
Headmaster	*Yes....thank you...um...I must have a think...Goodbye*

Sure enough – for the undoubted benefit of the girls - he found a way and no, he didn't suddenly get married[75] or borrow my wife; he simply employed some experienced female staff who had once been girls[76]. Where would we be without them? God bless them every one!

So, the dance goes on, girls and all!

Through the mid to late 1970s and into the 1980s, All Hallows continued to grow in pupil numbers, expansionist plans and reputation. Paul Ketterer knew about continuity with the past, and about the need to manage tradition and creative innovation in a carefully timed, sympathetic, yet pragmatic way. Stable courtyards looked good but let's put people in there. Dormer windows grew out of hay lofts; vegetable gardens sprouted sports courts; classrooms

---

[75] Mind you, Pope Adrian IV (died 1159) fathered two children on the grounds that he was meant to enjoy life since God had elevated him to the Papacy.

[76] As Dr Johnson's Dictionary didn't say: ***Girl. N. An exceedingly complex and powerful member of the human race.***

were created in colonnades. In July 1977 a six-figure surplus (converted to today's figures) was achieved and similar revenues enabled ongoing projects to be considered (although such returns were not repeated in some harder years ahead), so that prudent financial management could enable further developments to take place (conversions, dining room, sports facilities) whilst also establishing a healthy bank balance in order for confidence to be instilled. An Appeal Fund was launched in 1979 with a view to buying the Old Chapel of St James and parents supported various specific or general capital projects in a similarly generous and far-sighted manner thereafter. One does not wish to diminish the problems but they were more likely, in these years, to be connected to snow, influenza, dangerous cedars in the school grounds, even a small electrical fire, than any potentially life-altering concerns. But roof repairs became necessary and staff salaries continued to rise and capital projects (like the purchase of the Chapel of St James) did not always come off. It was not all about money, of course. There was a school to be run, an educational establishment that required academic management. In October 1977, succumbing to pressure from parental enquiries, Paul Ketterer circulated a serious questionnaire to parents canvassing their collective views on extending the school leaving age to sixteen in order to accommodate O-Level teaching. The Day Parents came out in favour and the parents of Boarding Girls could be persuaded but the parents of Boarding Boys were against any such proposals and, since they provided over 60% of the fees-income, their views prevailed. The idea of keeping pupils through to O-Levels or GCSE, as it is now known, has been mooted in more recent times, occasionally, by parents but in a slightly more light-hearted manner as a way of expressing their child's happiness at the school, and, in any case, the educational structure of the Key Stages doesn't really support what would be quite a radical change. It could be argued that pupils could stay for one more year in order to complete Key Stage Three as Year Nine pupils but that would have complex ramifications for Common Entrance and Scholarship exams. Equally, a number of schools in a geographical region would have to agree to follow suit in order to maintain a working fixture list on the sports field, not to mention senior schools having to agree to lose the potential income of their Year Nine cohort. If there are to be any changes that might be promulgated regarding the constitution of the 'Prep' schools, they are more likely to be concerned with ending at the end of Key Stage Two in Year Six, especially with the recent developments in 'pre-assessments' well before Year Eight, and, it should be noted, there are many independent schools that operate under this system at present. But, for traditional mainstream preparatory schools that is a potential development schools should resist.

The Governors, generally, took a keen enough interest in the school's achievements and 'everyday' preoccupations, even if the Minutes of meetings, as recorded, appear to be mostly concerned with business, finance, pupil numbers, revenue, capital expenditure and development. Having prepared for and sat through many such meetings, I can vouch for the fact that the Governors genuinely wanted to know about the 'everyday stuff' even if, it seems, that their comments seemed to stray towards the sports field rather than the academic performances. Perhaps the sports field was an obvious and easy target for the uninitiated and experts alike.

GEORGE SIMEY

(F.P. 1944-1950; Chairman of Governors 1968-1977)

George Simey started his All Hallows' life as a boarding pupil in September 1944 and he was still a Governor of the school in 1996, having served as Chairman for nine years through the Mortimer/Ketterer handover and assuming principal responsibility for managing the fluctuating fortunes of the school at that time. George features in school photographs as a large, friendly boy who passed very well into Downside in 1950. As a Governor, George brought his legal training to bear in handling many school matters, and his deep-rooted love of the school, which included all due recognition of the everyday concerns like cakes and courtesies and congratulations, as well as his measured judgement, ensured that his interest remained a positive force for good throughout his time.

"*All Hallows wins National Tournament*" tends to capture the public imagination rather more easily than "*Record Number of Scholarships at local Prep School*". I may be wrong – it has been known – but I suspect that there are many 'stakeholders' (aaarrrggghhh!) who would make any number of correlated deductions about the health of a school based on its sports results as opposed to its academic record. The two are not, of course, mutually exclusive and it happens to be my experience that the best sports teams tend to include quite a few players at the upper end of the academic spectrum, even if it is equally true that some of the best sporting pupils have found the academic lessons something of an interruption. I can certainly remember one All Hallows' second-row forward, who had only been selected for the first team for a school rugby team when he reached his final year, becoming really surprised when I replied "Yes" to his question: "Can we jump off the ground in the lineout?" I found it easier to tell him that he could jump at 'Two' and again at ten-past and then at half-past and so on and so on…. (a rugby joke for those who know). And then, of course, there was Will – a formidable wing three-quarter - who needed to be pointed in the right direction before taking off at great speed and leaving all would-be tacklers in his wake. Will once amused his Games master by spending most of the match running round the games field wailing because nobody would pass to him but he did go on to win a gold medal in the National Athletics Championships and, in 2012, as an adult, narrowly lost out on a place in the Belgium Olympic Team. The occasional chain-jumping Paul

Ketterer may not have been the most obvious champion of sport but he knew a good marketing opportunity when he saw one. He appointed Staff and developed systems and supported fixture lists that demanded the highest aspirations. One thinks of Moira Thompson, Sandra Gadsden, Katie Johnson-Jones and others on the girls' side, as well as Tony Rolt[77], Roger Smeardon[78], Robin Durant[79], Peter Booth[80] and others on the boys' front who all made their mark through dedication, enthusiasm, discipline and determination. Both at the time, and subsequently, their example and legacy was supported by the likes of Sue Kirby, Jayne Knowles[81], Ann Lydon, Pip Davies, Sammi Stride, Mary Brown, Peter Scotland, Dave Fuszard, John Murphy, David Clarke, Greg Jones, Mike Walsh, Shaun Phillips, Chris Godwin, John-Paul Renouf, Chris Bird, Mark Kennedy, Ian Murphy, Jody Wells, James Callow, Ben Coombes, Owen Lucas, Kevin Hanratty, Joe Emsley and so on and so on. In amongst that lot are international athletes, first-class rugby players, coaches of teams and individuals of the highest order, as well as experienced practitioners from up and down the country and across the games spectrum. Fixture lists took on schools like Millfield, The Downs, Sherborne, Clifton, Colston's, King Edward's Bath, and various tournaments were entered including the Rosslyn Park Sevens (semi- finalists in the inaugural year; about time we won it!), the National Catholic Sevens at The Oratory (at which we have won The Governors' Cup for non-aligned schools), local, regional and national competitions in hockey and gymnastics (in which we have been Champions and Finalists many times). Paul Ketterer might have found it easier to manage the female games staff than the male games staff, over the years – for it was a source of frustration, it has to be said, when it became administratively easier to cancel Games at 11.00 in the morning because of 'wet weather

---

[77] Tony Rolt was perhaps the second-finest teaching rugby coach I have encountered in a personal rugby-playing career that spans nearly fifty years (Elwyn Price of Saint Brendan's sits at the top of the pantheon) and he played an influential, charismatic role at All Hallows before becoming Director of Sport at Trent College (even if he did wear dodgy shorts); John-Paul Renouf pushes him close for the second spot, as does Jack Rowell, and they, it has to be said, never wore dodgy shorts. Sonia Ketterer remembers a daring gymnastics display in the late 1970s coordinated by Tony Rolt when he had pupils jumping off the roof outside a dormitory window some two floors above the Headmaster's Study, onto a trampoline on the Library Lawn, to undertake a few tucks and somersaults, etc, as you do, before running through to the middle of the lawn, bouncing on another trampette and vaulting the stone urn in the middle of the manicured grass. Health and Safety! What's that?

[78] Roger Smeardon was a 'visiting' coach from Downside who probably achieved greater fame on those particular playing fields but still left a considerably positive impact on the rugby at All Hallows.

[79] Robin Durant had a marvellous temperament, marvellous moustache and marvellous way with children, a fantastic rapport with his dog, Basil, but perhaps not always the best relationship with the Headmaster of the time; he went off to forage about in the foothills of Mount Kilimanjaro, I seem to remember. Where else do Games Masters go?

[80] Peter Booth was an international athlete in his own right, an inspirational coach, excellent administrator, who didn't 'get' Shakespeare, but who became a good friend, nevertheless, and who followed me professionally to Cricklade, Wiltshire, where we enjoyed hugely important formative times in several ancient coaching inns; we have sadly lost touch since.

[81] Jayne Knowles, Ann Lydon and Pip Davies were as fine a trio of coaches of Girls' Games as one could wish for and their sporting successes are legendary. Each, in their own ways, contributed distinctive and dedicated styles to the girls' development, as well as insisting on the highest standards of sportsmanship and courtesy established so firmly by Moira Thompson.

conditions' even though the Cranmore sun beat down at 2 o'clock in the afternoon whilst all the boys and girls were undergoing 'early prep'- but, nevertheless, the sporting stories of the school in their breadth of achievement, and in certain specialisms, compare well with other similar schools. Paul Ketterer might also, have found it easier motivating the pupils rather than the staff for most of his career – although there will be plenty of examples of both cohorts who think otherwise - but such an observation reflects as much, perhaps, on the individuals concerned, as on the Headmaster. It is never easy 'taking sides' between two core elements of a school – teachers and Headmaster – which are supposed to be pulling together but which, in reality, often occupy different places in the trench and, as for the pupils, - well – they are rarely in the same zone as the Headmaster.

Moira Thompson deserves a special box of her own (see right).

Sport had achieved a status of its own – particularly in Girls' Games and Gymnastics during these years – and it had been given a greater prominence in the building of the Sports Hall, opened in 1985 by the England and Harlequin Rugby Player and Coach Mike Davis.

Other reflections of the early 1980s, based on personal experience (since I spent five years at All Hallows between 1980-1985) include the following observations......

It gave the impression of being a 'modern' school. Admittedly, I had arrived from two years of living and teaching in my first full-time post in a privately-run, fully boarding school in Berkshire where all pupils were referred to by their surnames and where Harris i and later Harris ii were taught in small classes named 'Remove' by octogenarians or former colonial masters of the empire who sported walrus moustaches and smoking jackets, if not guns (those days are definitely for another story). But All Hallows in the 1980s was well-established, well-run (like a military machine) and well-regarded. There was a vibrant, professional Common Room with interesting and amusing schoolmaster characters like Peter Scotland who taught French to reluctant schoolboys even if he often felt his pupil-charges were *"not like other men"*. He it was who used to bemoan the fact that, in his view, he did *"all the work and they don't bring home the bacon"*. I joined the French Department briefly – even delivering the subject to Common Entrance – and he generously never commented upon my strange accent which must have seemed like a foreign language all of its own. Still, the pupils passed their CE under my care even if tapes recorded for their Orals needed some deciphering from decryption experts who might otherwise have worked at Bletchley Park. Mind you, quite what the Head of French at the relevant senior school made of one pupil some ten years later or so whose answers to Madame Doe-Wansey's beautifully phrased questions came back in perfect English but with an 'Allo, Allo' accent, complete with unseen but expansive hand-gestures, as in *"I 'ave twooo bruvvers and threeee seesters.."* we shall never know; (the story is better told aloud). Peter Scotland was a real gentleman; an old-fashioned schoolmaster with high standards; acceptably pedantic about the correct application of grammar and punctuation; interested in rugby; brewer of his own good, strong ale; purveyor of great good humour; wearer of a different tie every day of the year; well-practised dodger of Headmasters in case he was asked to do something; all in all, a

MOIRA THOMPSON

(A.H. 1987-1998; 1949-1998 RIP)

Moira was first employed as a temporary sports coach who made such a strong impression so quickly that Paul Ketterer was able to offer her a permanent and wider-ranging brief to develop the Girls' Games Department which led onto elite gymnastics coaching and an overseeing role as Director of Sport. Moira had already enjoyed a distinguished sporting background of her own and remained very modest about her own involvement in sport although she had once coached Merlene Ottey – the Jamaican world-famous athlete – in her formative years. Under her leadership, the Girls' Games programme saw unprecedented success in all areas of team sports. Gymnastics, in particular, flourished under her expert guidance with different teams winning national and regional championships regularly. Moira organised the most breath-taking gymnastics displays every year which became regular showcases of talent from the very youngest pupils to the more senior. In a Thanksgiving Service in December 1998 held at the Chapel of All Saints at the school, Headmaster Chris Bird made the following comments… *"Moira was always very modest about her successes but always seeking to improve the children's talents and performances. It is worth dwelling on those successes. Most sports coaches taste success in some form or another at some time, particularly in the natural order of things when one was lucky enough to have a strong year with gifted pupils. Moira's successes as a sports coach were different and they elevated her to another plane in the pantheon of teachers. Firstly, she was consistently excellent. They were no flashes in the pan; they happened year after year. Secondly, her achievements were exceptional and took her onto the national stage. It was her firm belief – which subsequently spawned an article in The Times – that Gymnastics was the foundation of so many other sports, as well as creating a sense of individual worth and confidence, in its focus on poise, strength, agility, balance and team work. And Moira, herself, had those attributes in abundance. I believe, however, that the true extent of her excellence is measured in the vast numbers of pupils who achieved a kind of excellence of their own in terms of their own more limited abilities perhaps defined by their more modest potential. Moira might have invented the notion of 'sport for all' long before it became a catch-phrase in the politics of education. Moira wrought these developments in young people and achieved these successes in many ways – enthusiasm, knowledge, skill, communication, organisational flair, motivation – but there were two principal strands to her approach: (1) she demanded the highest standards and had the highest expectations (2) she gave unstintingly of her time….she had no time for shirkers and she would not accept a lack of confidence in those who were shy of pushing themselves forward but she only drove on pupils whom she knew were capable of better. I remember encountering her, one Monday lunchtime, after the Sunday when her gymnasts had just won the National Championships, working patiently in the gym in her regular session with those children who had difficulty with physical movement and co-ordination. Such was her dedication to all children and her sense of perspective. To her colleagues, Moira will be remembered as an uncomplainingly, loyal, even-tempered friend whose sense of humour endeared her to us all. And yet she remained essentially shy, forever modest, certainly, about her achievements, fiercely protective of her pupils and passionate about the ethos behind All Hallows."*

She became ill towards the end of her time at All Hallows but coped bravely and with her customary good humour throughout that time. She made her final visit to the school at the Craft Fair in December, which was an event Moira had first conceived and arranged, and she died within a few weeks of that visit. She leaves behind the firmest foundation of sporting prowess and a lasting legacy, in the minds and hearts of those who knew her, of a decent human being.

much-loved colleague. The Common Room was full of strong characters, excellent and caring teachers and a good-humoured bonhomie which added to the stimulation of working in such an environment. Eve Jackson, Rob and Anne-Scott Ward, Greg Jones (see further details below), David Clarke, Dave Fuszard, Robin Durant, Jenny Elliott, and others, all added to the richness of life.

GREG JONES
(Head of Science)

Greg spent over twenty years at the school as Head of Science and Games Master from the early 1970s until 1995. He was a wholly committed member of staff who made the school his life. He was larger than life in his physical presence and his excitable, emotional nature which was always dedicated to the pupils in his charge. Whenever the snow came down, Greg would walk into school from Frome. He was a living example of a man who would do anything for anyone. His organisational skills and administrative efficiency were phenomenal; the Science Laboratory was catalogued, categorised and coordinated like a nuclear submarine and I have never seen a neighbour's garage so lovingly ordered either – he could have run Bristol Airport from his garage. Greg cared hugely about the pupils. He worked tirelessly on projects that did not always bear fruition, for example, designing a DT Centre where the present Art Room is currently situated, and his enthusiasm was unbounded. He built pretty much single-handed (with just a little ham-fisted help from the writer) the ambitious Adventure Playground mentioned above with great technical prowess and strength. Greg was a formidable rugby player in his own right and his coaching techniques belonged to that school of thought that believed a kick up the backside was probably the best incentive any boy could expect. If Greg occasionally blundered in where elephants fear to tread, his wife, Sheila, provided a gentler source of wisdom and also taught Science in the school, even, briefly, heading up the department before joining Greg after his departure to The Blue School in Birmingham where he was able to continue his pastoral care of children as a boarding Housemaster. Sheila, together with a willing group of pupils, planted the hedgerow which grows so splendidly on the front field along the lane towards West Cranmore. Greg and Sheila's two sons, Richard and Christopher, also excelled during their time as pupils at All Hallows. It is not surprising that one occasionally hears of pupils on Facebook sharing memories of their favourite teachers and recalling the name of Greg Jones on a regular basis.

One was able to teach one's subject in those days without interference from external agencies or from the Headmaster; Paul Ketterer made his appointments, trusted his judgements and let us get on with it. That is not to say, however, that one's teaching time was never interrupted by what Paul saw as higher administrative needs. If some aspects of routine – like sheet-changing – needed attention, all other niceties like allowing lessons to start on time were shunted sideways. The PFJK memos that appeared in our pigeon-holes or hand-delivered notes to our classrooms announcing the fact that there would be a 'Line-Up' south of the Cran Wall at Morning Break meant one could linger over one's coffee with impunity, confident in the knowledge that one's pupils would be otherwise engaged for an hour. Duty Staff were needed to attend the said 'Line-Ups' (although I suppose Peter Scotland would have called them 'Lines-Up). I mentioned 'sheet-changing' because memory doesn't seem to move beyond that particular aspect of boarding school life which Paul somehow turned into a mystifying process designed to test the brain-power of Einstein thus rendering the whole process rather more complicated than simply putting one's dirty sheets into the laundry basket. The pupils would line-up in their Year Groups, 'vertically', as it were, so that the naughty ones would be standing at the back of the line, or, sometimes 'horizontally', sitting on the Cran Wall, so that the oldest pupil in Form Six (Year Eight now in the nomenclature of National Curriculum years) would be far away to the Headmaster's left and the youngest pupil in Form One would be fidgeting someway off to West Cranmore village on the headmaster's right. Paul believed in fresh air. And in shouting instructions. Now, if there is one thing one learns in Teacher Training College it is that you never overload children with information. One should speak in simple sentences. Use vocabulary that can be understood by a dog. After silence had been achieved (this could take some time - not because Paul had no disciplinary presence but because he insisted on total, unwavering attention which usually required him calling out twenty or thirty names in admonishment before delivering his message), came the instructions....

"Right, it's been brought to my attention by Matron that some children don't seem to know the rules and are not following the correct procedures which are typed in three separate places in prominent positions on the dormitory landings, in the Linen Room and in the Main Cortile."
At this point, the youngest child is whispering to his neighbour "What's the Cortile?" and some of the older boys are trying to shoot each other with sticks picked up from the Library Lawn on their way to the Line-Up.
"Now we all know the rules, don't we? They're very simple," continues the Headmaster.
The Duty Staff are now looking down nervously at their feet in case Paul asks one of them to explain the rules and wishing they had read them in their prominent places on the dormitory landings and the Linen Room and the Main Cortile (where was that blessed 'cortile'?). I asked that question once and was informed it was through the Housemaids' entrance, outside the bain-marie, just before one stepped into the north-west corner of the stable courtyard. I was none the wiser.
"Sheet-changing. It's very simple. After you have been dismissed from here in height order, pick up your empty grundy bags from Miss Treanor, walk – don't run, go up to your dormitories via the principal route used in the event of fire (unless you are in T-More dormitory in which case you will use the back, wooden staircase), make sure you have your clean duvet covers from Matron, blue for boys and red for girls, stand at the foot of your beds and change your dirty duvet covers first, then your sheets and then your pillow-cases, but only do your duvet covers and sheets if you were one of the dorms who changed your pillow-cases on Tuesday. Fill

your grundy-bags with old socks and place them in a pile in the correct order in the south-east corner of the dormitory landing before going back to your dorms to collect up your old sheets and pillow-cases and duvets making sure they're NOT inside out then deposit the bundle in the Linen Room via the old drying corridor, if you are a boy or if you are in St Hugh's dormitory, and via the Small Cortile, if you are a girl or if you are using the back wooden stairs."

Now, the small boy is freaking out having discovered there is a Small Cortile.

"Right, any questions?"

One brave hand goes up. *"What do we pick up from Miss Treanor, Sir?"*

"LOOK! It's very simple…after you have been dismissed from here in height order, pick up your empty grundy bags from Miss Treanor…" and Paul would deliver exactly the same message from start to finish in perfect word-order in just a slightly irritated tone until the next question forced him to do the same thing all over again in a much louder voice – and more quickly – quite exasperated at the pupils' inability to follow simple instructions that had been triplicated on the dormitory landings and the Linen Room and in the Main Cortile, for heaven's sake!

The next day, we would have a Line-Up about shoe-cleaning (and Paul would check the back of the shoes on the grounds that anybody can quickly rub the front on one's socks or trousers but the polished backs would indicate that the shoes really had been cleaned).

But All Hallows was a well-run school. Not only would it have earned three-times over the old HMI accolade of being 'efficient', its efficiency meant that the school was clean, the living spaces well-ordered, the food sufficient, the health of the children (and staff) in good hands, the resources well-maintained, the estate well-managed, the finances well-ordered. It was a good place to be, a good place in which to live and work and play. Boarders and Resident Staff woke up every morning to a delightful setting and day pupils and staff arrived each day with a subconscious – if not more obvious – realisation that there were unlovelier places in the world in which to grow up or make a living. Jean Ketterer, of course, made many such perceptions possible with her unstinting support of the school, partly, at times, no doubt, in keeping Paul sane and sensible (qualities needed in all good Headmasters' wives), but mostly in her own right with her overview of catering, house-keeping and welfare of the school. Jean was also bringing up four children of her own and exuded a sense of grace and fragrant equilibrium as an antidote to the sense of rising storm that could occasionally emanate from the Headmaster's Study. Perhaps one should write a book about the storms that rise from Headmasters' Studies when all about them remains actually really calm and the birds still sing and the world keeps turning regardless.

There was something about the Christian character of the school which also left its mark. Most visitors and those who passed through the school either fleetingly or for longer periods of time felt something of this characteristic nature which is best expressed in Paul Ketterer's own words of the intermingling of Christian witness with daily life. The sacramental life of the school was important and the visiting priests and monks played their part but the daily routines of prayer and assemblies imposed, almost surreptitiously, a mostly successful stamp upon proceedings; one could not help but feel that people cared about each other.

Jamie Bradley was a confident, excellently-humoured, popular Director of Music who brought another mark of sanity to school life, and spent a good deal of her time teaching in the Dix Room which, previously, had been used as a dining-room, and now is known as the Dix Music Room, used, principally, as a meeting room for the Headmaster.

Paul Ketterer conducting lunch   *Jamie Bradley conducting the orchestra*

That Christian character of the school, mentioned above, also shone very deeply in the person of Jamie Bradley's successor, Roger Bevan..... (see box overleaf)

Another developing characteristic of All Hallows, also, in the 1980s was the advent of pupils from Spain. Many independent schools cultivated strong links with students and families from abroad and although these associations are sometimes considered as slightly cynical, marketing exercises to maintain pupil numbers and increase revenue, the links we have had with Spain from the time of Paul Ketterer up until the present day (that is, fully thirty years and more) have proved to be one of the most productive and positive developments of the school. I believe it all started in the 1970s with pupils like Antonio Valdes (1975) Sandra and Maria Perez-Juez (1981) and Gonzalo de Rivera (1981) and continued with Lourdes Huarte (1984) who arrived at the school as a charming, confident and stylish young lady who made an instant impression and established through her family and friends a growing network of other Spanish families interested in sending their children to an English school, ostensibly to learn the language, but also to develop personal strengths and cultural links which would serve them well in later life. Lourdes' brother, Javier, and sister, Elena, followed in 1986 and 1988 respectively. Later families included the likes of Jaime Urquijo Zobel de Ayala (Jaime is now an analyst on Wall Street and plays rugby for the Philippines national team as a strapping flanker having been introduced to rugby at All Hallows), and his sisters, Paloma and Monica. Jaime's mother, Bea Zobel, Jr, and her mother, as well as other members of the family, are generous and active philanthropists in the Philippines and elsewhere. It is a failure

ROGER BEVAN
(Director of Music at All Hallows until 1994; 1918-1998 RIP)

Roger Bevan died at the age of seventy-nine after a long career as a schoolmaster at both Downside and All Hallows, principally as the Choirmaster and Director of Music at both schools in his time. He was born into an Anglican clerical family in Middlesex as the First World War came to an end and for some time it was presumed that he would follow his father and grandfather into the Church of England but, after university at Oxford, and then Westcott House, Cambridge, he met the Catholic Chaplain Father Alfred Gilbey, read Cardinal Newman's writings and decided to become a Roman Catholic. Not long after, he met and married Cecilia 'Mollie' Baldock who shared his life for the next fifty years until her death in 1992. Together, Roger and Mollie brought into the world fourteen children who eventually formed 'The Bevan Family Choir' and many of those children, now grown-up, can be found in parishes and schools around Somerset and beyond, conducting choirs, singing, playing the organ and teaching, as a lasting human legacy to their father's love of music. Roger himself, however, said that he had enjoyed teaching most and that he was *"not a musician in the truest sense of the word…I only enjoy music to the full when I am taking part or conducting it myself"*. In fact, Roger and Mollie has started up a choir school of their own called 'St Mary's and St Benedict's' when Roger, perhaps only half-jokingly, said that the three elements of a good education were 'the Bible, Kennedy's Latin Primer and the cane'. Few people in education begin their teaching career as a Headmaster. No wonder he fitted in to the worlds of Downside and All Hallows although by those times the world was already changing! The Daily Telegraph, in its obituary of Roger, relates the anecdote that one of Roger's former pupils later became employed on the railways and became 'one of the few ticket collectors able to quote Xenophon'. At one point, Roger was holding down his responsibilities at Downside whilst also running the music at All Hallows but after he 'retired' from Downside following more than thirty years' association with the Benedictine-run school, he continued as Director of Music and Choirmaster at All Hallows for another decade. He translated into English and put to music the words written by Francis Dix which form, today, the official School Song which is sung with gusto at least once a year on the occasion of All Saints' Day.

In his autobiography *"A Quiver Full – memoirs of a family man"* he writes *"I enjoyed my last ten years at All Hallows almost more than any other period of my teaching life"*

in us that we have not travelled back to Spain ourselves more often to thank in person the many, many families who have supported and trusted the school so much over the years. The Spanish pupils have added immeasurably to the life of the school and we are surely ready to mark that association by taking the relationship to another level. We like their names and their enthusiasms and their confidence. We like their merry (and loud) chatter, their zestful presence, their sense of purpose, their heroic equilibrium and their contradictory passions. We are even now receiving children and enquiries from those same early Spanish pupils now grown up – which says something for continuity and long-lasting benefits; Maria Perez-Juez's niece, for example, is currently a pupil at the school. Ideally, one never really wants more than about ten Spanish children in the school at any one time – and spread out through the year groups - mainly for their own benefit so that they are not tempted to converse too often in their native language, bearing in mind that the principal reason for them coming to England is for them to learn to speak English. We might occasionally appear harsh to the children when we try to enforce a 'no-Spanish speaking' rule but if the children from Spain sometimes spend a few early times in tears because they are at All Hallows, away from home, it is always instructive to see those same children in tears at the end of their time because they do not want to leave! We should be sorry to see our Spanish friends and families slip away. Let us hope that in seventy-five years time there are still children from Spain wanting to spend some time at All Hallows. Perhaps a Spanish Head Teacher would seal the deal. Now we need a woman and a Spaniard. Maria, Sandra, Lourdes, Paloma, Monica…. your time has come!

If sport was making its mark, of no less importance was the development of the Learning Support Centre which quickly established for itself a regional, if not national, reputation for excellence in terms of assisting pupils who experience some specific or general difficulties in the learning process. Paul Ketterer began the process by converting the courtyard barn lofts into dedicated teaching spaces and then employing staff to manage the various programmes undertaken by the pupils whose academic needs had been identified as deserving of support. Chris Bird and Ian Murphy built on these foundations and maintained the traditions. The principles of Learning Support became enshrined as part of the mantra of the school and I can certainly remember leading a seminar at a national I.A.P.S. Conference for Head Teachers when approximately fifty other Heads across the country signed up for the session to find out how we did things at All Hallows. The principles were straightforward. The Learning Support provision in the school underpins all educational, pastoral and extra-curricular activities; it is a fundamental part of the culture of All Hallows and is entirely consistent with the Christian principles upon which this Catholic school operates. The terminology is important. At All Hallows we refer to 'Learning Support' deliberately. This is partly to do with avoiding any negative connections with the term 'special needs' or with the idea that children are being withdrawn from mainstream and therefore stigmatised. More importantly, the term has been chosen deliberately because it reflects a whole-school approach which encompasses the academically able, the mainstream pupils and those with learning difficulties. This is a matter of *philosophy*. Learning Support is available and intended for every child. Every child needs some kind of support, at some stage or another, to one degree or another. A casual recollection of our own schooldays will remind us of the 'special needs' we had at some point in our education (which may or may not have been met) and our own experience with the children of today underlines forcibly the fact that each child is an individual with his/her own unique needs and potential. Which of us has not needed support of one kind or another in our own education? Such a philosophy cannot be made effective in practice if an *environment* conducive to meeting key targets is not established. All too often, specialist learning support of the kind being described is set up in inaccessible places on a school campus, away from mainstream activity, separate from the curriculum and the community, marginalised in its location and utilising the 'last available space' that nobody else wanted. The Learning Support area should be central to the school in its physical situation as well as in its purpose. It should be warm and welcoming. There should be a sense of space, harmony and comfort. The business within should be calm, controlled, purposeful and rigorous. It should be an area that allows for free and natural movement to other key areas of the school. Its physical appearance, upkeep and identity should be as seamlessly accommodated within the school as any other vital function, yet specifically as distinct as, for example, the Library or the ICT centre, or any other clearly defined element of the school. Such an environment will not function to its best capacity without the appropriate resources. The department requires serious funding. Personnel should be specifically qualified and/or well trained. Whole-school timetable issues should be considered alongside the demands of the department rather than 'bolted-on' after the main event. Modern technological aids should be in place. Access to external specialists should be routine rather than exceptional or as 'last-chance' options. Individually designed programmes should account for the individual nature of the children's needs. There should be a carefully thought-out approach to integration. Within the department, and the school, there should be a wide mix of different children from different backgrounds with a clear emphasis on equality of opportunity and treatment. All staff should be well versed in the kinds of strategies adopted by specialist staff since such methods, in isolation, also work very well in group or class structures. Specialist staff should work with individuals, pairs and small groups on a withdrawn basis, alongside the opportunity to provide in-class support. Specifically designed programmes of study should co-exist with the demands of the mainstream curriculum. A whole-school approach of this kind encourages tolerance, acceptance, validation and approval with the resulting improvement in self-esteem. The psychology of Learning should be a matter of ongoing fascination for all educators, none more so than those engaged most actively in the learning support provision. How children learn; the various mediums for understanding, presenting and receiving knowledge: the visual, the auditory, the kinaesthetic; the various expressions of intelligence in areas like the linguistic, the logical, the artistic, the musical, the practical, the interpersonal, etc.; what we teach; the tone of presentation; the complete multi-sensory approach; - all such aspects of learning should inform our teaching. If a child cannot learn the way we are teaching, then we must teach the way he/she can learn. *Learning Support* is a central commitment which goes to the core of the educational process rather than the edges. It is not an extra; it should be an expectation, a right. It is for that reason that, at All Hallows, it is *free*; additional charges are not made for our potential scholars, and not for our mainstream pupils, and not for our children with specific or general difficulties.

Elizabeth Ballinger might be remembered as the first Head of the Learning Support Department and she was followed by notable successors such as Ann Crowcombe, Lynn Walker, Jill Shahbahrami, Debbie Caines, up to the present post-holder, Liz Renouf. I was even acting Head of the Department myself for a short time! All such personnel had the right mix of skills in empathy, subject-knowledge, administrative efficiency and rigour which has sustained the work of the department over the years. The present staff represented by long-serving personnel like

"

*The raison d'être of the school is
the integration of Christian principles
with everyday life*

"

Caroline Fear, Bridgette Weller, Victoria Somerville, as well as others like Anne Harries and Nicky Moulton, and many others, continue to foster those fine traditions. Caroline Fear, in fact, has been involved with the school since 1981 and is still providing one-to-one assistance to so many individual pupils who gain from her kindness, interest and genuine humility alongside her realistic and challenging aspirations. One would like to instigate a trophy in her name to commend pupils who have made obvious progress through dint of perseverance and endeavour in the face of passing difficulties but 'The Fear Award' would conjure up the wrong image. Fortunately, such an award exists already in the 'Menage Shield' named after a previous worthy 'winner' of that accolade whose family donated a trophy in recognition of his example and as a mark of gratitude to the school; so it is that the work of Caroline Fear and all those worthy Heads of the Learning Support Department is commemorated in this very special and very honourable award announced on Prize Day. Caroline became a very useful and welcome assistant to Paul and Jean Ketterer in helping them with their son Carl's upbringing and she has demonstrated remarkable personal qualities throughout her time, benefiting as much as the pupils in her own personal education, formation and growth, whilst also dispensing dedicated learning support to so many worthy boys and girls. Just as girls were welcomed to the school as a matter of conviction at a time when other schools, perhaps, weighed up market forces, so, too, 'learning support' became a visionary aspect of the school that anticipated modern watchwords like 'inclusion' and 'differentiation' without diluting the high academic reputation of the school. Paul Ketterer – who instigated the developing notion of learning support - had an educational vision that rose above passing trends and when he had been convinced about the rightness of a cause he pursued it with what had recently (and kindly) been described of him as his characteristic 'Teutonic efficiency'. The Learning Support Centre has named certain of its rooms after famous people who had experienced learning difficulties of their own in their schooldays such as Winston Churchill, Susan Hampshire and Tom Cruise. The All Hallows of old had received a handwritten note of thanks from Churchill after the school had congratulated him on his 75th birthday and it also welcomed Susan Hampshire to the school in 2002 when she visited the department when taking a break from her acting at the Theatre Royal in Bath. Let us hope she did not overhear the remark from one pupil saying "When is Tom Cruise coming?" But, who knows? Churchill and Susan Hampshire have come and gone, so perhaps it is time for Tom Cruise to drop in after all.

Hand-in-hand with the characteristic support of individual pupils encountering occasional difficulties has been the individual attention given to those pupils whose obvious or latent talents needed nurturing on the appropriate stages. It is a hallmark of the school: the recognition of the uniqueness of the individual. In one obvious way, this striving for excellence is registered by the Honours Boards dating back to 1942 where the number of names and range of schools record a wide array of awards in the fields of academia, sport, music, art, leadership and all-round abilities. As is also the case with general pupil numbers, each Headmaster has been pleased, in his time, to achieve a record number of awards. The year 2013, for example, has hit new heights with forty awards to nine different schools in six different categories of achievement for thirty separate Year Eight pupils. All Hallows punches above its weight in terms of the number and breadth of public achievements, at least, and it is a mark of the school's distinctive nature that it can accommodate and meet the demands and expectations of so many pupils, parents and senior schools consistently over the years.[82]

It is possible to take the view that the Honours System - with reference to educational establishments - has been devalued along with 'grade-inflations' and pupil performance and manners, etc, etc, but it would be a sad day, indeed, if those of us involved in education (that is, ALL OF US) jumped onto the comfortably-passing, disgruntled (and slightly-smug) bandwagon of popular fancy without examining the evidence or without being prepared to play a part in maintaining rigour whilst embracing the culture of our times. The pace of change may be almost overwhelming in this twenty-first century but humankind is nothing if not adaptable. We can all don with temporary alacrity the rags and remnants worn by prophets of doom but could usefully pause to wonder if we can aspire to wear the heavier cloaks of more lasting hand-me-downs[83]. My point is that the 'old days' would record scholarships that were genuinely – and mostly – academic. Pupils would excel in academic subjects with a liberal dose of the classics thrown in for good measure. Nowadays, the awards are broader in number and kind. There is no doubt that this trend is driven by the need to recruit pupils in a competitive market but, one likes to think that it also reflects a genuine and more-encompassing view of 'talent' and potential. To compare the regimes of scholars of old who knew their Latin and Greek with those, today, who gain triple awards in a breadth of academic subjects with sporting excellence or artistic talent or musical talent thrown in, alongside an all-rounder appeal which includes leadership, modesty and general good character, is like asking for the judgement of Paris, albeit without the attendant nudity and bribes. Nevertheless, there is a residual matter to be addressed concerning the diminishing number of pupils of the present who don't gain awards compared with the elite numbers of those who did from the past. Numbers have always provided comfort and challenges of sorts. We stray towards the equality of Melanie Phillips' 'All Must Have Prizes' or the madness of Alice in Wonderland. And yet we continue to inscribe our Honours Boards with public and promotional pride. And why not? Beguiling, seductive, romantic, accurate and cynical in almost equal measure, they tell their own stories too.

But, if you wanted to put a premium on an 'All Hallows Prize', choose the 'Unsung Hero Award' or 'The Menage Shield' or the 'Star Trophy' or 'The Paget Cup'. There you will find life's true winners.

In any reflection on the past, especially one involving education, there is bound to be some comment on technological advances. Mention has already been made of the epiadioscope, after all. Television forced its way into schools as we have seen. And then the race was on. Technology

---

[82] See Appendix D for full Honours details

[83] Fowler would either dismiss this as *'overworked labouring of metaphors'* or welcome it as an example of *'remarkable insights'*. I suspect it leans towards the former but, if this observation still remains in the footnotes, it passed the eyes of the editorial stylists.

changed the face of education at various times with the pace of change never so fast as the last thirty years or so. Paul Ketterer was proud to announce the fact that the French Department had developed live satellite links to French television with suitable recording facilities so that the children could see and hear the French language being spoken in an everyday way by natural French-speaking people (October 1988). It became a valuable resource (with only one or two embarrassments) as staff became more aware of the kind of programmes available for recording and subsequent playback in the classrooms – always check the recordings first! Computers grew even more exponentially. The widespread use of computers had yet to be fully realised in terms of application and it was certainly the case that the staff needed specialist training of their own before the benefits and range could be ascertained and utilised. As with all things, computer technology started slowly but the inevitable 'space-age' machines began to appear like a mutating rash. A Minute from the Governors' meetings in October 1983 approves the expenditure of £900 for a second computer. One can imagine some governors questioning the wisdom of such a purchase on the grounds that 'we approved the purchase of one computer only last year – now you want another one?' But the governors were not a problem, it has to be said, and only ever supported the latest demand in this respect. The problem would be much more of the order 'which computers to buy?' and 'where should they be situated?' and 'who gets to use them?'

Nick Somerville, Sam Thornton (who also provided early Cranes and Chronicles on which I have relied for detail) and, especially, Martin Green, have all played their part in training and managing systems. Each school probably has its own story to tell regarding the progress made and route taken but the simple fact of the matter today is that there are over 250 appliances in the school on the network including linked computers in dedicated locations, stand-alone computers at every work station, laptops, i-pads, mobile phones, printers, servers and the school telephone system all requiring integration and upgrading. The Internet is freely available – if governed by strict guidelines within the school – and the interactive whiteboards in every classroom are able to connect to the World Wide Web at the push of a button, as well as tap into a growing bank of educational software programs and facilitate power-point presentations at the drop of a mouse. Email communication has quickly become the internal mode of expression between staff and is increasingly becoming the favoured form of messaging with parents and external professional bodies. Just as the writing of cheques has been superseded by credit and debit cards (one awaits the day when public places say "No cash accepted"), so, too, the post-office letter – personal or professional – has almost become a thing of the past. Into one's pigeon-hole (another time-honoured item of staff-room furniture surely destined to be burnt) arrives, every day, fliers, promotional leaflets, catalogues, circular communications, advertising features, magazines but precious little worth reading. The administration time spent in filing these days consists of picking up the contents of one's pigeon-hole and dropping them into the bin. Examinations are undertaking changes as on-line assessments are becoming more common in terms of testing certain 'raw' information and learning potential; teaching and learning has already been adapted in style, if not in substance. Coursework has been word-processed for some time now and senior school students simply whip out their mobile phones and photograph their homework from the interactive whiteboard. Individualised i-pad provision for each pupil in the classroom is simply a matter of time (and cost). I wonder how long it will be before the teachers simply get to know the back of their pupils' heads as they all tap away on their computerised appliances whilst a stack of pens sit idly in the bin. Already we are used to ending many of our lessons with the words "OK, everybody, save what you have done, log off and close down". And off the robots trot to their next engagement with the virtual world out there. The signing-in Register for Day Pupils had been introduced for parents in October 1985 which had seemed quite forward-thinking at the time – imagine being able to know which pupils were on the premises at any given time! Other systems have since taken over to satisfy legal requirements but that Signing-In Register is still going strong; its days as a paper exercise must surely be numbered! Even the accounts sent to parents were computerised in September 1986 but perhaps the more 'human' an activity appears to be, the more resistant it is to computers (not that fee-payers aren't human, of course, any more than those responsible for increasing the fees don't always appear to be on the same planet). Nevertheless, such had become our dependency on computer technology the world over, we were sucked into the passing fad of preparing in advance for the Millennium Bug meltdown. I found myself attending meetings with the Bursar and select 'emergency committees' listening to various experts about the need to safeguard our systems in the event of the 'Millennium Bug' compromising all manner of things. The Boiler system would break down; the telephones wouldn't work; our catering equipment would malfunction; aeroplanes would fall from the sky; the inmates from Shepton Mallet Prison would escape; nuclear reactors would spring leaks; and, perhaps worst of all, the coffee-making facility in the Staff Room would give up the ghost. I sat in on those kinds of meetings. Somebody made a fortune in selling Millennium Bug Compatibility programs. And the jury remains 'out' on the hundreds of billions of dollars world-wide spent in averting the imagined catastrophe. The fact is that few problems were actually encountered when the date-change took place but the arguments run thus: there were few problems because so much money and time had been spent in remedial action; or, there would have been few problems anyway so the money and time spent was an over reaction. And, on the matter of virtual realities, I have just heard on Radio 4 that one can now book an appointment for virtual therapy with a virtual therapist who smiles and nods and probes and listens; I'm off to make my appointment now.

I have no formal school diary records to consult during most of Paul Ketterer's time as Headmaster since, as has been mentioned, that practice ceased not long after his appointment but, in order to maintain some kind of continuity with earlier parts of this book it might be appropriate to include some comments recorded by me in my own personal diary from 1985. At this time, I was coming to the end of my first engagement as a member of staff at All Hallows and I was running the English Department and the Library whilst also holding responsibility for Discipline and Estate Management. Being 'i/c Discipline' simply meant that one picked up all the pieces regarding pupil behaviour that nobody else wanted to deal with especially if it involved detailed action like interviewing alleged miscreants, informing the Headmaster, deciding on courses of action and contacting parents. 'Estate Management' meant that one became a coordinator by liaising with

academic staff, resident staff, grounds staff, the maintenance team, external contractors and the Bursar who would often point out that there was no money available for that particular project anyway. That last point is not particularly true – I included it as an attempt to play the traditional card regarding the parsimony of 'the School Bursar' – but one can recall encounters with one particular All Hallows' Bursar that were rather akin to seeking a papal audience or trying to bend the will of Attila the Hun when he was set on a course somewhat contrary to one's own (not that the particular Bursar I have in mind was male). In truth, the Bursars of All Hallows have always been facilitators even if they were, collectively, and very properly, highly successful in managing purse strings carefully. I like to think I was neither frightening, as far as discipline was concerned, nor particularly adept at changing light bulbs (never mind having views or skills to do with managing the estate) but both positions were extremely useful areas of involvement and I was able to draw on such experiences thereafter. A fairly casual glance through selected pages of my 1985 diary, therefore, records the following considerations through those days….

> *"…set up Lourdes and Isabel with EAL; do lesson planning: mini-sagas, desert islands, zebra; investigate stink bombs; boys swearing; stone-throwing; order shelves; change light bulbs; no water in toilets; contact electrician, builder, plumber; see Oliver Gibbs and Terry; squeaking doors; check floorboards; leaking overflow pipes; blocked toilets; grass-cutting; smells in music practice rooms; behaviour in boys' showers; contact Bath rugby players: John Horton, John Palmer, Gareth Chilcott, Richard Hill, David Sole, Nigel Redmond; phone Rentokil; why girls in cran?; fix loose flag-stones; fix missing fire extinguishers; who's stealing from the tuck boxes?; purchase water softener; order more creosote; three boys off sixth form privileges; see PFJK about testing state of stonework re. vibrations from quarry blasting[84]; rugby coaching course 26-30 August*

---

[84] Torr Quarry is one of eight active quarries on the Mendips and is situated within a mile of the school site. It has been described as "the biggest hole in Europe" although one would never know it is there since it has been sympathetically landscaped to nestle snugly, out of sight almost, into its surroundings, with even a bridle path weaving its way through its six hundred acres and any number of interesting examples of flora and fauna finding homes on the edges and slopes. The main quarry is already sub-water table level and extractions are poised to continue for another twenty-five years or so after a period of uncertainty as to its future. Limestone has been taken to build Wells Cathedral, Glastonbury Abbey and further afield across the country including infrastructures for the second Severn Bridge, The Channel Tunnel and Heathrow Terminal Five. Together with its headquarters at Marston House it employs over three hundred people and contributes many millions of pounds to the local economy. Future plans include allowing the main crater to fill with water to form a lake for recreational use, as well as providing a public water supply and a home for various wildlife habitats. Both Paul Ketterer and Chris Bird had commissioned surveys, from time to time, to assess any potential damage being done to the school's stonework as a result of the quarry blasting but the school's experiences have only been positive in the strength of the relationships established with the quarry owners, particularly when Angela Yeoman managed the site with her husband, when it was known as Foster-Yeoman's. Angela was the guest of honour one year at our Prize-Giving ceremony and she has been a good friend to the school and instrumental, over the years, in undertaking preliminary building work at the school, at no charge, as we have wanted to develop a playground area or clear space for car-parking or various other projects of this kind. There is an excellent picnic area and viewing point, overlooking the quarry, with good information plaques available to the public just a short walk from the school, via an underpass and bridleway, which is well worth a visit.

1985; renew cracked glass in pet rooms; arrange chimney sweep; why missing screwdrivers?; coordinate keys; dangerous yews in spinney – how dangerous?; order one ton of sand; see Joseph Merszei; see Joseph Merszei; see Joseph Merszei; see Joseph Merszei's father; look after Joseph Merszei in Easter holidays; etc, etc, etc..."

I cannot possibly know how that comes across to the reader today but it all comes flooding back to me now – as I read it again almost thirty years on - especially the bits about seeing 'Joseph Merszei' who seemed to find himself in regular trouble although it is with some irony that, having castigated and rusticated him on many occasions, Greg Jones (my Science colleague) and I shared nurturing responsibilities for him one Easter holiday by having him stay with our families for fully five weeks when he could not go home for some reason or other. Joseph Merszei, like many rogues, was a lovely house guest and a real charmer; he is probably running some major business enterprise now and, if he is, it's about time he sent Greg and me some money for his board and keep all those years ago. As for the mention of the zebra....I have no idea!

The rugby coaching course referred to above was a great success and I was able through my own playing contacts to invite many of those rugby stars mentioned to come across for parts of the course to provide expert hands-on tuition to the boys. The course had been deliberately open to local boys as well as our own pupils and the interaction and expectations were interesting to handle. One such likely bruiser from Frome (whom we would have liked to have recruited as a pupil for the new season) found the whole experience lifting him out of his comfort zone on occasions but he could play rugby and, as he became relaxed, his natural confidence returned. It had been reported to me that 'the boy from Frome' was smoking in-between the coaching sessions. I had made a solemn pledge to Paul Ketterer and, more importantly, the female bursar who might have been descended from ancient Viking marauders who took no prisoners, that I would assume personal responsibility for the success of the course and that nothing untoward would happen on my watch. Inside, I was panicking as I envisaged the headlines screaming from national newspapers "Independent Prep School Burns Down!" so it was with even more pride that I recall my masterful way (even though I say it myself) of dealing with the potential problem. Coming off the pitches for a mid-morning break, I fell in with our friend from Frome, wiped my brow, let out a huge sigh of mock-exhaustion and said "Wow! I could do with a fag!" whereupon he promptly took out his packet of cigarettes and said "Here, have one of mine". I quickly confiscated them for the rest of the course and said he could have them back at the end of the day if he worked very hard for the remaining sessions. We got on, of course, like a house on fire which, thankfully, was a legacy I managed to keep merely on a metaphorical level.

The late 1980s saw consolidation, growth and development. In September 1986, Mr Bonham took over as auditor and accountant from Mr Bassett who had provided wise counsel for more than thirty years; pupil numbers[85] were at the highest ever (230); BBC computers were in use now in the Geography room and the remedial department with the Science Department now wanting £1500 for Atari computers and related software; the school clock wasn't working (again); a new school mini-bus was purchased for £12130; in October 1986 the Headmaster was concerned about the high number of boarders and the lack of suitable dormitory space (this is not a problem for most schools in the modern age but see below); Hellmut Schutz was set to retire in July 1989 and died in 2012 (see details overleaf); the Common Room remained strong with long-standing members of staff like Dawn Kitchen and caring people like Caroline Dawnay adding typical solicitous affection and support; the staff salary increase under the Burnham Commission was 16% (ah! those were the days) - school fees went up accordingly; arrangements were in place to convert the old chapel into extra dormitories; a new chapel building was being commissioned to seat 250+ (it became an award-winning design by architect Norman Cant and was completed in 1988 costing just short of £200000) and £10000 was set aside for the replacement of the power mowers, tractor and gang-mowers for *grass-cutting* – (things had moved on since Mr Dix's efforts by hand on the Scorhill slopes); Paul Ketterer was pushing for a new all-weather pitch[86] in 1989, looking to level land in preparation for this project, and develop new tennis courts and netball courts south of the Cran Wall so that space could be freed up on the Upper Hard Court for a building development.

In October 1988, in celebration of the school's 50th birthday the following events took place:

- *27th October – a formal Dinner at The House of Lords*
- *28th October – a Buffet Lunch for Former Pupils*
- *29th October – a Supper Dance for Parents*
- *31st October – a Fancy Dress Party for the pupils*
- *1st November – the Dedication of the Chapel of All Saints by the Bishop of Clifton followed by a Cocktail Party*

---

[85] Paul had underestimated one summer term the number of beds needed for the incoming boarders so, not one to be put off by a challenge, he invented the concept of the "Best Dormitory of the Week' award which meant that the winning dormitory won the prize of camping in tents outside for a week; thus did he turn a potential crisis into a marketing strategy.

[86] The astro-turf pitch became a reality under Chris Bird's Headship from 1995 onwards and the Upper Hardcourt development saw the building of the Ketterer Wing with the completion of that space in a classroom block named the Crane Wing some years later, thus underlining the time it takes for wheels to turn sometimes, whilst also demonstrating the continuity of purpose in handing over from one Headmaster to another.

[87] Lord Hylton hosted a Formal Dinner in The Cholmondeley Room for approximately 60 guests at which Dom Philip Jebb, OSB, former Headmaster of Downside and Paul Ketterer made speeches of welcome. Paul teased Fr Philip that although the Benedictines could proudly boast of a tradition that went back fourteen hundred years, *"the group running All Hallows goes back two thousand years…yes, the Catholic Laity were in at the beginning…none of this sixth century stuff…in the square in Jerusalem at Pentecost there were three thousand Catholic laity and not a single Benedictine"*. He also pointed out that the year 1938 saw the foundation not only of All Hallows School but also *The Beano* and he wondered if the boys at Bognor Regis would realise how their education would be thus enlightened for the next few years or so.

Paul and Jean Ketterer, of course, attended every function and were able to celebrate in style even if Francis and Evelyn Dix were no longer alive to see their school in such good heart. The tight and busy sequence of days in celebration must have had some effect on future thinking, one feels, since a Governors' Minute at around that time raises the prospect of introducing half-term breaks, perhaps by way of arranging well-earned breaks, although perhaps that is just coincidental.

The opening of the Chapel by the Bishop of Clifton

Despite the genuine cause for celebration regarding healthy pupil numbers and positive building developments, however, and the worries about finding space to accommodate all the boarders (mentioned above), contrary forces gathered pace very quickly – as they are wont to do - and worries of a different kind started to surface in the 1990s. Perhaps as a sign of difficult financial times, the main building contractors employed to build what became known as the Ketterer Wing, went into liquidation in 1992 and new contractors had to be sought under a novation agreement. Even before this time, the Governors had removed the ceiling of 250 pupils as an optimum school roll since there were concerns about the less promising split between boarding and day pupils. A sense of greater accountability was in the air, partly from external developments like The Children Act[88] and

---

[88] The 1989 Children Act began with the legislative intention of ensuring that each parent fully understood his/her equal and independent rights and responsibilities to the child whilst their child was in their care but it broadened to set out processes whereby the welfare of the child became paramount so that, by working with parents, any possible harm to the child could be eliminated. Children were to be consulted and their wishes and feelings considered in matters to do with their development. The 2004 Children Act outlined these considerations still further and provided the legal underpinning to 'Every Child Matters: Change for Children'. It might seem a little odd for a modern child to learn that Acts of Parliament were considered necessary, within living memory (only twenty years or so ago) to protect children, but there were also such Acts in 1908, 1948, 1972 and 1975, as well as since 1989, so it is not a new phenomenon. Equally, when one learns that the 1908 Act established properly functioning juvenile courts, introduced official registration for foster parents, tried to eradicate infanticide, granted powers to local authorities to keep poor children out of workhouses, prevented children from working in dangerous trades, stopped them buying cigarettes and ceased the practice of sending children to adult prisons if a crime had been committed, one can see that there was a lot of work to be done.

the establishment of the DES List 99[89], and partly from the Governors' wish to become more involved in the management of the school, even if that desire was designed to ease the workload on the Headmaster. Paul Ketterer had served twenty years as Headmaster and a celebratory Dinner was planned by the Governors in May 1991 to commemorate his achievements but they were also concerned to plan for his successor whenever Paul decided he wanted to retire. In these early years of the 1990s they were looking ahead to the mid-1990s in order to manage any such transition. The Governors had minuted the fact in February 1992 that the importance of being a good employer was an undisputed part of their role and they wanted to take those responsibilities seriously for the benefit of all[90], especially since new staff contracts were in the process of being drawn up at the same time as redundancies were being considered as possibilities.

All of these observations – plus the footnotes below – might serve to provide a flavour of the kinds of business matters the Headmaster and Governors had to keep in mind when managing the school, alongside the core aspect of education in all its various forms. Tom Barrington was Chairman of Governors at this time.

If the Governors had weighty matters to think about, the pupils had their own preoccupations. Just as those responsible for acrobatic aerodynamics had 'forgotten to tell the bumble bee', so, too, it seemed, those dealing with the grim realities of recession and redundancy had not shared the gathering potential gloom with the children. The school was enjoying significant success in gymnastics under Moira Thompson's expert and exacting direction and the commentary below simply highlights selective achievements of those particular times. In 1993 the Under-13s Boys' team – consisting of Christopher Jones, Folarin Alakija, Daniel Gadsden, Stuart Thompson, Robert Wynn-Jones and Patrick Middleton – won the national schools floor and

[89] List 99 was for many decades, going back to the early twentieth century, a confidential register of people barred from working with children in schools, social work and/or voluntary settings. The List included adults found guilty of sexual offences against children, as well as those who had been violent towards the young, or who had abused any kind of trust with young persons, or who had been guilty of drug offences or any violent crime, e.g. rioting and football hooliganism, or who had stolen school property or who had any form of mental illness. From January 2009 all referrals were handled by the Independent Safeguarding Authority. Schools are bound to refer potential applicants for jobs to the ISA and prospective candidates have to agree to their personal details being examined before appointments can be made.

[90] An example of the Governors making benign plans for staff benefit was their forward-thinking provisions in case the findings of what became known as 'Pepper v. Hart' in the highest law courts in the land went against them. Pepper was Her Majesty's Inspector of Taxes and Hart was one of nine teachers at Malvern College receiving staff fee concessions in educating their children. Such arrangements applied across the independent sector so the ramifications were significant. Not without some dispute and subsequent appeals, the law lords eventually decided in favour of Hart thus eliminating the need for substantial back-payments in tax for teachers with children in independent education which would have militated against this benefit in kind. The teachers' case, however, was merely the catalyst; the principle behind the court hearings was one of parliamentary privilege being compromised if such disputes could be settled by consideration of debates in the House of Commons and/or the House of Lords (through reference to Hansard) to clarify primary legislation where doubts existed. Nevertheless, the point is that the Governors of All Hallows had made some provisional arrangements to assist staff if such retrospective legislation counted against them.

HELLMUT SCHUTZ
(1925-2012 RIP)

Hellmut Schutz, who has died at the age of eighty-seven, was a much loved and respected schoolmaster at All Hallows having first been appointed in September 1958 and, although he left in 1970 to further his teaching career, he returned to the school not many years later and carried on exerting a benign influence until 1989. Even then he had not quite finished his long association with the school because he often re-visited, always showing a great interest in people, particularly the children, and was asked in the mid 1990s to fulfil the function of the school's 'Independent Person' to whom the children could communicate their worries if ever they felt they might prefer to speak to somebody not employed at the school. To that role he brought all his customary friendliness, confidentiality and gracious good humour. Hellmut remained almost obsessively modest and self-effacing but his benign exterior hid some anxious and ultimately tragic wartime experiences when his parents evacuated him from Austria just as the Nazi forces were occupying that country. He became attached and grateful to Downside for assuming a strong, formative influence on him and he showed the same loyal and kindly characteristics thereafter, infused by a strong Christian faith. Hellmut taught a variety of subjects, even if his classroom disciplinary instincts were not his strongest attributes and, for many years he was the unacknowledged and amusing writer of substantial numbers of old chronicles on which this present writer has drawn for many resources and anecdotes. He was one of life's gentlemen.

TOM BARRINGTON
(F.P. 1954-1960; Chairman of Governors 1982-1989 seated front left)

Tom Barrington was part of an All Hallows' family tradition which began with his father, T. J. Barrington, who was on the Board of Governors between 1962-1972, continued with Tom's brother Christopher (Kit), who was also a pupil at All Hallows, (and who excelled in sport, crowning a fine year in 1956 by winning the Wimbledon Prep Schools Doubles Tournament) and with his other brother, John, who also attended All Hallows from 1957. Tom was no mean sportsman himself since he represented the 1st XI Cricket for four years from 1957-1960 and played for the 1st XV Rugby team in 1958 and 1959. Tom became a Governor of the school in 1980 and continued on the Board until 1995. He presided over the halcyon years in Paul Ketterer's Headship and saw through the handover from Paul to Chris Bird in 1994/1995 as a member of the Board under Sue Goodson's leadership.

vault competition in the Under-16 age bracket. This accolade came on the back of a number of pupils' successes at regional and county level, both individually and in group categories. For example, Patricia Moxey, Sarah Roberts, Zoe Parkinson, Victoria Thompson and Victoria May made up the Girls' Under-11 team that took the gold medal in the Somerset Schools Gymnastics. Peter Moxey, in the same year, became the Under-11 Boys Champion in the South West Schools Trampolining Competition, winning the gold medal for the third year in a row. Laura Branscombe (pictured left) won the gold medals in the Girls' Under-13 Hurdles and the 100m sprint at the South West Prep Schools' meeting, with Victoria May winning gold in the Under-12s Sprint, and Adejare Doherty (Triple Jump), Francis Ventham (800 metres) and Lawrence Lagnado (Long Jump) also winning gold at the same meeting. Enrique Mora-Figueroa won the gold medal at the Under-14s 75-metres Hurdles at the National Prep Schools' Athletics Championships in 1993. Rebecca Goodson (pictured right) played as a twelve-year-old pupil in the Under-14s Somerset County hockey team which finished joint first in the West of England Tournament in 1993 and, the previous year, Laura Branscombe won gold in the 70-metres Hurdles in the National Prep Schools' Championships with Bernard Franklin winning the gold medal in the Under-14s Triple Jump in the South West meeting. The Girls Hockey teams were winning tournaments, for example, at Claysmore, and the Boys' rugby teams were enjoying success over several seasons winning all but a few of their matches against strong opposition. Nor was it all sport: Anna Boyd, Daniel Britten, Duncan Brown, Meriel Buxton, Honor Conroy, James Gay, Anna Grundy, Seamus McNulty, Felix Moreno and Miranda Pountney all achieved awards to their senior schools in 1993 and in 1992 the school won eleven trophies at the Frome Music Festival with fine performances by Edward Hare, Anna Boyd, Sharon Mitchard, Gemma Dudgeon, Patricia and Peter Moxey, Katie Martin, Nicola Brown and Victoria Lomas.

CATHY CARDOZO
(1993-onwards)

In January 1993, Cathy re-joined the school, having spent one year as a resident assistant from 1986-1987, and with a music degree behind her in those intervening years, she had gone on to achieve Qualified Teacher status whilst at All Hallows and has taught music, mathematics, science, geography, as well as assisting in the Learning Support Centre, and, of course, heading up the R.E. Department. Cathy has prepared candidates for First Communion and Confirmation, liaised with many different priests and chaplains in the course of her time and co-ordinated all Chapel services. She has been a resident Housemother, helped with the Brownies, supervised bath times and sung beautifully in chapel and musicals in the school. She is related to several former pupils who have been at the school like the Gaggeros and the Isolas and the Cardozos. Cathy became Mrs Wolf when she married OG Sebastian (himself a former Gap student at All Hallows) and they now have a bonny baby boy, Max. (*John-Paul Renouf, Trevor Richards and I were pleased to cover Cathy's R.E. lessons during her maternity leave, self-styling ourselves as 'The Three Wise Men'*).

Despite such conspicuous success at so many levels, however, so it was, in the economic climate of the time, that pupil numbers fell from a record high of 273 to round about the 200 mark in the summer of 1993 and the cloth needed to be cut accordingly. Several members of staff were made redundant in these years and others found their hours being cut to part-time employment whilst major projects (like the building of a new swimming pool in the region of £500000) had to be shelved. And the Governors still wanted to plan for Paul Ketterer's retirement despite their confidence in him and their recognition of his achievements. They had expressed concerns about Paul's health and his ability to delegate in the early 1990s and they were aware of unease that existed between the Headmaster and some members of staff. Delegated senior teachers were invited to attend some Governors' Meetings to articulate Common Room views and support Paul in his management of the school. Various sub-committees met to discuss issues arising including the organisational structure of the school. Senior Teachers were also charged with the task of conducting a confidential Staff Survey which led to a Report which was presented to the Board of Governors.

It was against this background that the Governors' Minutes start recording the fact that a Deputy Head would be a good idea to support all that Paul Ketterer was achieving and, after a few years of consideration of all these matters, it was decided that approaches should be made to the present writer regarding his willingness to assume such a role. In a meeting of April 1994, financial losses were being contemplated on the basis of a school roll of 187 for the forthcoming September; yet, at the time of the meeting, numbers stood at 164 with the school losing pupils at twice the rate of recruitment. Much of this developing trend was due to the fact that 'bulge' years look good at the time of engagement but need to be managed carefully thereafter, since, when they work their way through the school and then leave, they create huge pressures in filling the gap. And bulge years at the top had stacked up in the 'years of plenty'; now that the recession had taken a grip, future projections looked grim.

But the school remained viable and its immediate future could not be compromised by the present lean spell. Finances were still strong and the essential core of the school – established by Mr and Mrs Dix and consolidated brilliantly by Paul Ketterer – was not about to succumb to passing pressures.

Some Ketterer Years

Some Bird Years

In May 1994, Chris Bird, the Assistant Headmaster Designate, attended his first Governors' Meeting, in preparation for taking on the post from September 1994, to work alongside Paul Ketterer in spreading confidence about the future. An unusual arrangement to be sure but one that suited the unusual times and one which, perhaps, prefigured the similarly unlikely scenario when Chris Bird, as ex-Headmaster, worked alongside his successor, Ian Murphy, in 2006, albeit in a different role.

I duly attended an 'interview' for the post of Assistant Headmaster which must have been in the Lent Term of 1994 when I found myself in a short-list of one. The position had been advertised internally and various candidates, I believe, had been considered but even I – with all my misgivings about taking on a Headship – came to realise that short of arriving without any trousers or possibly dropping a few empty bottles of whisky onto the floor as I shook hands with the interviewing panel, might stand a reasonable chance of being appointed. There was no mocked-up typical 'In-Tray' to sift through (which I think is standard fare for prospective Head Teacher candidates these days) but the log fire in the Dix Room was blazing and the interviewers had thoughtfully positioned my chair within about two feet of the fire so that the back of my suit slowly started to smoke as my face took on the hue of a startled beetroot. Who needed the pressure of an 'In-Tray' exercise? I remember very little about the process except one question from the Chairman of the Finance Committee, who was a plain-speaking man from Yorkshire with many years of experience in running County Councils and, possibly, small countries, such was his faintly intimidating presence in that room. The question he asked (which stuck with me throughout my eleven years as Headmaster) was this: "Well, Mr Bird," – his eyes now looking over his glasses which were perched on the end of his nose, "What makes you think you can make the step up from Deputy Head to Headmaster?" And that may well have been a question that everybody else was asking for the next eleven years too. History records, however, that I was appointed and as I left the room, complete with singed jacket and with the demeanour of one about to reach the status of gibbering imbecile, I came upon the portrait of the Founder, Francis Dix, who stared disapprovingly from his bushy eyebrows back down at this puny successor standing before him. And it had been raining, of course, all morning long. No doubt with these symbolic impressions burning strongly in our collective minds, we all rolled up our sleeves, took a deep breath and prepared for the dance.

Nothing can prepare one for Headship. Later, I accepted an invitation to talk to about fifty assembled Deputy Heads who were attending a conference at King's, Bruton. I had been invited as one of the keynote speakers to explain the role of a Head Teacher and to encourage them, presumably, to make their next applications. Instead, I urged them all to think very carefully before they put in those applications and, with only a slight trace of guilt, looked at them over my glasses, to ask them to answer the question: "What makes you think you can step up from Deputy Head to Head?"

Deputy Heads are well-known for having deputy headaches and for fielding all kinds of things that nobody else wants to do (given to them usually by the Headmaster) and they are genuinely the life-blood of the school. A good Deputy Head knows everything that is going on at all times of the day and night and probably has anticipated events that have not yet even happened. He (or she) is particularly good at guessing what boys (or girls) are going to do next and where they have been and what they have done. Perhaps the very best Deputy Heads are not suited to Headships after all. The ideal ticket would be for a school to appoint one of those 'best' Deputy Heads and hope that the Head appointed would be able to function sufficiently competently alongside to avoid messing things up. Perhaps the two roles should always be advertised together with the two appointments being made at the same time after the application of some sophisticated psychometric tests determining the 'best fit' of the dream team. The point remains, however, in my contention at least, that being a Deputy Head does not always qualify or prepare one for becoming a Head Teacher. One can read booklets on the matter (as I did) or attend various training courses (as I did not) but the simple truth is that one has to learn as one goes along. That might not be a particularly scientific statement to make with any firm guarantee of reassuring parents but there is something in it. If reassurance is wanted, it is usually the case that the appointed Head is so terrified of messing up that he/she invariably gets it right. Perhaps it is only when the Head loses the terror that things start to go off.

Chris and Jan Bird, then, moved into residence at All Hallows into the newly-converted Staff Flat, (hitherto St Luke's dormitory[91]), which had previously been the old school chapel, and had always been situated above the dining room, thus ensuring that the lingering smells of boys' socks, incense and cabbage provided a heady olfactory tonic at the end of the day. We moved in during the last few days of August 1994 to an empty school, trying to feel like Lord and Lady of the Manor, but really feeling a little like tiny mice scampering about the rafters. Incidentally, it was literally in those rafters that I discovered the statue of Our Lady lying on its side having presumably been deposited there for safe keeping during the last change of use from a chapel to

---

[91] Former pupil, Mark Bassett, who straddled the Ketterer and Bird years, remembers being shunted out of the dormitory to make way for the new Assistant Headmaster – sorry, Mark! – and also remembers building a "dodgy" wooden bridge over the Cran down by the Pet Room – which might not have been that dodgy since I seem to recall it surviving for years thereafter. He also mentions the "creepy" statue of Saint Francis on the other side of the Pet Room, which he might like to know now only frightens wild animals and garlic in Scouts' Wood (although Saint Francis, of course, only loves and looks after all living things and is never 'creepy' at all).

a dormitory. I brought it down, reverently, and cleaned the statue with a new toothbrush like some awe-struck archaeologist handling the Holy Grail and duly positioned it in the new school chapel of All Saints where she truly belonged and where she stands still today; there cannot be many Headmasters who remember their very first job with such pride and awe.

It is that aspect of awe that becomes the first realisation of the new Head Teacher, certainly in free-standing, day and boarding, independent schools like All Hallows. Typically, with 300 pupils, 600 parents, 100 employees and sundry other personnel with vested interests in the success of the school (not to mention 20 or so Governors), one quickly wakes up to the fact that there are over 1000 people whose lives and livelihoods depend on one person doing the job well. I don't suppose those one thousand people thought of it in terms like that – or at least not overtly – but I believed this personal interpretation of my role to be one of the singularly sobering driving forces throughout my years as Headmaster. People react differently when a Headmaster is about. They accord surprising levels of respect to 'The Headmaster' perhaps remembering their own Head Teachers from days gone by. Perhaps they recall guiltily their own undiscovered misdemeanours and worry in case all Head Teachers have access to an eternal Disciplinary Log Book that has recorded all pupil crimes ever committed.

I recall one supper party early in my Headship when I had been invited to 'just a quiet meal' to find about twenty parents in attendance whose conversation flowed freely until somebody asked me, on some matter, '*what did I think?*', whereupon the room fell silent. Parents soon found out, perhaps, I did not think very much at all. But the long arm of the Headmaster stretches beyond Somerset supper parties. I was always amused and impressed to receive very respectful emails from the Chief Operating Officer of 'Surface Transport', Hammersmith Flyover, who went through a phase of sending me detailed updates about the state of the repair work and apologising for the scale of the disruption. It is easy to feel important. I was disappointed not to hear from Bristol Airport about their flight changes or to be consulted by the custodians of Stonehenge about their plans to transport the monument to the children's playground in West Cranmore; one becomes used to receiving such news, you know. In amongst the flippancy, lives the profound, however, and one is never far from first and last things that touch people's lives. All the Headmasters at All Hallows have had to handle sensitively, and with strength, the death of a pupil or teacher or parent, often in particularly tragic circumstances: armed conflict, suicide, murder, road accidents, untimely illnesses. It is not surprising there are counselling courses in bereavement these days. There was a time when one had to go with one's instincts. Such deaths affect the community of the school; "*No man is an island, entire of itself. Each is a piece of the continent. A part of the Main...Each man's death diminishes me, for I am involved in mankind.*" Headmastering is a challenging task on personal and professional fronts.

And the day-to-day management of a fee-paying school is similarly complex with many overlapping strands and sometimes counterpoised tensions. The central vested interest of all parties, of course, – pupils, staff, Head Teacher, Governors, parents, outside agencies, business associates – is for the school to remain successful, and yet those different parties can often operate from such different starting-points or generate such potential conflict that complexities can easily arise. The characterisation of a typical term, or week, or even day, is that there are no such typical occurrences, although the routines of the timetable and the rhythms of the calendar dictate a certain predictability about proceedings. Yet everything is calculated to surprise. It is the richness of this dynamic that provides the lifeblood of the school. I made a firm commitment to myself early on that I would not be buoyed up by the seduction of instant successes nor weighed down by the depression of real or imagined fears and I am pleased that, by and large, I managed to achieve a kind of internal equilibrium despite, perhaps, any public impressions I may have been giving to the contrary. It is a good recipe for life. I kept Kipling's 'If' nearby and sang Frank Sinatra's 'My Way' loudly to myself before stepping into any potentially unpleasant encounters. Having made those points, it is genuinely the case (at least as far as I was concerned) that the unpleasant encounters, whilst living on in the memory, were few and far between. Such meetings have never involved the pupils and never the Governors. Very occasionally, there were some staffing matters that required firm attention and, just a little more frequently, some appointments with parents created tensions. Staff matters were relatively easy to resolve since one hopes one was working from a solid base of constant and conspicuous support so that one could draw on a strong working relationship that had already dealt mostly in the realm of the positive. Parental encounters were more unpredictable, possibly because the relationship, by definition, was not bound by 'professional' codes and parameters but, again, to myself, I explained away a lot of parental discontent on the grounds that fee-paying parents were under huge pressures often for financial, marital, work-related, lifestyle reasons and they naturally wanted to get things right for their children. That is not meant to sound pious or condescending; I naturally had a strong sense of empathy for our parents and valued hugely their support over the years. Indeed, I can think of only a few occasions, and with one particular parent only, when his disagreeable manner was directed at me personally. Recent external Inspections during my time only ever produced overwhelming endorsement from the 'parent body' regarding the school and their experiences of the education offered. And parents formed important social and support groups through various committees and associations led by people like Anne Dalgety, Veryan Gould and, in more recent times, Jess Hyde. The worst encounters with parents, actually, were not connected to complaints but much more to do with the occasions when one was drawn into the huge pressures they were experiencing in their private lives and I have never encountered yet a Training Manual that tells you how to respond when parents break down and weep in the privacy of the Headmaster's Study. Despite the discomfort of such occasions, one also feels extraordinarily humbled - and even privileged - that one is being trusted in this way. It is a reflection of the unique status often accorded to that of 'Headmaster' which does not always have any connection to the particular person occupying the role. I do remember a time when it seemed I had had just such a sequence of parental meetings, interspersed with a number of occasions when staff, also, became somewhat emotional behind the closed door of my study and I suddenly realised how it must have looked to casual passers-by as I gently escorted off the premises variously tear-stained adults after a meeting with me. I wanted to shout out "It's OK – everything's alright – it's not me – they're really very happy – I've actually been helping them!" All this reminds me of the ambiguous and apocryphal notice in a Staff Common Room that proclaimed *"If you think you have a problem, you should see the Headmaster"*. A notice which is not apocryphal and one which I blundered into delivering verbally to the Common Room followed a series of meetings I was having with younger female members of staff. As if by design, several of them seemed to be seeking maternity leave at overlapping times and whilst I was naturally pleased for them, it occurred to me – as I tried to arrange suitable but complicated maternity cover during their absence - that things could be coordinated a little better rather than simply leaving things to chance. My announcement to the Common Room, therefore, was meant in that light and needed to be understood in that context although even I realised that it was an area I could not control. Nevertheless, it seemed a point worth making so I finished one staff meeting with the clear advice that "if any members of staff were thinking of having a baby, they should come and see me in my study first". My wife, later, sweetly but definitely firmly, informed me that I should think before I speak.

In those interesting times in 1994, therefore, Paul Ketterer and I picked up again our professional relationship, working in the same school, for the good of the pupils, staff, parents and governors. Perhaps the relationship was not the same as the one we had left in 1985, since the expectations of our two roles had been significantly altered, but there was a sense of tentative hope in the air. Paul was working towards retirement and I was anticipating taking on the Headship at a point to be decided by the course of events. There had been no fixed time set out although Paul had indicated to the Governors that he would like to continue in post until 1997 when he would have reached the age of sixty-five. Those events, however, determined their own timing – as events often do – because in the November 1994 Governors' Meeting, Paul was offering his own notice to relinquish the post of Headmaster at the end of that academic year on the advice of his medical consultants. Given the circumstances, although Paul and Jean remained on site until July 1995, Chris Bird was offered the position of Headmaster from the point of Paul's submission of notice which, in theory, meant there were two 'Heads' operating together on the same site at the same time, albeit in different roles, in what was becoming an unusual trend in the history of All Hallows, even if the precise details of the Dix/Mortimer collaboration and, later, the Bird/Murphy handover had their own peculiar characteristics unique to them. Paul carried on in a marketing capacity, principally, whilst also acting as general consultant, whilst Chris assumed responsibility for the budget and all other internal and external matters. The Governors who attended that November meeting in 1994 might have wondered at the unfolding drama as first one Headmaster, unexpectedly, handed in his notice to leave with immediate effect and then, another Headmaster, possibly also unexpectedly, requested a few hours before deciding to accept formally the vacant post offered. In keeping with the unusual turn of events, despite the fact that 'two Heads' had theoretically existed for a time, there was also a brief period of almost fours hours, therefore, when there was 'no Head' at all! Being a School Governor was never meant to be a straightforward task!

BURSARS WE HAVE LOVED - CHRIS COYLE
(1990-2003)

Ironic juxtapositions aside (can one love a Bursar?) Chris Coyle was a much-loved Bursar, at least by the Finance Governors, and, certainly, by me. It was a professional relationship that grew to personal warmth and respect. There have been other financial personnel who have made significant impact upon the good health of the school. One thinks of Bob Bassett who retired in the May 1984 Governors' Meeting after providing over thirty years' service to the school as Accountant, Eric Fieth, Clerk to the Governors and Appeal Director, Margaret Carter, a formidable Finance Secretary and Clerk to the Governors, John Whittaker, Chairman of the Finance Committee, Peter Greenrod, his successor, and many others, right up to Mike Gardiner, the present-day Bursar and Clerk to the Governors. We salute them all in this personal tribute to Chris Coyle who represents all that is best in that great tradition, without whom, the school, as a business, would cease to function.

Chris possessed a rare combination of professional acumen, administrative efficiency, dogged determination, saint-like humility and understated humour. It is difficult to imagine a man more suited to his post or his times. I never knew him to make a mistake. Rather like the famous Australian second-row forward, he could have been nicknamed 'Nobody' – keep up....'Nobody's perfect'. He

accommodated, generously, the rather callow Headmaster forced upon him by the Governors when they appointed me to that role and guided me, gently, down the intricate path of school finances. We even shared a delicious moment when he realised five minutes before a meeting of the Finance Committee was due to start that I had forgotten entirely about the meeting. He led me skilfully through the initial exchanges until I had recovered sufficient inner resources to lead my portion of the meeting with a quickly-acquired presence of mind and our mutual respect for each other remained in place for the rest of our professional relationship. Chris was consistent, courteous, fair and uncompromising with staff; he exerted a benign despotism over the parents in gathering in fees; he remained loyal, wise, robust and good-natured in his dealings with the Governors, despite a rather austere and forbidding demeanour which made people think twice before offering reckless financial proposals. The school's finances were managed prudently under his careful watch, yet he supported every initiative and proposed every development with sympathetic, if cautious, enthusiasm. He appreciated, entirely, whatever vision it was that I was trying to develop for the school and he became the closest confidante in advising me on the art of the possible. That he was able to enact all his duties so competently and surely, even in the face of growing difficulties with his health towards the end of his time at All Hallows, is a fitting tribute to the gentleman professional he remained right up to his retirement. Chris is another of those 'unsung heroes' of whom we occasionally hear but rarely fully appreciate. Chris was a gentleman and, actually, loved by many, which just goes to show that one can effect and determine hard-nosed financial decisions without losing one's humanity. The school was lucky to have gained from his services and fortunate, generally, in the dedication offered by all other finance clerks and bursars mentioned, or not mentioned, above. Heads and Bursars have to work well together

In practice, of course, for the benefit of pupils and staff, if not parents and Governors, there could only be one Headmaster directing school business and that dispensation was duly delivered by Chris Bird who assumed the mantle with a mixture of trepidation, excitement and conviction, mindful of the excellent legacy left by his predecessor's hugely successful twenty-four years. From January 1995 until the first Governors' meeting in February, over a period of 48 calendar days, my diary records the fact that I met with 50 sets of parents – current and prospective – trying hard to 'keep my eye on the ball', recruiting, reassuring, re-building. Thankfully, in a new climate of hope, the recessionary fears receded, pupil numbers recovered and the anticipated financial losses for that current academic year actually turned into a small surplus, thus generating its own impetus for managed change and development within the traditions of the school.

A Development Committee was formed which included relatively new Governors in the persons of Diana McNulty and Ken Brown and various everyday initiatives were considered and then implemented alongside planning for major projects. For example, advertising brochures were sent to local parish priests – both Catholic and non-Catholic - , a sequence of Cheese and Wine Receptions were held at the school to foster strong relationships with current parents, new daily transport services were set up to escort pupils to school from various locations and even a school directional sign was installed on the main A361 road since one heard, time and again, that 'people didn't know where All Hallows is!' Diana McNulty became a key figure in driving this latter development home and, as is often the case with seemingly straightforward matters, this particular idea took a gargantuan amount of time and effort out of all proportion to the simplicity of the concept which, essentially, involved a road sign pointing to Turnpike Lane

---

[92] **Bob Bassett** was clearly an important financial figure in the early days.

Eric Feith was a superb supporter of the school for many years, not only serving as a Governor, Chairman of the Finance Committee, and Clerk to the Governors, but also acting as a dynamic and meticulous Appeal Director responsible for bringing in many commitments from generous benefactors when the school was launching various projects that required serious finance. He was also a modest, self-effacing man. He had sufficient faith, also, to send his son, Robin, to the school as a pupil.

Perhaps less self-effacing was the equally effective and powerful **Margaret Carter** who made Margaret Thatcher look like a fluffy pink teddy-bear. Miss Carter had possibly founded the SAS or, in a previous life, might have acted as training officer to Boudicca. I believe she was soft and lovely – really - but she knew how to protect a cheque-book and she knew how to live in a world of men.

John Whittaker was the straight-talking Yorkshire-man who asked me on interview, whilst I was still a mere junior Deputy Head, whether I agreed with the commonly accepted notion that some Deputies could never really aspire to Headship. He reminded me a little of my father-in-law who perhaps wondered whether I agreed with the commonly-accepted notion that some suitors could never really aspire to some daughters. John turned out to be the most supportive, most reasonable, most gentle of men one could wish to meet. And he also knew his stuff.

Peter Greenrod applied stringent financial controls and also saw through his own children in the school who went on to gain scholarship success at the transfer stage. I remember him also for always asking permission to dig up 'spare garlic' from Scouts' Wood; he could have taken the lot as far as I was concerned.

Mike Gardiner arrived not knowing the intimidating foreground and promptly set about throwing out the old. The fact that he is still in post speaks volumes for his financial management and just goes to show that there is more than one way to cook the books – *that is a totally cheeky and totally untrue joke I could not resist* – I meant, of course, cook the goose.

saying 'All Hallows School'. Diana found herself negotiating with the Planning department of the Highways Commission and fell tumbling like some entranced Alice in Wonderland into the circumlocutions of having to fill in forms to qualify for filling in more forms before the application could even be processed in the right offices by the right people at the right time. It is an interesting reflection that the successful erection of the road sign almost became our greatest triumph. After we had by-passed the three hundredth objection, it was with some relief that we did not have to clear away from the entrance to the front drive, spiteful rubble-loads of twenty-five quarry lorries, commandeered by the Planning Authorities, who might have been put out that they could find no further reasons to procrastinate. Whilst awaiting permission to install 'our sign', I had even considered standing at the top of the road myself in my best suit and tie, directing down the lane would-be prospective parents (who were, perhaps, only driving to Sainsbury's or church or Glastonbury) but it was pointed out, gently, that we did not want to be counter-productive in our recruiting efforts. Somebody said something about 'not wanting to put off parents unnecessarily'. As gimmicks go, I still think it might have worked. Mind you, it would not have been as successful, one imagines, as the relatively local senior school which definitely attracted a certain kind of boy to their school by insisting that all new pupils should take possession, on arrival, of not one, but two, ferrets. If ferreting Headmasters standing forlornly on the A361 never took off, we also looked again at the viability of building a new swimming pool and/or creating an all-weather pitch particularly for hockey. Swimming Pool plans were significantly altered when the preliminary costings quickly raced above the one million pounds mark, so all planning efforts went towards the provision of an astro-turf playing area, subject to the necessary confidence and funding coming through over the next few years. Sue Goodson was the Chair of Governors at this time having taken on that role in 1990 and her benign influence and genuine interest in the workings of the school ensured a high level of support for the new Headmaster. Sue was followed by Chris Dick and Patrick Nixon, both former pupils of the school, thus maintaining that tradition established by excellent leaders and communicators like Tom Barrington, George Simey and John Jackson from an earlier time. In a slight re-working of the old joke, it could be presumed that Headmasters should keep their friends close and their Governors closer, but, in absolute truth, that implied watchfulness has not been a factor in the various Headmaster-Governors' relationships over the years, at least in my view. The Governors have offered total support, albeit sometimes in robust and determined ways, and have always had the interests of the school at heart.

The Governing Body, over the years, has produced strong, successful, charming individuals, as well as providing a consistently corporate and professional mixture of support and direction, as times dictated. All Hallows has been extremely fortunate in those who have represented the Governors from its own formation in 1962 when Francis Dix first handed over the school to the Charitable Trust. One hears and knows of the horror stories elsewhere. It became a fairly common complaint at Head Teachers' Conferences to learn of others' misfortunes in dealing with governing bodies that acted with almost brutal disregard for the people involved in their

SUE GOODSON
(Former parent and Chair of Governors)

Sue wrote in the 2001 Chronicle.....

"My first contact with All Hallows was in the late 1970s when the first of our four children came to the school as pupils. Second and third followed soon after and, after a long pause, number four arrived in the 1980s. Brian, my husband, and I were delighted with the happy atmosphere permeating the school, which created opportunities for encouraging academic, sport, music and a large range of other activities in equal mix. In the mid 1980s I was invited to be a Parent/Governor which became a job I found both interesting and rewarding. Seeing how a school is run from the other side makes you realise just how difficult it can be juggling the available money, with dreams only possible if finances allow. Over 60% of our income goes out in salaries – the remainder has to be used to keep the fabric of the building in a good state of repair and buy equipment for classrooms, as well as many other pressing calls, including the major capital expenditure projects. Over my time as Governor, the campus facilities have vastly improved...and many other internal alterations and decoration have taken place to update the school. The shopping list remains endless because ideas for improvement keep coming – there is no risk of complacency! It is really impressive to see the dedication of the staff who give so much of their time to encourage the children in developing their individual talents within such a happy environment. In fact, one of our sons found the ambience of the school so much to his liking that we discovered from his school report he spent more time distracting his friends in class than actually working. A father-and-son bonding session along the lines of 'I don't see why I should work in a subject that doesn't interest me' was countered by 'I don't see why I should spend good money educating you if you don't start applying yourself'. The threat of removal from the school seemed to do the trick since the son went on to pass Common Entrance and achieve three good A-Levels. So - parents - don't despair! After an association of over twenty years with All Hallows I now find I have gone full circle as our elder daughter teaches here and her two children are also pupils. All Hallows remains an extremely happy, welcoming and fortunate school."

stories when business interests appeared to override basic courtesies. There is no place on a Board of Governors for ego or self-interest or vested interests or private agendas. It can be one of the hardest 'jobs' to outline and yet, at its simplest, the Board needs to appoint its Head Teacher carefully and then support him or her in whatever ways possible. All Hallows was indeed fortunate. The Friends of All Hallows' Association continued for a few more years with

Chris Bird – as the new Headmaster - trying to maintain the format of that group although contacts and external interest began to wane, especially as some records were lost in the handover. Nevertheless, I wrote a letter to as many former contacts as we could find in June 1995 assuring former parents and friends of the sense of continuity and the pace of change that might be anticipated in the years ahead in the hope that communication channels could remain open[93]. On Saturday 1st June 1996 Richard Arnold- Jones chaired a subsequent meeting when all those present had an opportunity to view the re-named Ketterer Wing which housed the new classrooms and Art studios (the suggestion for its name had come from the staff) and kind donations from parents had arranged for a photo-portrait of Paul and Jean to hang in that wing of the school. The meeting could also view the new prospectus which had formed part of our marketing strategies, as well as see the various decorative upgrades to the front of school which formed a crucial part of 'first impressions' for visitors. Members present at that meeting also heard, at this time, of an extension to the pre-prep department being planned to take in the old Linen Room because of the increasing pupil numbers at that end of the school, as well as the advent of outside caterers for the first time in the school's history. Jean Ketterer's role had been very much involved with catering and domestic arrangements but, whilst Jan Bird was to continue overseeing such aspects of the school in her capacity as Headmaster's wife, she had also been appointed to teach in the classroom and, as we shall see, took on various other roles as time went on, including the important administrative and promotional task of Registrar. It was surprising the uninformed passions that were generated by the idea that 'outside' caterers might have a role to play. A select group of Governors, the Bursar, Jan and I had to arrange a considerable number of interviews and meetings to bring staff and general opinion with us in order to 'sell' the idea philosophically, as well as reassure some about such fine details as the continuity in size of the usual sausages. One knows from history about imaginatively named conflicts like 'the war of Jenkins' Ear' but one wondered at the time if we were about to be drawn into the 'the war of the two-inch sausage'. Nevertheless, sanity prevailed. All existing personnel were re-employed under the same working conditions with the added bonus of being re-trained along more 'professional' lines, the quality of the food 'on the plate' improved and the school became better off financially without providing a diminished service. Another level of management was installed and we had excellent experiences with the Catering Supervisors chosen. The company selected also provided corporate 'know-how' to the expanding school which had become a much larger enterprise, especially as catering for regular events like 'team

---

[93] Mary Emsley picked up a lot of the administrative tasks of managing and updating the data base of former pupils, teachers and friends of the school that had been first put together by Sue Hiller (see later box details). Mary had enjoyed a long and healthy association of her own with the school, as mother of Daisy and Joe, then as an employee in her role as secretary, and finally as the Boarding Independent Person to whom boarders could refer, confidentially, if they wanted. I always suggested to her that her work in this latter department was not so very different from the work she undertook as a Prison Visitor. Mary displayed excellent humour, good common-sense and friendly charm in all her dealings.

teas' and other receptions became another part of our deliberate marketing. We even – or perhaps especially – set up a Catering Committee consisting of pupils and whilst children never merely dislike school food (it is always 'disgusting') they were able to have a genuine input into menu planning and food selection including theme days, requests for garlic bread and more ice-cream days. Received wisdom had suggested that the favourable treatment and service we were receiving from the catering company would 'tail off' once the contract had been won but, through the efforts of Jan and the Bursar, those high standards were maintained for as long as we were content to manage the whole business; once key personnel needed to shift their priorities onto other areas of school life, we made the subsequent decision to take everything 'in-house' once more with a more sophisticated management structure of our own. When that decision was made, all catering staff were again re-employed once more by the school foundation and the quality of the food continued seamlessly. Parental, pupil and staff views are rarely engaged so actively, one learns, as when the catering provision is under the threat of change. Incidentally, when Ian Murphy took on the Headship in 2006, the first decision he made with a financial implication was connected to the Catering Department; he authorised the purchase of larger plates and promptly supported the policy by piling his own plate sufficiently high, just to show willing. The personal example and sacrifices made by Headmasters are important 'pour encourager les autres". 'The management of change' is, I am sure, one of the key considerations on training courses for new Head Teachers. Rarely, one suspects, do new Head Teachers assume the role without the explicit or subconscious drive for change. This desire is not driven, usually, by professional or personal ego, even if new Heads, naturally, want to make a personal mark. New Head Teachers bring in a wealth of experience and good ideas from 'outside' and it is often the case that old regimes need invigorating from time to time with fresh air. One genuinely wants to build on successes and maintain traditions that have worked. One respects the history of the school. Inevitably, however, new Head Teachers are likely to be inheriting the mantle after a previous incumbent has been in post for some considerable length of time or after a relatively quick turn-around and both scenarios bring their own challenges. And, equally, it is likely that a new Head Teacher will develop his or her own view of how the school can move forward. The whole process is about becoming knowledgeable about strengths and weaknesses before determining the priorities. I had been in the fortunate position of knowing the school rather well, both from previous experiences and from my detailed and recent contact with Governors regarding the likely nature of my appointment. I was also fortunate in that Paul Ketterer and I were able to fall back on our good working relationship from the 1980s, as well as by the fact that Paul had authorised any changes I felt were reasonable when I first re-joined the school, especially since he spent that summer in France working on the timetables, leaving me free to attend to practical systems applying to the dormitories, for example. Those early weeks provided excellent preparation in terms of dealing with staff as I introduced a system whereby more dormitory staff were employed in 'Houseparent' capacities with senior pupils in the top year no longer having to operate as Dormitory Captains, but one encountered the "we always do it this

way" mentality at the very beginning as some personnel found themselves resistant to change of any sort. To their credit, however, most staff came round and embraced a new order; those who preferred not to, pursued careers elsewhere. Both alterations to the existing regime were intended to make the boarding experience more pleasurable for the pupils which, as has been noted, was entirely in keeping with recent moves to consider the child's point of view through legislation like the Children Act. Senior pupils might have lamented, partly, the loss of authority for, as Dormitory Captains, they were expected to maintain discipline and take responsibility for escorting younger boarders out of the building to the assembly point in the event of a fire alarm. The system also depended on them going to bed at a later time into dormitories filled with younger pupils where the lights had already been turned out. The Houseparents, therefore, took on these roles, allowing the senior boarders to enjoy each other's company through the night-time routines of preparing for bed and settling into sleep at the same time, and in the same dormitories, as their peers. It did mean, however, that the discipline books that had been maintained by the senior pupils were now passed onto staff so that previous entries - such as *"He was talking constantly and when I told him to stop he said he was only talking to God"* - were no longer recorded; which became a loss, indeed.

Some matters, as I have indicated, forced themselves upon proceedings without much sense of strategy or ground-breaking innovation; they simply had to be done. I am thinking of the need to produce curriculum documentation and related policy statements. It seems inconceivable today that such printed matter did not exist in any shape or form in 'the old days' but those requirements grew from external agencies exponentially and assumed legislative force in the course of time. Equally, the idea that one should attend professional in-service courses and training was not common-place. Preparing lesson plans, subscribing to corporately understood whole-school policies, taking into account Health and Safety considerations (apart from those connected to common-sense), producing detailed schemes of work and programmes of study, wrapping everything up in departmental and subject handbooks – all seemed 'modern' inventions. The National Curriculum was introduced into the Maintained Sector in 1988 and although independent schools remain exempt from the strictures, most have adopted a good working understanding and knowledge of the core components and certainly make use of aspects considered to be helpful in the teaching and learning process. In any case, greater accountability and inspection regimes now make it compulsory, in effect, for all schools to be able to prove that they achieve what they set out to do and record-keeping, paperwork, policies, etc, all underpin the more obvious evidence that can be gleaned from on-site visits by inspectors. Such prescription and accountability ushered in undoubted benefits but one cannot help feeling sometimes that something else was lost in the process. And some of this prescription has undoubtedly spilled over into the matter of teaching styles. There seem now to be fewer idiosyncratic, eccentric lessons that turn out to be memorable and inspirational, although I'm not sure how one would produce the evidence for that observation. Whether that means that there are fewer inspirational lessons today is a moot point; perhaps there is just more conformity, a corporate approach which guarantees safety and competence albeit one that is somewhat predictable and compliant. As it happens, the 'chalk and talk' approach associated with dogmatic pedagogy which was more obviously practised some years ago has never actually been proven to be ineffective, to my knowledge, but it is discredited nowadays and it is out of fashion. And as we know, education is always subject to passing fashions.

Of course, the best schools are able to accommodate and exhibit personal style and traditional practices of note alongside innovation and uniformity of approach at the same time, and it is almost certainly the case that the developments in curriculum planning alone have probably weeded out schools that were not performing as well as others. All Hallows had been inspected by HMI in October 1991 and its strengths had been recognised along with a favourable entry in the rather more idiosyncratic *'Good Schools' Guide'* which picked out many positive and distinctive features of the school including Paul Ketterer's 'avuncular' style and charisma. But the inspectors had noted some criticisms of dormitory arrangements and common room space which required attention with a subsequent D.S.S Inspection also due between May and October of 1992. Furthermore, all teaching staff had been asked to help formulate their own Job Descriptions, and Heads of Department had been directed to establish curriculum documents. Fresh on the heels of these inspections, the ISJC (Independent Schools' Joint Council) had also informed schools of its intention to undertake whole-school inspections following the demise of the HMI regime and All Hallows had been selected for inspection in the near future along with the expectation (levied on all schools) that it should pay several thousand pounds for the experience. Attempts to waive this requirement in the light of the other inspections already held came to nought, however, apart from the granting of a postponement which meant that the ISJC inspection would take place in 1995, although I was able to negotiate a further 'stay of inspection' until October 1996 on the grounds that I had only recently taken on the Headship. Having come through a thorough inspection at Prior Park Prep School not long before joining All Hallows, in my capacity there as Deputy Headmaster, I felt reasonably assured of my understanding of requirements and set to, therefore, with a will, to establish the kind of paperwork evidence which would satisfy inspectors whilst also having some direct relevance to our everyday work in the classroom in the business of education. It was at times like these that one sometimes felt that one could run the school without ever really having to see children and that their arrival at the beginning of term was something of a distraction – we were too busy setting out the principles and policies! One felt vindicated and energised by the subsequent successful report from the ISJC and later inspections from the SSD and Ofsted which had taken on responsibility for Nursery Education, as well as later inspections again by ISI which superseded the ISJC. In the course of just fifteen years or so, modern inspections are part and parcel of normal school life and any school that finds itself 'wanting' only has itself to blame. What used to take a great deal of time, as a 'one-off' exercise, in terms of specific preparation, now applies all of the time – or should do – which is probably the best development that has emerged from this inspection regime; schools can receive merely a few days notice of a visit from external inspectors and we are all much more relaxed about the process because we are more confident about the outcomes due to our own internal monitoring and assessment procedures. I am boring myself writing about these matters so it is time to move on to other things.

The Friends of All Hallows[94] met in June 1997 and the following points were noted:

- Pupil registrations had improved.
- Lynn Walker[95] – current Head of the Learning Support Department – had been appointed as Head Teacher of St Antony's, Leweston.
- Janet Rose (teacher) and Bruce Mein (school doctor) were both retiring after 19 years of association with the school.
- Peter Scotland, former teacher of French and Games, had died earlier that year.
- The Science Laboratories had been modernised.
- The Internet and an email system had been installed.
- Eleven scholarship successes had been gained to eight different schools.
- The Under 13 Boys, Under 12 Girls and Under 11 Boys were South West Hurdles Champions.
- The Under 13 Boys won the St John's, Beaumont, rugby seven-a-side Tournament.
- The Under 13 Boys, Under 13 Girls were South West Long Jump Champions.
- The Girls Hockey Under 13s (pictured right) recorded their third undefeated season in a row and became Champions at tournaments held at Canford, Blundell's and Prior Park with the Under 11 Girls winning the Somerset Schools Tournament and at Port Regis.
- The Under 13 Boys became Champions of the National Gymnastics Competition and also became the British Schools' all-comers Champions made up of Tom Bishop, Charles Hare, Tim Wynn-Jones, Chukwudi Phil-Umunnakwe, Mark Byrne and Andrew Edwards.
- Misa Vernon rode for England in a three-day Equestrian Event in Paris beating France in their own arrière-cour.
- The Duke of Norfolk had accepted an invitation to give away the prizes on Prize Day (ill health around the time of Prize Day subsequently prevented him from attending).
- News was circulated about the impending visit from Cardinal Basil Hume to All Hallows to celebrate the school's sixty-year jubilee in 1998 (see right).

---

[93] The thirteenth and last meeting of the Friends of All Hallows Association took place on 14th June 1997 after only 14 people turned up out of 1000 invitations sent out. Mind you, if one thousand had turned up that would have presented problems of a different sort. A new Parent Organisation was set up in its place which consisted of parents of a more recent vintage as well as, mostly, current parents and that committee exists today in a slightly different format but with the same overriding principles of raising funds and organising social events. (It has been noted at various times with some wry amusement that one used to become a 'friend' of All Hallows only after one had left).

[93] In addition to Lynn Walker, the following staff also went on to Headships after a career at All Hallows: Jocelyn Trappes-Lomax, Richard Arnold-Jones, Derek Henderson, George Robertson, Caroline Riley, David Clark, John Murphy, Chris Godwin, Chris Bird and Ian Murphy (apologies to anyone missed off the list).

On 8th May 1998, Cardinal Basil Hume visited the school for the day, having been invited by Richard Arnold-Jones, and not only said Mass (which was recorded live on the Internet) but took part in many activities. He visited, for example, ('uninvited' as recorded by Alex Cotterell of Form 1W), the Greek Taverna that had been set up for the day as part of their class project, and, taking Alex's advice, he sampled "a small snack of pitta bread, taramasalata, black olives and Greek lemonade – the Cardinal said it was delicious". His sermon was memorable for keeping things simple when he reminded the children that all they had to remember from his visit were five words: "Jesus loves us very much". The children had become very excited before the Cardinal arrived even if one pupil in Lower Prep informed one of the dinner ladies that a very special cardigan was coming to the school and Archie Baker, in Upper Prep, wanted to know when the carnival was arriving. They remembered a lot more, however, than simply those five special words for when they had been asked to write or talk about the Cardinal's visit after the event they came up with the following comments.....

"I think the Cardinal is a kind man. He helps keep people safe. He must go to other places like Australia to help street beggars".

"A Cardinal cleans the place up. After the people have gone home, he goes home too to visit people who are ill".

"We can tell him our problems and he often draws a little cross on us".

"He goes to church on Sundays but not the other days because he is too busy".

"The Cardinal tells everybody about Jesus and his friends and he cleans the bells and he tells everybody what to do".

"I think a Cardinal wears a long gown. He has a house just next to his church and I think he will be very crinkly and old and I think he has a pet dog or a cat" (to which Basil Hume added in his own handwriting "and he likes All Hallows' pupils".

The children were invited to compose a prayer to commemorate the visit and we sent the 'sixty best' prayers to Cardinal Hume. Quite what he made of one prayer (in which a girl asked God to *"look after our parents, especially our mothers and fathers"*) one never knew but he wrote back to the school to thank us in April 1999 for a copy of the school magazine in which were recorded many details of the day. When he left us the whole school lined the front driveway to wave him off and it was with great sadness when we heard of his death in June 1999.

Basil Hume OSB, OM, R.I.P. (2nd March 1923 – 17th June 1999) was a monk of the English Benedictine monastery of Ampleforth Abbey and for 13 years its abbot until his appointment as Archbishop of Westminster in 1976. His elevation to a cardinal of the Roman Catholic Church followed during the same year. From 1979 Hume served also as President of the Catholic Bishops' Conference of England and Wales. He held these appointments until his death from cancer in 1999. His final resting place is at Westminster Cathedral in the Chapel of St Gregory and St Augustine. During his lifetime Hume received wide respect from the general public which went beyond the Catholic community. Hume's time in office saw Catholicism become more accepted in British society than it had been for 400 years, culminating in the first visit of Queen Elizabeth II to Westminster Cathedral in 1995. It was also during his tenure in Westminster that Pope John Paul II made an historic visit to England in 1982. In 1998, Hume asked John Paul II for permission to retire, expressing the wish to return to Ampleforth and devote his last years to peace and solitude, fly fishing and following his beloved Newcastle United Football Club. The request was refused. Hume was diagnosed with inoperable abdominal cancer in April 1999. On 2nd June of that year, Queen Elizabeth awarded him the Order of Merit. He died just over two weeks later in Westminster, London, at age 76. Following his death, a statue of him in his monastic habit and wearing his abbatial cross was erected in his home town of Newcastle upon Tyne outside St Mary's Cathedral which was unveiled by Queen Elizabeth II. He remained a modest, unassuming man all his life and was perhaps never happier than when living within the monastic community at Ampleforth; "*Like the deer that yearns for running streams, so my soul is yearning for you, my God*" – Psalm 41.

Ironically, for a man of such humility, he inspired awe in those around him, certainly in those of us at All Hallows on the day of his visit. But not for pupil Camilla Jennings. As the Cardinal walked down the drive, Camilla stepped over the prostrate figure of former Headmaster Paul Ketterer, who was expressing old-style devotion of a Catholic kind by lying down at the Cardinal's feet, sidestepped the present Headmaster, who was dithering about the correct form of address, and expressed an awe of her own by grabbing the Cardinal's hand and saying with utterly genuine admiration, "Oh, I do like your ring!" She might as well have said, "Bas, come and sit down by me with a nice cup of tea and we can have a natter." His Eminence Cardinal Basil Hume, OSB, OM, Archbishop of Westminster, 'the Queen's Cardinal', President of the Catholic Bishops' Conference of England Wales, Abbot of Ampleforth, was, of course, like the rest of us, charmed by the force of nature that went by the name of Camilla Jennings. Camilla could almost fill a chapter of her own but we'll allow her a few lines which she emailed to me recently: "*I miss All Hallows with all my heart, this school changed my life in more ways than one. I never believed my dreams would come true of joining my sister at her secondary school as my grades wouldn't allow me. However Mr Bird made it possible. He told me if I work and try my hardest and kept my head down (most of the time - as it's clear I like to talk) then maybe you might just see what happens. Mr and Mrs Bird taught me to never give up no matter what. If anything they taught me to believe in myself. I did and it paid off and I owe it all to them.*

Cardinal Hume was a lifelong supporter of Newcastle United FC and the boys are showing off their project

This school was just wonderful inside and out."

The wonderful Camilla – inside and out.

And just by way of contradistinction, I'll sandwich Camilla between a Cardinal and a Major-General. I received an email recently from former pupil Patrick Fagan who attended All Hallows in the 1940s and straddled the years at Scorhill and Cranmore like a few others already mentioned. He tells me that every so often he walks the familiar pathways of Dartmoor from his schoolboy days and that he had immense pleasure in returning to Cranmore on the occasion of the Cardinal's visit. He outlined the fact that *"mountains, music and cricket"* became the three *"non-human"* loves of his life as a direct result of his experiences at All Hallows, both at Scorhill and Cranmore. He remembers bowling to the cricket master - Mr Gorman - who had placed a sixpenny piece on the middle stump as a reward to any boy who could bowl him out - which Patrick duly did, of course, thus surrendering, as he puts it, *"his amateur status"*. Furthermore, with typical All Hallows' Major-General modesty, he describes his love of mountains.... *"My first four terms were at Scorhill, and I believe marked my life. I had never before experienced wild country, and I loved it. Years later it led me to wander amongst the mountains of Wales, and this in turn led me to meeting Chris Bonington, much my age, and started me mountaineering. I was never a great climber, but I did love the mountains and eventually went nine times to the Himalayas, and also to both polar regions. (I have a little mountain in Antarctica called Mt Fagan after me!)"*

All Hallows continued to move forward towards the Millennium. Systems, facilities and personnel were all transformed in a continuous development programme which built upon all the sure foundations of the school and its typical characteristics whilst also adding some

JOHN-PAUL RENOUF

Into this world stepped John-Paul Renouf, one of the great men in the history of the school, who took on the role of Deputy Headmaster in September 1995. Whilst checking the dictionary for definitions of the word *'deputy'* I came across *'substitute, replacement, makeshift, apology, stand-in, stop-gap, baby-sitter, vice, stooge, scapegoat and dummy'*. Now, I make no conclusions about those descriptions (I was once a Deputy Headmaster myself, after all) but many Deputies might find some knowing correlation with the nature of their jobs and

the definitions alluded to above. Interestingly, my dictionary trawl for definitions of 'deputy' also threw up the word 'metaphor' which might mean that such men and women are not to be taken literally. But John-Paul could not have been taken any other way. Good Deputy Heads loom large in the life of a school and make a real difference to the pupils, staff and parents they encounter; John-Paul Renouf was one such man. His charisma, good humour, experience, wide-ranging talent and humanity carried all before him. And like all caring disciplinarians, his bark was worse than his bite, although some boys might have other memories after a few times in his study. I had known John since 1985 when we worked briefly together at Prior Park Prep School and had quickly recognised his professional talents and his personal qualities. John had had a wealth of experience in teaching many different academic subjects, as well as enjoying unparalleled success at coaching rugby with his sevens teams, in particular, winning many prestigious tournaments across the country. He was also extremely musical and possessed the richest baritone singing voice which embellished so much of the school's chapel life at Mass and other assemblies. He was the kindest, most sociable man one could wish to meet and, in those midsummer months of 1995, when John joined the school a term early whilst his wife, Elizabeth, was concluding family business with their three children in Leicestershire, John made it his own business to meet as many of the local inn keepers as possible, such was his bountiful way with people, particularly if they liked to talk and sing in wayside alehouses. The job of a Deputy Head was wide-ranging. I once went through John-Paul's pigeon-hole in the Common Room (in the days before emails) and found letters addressed to The Communications Officer, The Key Skills Manager, The Inset Trainer, The National Curriculum Expert, The School Policies Co-ordinator, The Head of Media Studies, The Outward Bound Co-ordinator, The Travel Officer, The Health & Safety Manager, The Timetabler, The Person i/c Drains, etc, etc. Mind you, I had arranged for most of those letters, in the first place, to leave my pile and go straight into John's; I'm not quite sure what he did with them thereafter. John often referred to his role as 'The Deputy Headache' but, as I tried to point out to him, his principal job was to make me look good. I had, after all, once received a letter in my pigeon-hole, addressed to 'The Hamster' when it was clear the typist was having trouble with letters e, d and a (I think) but there was

something in it, in that the treadmill goes round and round, without much sense of progress or purpose sometimes, so it falls to the Deputy Head to keep the Head grounded and prevent him from becoming isolated. Being addressed as 'the hamster', whilst not portraying the particular respect one might wish for, I have to say, is infinitely better, however, than the term used by one parent whose true feelings, perhaps, came out uncontrollably when he had written a letter to the Bursar with the envelope addressed as 'The Bastard'. As I have suggested elsewhere, the role of a Deputy Head, however, is not to be seen as a stepping-stone to Headship; it has an identity, importance and definition of its own. And, of course, there are occasions when the Deputy has to deputise for the Head Teacher which means acting with all due force and authority, as occasion demands. John taught music, Religious Education and Games at All Hallows before heading up the Mathematics Department for many years, a role he continued even when voluntarily stepping down from Deputy Headship at the end of 2012. John had been a Deputy Headmaster in the Maintained Sector, as well as filling a senior master role at Ratcliffe College, before joining All Hallows where, one presumes, he will finish his career, for he is still teaching maths at the time of writing. But John has a life outside of All Hallows. He writes music, sings, and keeps the community of Shepton Mallet happy in his jaunts to the local watering-holes. He dreams of becoming a commercial courier ferrying documents and packages of national importance to London, the North of England and The Dordogne and back. He skis. He runs farms in Devon during half-term by shearing sheep bottoms, administering healing ointments thereto, cleaning pigsties and making sure that Rufus, the Bull, has all he needs in order to service four dozen cows twice-daily. Rufus might have thought he could get by without the assistance of John-Paul but for schools like All Hallows it is a different story: they need men like John-Paul Renouf.

softer touches to relationships and communication. The spirit of the times demanded a more consensual approach than might have been the case in previous years with certainly a greater sense of accountability. The need to be more transparent is not a veiled criticism of previous regimes under Dix-Mortimer-Ketterer but simply a reflection of the age and of the society in which we lived. Equally, parental expectations had moved on too. More and more parents were choosing independent education who had not necessarily 'gone through' the private system themselves and one found oneself dealing, on the one hand, with those who seemed somewhat nervous and unknowing about all connected matters, as well as maintaining a working relationship, on the other, with those who banged their fists on the metaphorical table as 'paid-up' fee-payers who had bought a commodity like any other with rights and demands of their own which they expressed confidently on a regular basis. The trend towards day pupils and the shift away from boarding continued which brought a dynamic of its own also, although many parents and pupils bought into the school on a day-basis because of the school's boarding traditions and status. But it remained a full-time occupation and lifestyle.

One's early years as Headmaster are always likely to remain long in the memory as one tries to grapple with the giant's robes that have been draped over uncertain shoulders and, I suppose, mine are no different in that two incidents spring to mind in 1995. Firstly, perhaps echoing a similar experience of Paul Ketterer's, in March 1994, when a Governors' meeting records the fact that *"three boys had taken to the high road"*[96], my first 'official' day and night as Headmaster was marked by the fact that a boy, new to boarding, decided at midnight to escape via a dormitory window and run up the lane to hitch a lift from a passing lorry back to Bath, where he lived. His mother, showing a remarkable level of sangfroid (although perhaps she expected it since she knew her independent son was not minded to remain a boarder for long) phoned me rather teasingly to ask how her son was coping knowing all the time that he had absconded and was tucking into bacon and eggs at home. The boy – now a young man – smiles charmingly every time I see him, hardly realising, I think, the role he might have played in ensuring that my career as Headmaster almost never got off the ground. Paul Ketterer's absentees decided to take themselves off at the same time as the Governors' minutes also recorded the replacement of Greek on the timetable with Information Technology – perhaps they were budding classicists in revolt; my young man simply had no wish to board, so he didn't, and that, mercifully, was an end to it. But, Freddy, I shall never forget you. I was somewhat reassured only recently, as I near the end of the writing of this book, to have received an email from the splendidly-named

---

[96] I think these must be three different pupils from the three or four called Mark, Simon, Tom, and one other, whose facebook entries record the fact that they were *"caught venturing off the footpath towards the local train station"*. Their punishment for the rest of term was to pick up stones by the old Long Jump Pit. And these must be different again from the boy who remembers that for some misdeed he had to creosote the athletics track or others who recall *"sweeping snow in the winter and picking up leaves the rest of the year."*

Hadrian Teasdale, a former pupil in the later 1960s of Mr Mortimer's time, who ran away from All Hallows never to return. Hadrian was not happy at the brutality of the regime he encountered, although he admits that a sudden move from Peru to Shepton Mallet was not guaranteed to ease his transition, and he remembers fondly his maths teachers, Colonel Yule, and *"the kind gentleman"* that was Major Carslaw. Hadrian went on to Downside in 1972. At least, pupils of mine - and those of Paul Ketterer - who ran away, returned! It reminds me of the parents of another ex-All Hallows pupil, who had just returned home after dropping off their reluctant son at his new senior school – as a boarder for the first time - only to find him emerging from the boot of their car into which he had climbed, unseen, before they departed. Sometimes, boys just don't want to board. Incidentally, my first night at Prior Park Prep School as a resident Housemaster, charged with the welfare of thirty or so boys whose parents had placed utter faith and confidence in my ability to look after their sons, was notable for the fact that one James O'Brien decided to fall out of the top bunk in his sleep, gash his head and pump blood all over the dormitory floor which necessitated a midnight dash to Casualty. I put it all down to 'First Night Nerves' although, it has to be said, the nerves were not mine for I slept like a baby. My second early memory as Head at All Hallows concerns the time I finally decided to leave the premises on an official visit to Sherborne School having spent a ridiculous period of twenty-four hour/seven-days-a-week vigilance on site for what seemed like months on end in case 'anything should happen' that nobody else could manage. This was my school. It was my watch. Only I could deal with all eventualities. I dare not leave the premises. Or so my theory went. But, I had to leave it, of course, and trust that all would be well without my protective hand. Hah! I duly went for a tour of Sherborne School and spent the afternoon being a grown-up Headmaster only to return towards early evening to find three fire engines on the front drive and the whole school crammed into the Chapel whilst yellow-helmeted firemen combed the dormitories for a non-existent fire. Memo to self: don't leave the school premises.

Back to those 'systems, facilities and personnel'. The Curriculum received a major overhaul. Inspection regimes expected nothing less but, notwithstanding the requirements of inspections, rightly and reasonably, professional educators in the modern world needed to set out on paper their considered rationale for what was taught and, perhaps more importantly, how such things should be taught. Gone were the days when one Headmaster known to me in another school could proudly proclaim his academic philosophy to a highly intellectual Chief Inspector that 'we teach the children to read and write', thereupon turning away to light his fat cigar saying, dismissively, "if you need any more detail, see my Deputies". The National Curriculum, as we have seen, was very much in the public eye and the independent schools' regulatory bodies were busily revising Common Entrance and the Public Schools' Scholarship exams. Our reporting and assessment procedures needed to be upgraded in the light of the curriculum developments. The timetable had to be adapted to fit new requirements. Information and Communication Technology (ICT) was introduced across the school and the sum of £25000, in 1995, was readily set aside by the Governors to purchase a suite of Acorn computers in an appropriately converted room with full training opportunities for dedicated staff. Nor were the extra-curricular activities neglected as the school day was reviewed to accommodate over sixty clubs and hobbies between the end of formal teaching time and the bed-bells for boarders.

A spate of school inspections included the ISJC (October 1996), the boarding provision under the auspices of the Social Services Department (October 1997) and the Lower Prep arrangements by Ofsted (September 1997), with a separate, two-day HMI visit in November 1997, when the Inspector found All Hallows in excellent shape with 95% of lessons observed showing the children working well above National Curriculum norms, specialist teachers *'knowledgeable and inspiring'*, the extra-curricular provision *'outstanding'*, display work *'first-class'*, and pupil responses *'excellent'*. Nor could he recall a school coming through a Social Services Inspection with the final adjudication of 'no recommendations' as All Hallows had done earlier that term.

Form Tutors took on greater responsibilities; Personal and Social Education programmes were introduced; developments took place in Speech and Drama (both in terms of whole school productions[97] and personalised opportunities through LAMDA and external festivals[98]), as well as in regularised Music Concerts. Sports tours[99] abroad took place for the first time in the school's history with hockey trips planned to Holland and skiing trips departing for Europe. The Merit Championship and House system was given life – with a new fourth House, Wanstrow, introduced (although, as it transpired, and as has been recorded elsewhere, it was simply a re-introduction of The Wolves pack from many years earlier). Open Days were built into the Calendar; school mini-buses and other forms of transport were utilised to bring pupils to school from far-flung places; B-teams, C-teams and even D-teams were introduced into the games programme with competitive matches for all which went a long way towards galvanising

[97] John-Paul Renouf directed a stunningly good production of *Bugsy Malone* and a moving performance called *Carrots* about the story of Dr Barnardo which was notable for its employment of staff actors and singers in the persons of Renouf, Cardozo and Bird (I know, I know!) alongside the children (interestingly, that experiment has never been repeated). Sophie Ball maintained the high standards with her own creation of *A Shared Dream* which saw the alien Mismi land on the Library Lawn and those renewed traditions from the time of Mr Dix now live on through the excellent efforts of Naomi Holland with mesmerising shows like *Alice in Wonderland*, *The Wizard of Oz* and *Fame*.

[98] Sue Holland (now Cook) and her daughter, Naomi, developed and have maintained a wonderful recent tradition which has established the name of All Hallows firmly on the map of Speech and Drama in the South West as cherry jersey after cherry jersey goes up to deliver distinctive solo and duet performances in centres like Bath and Taunton to take away gold medals and individual trophies in delivering captivating showcase performances in verse and prose speaking and acting.

[99] For example, the Easter Holidays, 1999, saw forty pupils in two boys' teams and one girls' team embark on a hockey tour of Scheveningen, Holland, organised by a certain Ian Murphy, in his guise as Sports' Director at that time, aided by the incomparable Jayne Knowles. Although results went against us and the usual observations about over-age players in the opposition teams along with idiosyncratic umpiring decisions were manifold, players like Matthew Cross, James Brackley, Aaron White, Richard Morgan-Jones, Carlos Flores, Tim Ball, Joe Emsley, Inigo de la Rica, Sebastian Luckman, Oliver Mellotte, Flora Robertson, Anna Walker, and many others, all featured from time to time. One of the principal learning curves involved the fact that we needed to practise on an astro-turf of our own if we were going to compete on 'level playing fields' and such a touring experience, no doubt, added useful ammunition to the impetus gathering pace for a suitable all-weather playing surface at All Hallows.

Early computers in use

the broadest possible pupil interest in sport, as well as improving the standards of the school A-teams because of the greater sense of competition for places. Nor were the staff forgotten. The classroom contact time was gradually reduced, partly to recognise the broader range of additional responsibilities and commitments many staff took on as the bureaucracy of education became more demanding. Half-days were instigated by combining in a sequence such non-contact lessons, also as a means of recognising the value of the teachers, as well as the practical reality of Saturday mornings, and other weekend duties, which involved many of the staff. One can focus on the children, of course, as a primary responsibility, or make a case for the parents as our fee-paying clients to occupy our thoughts most of the time, but I hope it is accurate to state that my priorities were the staff. I recall my father, in his role as the Regional Chief Pensions and Welfare Officer at British Aerospace, telling me that one should always look after one's staff and I tried to keep that mantra in the forefront of my thinking. My reasoning was partly because colleagues should be motivated and their achievements recognised, as well as because support should be offered where it was needed, but, also, because if the staff were operating at high levels of engagement, the other key personnel in the 'triangle', that is, parents and children, would be happy and fulfilled anyway. A great deal of my time, therefore, was spent in wandering round the classrooms, showing a genuine interest in what was going on, arranging personal meetings with staff in the privacy of my study and making it my business to know what was happening in the school. Looking back, such an approach hardly seems ground-breaking but it is surprising how quickly disgruntlement can set in, with the attendant power to create further problems, if a genuine interest in people and the simple common courtesies are not maintained. Ted Wragg, the late and much respected professor, teacher and educational commentator and satirist, once asserted that if children were to get a good deal, teachers had to have one too, and that he occasionally meets *"people who have been shredded of their humanity but the good news is that many teachers and Heads have managed to retain it*". It is in trying to help people retain their humanity that we encourage the best out of the grown-ups so that the best opportunities can flow towards the little ones. And, in a boarding school, with mouths to feed and toe-nails to be clipped and roofs to be mended and wickets to be cut and egos to be massaged and individuals to be recognised and hearts and minds to be engaged, it's not just about the grown-ups who are teachers. 'Keeping people gruntled' is not a particularly 'sexy' mission statement but it will do for the moment alongside 'keeping one's eye on the ball'.

All Hallows of Cranmore Hall was also sitting on a peach of a site and it needed to be shown off to the world and inhabited happily by its inmates in the very best possible light. There were twenty-five acres or so set in beautiful Somerset countryside (even if it did rain quite a bit). Cranmore Hall, former seat of the Right Hon. Sir Richard Paget, Bart., was described in the 1899 edition of 'Country Life Illustrated', as *"a fine, and in some ways, ornate mansion of Jacobean aspect much of it dating from thirty years ago though the location is very old. The general character of the house is striking and effective and the long and handsome arcades form a very unusual and picturesque feature. They seem somehow to give an impression of summer, with their temptation to live out of doors, with a summer garden as the picture they command. Here we are in the midst of a pastoral valley, on the slopes of the Mendips, and the little rivulet known as The Cran, from which the place takes its name, flows at the foot of the lawn. It is indeed a pleasant meeting of garden and stream, where the sward is greener and where many opportunities for water-gardening are to be found. The entrance front of Cranmore Hall faces the open park, with its broad grassy sweep, and across a charming vista of wood and meadow is seen the distant tower of the old church at West Cranmore. It is a very noble and spacious outlook. To the south of the carriage drive the wooded park rises abruptly to an eminence, upon which stands a summer-house fashioned after the style of a Grecian temple. The situation is very fine and commands a splendid view of the hall, the winding valley, and the wooded heights, with a further prospect down the stream, ending in an elevated pine-clad knoll, near which is the site of a Roman camp"*. (The site of the Manor House dates back to the Middle Ages and Cranmore Hall was actually built in 1611 but it was much altered, restored and added to in about 1860 by the Paget family. It also had a fine pair of panelled stone gate piers on the old 'back' drive way off the A361 which dated probably to the seventeenth century - known locally as 'cat and dog' - but these were cut away and stolen in the middle of the night in the late twentieth century).

Even a monkey, as Headmaster, could sell the place! I am going to remind my pupils that *"the sward is greener"* at All Hallows lest they fix their inward eyes too firmly on those blessed computer screens. And if you want a touch of history connecting to the past still farther back, how about this description from the same publication of 1899, lingering over the old stable courtyard and the old chapel, *"here, by the glass-houses, are the evidences of the older Cranmore, in a two-storied cruciform building, known as the Cross House, carrying us back to the days when this was a possession of the great Abbey of Glastonbury, which lies some twelve miles away. The mitred abbots of Glastonbury were great men in their day in the West Country and even now the*

The Library Lawn c.1890

horror of the judicial murder of the last of them[100] *casts a shadow upon the land. Thinking of this, we recall, in this old garden at Cranmore, the days when the monks of Glastonbury, living at their house on the Mendip slopes, tended their gardens and tilled their fruitful fields."*

Francis Dix had chosen well. If D. H. Lawrence's Tom Brangwen had raised his head from the earthy soil with a kind of wistful longing for elsewhere towards the *"church tower at Ilkeston in the empty sky"*, there was a sense that the *"expectancy and the look of an inheritor"* was bestowed, in reverse, by those who gaze towards Cranmore Hall, on the spirited children and adults who live and toil and play in the gardens and grounds of All Hallows. But the gardens and grounds and buildings now serviced a school, the needs of which were specific and full of intent. An astro-turf[101], dedicated to the memory of Moira Thompson, was built into a newly-landscaped level surface to the south-west of the main building (see pictures overleaf), and Scouts' Wood, as it was known, was given a sympathetic make-over with managed pathways and picnic-places and a central reading/drama circle, as well as areas dedicated to children's sculptures like their gothic totem-poles, all produced so expertly by Nick Somerville.

---

[100] The last Abbot of Glastonbury, Richard Whiting, was executed in 1539, at the age of eighty, on a trumped-up charge of treason and hanged, drawn and quartered at the Tor beside St Michael's Church and his dismembered head was displayed thereafter on a pike at the Abbey gateway whilst his limbs were exhibited at Bath, Wells, Ilchester and Bridgwater as a salutary lesson to others who would stand in the way of the King's men. Cardinal Wolsey had described him earlier as *"an upright and religious monk, a provident and discreet man, and a priest commendable for his life, virtues and learning"*. Despite his ill-health, great age and innocence (!), Cromwell's own handwriting records the note that *"The Abbot of Glaston to be tried at Glaston and also executed there"* – such summary justice was the order of the day! The abbey was broken up: *"the exquisite panelling served to make great fires by means of which the bells were melted: the metal was then sold. The stained glass in the windows was smashed, the arches and pillars hacked away, the tombs desecrated. The sculptured stones were disposed of at sixpence a cartload to any countryman who might desire to build a pig-sty or a cattle-shed. The manuscripts from the precious library were torn up to light fires or make parcels or were sold to book-binders at nominal prices"* – The Glories of Glastonbury by Armine le Strange Campbell.

[101] The astro-turf pitch was part of a major project which involved numerous meetings with planners, sports architects and other technical advisers to create an all-weather playing area on a surface which could accommodate hockey, as well as tennis, and, at the same time, realign the natural contours of the sloping land in the south-west corner of the playing fields by, essentially, dumping the top slope soil onto the bottom portion and levelling everything into a two-tiered arrangement. A separate grass pitch could also be utilised, therefore, into the bargain. As the diggers moved in, I was half-hoping we might encounter some Roman remains or perhaps the Holy Grail – thus bringing some potential revenue into the school - but our only treasure concerned the discovery of an abnormal amount of arsenic in the uncovered soil which needed extensive treatment. A further major set-back occurred a few months after we had started using the new surface when a flash-flood swept down the Cran in a Somerset tsunami and corrugated the astro carpet as if it was made of cardboard so we ended up with a concertina-effect at the school end of the pitch. Fortunately, the insurance covered the costs of a totally new surface being installed hardly five minutes after the first one had been laid. Our own mini-flood prevention scheme, subsequently put in place, ensured that such a phenomenon could never happen again. All these logistical manoeuvres took time and necessitated several meetings with experts. One such meeting memorably involved the Chairman of Governors, the Headmaster, the Bursar, the Engineer and the Project Manager. It was memorable mostly for the fact that each of the gentlemen mentioned possessed the Christian name 'Christopher'. The Minutes of that meeting referred to the fact that *'Chris had suggested such-and-such but Chris felt this would be too costly so, on Chris' recommendation, the idea was adopted to do so-and-so and Chris was charged with bringing it into action after consultation with Chris'*. It was a wonder anything was actually achieved at all.

Julian Silk, scorer of the first goal on the Astro

The re-ordering and subject-specific development of two new science laboratories enabled the Head of Science, Sue Forshaw, to make better use of the good facilities already in existence, which had been so well marshalled by Greg Jones over more than twenty years, and new classroom sites were also established for what became Martin Green's ICT suite, the History room, under Hilary Adams' dedicated eye, and the French rooms to modernise the excellent work being undertaken by Libby Doe-Wansey. Pupil numbers in the junior department were increasing again which necessitated the conversion of two former garages into additional classrooms; new music practice rooms were established; common room space provided for (in the cellar, for example); new staff flats were converted in the boarding houses; a cycle track was created around the perimeter of the grounds and a new, safety-conscious Adventure Playground replaced the rather risky but fun version Greg Jones and I had first constructed back in the 1980s when we instituted the 'All Hallows Challenge', a competition which was taken on and developed by Moira Thompson, but which now seems to have faded away – more's the pity. Internal communication systems were also improved, including a whole new telephone network, and additional and enhanced office space for secretarial staff and key personnel were made available. And the knotty and perennial problem of the swimming pool was finally resolved with a cost-friendly solution of approximately £40000 which compared extremely favourably with the £1 million projections we had also been considering; this consisted of a sliding, 'concertina' roof structure which could be opened up in the summer to retain the outdoor pool appearance whilst also allowing for prolonged swimming activity through all but the worst of the winter months. New sports changing rooms were also built alongside.

The School Library finally moved into purpose-built surroundings in the Ketterer Wing thus freeing up the old Library for an enlarged Staff Common Room which, nevertheless, still looks out onto 'the Library Lawn' although no library remains in that vicinity. Some names just stick.

But facilities and systems are only part of the story; people have to utilise the 'bricks and mortar' and operate the systems, so new appointments were made like a Second Deputy Head, first in the person of Ian Murphy, when he and his wife, Rachel, joined the residential team, and then with Jeff Peabody and his wife, Becky. Jeff went on to assume the title and role of 'Assistant Head – Operations' and kept a good handle on the day-to-day running of the school thereafter, including organising the almost daily (it seemed) Cover arrangements which arrived in email form into our in-boxes with an amusing quote each day, lest we lose our sense of humour as the need for more cover pinged in. A Director of Studies was considered necessary to coordinate all curricular matters so Trevor Richards was promoted, from within, into this role and he looks likely, today, to assume many of those same responsibilities, along with an enhanced senior position as Director of Learning, in his second stint of service at All Hallows following a brief professional 'sabbatical' whilst gaining educational psychologist qualifications.

The Junior Department had grown sufficiently for a specific departmental co-ordinator to be appointed at that end of the school and Mary Whittleton developed all connected matters in a highly efficient and professional manner before moving onto a Deputy Headship at Stonar School, thus paving the way for others to take on that role, until Kevin Hannah arrived in recent times to become Head of the Junior School under Ian Murphy's Headship. Many more staff were appointed as pupil numbers grew to record levels yet again towards the end of my Headship years which brought in renewed staff contracts and more sophisticated appraisal systems. Just as inspections initially created tensions, so, too, the idea of Staff Appraisal programmes created some uncertainties as some staff felt that it would have the effect of undermining performance rather than enhancing. Careful and sensitive management ensured that the whole process only came to be seen as positive and uplifting; there was no doubt that it helped hugely in the professional development and better performance of teaching which led to improved learning. Perhaps the single most reassuring decision that eventually persuaded staff that there was nothing to fear was my explanation that I would undertake, as Headmaster, an appraisal of my own, first, and subject myself to external appraisers who would be conducting a confidential survey amongst staff as to my own credentials. As the good and the great from the Catholic world of education were wheeled out to scrutinise my every move over the next term or so, I wondered why it was that the Holy Father in Rome had not been approached to add his infallible input into proceedings, so 'good and great' were the men and women chosen to appraise me, but, somehow, I came stumbling through with an endorsement, after a far more rigorous procedure than the one I was proposing for staff, so everybody relaxed and we carried on. Pupil numbers were racing towards 300 and just as Paul Ketterer before me had had to raise concerns with the Governors about the expansion of the school in his day, so, too, I felt it important to bring to the Governors' attention the question of optimum numbers. Governors' Minutes over the years had committed themselves to 'no more than 250', 'absolutely no more than 270', and as long ago as Mr Dix's time there was a feeling that the school should not go above 200. All such considerations had two points in mind. The first was practical. Every time the school roll went above a certain number, additional classrooms would be necessary, extra staff should be appointed, and some of the fixed communal areas could start creaking at the joints (for example, the Dining Room, the Chapel, performance areas, etc). Secondly, the concern was more one of ethos and style. Schools like Millfield and Port Regis and The Dragon School, say, survived very well with as many as 500 prep school pupils, but they had developed their own traditions and campuses, for that matter, to accommodate such numbers. All Hallows is renowned, one feels, for its small, family atmosphere, its attention to each individual child and its homely, more intimate touch; 'we know thee by thy name' (see earlier comments). Some of that familiarity can, inevitably, become lost as the business enterprise takes over[102] but other research suggests that there can be benefits in large schools such as reduced bullying. It was a direction that needed to be discussed at Governor level. Strategic planning needed to be employed. Under my Headship, at least, the decision was reached to limit numbers to 299 (and even then we broke through the 300 barrier for a time) so that traditional characteristics could be managed and maintained. Even today, I think a floating number of pupils between 250-275 would be a norm to which we could happily cut our cloth, with a contingency for up to 299 as demand dictated. Complications concerning 'income-streams' occur when the balance between boarding and day is taken into account but, again, this is a matter of analysing expenditure in all its forms against income. But who am I to put forward future planning of this order? Future regimes might well decide that 400 pupils is a reasonable target; that All Hallows will become a school for Day Pupils only; that a separate international school will occupy the residential quarters for eighteen weeks a year; that a stand-alone nursery will take on children from the age of six months who are not yet out of nappies; that corporate events and business enterprises will have exclusive use of school facilities at designated times; and that some of the grounds are given over to a 40000 seated sports stadium to support Shepton Mallet Rugby in its bid to become a Premiership side. I think it is time I retired.

Meanwhile, there were children at the school who were continuing to confound and inspire and delight in equal measure and I hope we never lost sight of them. Luke Siese, who was one of the nicest boys one could hope to teach, recalls his dog, 'Digger', in one of The Crane editions of 1999:

---

[102] School numbers occupy hearts and minds in the year 2013 in The Maintained Sector as 'Titan' primary schools emerge in London. One such, in Leyton, anticipates 1600 pupils in 2014. It has a School Hall that can accommodate all its pupils in one sitting which must make the task of running Assembly rather like organising a State occasion at Westminster Abbey, but doing it every week, instead of on the rare occasions, these days, when a new monarch is crowned. Impressive, indeed, would be the Head Teacher who could boom across the tannoy "Michael! Please don't do that! Sit up straight!" But 'Titan' schools are emerging elsewhere around the country with a 60% increase in the last three years of primary schools of more than 1000 pupils. 'Swelling schools are a product of England's rising birth rate and a rise in the number of young immigrant families entering the country' according to The Guardian which goes on to assert that such 'super-sized primaries are clustered in the most deprived areas of the country' suggesting that politics, rather than principles, are at work.

Digger, RIP

My dog was called Digger. He was the best animal ever. He was very calm and he LOVED raiding bins and exploring. He got run over. I think it was deliberate. Everybody else thinks it was an accident. When Digger sometimes got out he went to a place down the road. They had guinea pigs and Digger caught them. The woman who owned them could not catch him because he was too fast and always escaped. The woman rang us up and said: "If you cannot keep your dog under control I will have to report you to the RSPCA thank you". I remember every word of that message. I was so annoyed I felt like ringing them back and saying something really horrible like: "Can YOU keep your children under control" but I must admit she was right about keeping our dog under control (we didn't really do that). When we bought him he was so happy but when he died I was so unhappy. My mummy and daddy tried to cheer me up but it was no good. For two miserable years I have prayed for him but he never came back. I think he will but my mummy says he won't. I have so many photographs of him and I am missing him so much, too much. I have never let my feelings out before. He used to take a long stick and take it past us and we would all have to jump but my brother, Marc, could not jump so high and he would start crying then Digger would dump his stick and see if he was alright. He hated it when other people hurt themselves. I hope you now know how I feel about never seeing this dog of all dogs (man's best friend) again.

Whilst our email system did not quite ease our communication levels – as promised when paper memos and pigeon-holes were anticipated as things of the past – it is a point of strength, on balance, that internal news is circulated on a regular basis regarding matters of great importance as well as the fact that 'Michael' in Form One is upset because his pet stick insect has escaped. I'm not sure if stick insects can actually escape but I use it as an illustration, you understand, just as Luke felt comfortable enough to express his inner feelings in The Crane extract above. The children, I think, appreciate the fact that the staff are well-informed about their world and we try to communicate our understanding and empathy to them. And, Luke, for the record, I think Digger had the best life ever because he was loved by you.

The year 1999 seemed to mark a number of events of distinction including the departure from the school of long-standing and successful staff like Ros Boyd, who had been a popular and cultured Head of English for thirteen years, Jenny Shackleton, who had provided such benign but sure foundations in the Junior Department and Angela Moore whose French teaching to the juniors was inspirational. Mark Wood, who had taken on the baton as Director of Music after the incomparable Roger Bevan, decided to resign from his post to concentrate on becoming an Anglican Vicar and looking after his newly-born daughter, Deborah; he stayed on at All Hallows in the capacity of a peripatetic music teacher, much to our delight. Two other members of staff, Mary Whittleton (Head of the Junior Department) and Jill Shahbahrami (Head of Learning Support) also

PATRICK KAYE
(F.P. 1989-1998 RIP)

Alongside the celebratory events of recognising careers well developed, we entered, with the family, into a memorial celebration tinged, of course, with great sadness at the tragic death in a car accident of pupil Patrick Kaye, who died just before Christmas. Patrick was a quiet and sensitive young man who was beginning to blossom and flourish as he became more comfortable with the challenges and opportunities at All Hallows. He was making a mark on the rugby pitch with great determination and clear evidence of silky skills and he had become a popular boy with staff and peers for his commitment and friendly bearing. Close classmates were invited to attend the Memorial Service to celebrate his short life and the Headmaster was privileged to deliver the eulogy. The Patrick Kaye Memorial Cup continues to be awarded to the Colts rugby player who shows the most promise in a season.

Other former pupils who died in car accidents as boys or young men include J. F. P. Pearson, Nigel Messery and Robin de Guingand.

went on to pursue their careers elsewhere after achieving significant results in a relatively short time.

On the theme of sport, other pupils, in 1999, also excelled as individuals and as members of teams in various competitions. Tim Ball (Triple Jump), Ian Byrne (75m Hurdles), Eve Harvey (Long Jump, Shot Putt and 100m relay), Katherine Roberts, Flora Blathwayt, Camilla Jennings (all 100m relay) and Will Oyowe (100m and 200m) all won their events in the South West Championships, thereby qualifying for the National Finals. It was in these championships that Will Oyowe covered himself in glory by becoming the National 200m Champion for his age group. Will was a real character during his time at All Hallows and delighted all of us with his idiosyncratic showmanship in improvised talent shows over the years. He also had a move named after him on the rugby pitch; it was called "Give it to Will!" Stephanie Newmarch broke all kinds of running records; Charlie Pearson recorded a hat-trick when bowling against The Downs; Tim Ball represented Somerset in both rugby and Hockey; Gus Allen, as an Under-9, showed brilliant character and technique when batting memorably for 22 overs against a rampant Hazlegrove team to force the draw; the rugby 2nd XV showed off our strength in depth by winning eight and drawing one of their eleven matches; and Ian Murphy, as Director of Sport and ex-Wimbledon AFC, battled gamely in trying to re-introduce soccer into the sporting calendar. 'Sport For All' was an overriding preoccupation and it is with some irony that one reflects on the occasional disgruntled parent who believed that there were not enough sporting opportunities for his child at a time when we were selecting more teams in more sports in wider age groups than ever before. We knew full well that the ability of the 1st team was only ever defined by the ability of the 2nd team and huge strides forward were made in coaching and establishing teams down to 4th and 5th team levels when numbers allowed. Thus did 'sport for all' become something of a slogan even if this didn't really happen properly until the late twentieth-century. The difficulty was in trying to arrange suitable fixtures for so many teams but, by and large, we overcame these logistical problems, and schools with larger pupil numbers like Millfield, Clifton and Port Regis were very accommodating in putting out suitably matched teams, and their coaches were always very fair in adjusting the strength of their teams in individual matches, so that the flow and score-line remained honourable. For our part, we did not seek to gain any trumpeting publicity when our 4th team beat Millfield, knowing that the game had been managed in an extremely sportsmanlike fashion. By these means, we tried to ensure that every boy and girl who was keen to take part could represent the school with a proper sense of enjoyment and participation. Mind you, even with such all-encompassing opportunities, such provision did not suit everybody and we didn't always get it right. Luckily for Jack, you might think, (who did not originally take to team sports), another school mantra kicked in – that of 'attention to the needs of the individual' – which later became re-fashioned as 'personalised learning'. So, when Jack's mates were charging about on the astro in gales and hailstorms playing hockey, he was playing table-tennis with a Gap student under the cover of the Colonnade (I even played ping-pong with him myself a few times – especially when it was howling and hailing on the astro-turf). One day, however, the 4th XI was struggling for numbers and Jack had been pressed into service as 'reserve goalkeeper'. Now part of the fun, for the hockey goalie, is getting kitted out; one was able to wear some cool extras like kicking boots, massive gloves, protective body armour and a mask. And it usually meant missing the lesson before lunch in order to get ready. Jack even felt quite good about joining the team even if – possibly especially because - he was destined to spend most of the game-time on the touchline. All was in place. Except favourable playing circumstances. The 4ths had battled manfully to keep the score at 0-0 with only five minutes to play. The players were focused. The watching parents were expecting Churchillian fortitude for just five more minutes. And then – disaster! – our regular goalkeeper was injured. The kicking boots and the massive gloves and the body armour and the mask could not prevent a sprained ankle. Cue the substitute. Jack was awoken from whatever place he had been occupying in his mind and was forced to stumble towards the goalmouth, stepping on a few team-mates' toes as he went and bumping into the Umpire on the way, since he couldn't actually walk very well in the kicking boots and the massive gloves and the body armour, and he couldn't actually see very well from behind the mask. The game resumed, the clock ticked and the opposition attacked. Nil-nil for forty-nine minutes of a fifty-minute match was a fine achievement. Sadly, for Jack, a last-minute ball screamed into the top left-hand corner of the net whilst our press-ganged goalie was thinking of iambic pentameters and purple prose. Luckily, for Jack, he was wearing a mask which hid his embarrassment and prevented him seeing the full range of expressions on his team-mates' faces. Let us record a salutary message for the Games Teachers' Manual based on this true anecdote: 'Put your substitutes on the wing'. Jack, by the way, went on to become a forceful, confident, driving second-row forward in rugby and wrote the most colourful, insightful and engaging prose in his English classes which I have ever had the pleasure to read.

"

The school is just wonderful,
inside and out

"

If Jack's goalkeeping skills could be seen as an act of charity towards the opposition, in that year of 1999, the school also continued its charitable support of local causes by donating £1000 towards the St Bartholomew's Church Bells Restoration Appeal in West Cranmore and I was pleased to learn only recently that every Tuesday night a table is booked in The Strode Arms for 'The Bell-Ringers' who make a well-earned visit to that hostelry after an early evening's ringing of the bells. I know this because I was part of a Wednesday evening table-booking of teachers who were occupying the same table just twenty-four hours later. We pondered on what other groups of professions or friends might occupy that table through the week: farmers, Village Councillors, Gap students, steam railway enthusiasts, quarrymen, prison officers, monks from Downside, Gap students/teachers (they tend to go down twice) – there just aren't enough days in the week. Incidentally, on the occasion to which I refer, the teachers sitting round that table confided to me that, if they had not been teachers, they wished they had followed their ambitions to be an astronaut, a pilot, a lawyer, a musician, a doctor, a midwife, a gardener, a writer, a Good Samaritan and The Pope – children, live the dream!

In 1999, I mentioned on Prize Day to anybody who would listen (which was relatively easy since I was standing on the dais and everybody else was sitting facing me) *"we are engaged together in completeness, raising expectation, fulfilling potential, opening doors and living life to the full...my predecessor coined a marketing slogan as good as any you will hear 'Your Child Deserves The Best'...at All Hallows, we strive to provide the best for our children which aspires to the best in the country and it is right on your doorstep"*.

It seemed to me that if I was to fulfil my function as the Headmaster of a Catholic School, I should know something about its distinctiveness in the world of education, and, after thinking over such considerations, as they applied to All Hallows, I came up with the following characteristics: (1) A Recognition of Uniqueness (2) A Culture of Forgiveness (3) A Pattern of Service (4) A Sense of Sacramentality (5) A Place of Prayer (6) A Beacon of Christian Witness (7) A World of Community. I hope we were successful in transmitting those messages, particularly in recognising the children as unique individuals and in establishing a 'pattern of service' which allowed them to grow in a 'culture of forgiveness'.

I think it is that aspect of forgiveness I find most compelling and comforting in a school, in terms of the here and now, and the hereafter, and the Hereafter. Teaching monks at Downside have been known to say that they are preparing their pupils for death; I think I prefer 'we are preparing our pupils for forgiveness'. Father Edward Corbould OSB, an erudite and respected monk at Ampleforth, and, as Michael Corbould, a former pupil of All Hallows, was invited to speak at a Legal Service at which were present bench after bench of lawyers, barristers and High Court judges. He took as his theme 'Forgiveness'.

" 'Do not judge and you will not be judges yourselves' – Luke 6:37...
That might seem a pretty odd text to read at a Legal Service but I do not think that
Jesus is condemning Judges! Indeed, Judges have a sacred duty to perform and must

uphold the just laws which are necessary in an ordered society, which must give peace and protection to the members of that society. That is, of course, why we are here today, to pray for those who are responsible for exercising that sacred duty. But it is on ourselves, as self-appointed judges, that we might reflect for a moment, and in particular on Jesus' words, 'Be compassionate as your Father is compassionate, Do not judge and you will not be judged yourselves'. They are powerful and challenging words and are important to the way we conduct our lives. For we live in a society which is extraordinarily judgemental, with the media lacking in compassion. In each of us there is a desire to show that we are God rather than we need God. I think it is true that in order to find God we have to discover our own weakness and vulnerability. I want to read you a short extract from a letter written by a condemned man in South Africa shortly before he was executed. It was written to a German nun who had greatly helped him.

'All of us who have been crucified on beds of pain remember that an hour will come when we will be taken down from our cross and Our Saviour will look upon our hands and feet and side to find the imprints of His wounds which will be our passport to eternal joy'.

The experience of failure, of sickness, of weakness, of suffering, of loneliness, shows us our need for God, indeed, draws us to God. Then we become more conscious and more sensitive to God's love for us, his forgiveness of us. So we in turn learn to love, to be compassionate, to forgive. It is those virtues that are the hallmarks of a healthy, moral society. It was that great Spanish mystic of the sixteenth century, St John of the Cross, who said, 'Where there is no love, put love and you will draw out love'.

We are called to be men and women of compassion and forgiveness. When we pray the Our Father we say 'Forgive us our trespasses as we forgive those who trespass against us'. That is an extraordinarily challenging statement and we should take it very seriously. Forgiveness is an essential quality of true love; that is why it is central in marriage, in family life, in human relations. Even in a Court of Law justice must always have as its motivation a justice that heals and not as a retribution which breaks and destroys. The Prison Service, too, needs to have that constantly in mind. It is only when the broken in our society[103] are treated with respect, with compassion, and with their dignity recognised, that they will be healed.

---

[103] Downside School offers many benefits to its pupils which they take on with them into later life but the feature I like the most is 'The Broken Reed Society' which they have set up to look after those former pupils – and others – who have fallen on hard times and who need support.

But it is very easy to be critical of institutions and not to look at ourselves. It is we who have to be men and women of compassion and forgiveness. It is only then that we shall be close to God. It is only then that we shall be at peace."

Forgiveness should be embedded as a central aspect of our school culture. Young people 'get it wrong', inevitably. They are learning, experiencing, experimenting, growing, developing, changing and maturing. Mistakes will be made. Mistakes demand a reaction and it is up to us – the adults in the school – to react with wisdom, and forgiveness so that reconciliation can follow. We set the example. Just as we don't bully, don't shout, don't intimidate, don't exhibit prejudices, don't provide negative role models, so, too, we should not condemn. The teachers we remember fondly don't do these things. We are told in the bible that we should forgive 'seventy times seven' (Matthew 18:22) – in a thirty-four week year at All Hallows that means we should be forgiving others on over fourteen separate occasions through a week which adds up to thousands and thousands of times in a career. But forgiveness doesn't mean adopting a laissez-faire attitude or a loose sense of discipline. It is a robust and exacting process. It makes demands on both parties. It includes understanding, self-knowledge, contrition and remedial support. And it requires guidance, monitoring, reviewing and evaluation if growth and reconciliation are to occur. Most of all, forgiveness should be dispensed unemotionally and unconditionally, in principle, even if it is subject to conditions in practice. It should be consistent and consensual. Another Benedictine monk from Ampleforth, Father Henry Wansbrough, formerly Master of St Benet's Hall, Oxford, said *"The Christian knows that healing and forgiveness are the business of daily life and nowhere, it seems to me, is that more true than in the life of a school. It is the Christian lesson which children find most difficult of all to put into practice – as often remains clear, also, in adult life"*. Forgiveness lies at the heart of this book because it lies at the heart of what we do (which is just as well for all of us).

Trawling through those past editions of The Crane, I came across mention of *Thomas Henry Ball - 'Baby Boy for Mrs Ball' - born on Monday 2nd July who had already made his first visit to All Hallows on Friday 6th July*, 2001, thus possibly becoming our youngest prospective pupil ever. Tom went on to become an actual pupil as he grew older but a lasting memory of him was of the time he appeared, as baby Jesus, in our Nativity Play (he was all of five months or so). Our Nativity Play each year follows traditional lines (albeit with a few fighting angels at the back of the stage being 'exited left' by a shepherd's crook wielded by an irate Director) and the boy playing Joseph usually slinks across stage, from the crib, to the girl playing Mary, dragging, unceremoniously, by the toe, a fairly obvious doll dressed up to look like Jesus, saying, "'Mary, 'ere's yer baby!", as he throws the doll Jesus towards her. Sometimes Mary caught it, sometimes the doll crashed to the floor, much to the amusement of the parents watching. On this occasion, baby Thomas Ball played the part of Baby Jesus. Joseph duly arrived at the crib and carried that live baby with such love and care across the stage, step by loving step, so slowly and reverentially, we could hear baby Thomas breathing and we, too, caught our breath as we willed

Joseph on his way towards his beautiful Mary, Mother of God, who took up the baby into her arms and cradled him in her lap whilst the parents sat in awe, with tears streaming down their faces. That year, the magical Christmas message came across live and well.

The Year 2000 seemed to be as propitious a time as any for the Chairman of Governors, Chris Dick, to announce that it was the 'Year of the Former Pupil' and, in addition to inviting Sir Henry Keswick, himself a former pupil of All Hallows, and internationally known for his business interests, principally as Chairman of Jardine Matheson Holdings Ltd, but also as proprietor of The Spectator from 1975-1980, we hosted a 'grand reunion' of former pupils on Saturday 22nd July when almost one hundred former pupils attended. Twenty internal awards were made to pupils as part of the ongoing Jubilee Scholarships Scheme that had been set up in 1998 and, although they were genuinely designed to celebrate talent across a wide spectrum, they also had the value of retaining pupils who might otherwise have left, as well as attracting external pupils who might not otherwise have joined. The Astro-turf was handed over for use on Saturday 29th January and my Headmaster's Report to the Governors dated 1st March records the fact that "*it had been played on, every single day since that time*"; the landscaping and preparation of the grassed top pitch was set for the Spring. Incidentally, records show, lest anybody wants to dispute this fact in years to come, that Julian Silk scored the first goal on the astro-turf in a competitive match. The annual St Cecilia's Music Concert was held in November with over two hundred in attendance whose spirits were not dampened in any way by the incessant rain falling outside, which caused a major power cut, necessitating the rest of the concert to be conducted under candle light – all involved agreed the occasion was enhanced by the drama and the subdued lighting. With some horror at my own temerity and ambition, I read, in that same Report dated 1st March 2000, of over thirty development projects I was putting before the Governors for their approval totalling almost £900000. Interestingly, all bar eight of those ideas came to fruition, even if the £500000 designated for a Performing Arts Centre subsequently went towards covering the costs of The Crane Wing. Naturally, I am delighted that Ian Murphy, as the Headmaster in 2013, announced in an Easter Newsletter to parents:

"I have some very exciting news to share – plans are now very much afoot to create, thanks to a generous donation, a brand new All Hallows Creative Centre to be located in the heart of the school – the area currently housing the Theatre, the Music Department, the Orangery and Junior Common Rooms. Our creative centre is set to include a brand new acoustically friendly Music School, a Digital Room designed to offer instruction in Photography, Animation and Film Production, a re-located large and well equipped Art and Ceramics Department, as well as a Design Technology Centre which will encompass state of the art 3D laser printing equipment. Our intention is for these new facilities to surround the Orangery area on the Colonnade, which it is hoped, will be allowed to expand into the Cloisters and be used as a stylish Display Area to showcase the children's work and also host exhibitions and receptions. We hope, subject to planning permission, to have our Creative Centre available by September 2014".

Yet another example of continuity being maintained in the course of time, even if temporary expediencies change the focus, according to circumstances, and even if it falls to new Heads to out-do their predecessors in their ambition and vision although I do not mean to infer that this is a deliberate strategy but merely an effect brought on by the demands of the age for 'bigger and better and newer'. The development projects alluded to above included various building expansion and conversions to accommodate extra pupil numbers; additional staff appointments; enhanced internet and email facilities; a new school prospectus; pupil common rooms and playing areas; covering the swimming pool; a grand concert piano; new office space, etc, etc. Those ideas that did not see the light of day include the acquisition of new adjoining land and the advent of horses, goats and pigs, although who is to say that such projects are dead and buried? I think I'll push for pigs again before it's too late – the Bird Sty has a certain style. Mention was made of a leaving cohort of staff; but, inevitably, suitably qualified and excellent successors arrived in the persons of Sara Loughlin, Liz Green, Martin Green, Debbie Caines, Pip Davies and James Callow, all of whom added their particular skills and commitment to the school, thus proving that the cycles of change are to be embraced with confidence. That confidence and commitment to All Hallows was felt palpably on Saturday 27th May 2000 when approximately three hundred guests attended the Millennium Ball held under canvas on the Library Lawn. And in the spirit of 'what happens on tour, stays on tour', there were no minutes recorded (nowadays, of course, that particular brand of benign 'omerta' seems all but abandoned as the communications media becomes ever more accessible to all; one thinks of dwarf-throwing, for example, and jumping off boats into harbours on recent rugby tours).

An outline of the school roll over the last years of one century and the early years of the next is extremely instructive in terms of gaining a better understanding of the sometimes unpredictable fluctuations in trends which, inevitably, affect the nature of the school and its ability to develop. The chart below shows the year on the top line and the number of pupils in the school on the bottom line:

1989	1990	1991	1992	1993	1994	1995	1996	1997	1998	1999	2000	2001
244	267	272	255	220	192	212	187	201	241	256	267	289

As both Paul Ketterer and I explained to Governors at various times, parents were registering their children increasingly later in the year which meant that there were more difficulties in planning and predicting what could be needed and achieved within reasonable budgets. The theory is quite simple: balance the known leaving pupils with an anticipated number for recruitment, in order to maintain a status quo, with additional pupils needed if it happens to be the intention. In practice, many unknown variables come into the calculations, even before one can begin to consider optimum numbers and ethos, and one often found oneself seeing prospective parents right the way through the summer holidays up until the first day of the new academic year. For example, one year, with revenue up, as numbers crept towards 300 (the Michaelmas Term 2002 started with 290 pupils with the Lent and Summer Terms taking in additional pupils), saw the following year (2003) with 'only' 275 pupils, after an unexpected leave of twenty more pupils than anticipated, plus ten pupils deferring entry until the following year and fifteen others, who had been registered, subsequently dropping out. That was a swing of forty-five pupils whose names might reasonably have been on the school lists. The irony at that particular time was that we had refused entry to almost twenty other pupils because we were sticking to our self-imposed maximum and there were no places available when those enquiries had come through. And who knows whether or not those twenty or so pupils who did not arrive might have included a modern-day Milton or Cromwell in contradistinction to Gray's elegiac churchyard? Who knows what opportunities were missed and what characters developed in different ways through not coming to All Hallows?

I make no apologies to the general reader for these reflections since such pragmatics have to apply each and every year if the school is going to be able to fulfil its stated intentions and hopes; this is at the core of the school's business. Parents and pupils, of course, (not to mention Governors) want continuity and consistency but with perhaps as many as 70 pupils potentially leaving each year (approaching one quarter of the school) one can see the need to add 'clairvoyancing' to the skills of school managers. Would that all pupils were like Charles Willis, shall we say, who represents a kind of staying-power beyond the call of duty since, in my guesstimate, he is possibly the longest serving pupil of all time in the history of All Hallows having 'done' ten years. Nobody ever stays ten years in their senior schools, nor ten years at university (unless one becomes a seamless professor), nor ten years in prison, one might add, unless one has committed the appropriate crime, but Charles did his time and left a lasting mark. Since we don't tend to take three-year-old pupils, or younger, and they have usually left before the age of fourteen, Charles' achievement will take some beating. I think we'll give him a box of his own (see overleaf) to represent all those pupils who have managed to stay nine years but it could well be that some other former pupil out there is screaming right now that they also managed ten years (if so, many apologies!).

Early, in my Headmaster's 2002 Reports to the Governors, I referred to the School Choir's memorable trip to Rome, on 20th October 2001, when All Hallows sang in the only medieval gothic church in Rome, Santa Maria sopra Minerva, on the occasion of the dedication of that church to the English Cardinal, His Eminence Cormac Murphy-O'Connor, whilst also having the opportunity to visit the Pantheon, the Colosseum, the Forum (where Phocas' column stands firm as a symbol, perhaps, of All Saints' Day), the Arch of Titus, the Temple of Julius Caesar, the Catacombs of St Calixtus, the Spanish Steps, the Trevi Fountain, the pink abode of Shelley and Keats, and so much more. As reported in the Catholic Independent Schools Conference (CISC) Newsletter "*Paul Dowbekin* (Director of Music at All Hallows) *had been the organist to the Cardinal when he was Bishop of Arundel and Brighton and he led the choir in settings of 'Christ be beside me' and 'Ave Maria' to a packed church of over one thousand local parishioners,*

CHARLES WILLIS
(F.P. 1992-2003)

We'll let Charles speak for himself.....as he did in the 2003 Chronicle....

"Having been at All Hallows for ten years from 8th September 1992 until 13th July 2003, I have seen All Hallows go from strength to strength, changing all the time, always for the better. But the thing that strikes me most about my time

at All Hallows is not the facilities improving (such as the refurbishment of the science labs, the new astro-turf and new changing rooms) or the better quality teaching, or even the much improved extra activities for pupils; the thing that strikes me most about my time is the school's spirit. From my time in Reception, aged three, to my leaving All Hallows in Year Eight, now aged thirteen, I have seen countless sets of pupils all possessing the spirit and determination that keeps the school running and flowing the way that it does. The spirit and determination that makes sure everybody always gets into the senior school of their preference, the determination that wins us sports matches, the spirit that makes us win Speech and Drama cups, and the spirit and determination that takes us through All Hallows and onwards for the rest of our lives".

Charles had hugely supportive parents and a sister, Rosie, who followed on, becoming Head Girl in her own right (not that Charles was Head Girl) and who won many of those Speech and Drama cups mentioned by Charles. Charles was no slouch himself. He had an admirably horizontal mental equilibrium possessed by many boys throughout history but he emerged as a true star on the games field and threw in an academic scholarship to King's, Bruton, for good measure.

English Catholics in Rome and many others who had made the journey from England, as well as various dignitaries including the British Ambassador to Rome, and other papal representatives, Bishops and priests. Headmaster Chris Bird said: 'I have never heard the choir sing better; a fitting tribute to the Cardinal's celebrations on his special day in these magnificent surroundings. We are truly privileged to be part of this splendid occasion'." The Choir followed up this unique occasion with further moments of distinction in 2002 when singing the Mass setting at Westminster Cathedral, joining forces with Loyola School in Essex, before hosting the Catholic

Rosie MacKean and Harry Smith with their trophies from the Bath festival

Preparatory Schools' Choral Festival when choristers from All Hallows, Loyola and Farleigh, now some 120+ strong, contributed to a magnificent sound in Downside Abbey and Clifton Cathedral in the same year. The opening hymn, '*Dear Lord and Father of Mankind*' was specially arranged for brass and choir by the All Hallows Music Gap Student teacher, David Hawkins; the Kyrie and Gloria were arranged by Paul Dowbekin from a setting by Perosi and Paul also composed the Alleluia; at the Offertory the choirs sang '*Lead Kindly Light*' by Mark Wood, Paul's predecessor as Director of Music at All Hallows; the acclamation, '*Christ Has Died*', was composed by Roger Bevan, the illustrious All Hallows Director of Music; and the final hymn, '*Praise the Lord, ye Heavens adore Him*', was arranged by Downside's Chuff Byrne who was an old boy of All Hallows.

Following hard on the heels of the Rome Trip (which was repeated in 2006 – see diary extracts below – and, again, in 2010) came a skiing excursion co-ordinated by John-Paul Renouf with a total party of 72 including children, staff and parents; the French Exchange visits for our senior pupils went ahead between 14th and 18th March; and the annual Trip to Normandy took place between 6th-12th April with 32 children, plus staff, to take in excursions to the Normandy beaches, some military cemeteries, various museums, the Bayeux Tapestry, Mont St Michel, the Eiffel Tower (where yours truly was stuck, alone, for forty minutes in a broken-down lift with the afore-mentioned 32 children) and, finally, a well-earned break down the Seine when the staff fell asleep. By way of some odd coincidence, it was remarkable how often the Normandy trips ended up with exactly thirty-two pupils; perhaps our roll-call accounting could never master 'trente-trois'. And, on the subject of trips, approval was sought for a Girls' Hockey Tour to Cork and Dublin (see below).

My Headmaster's Report of November 2002 revealed that the 'perfect' school roll should be set at a ceiling of 300; in the six years from 1996 to 2002 there was a steady increase in the numbers of boarding pupils until it reached a recent high of 92 in the summer of 2002. Given the fact that a survey at this time had assessed the boarding capacity at 100 (due to conversions of accommodation for resident staff) and that pupil numbers, in total, were nudging record levels of 300, serious thoughts by the Headmaster and Governors were being given to the future direction of the school and how best to manage the expansion; that 37% of the leaving cohort gained some form of award to their senior schools; twenty sports teams had represented the school at different ages and levels with every single girl and boy playing for the school in the top four years in 98 competitive matches; the girls had returned from a successful hockey tour to Dublin during which they won five matches, drew two and lost only one (thus showing the benefit of the astro-turf after a first foray abroad to Holland); pupil Archie Young[104] had been appointed as Her Majesty's Page (he was to continue in this role for as long as he remained shorter than The Queen) and had conducted his official duties at the state opening of parliament (thus going one better than former pupil Julian Ormsby-Gore in 1953 who was merely page to his grandfather, albeit at the Coronation).

Ian Murphy was now residential Deputy Head and living in Home Farm alongside the school; Nick Somerville attended the Johannesburg World Summit with Robert Swan following their Mission Antarctica project; and some of the bureaucracy of school management was taken up with issues like: charitable status, the Parent Contract, new Staff Contracts, Residential Contracts, Employer's Pension Contributions, Disability Legislation, Age Discrimination and the Cranmore

---

[104] Archie's abiding memory of the occasion was dominated by the seven-course meal he was forced to endure afterwards when he had been granted royal permission to sip some wine between each of the seven courses.

Parish Development Plan. Incidentally, early on in my Headship, I had made inroads into the Cranmore Community by introducing myself and attending a Parish Council Meeting to show that I was keen to establish the strongest links possible and although I believe we managed to maintain good connections thereafter – especially in terms of encouraging our parents to slow down when driving through the village (perhaps at the beginning of terms when they were keen to drop off their children after eight weeks of the summer holiday) – my willingness to adopt a higher profile fell short of accepting their invitation to open the Summer Fete and judge the vegetables. It also transpired in 2002 that as we celebrated the Queen's Golden Jubilee, one pupil, when asked what he thought The Queen did in her spare time, offered the suggestion that *"she played ping-pong with Prince Charles"*. You see what we are up against? Although, on reflection, perhaps that is exactly what she does. Hardly on a par with fifty years on the throne of England was also the occasion when the hirsute Headmaster was bullied by the senior girls into having his beard shaved off, publicly, in front of the whole school, as a ruse to raise funds for the Girls' Hockey Tour to Dublin. I am confident in the assertion that no other Headmaster in the history of this story has done the same. The money raised came to over £1000 and I like to hold onto the idea that my beard is worth that sort of money (as I contemplate retirement, I would consider doing it again as long as I received the hard cash this time).

Ongoing Headmaster's Reports, through 2003 and 2004, covered the following details: another highly successful School Inspection had endorsed so much that was good (ISI October 2003) with *'teaching, pupil welfare, learning support (as a culture throughout the school), many academic departments and the Headmaster's firm leadership (!)'*, all receiving especial commendation. *'Unusually strongly supportive parents'* were also noted following a confidential questionnaire, *'no evidence of bullying was found'*, the extra-curricular programme was *'excellent'* and English, French, Geography, History, Art, Music, ICT, Learning Support and P.E./Games, as well as some aspects of the Junior Department all came through with *'flying colours'*. Recommendations included some refinements to our assessment procedures, the advice of producing a Business Plan with future projections and some minor suggestions like installing keypad security to dormitory areas...all, perhaps, signs of the times. The sense of accountability and the need to cover all aspects of being seen to be accessible and fair to all, even up to legislation, included considerations of the following: a formal *Complaints Procedure for Parents*, our *Disability Rights and Access* provision, the further implications of *'private action/public benefit'* re. *Charitable Status, and the Employment Equality (Religion and Belief)* Regulations whereby employees could not be treated differently on religious grounds unless there was a proven and genuine occupational requirement to do so. The boarding numbers remained buoyant, even 'kicking against the trend' a little, and there was an upsurge of interest in what we called 'Day-Boarding' whereby well over 90% of eligible day pupils (i.e. those aged seven or over) took advantage of the 'wrap-around' educational opportunities which was rather more than a simple sleep-over. Four successive terms tracked the fact that almost 200 children spent a combined total of 12000 nights at the school in this way, adding hugely to the richness of the boarding experience and dynamic and, perhaps, showing a way forward. The school gained a significant five-figure sum into the bargain which was used to enhance future developments in the same area. This was a successful period of time that needed articulation to a wider audience although my attempts to proclaim the message from the dais on Prize Day 2003 came to nought when I awoke that morning having lost my voice. I had to pass a written note – literally - to the Chairman of Governors to explain that I would not be able to deliver my speech and that he would have to carry the show by himself. It seemed to me that pupils, staff and parents were all very happy that day as they moved a little sooner than anticipated towards the refreshments on the Library Lawn. Academic staff had come and gone over these years, at least as members of the residential team, including Libby Doe-Wansey, John-Paul and Liz Renouf, Sara Loughlin, Debbie Caines, Charlotte Knowles, Ian and Rachel Murphy (Ian had moved on at the end of the Lent Term 2004 to take on the Deputy Headship of St Bede's, Eastbourne), so new staff like James Callow, Jody and Lucy Wells, and Jeff and Becky Peabody were appointed to keep the boarding flavour of the school intact. Jeff Peabody was appointed from September 2004 to assume the Residential Deputy Headship and he had a fine pedigree behind him of schoolmastering in various prep and senior schools in the region. Inspections continued to occupy our minds one way or another: Ofsted decided that Nursery Inspection fell outside all other parameters and required specialist scrutiny of its own but we were delighted to receive an excellent Report in March 2004 with all due credit to Mary Whittleton, Jenny Gritten and Julie Blakeley (the latter also offered many years of devoted pastoral care in the boarding wing). The years 2003, 2004 and 2005 saw great distinctions in the sporting arenas as the Rugby Sevens team strove manfully to reach the highest pinnacle and fell only a little short of national success whilst individuals and pairs started to emerge on the tennis courts once more. Musical accomplishments featured strongly and individual poets exercised their literary talents. The 1st VII, with a squad made up of Arthur Shepherd, Tim Batt, Peter Januszewski, Olly Newton, Johnny Neville, Edu Minon, Sam Ferguson, Tom Ukleja, Olly Aplin, Sebastian Isola and Freddie Mercer, became runners-up in The Sherborne Sevens Competition two years in a row, finalists and then semi-finalists in The National Catholic Sevens and winners of The Governors' Cup at The Oratory. Tom Wilkinson and Peter Januszewski wielded mean tennis rackets in winning through various regional rounds to reach the semi-finals of the IAPS Tournament at Wimbledon and set the stage for a resurgence of interest in tennis that runs through to the present time in the guise of The All Hallows Tennis Academy with its national accreditation. Toby Owen, Gus Allen, Matthew Budd and Tom Doe – the latter on three occasions – all scored over 50 with the bat. Meg Opie (High Jump) and Emma Burgess (Shot) won gold medals at the South West Athletics Championships with record performances in 2004 with Meg Opie going on to win gold the following year at the National Championships. The girls had no less than four unbeaten hockey teams on the astro following their successful tour of Dublin where, incidentally, they were denied one particular victory by the brilliance of a giant goalkeeper who made magnificent save after magnificent save only to reveal at the end of the match, as the mask came off, that he was, in fact, a great big strapping boy several years older than our girls. These things happen on tours. In Ireland. Thomas Veitch and Henry Spencer[105] became National IAPS trumpeters in 2003 and William Morrison, in 2005, won a prestigious bursary from the BBC Fame Academy, worth £1500, with which he purchased a Double Bass and then attended a grand reception in London where he mingled with celebrities like Paul McCartney and Bruce Forsyth. The All Hallows Choir might have mingled with celebrities of a different hue in the same year, when they performed, if not quite headlined, at The Glastonbury Pop Festival, although it is not known what the rousing sleepers from the night before thought of the fully-robed choristers in full voice right next to their pitched tents. George Dawson's 2003 poem 'Peace', reproduced below, was honoured at The Prior Park Regional Poetry Competition and in 2005 William Malin became 'Poet of the Year' in the same competition.

PEACE

At peace they lie,
Dangling from the wire
Though they must have had a jolt
When the rolling guns
Ceased their fire.
The silence crushes in
After what seems to have been
Years of infinite conflict.
In trenches, skeletons stare and
From beneath their caps of rotting cloth
Gaze shattered bones.
Pools of stagnant water become
Merged with deep red pools of blood.
The stumps of trees blaze merrily,
Their summits blown clean off by shells.
This is what has happened
To the green plains
And the lush forests of France.
The land is ruined
But, at peace, at last.

---

[105] Henry was the brother of Flora who were children of the Hon. Catherine Spencer and Charles Spencer who was a former pupil of All Hallows during Mr Mortimer's years. Charles went on to Downside having featured in school sports teams and continued to demonstrate his sporting prowess in events like the All Hallows Challenge and could even be seen playing competitive rugby until the age of 57 – well played, Charles! In his 'Valete' entry in the 1970 Chronicle one reads of Charles as *'Prefect...Scout Patrol Leader...Captain of Colts Cricket...4 gold medals...Science Prize and Industry Prizes'*

Preliminary proposals were now in place for the much-vaunted major development on the Upper Hard Court Pitch between the Headmaster's House and the Ketterer Wing which had been highlighted as a key area for further building from the time of Paul Ketterer's years as Headmaster. What had once been a garden allotment of some substance during the Paget years and which had served many useful years as a hard-playing surface for the hard-playing children ('Bugga Ball'[106] seems to be a lasting memory) was now about to receive its next make-over as a new classroom block (subsequently named The Crane Wing[107]). The need for additional, purpose-built, specialist classrooms had overtaken the previously held hope that we would build a Performance Arts Centre but, as has been mentioned earlier, that particular project seems destined to be given a Murphy modern twist of its own. The Crane Wing (and the new Library) was opened officially on Saturday 25th February 2006 by Bishop Declan Lang of Clifton, although classes had taken place in the various subject rooms in mathematics, geography, history and Religious Education before that time, as staff and pupils became accustomed to their new surroundings. Nick Somerville had invited into the school a local artist and sculptor, Laurence Tindall, who had previously restored, as a carver-mason, thirty-five of the stone figures adorning the West front of Wells Cathedral and he had also worked on Exeter Cathedral and Bath Abbey. In September 2005, Laurence Tindall started work at the school and, with his own Christian identity, literally fashioned metaphorically out of his work at Wells, he was able to draw on a rich seam of imagery and spiritual sensibility at All Hallows. Laurence says that *"the testament of the medieval craftsmen is strong and I found Christ through it. I have sought to speak about my faith both in my own sculpture and also by restoring historic work thus keeping the testament of others alive. Churches are…a living expression of people's faith (and) people past and present are giving us a coherent vision in an increasingly fragmented world"*. Laurence swapped, therefore, his work with churches and people of the past by taking on a modern challenge, in an educational setting, with young people, particularly, of the present. Laurence began with the raw material of a human kind by asking the children how they wanted him to help them commemorate, in the form of stone, the new teaching classrooms. From detailed

---

[106] 'Bugga Ball' was a playground game invented by the hardy pupil souls who could rarely wait for children's playtime to arrive. It was born in the 1980s – possibly earlier – and certainly in a time when health and safety did not feature so strongly in a school's (or society's) consciousness. The rules were as follows: there were no rules. The object of the game was to throw or kick the ball into one's opponents' goal area which was marked by a triangular fence. The two goal areas were perhaps forty metres apart across the diagonal playing surface. Any number of children could play from any age group of either sex. I suppose it resembled something like a cross between British Bulldogs and rugger in Tom Brown's schooldays or perhaps that bloody and brutal game they play on the streets of Orkney on Boxing Day when participants often find themselves spending a few days, thereafter, in the Casualty Department at Kirkwall. Any and every form of tackling prevailed; yellow and red cards did not feature.

[107] I seem to remember in one Governors' Meeting that the suggestion came up that it should be called 'The Bird Wing' but I was able, successfully, to prevent that particular idea taking hold. The Sun Dial that was erected instead to mark my Headship years was rather spectacularly demolished one day by a reversing van in 2013; its subsequent replacement was something altogether more appropriately modest.

discussions in the art classes with a range of pupils, Nick and Laurence were able to decide on the production of two complementary stone panels to be attached opposite each other at the main entrance to the new building. The children were consulted at every turn and their ideas were incorporated into the subsequent designs; they were asked what All Hallows meant to them, what did the school stand for, what were its values and how could those attributes be represented in art? The English Department also became involved in a separate project, when Laurence used local Doulting stone, through the generation of ideas and symbolism that were being put forward by pupils, to carve a 'stone-mountain' which took on a narrative of its own. For the panels, Laurence felt that the children's ideas broke into two related halves of 'nature and nurture'. Laurence chose The Creation Story to represent 'nature' and the school story at All Hallows to signify 'nurture' so that the two stone panels would present almost mirror images of each other. Thus the male and female figures in the centre of the first panel, perhaps representing Adam and Eve, are paralleled in the second panel by a boy and girl figure clothed in the uniform of All Hallows. One of the best features of the work undertaken, apart from the obvious fact that the stone panels would hang as a permanent reminder of the school's central message, was the method and processing chosen by Laurence Tindall. He worked almost entirely out-of-doors for five months just outside the Library, albeit under occasional temporary cover, for this was the Cranmore climate after all. Every passing pupil could stop and ask him what stage he had reached and alongside the creation of the stone panels ran hand-in-hand the work on the Doulting Stone. This huge block of stone looked like a miniature mountain and, with the willing story-telling support of the English Department, children and staff were invited to try their own hands at fashioning edifices out of stone by producing various shops, churches, houses, towers, etc, to be moulded into the 'mountain'. The only criterion was that they had to produce details of the inhabitants of the building and offer suggestions as to how they might connect in a story of their own. Thus was born *The Story of The Stone* which I weaved into a coherent narrative of some seventy pages beginning with the preface: *"All along, down along, out a long time ago, in another age, at another place, by the swirling shores of the Great Glastonbury Sea and the isles of mists that shielded its many secrets this story of enchanted and dark magic took place. It is a story of pain and pleasure; of grace and great beauty; of laughter, mercy and growth. Discover in these pages, if you will, the story of life and enter into the lives of these redoubtable and remarkable characters who are made all the more remarkable because they are just ordinary people like you and me. But remember – every time this book is opened, the Dragon stirs, the Crane awakes and another chapter begins for our own age....."* Now if that whets your appetite at all, go and look at the Stone Mountain, which can be seen by the footfalls to The Crane Wing, with its houses and its churches and its towers and its shops and its prison, and go and read the book which is kept in the School Library. It contains splendidly-named eccentric and distinctive characters like *Pansy, the Cobbler's daughter; Roger the Artist; Isha, who has been incarcerated in the Magic Mountain Prison; Mr McGilliwilly the Schoolmaster and Astronomer Royal; Boris the Alchemist; Norman the Dwarf, who liked supping ale at The Crane Inn; Sydney the Monk;*

Rufus, who was 'special' and mute; Father Benedict; Lily Summers, the Inn Keeper's Maid, who served Stan Summers' ancient ale 'Summer Lightning' which drew men from far and wide; Penelope the Princess and Olive the Servant Girl; The Hermit; Hugo the Postman; Clive the Well-Keeper, and Sassy, his daughter; Gilbert the Baker; Marvin the Music Man; Tomas and Dylan, the Orphans; Brandon the Blacksmith; Bill the Apothecary; Socrates the Librarian, (who really wanted to be called Bob); and The Stranger, Joseph Crane; and The Caretaker, who guides the children, Francis and Evelyn, through the various strands of the story; and, of course, The Dragon! The original contributors – who will all receive a credit (but no more) when it is made into a best-selling film, include the following pupils and staff: Lily Bennett, Chris Bird, Mia Blain, Joe Brown, Clare Colgan, Helena Constable-Maxwell, Libby Doe-Wansey, Timothy Drewett, Georgina Dunlop, George Ellwood, Katherine Eyles, Kit Hardy, Stuart Kaye, Sarah Keeling, Harry King, Philippa Loakes, Grace Logan, William Malin, Joel Somerville, Nick Somerville, Angus Stewart, Louise Tavener, Laurence Tindall, Rebecca Turner and Kirsty Wombwell. Best of all, it is a deliberately unfinished story, so if you fancy writing the last missing chapter, have a go! But you will need to be inspired by an 'All Hallows Imagination' which is not easily acquired by the sceptical or by those set in their ways. Incidentally, when Laurence Tindall asked the children what the new classroom building should be called they came up with dozens of suggestions including: *The Lesson Block, The Sancto Block, The Sun Block, The Saints Wing, Inspiration Corner, The Court Rooms, The Sanctuary, The Rookery, The Old Court, The Pitch, The Academic Wing, School House, The Life Wing, All Saints Corner, The Stone Building, The Crane House, The Bird Wing* and, my particular favourite, *The Work House*. Perhaps fortunately, or perhaps as a result of a lost opportunity, we settled on **The Crane Wing**.

In the May Report of 2004 there was also mention of the fact that Sara Loughlin, the Head of English, was leaving at the end of the Summer Term 2004 to take up a post at Bruton School for Girls which sparked off another major shift in the Headmastership of the school because, as it happened, the Headmaster rather fancied a return to full-time teaching.

In the course of my eleven years as Headmaster, I managed, occasionally, to timetable myself to teach. In theory, it is good practice for a Head Teacher to teach. It keeps one 'honest'. One is reminded of what the children are like in the learning environment and what one's colleagues go through many more times in a day than the hand-picked classes which the 'occasionally-teaching' Headmaster undertakes. It could be argued that the Head's pedigree, integrity – validity even! - is elevated to a slightly higher plane in the views of teachers and parents and children by teaching. It is the core aspect of one's professional make-up which inspired and characterised one's career before moving into the liminal world of Headmastering. Now, it is just possible that some Heads might admit they couldn't wait to leave teaching behind them and, it could be argued, that the modern business of running a school, in any case, demands just that: a business person. But there is something illuminating for all, if the Head can occasionally say to other parties who want his/her time, "I'm sorry, I'm now going off to teach 8W". When I couldn't actually find the time to teach according to a designated timetable, I willingly took on temporary leadership, or co-ordination might be a better word, of various departments that were undergoing a time-lapse between the departure of one Head of Department and the arrival of the next. So it was, therefore, that, whilst Headmaster, I also became Acting Head of Learning Support, Acting Head of Boarding, Acting Scouts' Wood Co-ordinator, as well as picking up some Games Coaching, attending summer camps, preparing Confirmandi, accompanying school excursions to France and Rome, acting and singing (mmm!) in school plays and, of course, acting as Acting Head of English. All such activities kept one grounded and connected to the children and the staff. In fact, in a teaching career spanning almost forty years the only subject I cannot ever remembering teaching is mathematics, not, I hasten to add, because I'm useless at maths, but, due, I think, to the fact that my methodology is rather different to the modern way of working things out[108]. Perhaps there are some who would say that the nomenclature 'Acting' was particularly appropriate in my case (since I was only ever really 'acting') but such forays back into teaching situations only served to whet the appetite, as far as I was concerned, even if others might have contrary opinions on that point. All in all, my Headship years were extremely stimulating and I was happy enough, looking back, with what I came to think was a suitably effective discharge of my duties in that role, even if I retained constantly the feeling

[108] I am well known in my family for 'helping', each of my children, in turn, with their difficult maths prep and for being the architect of the correct answer subsequently handed in to their maths teachers of the time, along with twenty or so pages of my working out. Many a maths teacher of my children has ended up impressed, but bemused, as to how the correct answer can possibly have been reached after so many numerical meanderings. My children learnt not to ask me to help them with their maths prep and I learnt not to become a maths teacher.

that I might not have been especially 'cut out' to be a traditional, typical Headmaster. With Sara Loughlin's departure as Head of English and the convenient need to occupy that role myself for a potential interim period, the ground was thus set for me to change direction. My thoughts turned, inevitably, to the need to advertise for a new Head of English but then I realised I was rather enjoying the prospect of teaching the English classes myself and even wondered if I could do both jobs. At the same time, grandchildren were starting to arrive and other family preoccupations emerged which all led to the same conclusion: appoint myself as Head of English and persuade the Governors to advertise for a new Head Teacher. In this modern age, looking back, I suppose I should have advertised the English post, interviewed myself along with other candidates, watched myself teach in an 'observational lesson', written a reference for myself and then phoned myself for further clarification before appointing ME (of course) and then contacting the other candidates to explain that they had come very close but they weren't just the best fit and it was nothing personal. The Governors listened to my rationale with remarkable equilibrium although I suspect no governor would have woken up that morning (on the day I decided to inform them of my hopes) with anything like that peculiar anticipation in their minds. My voluntary change of direction was not unprecedented but it was unusual and the idea of a former Headmaster continuing on in a different position in the same school obviously creates all kinds of potential delicacies for pupils, staff, parents and any succeeding Head Teacher. Nevertheless, as has already been asserted earlier, Alistair Mortimer and Paul Ketterer and Chris Bird, for that matter, all experienced some of those interesting and possibly conflicting dynamics when starting their own Headship years, so why not my successor too? Downside was a working example, of a kind, on our own doorstep, whereby former Heads became assumed once more into the educational and monastic fabric, even if the particular circumstances that apply there are brought about by considerations unique to them. And some schools operate with two Heads, as was briefly considered by the Chairman of Governors at the time when I made my announcement, although that idea never really gained momentum. Given the situation and the potential for presenting it in a clumsy or even damaging way, however, I believe that we handled all matters quite well, though I say it myself, which is testimony, also, to the intelligence, maturity and support of children, staff, Governors and parents. Chris Dick wrote in the 2005 Chronicle: *"I took over as Chairman of Governors at much the same time as Chris became Headmaster, so I am well qualified to assess his achievements. When he took over, school numbers were falling, but such has been the success in the last decade we have had to set an absolute limit of 300. When Chris took over we had six scholarships; this year there are twenty-nine. In respect of building developments we now have a covered swimming pool, an astro-turf pitch, better games fields, improved dormitories, refurbished changing rooms, a new science laboratory and...a brand new state of the art library, five new classrooms and properly equipped music rooms....Chris Bird's greatest achievement ...the 'All Hallows factor'....fit, happy, smiling children all learning to the best of their ability in a Christian environment. Potential parents visiting the school sensed the atmosphere when they were walking around...I am convinced that this special loving, caring and Christian atmosphere generated by the Headmaster is the secret of All Hallows; it is a great legacy and we are all indebted to him."*

I rather like, however, two remarks from Year Eight Leavers who were asked to comment on their memories of me: *"I shall always remember Mr Bird for jumping into the skip to get my ball back. You hurled yourself into the skip and threw the rugby ball out. Then you fell over. I knew I could rely on you"* and *"Actually, I always preferred Mrs Bird".* The first remark was from Freddie Mercer and if I can find out who wrote the other one...! That just about sums up things for my professional obituary; it seems to me that I spent quite a lot of my time in metaphorical skips, throwing things out and falling over, and as for Mrs Bird, well, as I have said on many public occasions, 'behind every great man there's a great woman and behind only ordinary men there are even greater women'. To be fair, there were some other complimentary comments which I include because it would smack of false modesty if I left them out and because they are so lovely and because they include some parental observations[109] which are a little thin on the ground in this book, I fear. These remarks were recorded in a presentational booklet produced by the leaving pupils at the time of my relinquishing the post of Headmaster.....

"For the last two weeks I have been watching the swallows swoop past the kitchen window, at times perilously close to the ground, at others, soaring up and away as they fly further afield. I watch them and think of our children and of all that you and Jan and All Hallows have done for Caroline, Thomas and Harriet...Graham and I give our heartfelt thanks" – Rosemary Veitch (parent).

"I remember Mr Bird first showing me round All Hallows in 1995. It was obvious he was being bullied by the girls in the Reception Class" – Angela Vick (parent and Governor)

"Cheers, Mr Bird...I remember when I was younger and seeing my little brother Elliot kick your shin on my first day at school but you just laughed" – Olly Cotterell (it's OK, Olly, I had pinched him when he was a babe in arms at a social function in the Old Library and he had never forgotten).

"Sir, I would like to remind you of a famous Midsummer Concert when you were a 'vital' part of the orchestra with your very impressive triangle. The only problem was you only had one

---

[109] Parents have been referenced, obliquely, I suppose, by the fact that they sent their children to All Hallows. I have deliberately not sought to highlight their profiles and reputations, for the most part, in order to avoid embarrassing them and in order to avoid any sense of name-dropping. It is the case, however, that some parents of All Hallows pupils have included those with links to royalty, nobility, prelates of the church, politicians, philanthropists, intellectuals, media figures, high-ranking military officers, fashionistas, renowned actors, artists, musicians, oscar-winners, etc, etc. The important point to note is that *all* parents have been hard-working, self-sacrificing, successful and loving people who have shown a faith and trust in the school and we are extremely privileged to have taken on that responsibility for the children in our care as they have passed through the school.

note." Thus the cheeky Archie Pearson, who redeemed himself with a P.S. "*The best Headmaster anyone could wish for*". Even a cheeky nephew, in the person of Henry Bird, got in the act as he contemplated my change of role: "*Then one day he called us round/And said 'Another job I've found/I no longer want to be the Head/I want to spend more time in bed'/ 'Oh no!', we cried, 'This can't be true!'/ 'Please don't weep and please don't cry'/Came his happy reply/ 'The job I've found is very near/It's Head of English – so I'm staying here'.*" But I think I'll settle for Emily Jennings' summary when she pronounced that I was "*steady, funny, kind and inspiring*". Emily, you weren't so bad yourself.

One final set of memories from the Head Boy's mother of the time....Helen Mercer...

"*The end of a wonderful time at prep school: four children at All Hallows School and eighteen years later! Days at All Hallows, with extended family and friends, have been so very special – we have been welcomed into all parts of school life and shared many wonderful times together. Melanie was chosen to represent England at a children's peace council in India where she and sixty other children from around the world presented a peace pact to the Prime Minister – and she was only eleven! Leah won two national photographic competitions in Year Six at All Hallows, winning a computer for herself and one for the school. Alice and Mrs Hand spent a year together in Form Remove during which time I learnt a big lesson as one day Alice came crying out of the classroom after school telling me through her tears that Mrs Hand had not been very nice to her... 'Mummy I have been told off for cutting Charlotte's hair – I promise I didn't!'*

'Now, then, Mrs Hand, why is Alice so upset?' says Mummy Mercer.

'Well, Mrs Mercer, I had been told that Alice cut Charlotte's hair'.

'But that's just hearsay', I said indignantly.

Mrs Hand went to her desk drawer, pulled out two pairs of scissors and placed them on the table. 'Mrs Mercer, I said to Alice, 'which pair of scissors did you use to cut Charlotte's hair' and Alice said 'this one', pointing to the red pair'. Guilty as accused! I gained much respect for Mrs Hand and Alice went from strength to strength, loving her time in the school and missing it badly when she went.

Freddie joined the school at six years old, spontaneously taking your hand on his induction day and becoming part of the school in every way from the very beginning, proving to us all his love of sports and then later, to our wonderful surprise, his singing. I knew then that All Hallows would help create in him that special zest for life...at this very special school. Chris, may you long be part of it. Thanks you so very much. We'll miss you."

In my last Headmaster's Report, dated November 2005, I offered some reflections on 'Past, Present and Future' and began by genuinely thanking the Governors for their support over the years. One was always aware of the 'horror-stories' that existed regarding the relationships between Governors and Head Teachers but I had been in the fortunate position of having had no such negative experiences with the Board of Governors during my time as Head. I can only recall two occasions when they said "No" to requests of mine: the first, when I offered to move into a smaller flat on the premises in order to accommodate a larger school family in The Headmaster's House, and the second, when I proposed that my salary should remain at a previous year's level by not accepting an annual increase. As it happened, the Governors didn't have to push ahead with their intentions to increase my salary because I resigned; it is an erroneous conclusion to make but there is something rather piquant about the idea that I must be one of the few Headmasters in the country who resigned as a result of the offer of more money. Having enjoyed such a good working relationship with the Governing Body I was keen to draw on that goodwill and also do all in my power to secure such an arrangement for my successor. I wrote to the Governors: "*Whilst it is recognised, unequivocally, that an independent, fee-paying school needs to remain commercially viable, my contention is that the school's primary purpose should be to educate young people, create a purposeful atmosphere, with happy children, motivated staff, satisfied parents, and that all the connected indicators that go with these core values are more valid in assessing the success of the school than a simple analysis of the financial balance sheet. It follows, of course, that if the core values are successful then the financial returns become secure also. I make this point because there are many wider external pressures in the current educational world that could easily be applied at All Hallows with the ultimate result of being counter-productive. These have been variously described at different times but, at present, they have been referred to by other commentators as 'perverse incentives'. Such matters refer to the pressures created by League Tables, Special Needs inclusion, university admissions, legal developments, the climate of accountability, the concept of blame, inspections, health and safety checks, community roles, financial constraints, etc. The counter-productive nature of such present-day pressures may be illustrated by just one example: the present government wishes 50% of school leavers to attend university by the year 2010 even though this is set against the rising percentage of students who drop out during the course of their first year (now reaching 40% in some institutions) – this is a perverse incentive! Some of the factors mentioned apply with greater urgency in the Maintained Sector and/or at the senior end of education but similar pressures can and do exist in preparatory schools, and, at All Hallows, in particular. I am thinking especially of the financial expectations regarding surpluses, teacher:pupil ratios, the percentage of teachers in relation to income, future fee levels, staff salaries, capital expenditure and the targets of pupil numbers linked to the subsequent fees accrued. The Charity Commission may develop real teeth also in its review of the financial activities involving independent schools and may well express a definitive position on the amount of surpluses and monetary reserves such 'charities' generate. Equally, our fee-payers, i.e. the parents, may well develop their own views also on the amount of money the school holds in the bank based on the fees we charge. In crude terms, if All Hallows had insufficient funds it would cease to be but if the school did not satisfy the terms of its own raison d'être it would have even less validity. I am sure that the Governing Body will maintain its clear understanding that the support given so freely in the past to the higher management of the school needs to remain firmly in place; only the Governors can sustain the morale of the Headmaster, so that he, in turn, can provide the positive leadership of the school....this year's theme, interestingly, for the Independent Association of Preparatory Schools (IAPS) is 'Brave New World, Brave Old Values'!"*

Some Murphy Years

S o, the position of Head Teacher was advertised nationally and an interesting crop of applicants was finally narrowed down to two outstanding men, one of whom – who was subsequently appointed – was former Deputy Head, Ian Murphy. Lest there are any sceptical observers out there, Ian was appointed after a gruelling selection process which started with all possible doors open for all applicants and was a process which, rightly, I had no part in - and Ian Murphy has gone on to put his own particular successful stamp on the school ever since.

'Preparation for Headship' courses were very much in vogue at the time and with the months available between Ian Murphy's appointment and his subsequent taking on of all responsibilities, Giles Mercer (Headmaster of Prior Park College and Governor) and I were asked to coordinate a training programme in consultation with Ian. We wisely used words that could be more easily digested than the advice issued in the January issue of '*Headteacher's Update*' in the matter of training: "*Flintham proposes concentrated development with structured, legitimized and funded opportunities for Headteacher support through peer networks to run alongside ongoing professional development for other staff in a model that engenders mutual sustainability. It is clear that portfolio Heads, practising a model of distributed leadership which empowers middle and senior leaders, have the potential to provide a robust environment for learning and teaching.*" As modern politicians are wont to say when they have absolutely no wish or intention to elucidate: '*Let me make it absolutely clear*'. Incidentally, at about the same time, a course was advertised in Sussex which took as its theme 'teaching as an educational activity'. We like to think that the kind of teaching at All Hallows is of the educational kind. Ian kept a detailed diary of this period of time when he attended conferences, embarked on an extensive reading programme of relevant documentation, built up a dossier on local and regional senior schools, familiarised himself with new and impending legislation, played a full role in the re-negotiation of Staff Contracts of Employment, met members of the local community, tracked other serving Prep School Headmasters, met with key members of the Governing Body and Finance Committees, met key members of the school's Senior Leadership Team, visited the Bishop's Office in Clifton, made plans for separate presentations to All Hallows parents, sat in on various internal meetings, planned and collated the results of a Parents' Questionnaire, and, of course, met with me, and tracked me regularly, as I completed my final term before the handover, if only to learn how not to do things. Ian, of course, met also with staff and pupils in countless ordinary, everyday events whenever possible. I mention above the 'extensive reading programme of relevant documentation'. Part of that reading programme included familiarisation with School Policies which had grown to well over one hundred. One Headmaster I worked for many years before told a visiting inspector that 'our policy is to teach them to read and write'; I don't recall there being many other policies. Go back to another age and we are straying into the 'Bible, Kennedy's Latin Primer and the Cane' territory. There is the apocryphal story of two ancient members of staff sitting smoking with their coffees at an adventure park for four hours or so whilst being dimly aware of their pupils occasionally screaming by on the backs of tractors or running half-naked through the undergrowth shooting arrows at each other but that was another age when health and safety had not been invented. That was at a time when as long as one had approximately the same number of children on the return journey as when one started the day, a successful time had been had by all. Policies today concern Equal Opportunities, catering for the disabled, Health and Welfare, Children's Rights, Employment Law, The Parents' Charter, etc, etc, and cover all manner of things in written guidance sheets appropriately positioned around the school such as 'The Five Steps When Washing One's Hands' or sticking labels on the hot water taps proclaiming the fact that these taps dispense hot water. It is rather like the airlines providing small tins of peanuts with the 'let-us-be-absolutely-clear' advice that 'this product may contain nuts'. I suppose all institutions can become a little inward-looking and the little things of life sometimes take on disproportionate hues such as the time I sat in on a 90-minute meeting once with residential staff, as we approached midnight, trying to determine a corporate policy on the siting of face flannels.

One recent trawl through our administrative systems revealed the fact that we had over 120 policies (I stopped counting at this point; blood was coming out of my eyes). They included statements and guidance on Admissions, Mobile Phones, Appraisal, The National Curriculum, Assemblies, Pastoral Care, Assessment, Play (yes, Play! - for a time we even had a teacher i/c Play), Boarding, Classroom Management, Record-Keeping, Crisis Management, Smoking, Disability Rights, Catholic Ethos, The Gifted and Talented, Handwriting, Car Parking (I know!), Learning Support, Medical Matters, and policies burdened with the inevitable abbreviations such as PSHE, IPC, CE, THRASS, HACCP, CRB, CATS, EAL, ISI, COSHH, ECO, IEP, SRE, SEN, NQT, GTP. Parents and educationalists reading this paragraph might be reassured to know that we also have a *Teaching and Learning Policy* but my favourites remain the *Bodily Fluids Policy* and, of course, the policy we have devised for guidance on how to write policies (I am still being serious). Why do we have policies? Why is it necessary today when it might not have been necessary many years ago? I suppose the easiest answer to the second question is that *because* we didn't have policies years ago we need them today. Without policies and protocols, things go awry. Guidelines are needed for the uninitiated and need to be applied by those whose job it is to apply them (that's policy-speak for you). But, in days gone by, life was easier then. Things were more straightforward. People knew what to do. Everybody played their part. Common-sense used to be commonplace. Or so the argument goes. Perhaps the following points are more relevant: the need for transparency and accountability is greater today; the world is more complex, more dangerous; our interpretation is more sophisticated; social and education changes have created a much larger group, i.e. all of us, who are discerning, disparate, often disputatious characters whose differing opinions and rights need regulation; we are all craving for direction; we are all often stupid; idiosyncrasy is now a dirty word; words like *innovation, distinctive, individual* have been replaced by words like *conservatism, congenial, corporate* – one takes one's choice.

Google in '*Why do we have policies in schools*' and the response (as a '*GREAT ANSWER*' please note) pings in as follows:

"*Policies and Procedures are the strategic link between the Company's Vision and its day-to-day operations. But why is that so important? It's because well written policies & procedures allow employees to understand their roles and responsibilities within predefined limits. Basically, policies & procedures allow management to guide operations without constant management intervention. In order to understand why policies & procedures are so important we need to know what they are and differences between them. So let's start by taking a look at policies: A "Policy" is a predetermined course of action which is established to provide a guide toward accepted business strategies and objectives. In other words, it is a direct link between an organization's "Vision" and their day-to-day operations. Policies identify the key activities and provide a general strategy to decision-makers on how to handle issues as they arise. This is accomplished by providing the reader with limits and a choice of alternatives that can be used to "guide" their decision making process as they attempt to overcome problems. I like to think of "policies" as a globe where national boundaries, oceans, mountain ranges and other major features are easily identified. With that concept in mind let's talk about procedures next. The ultimate goal of every procedure is to provide the reader with a clear and easily understood plan of action required to carry out or implement a policy. A well written procedure will also help eliminate common misunderstandings by identifying job responsibilities and establishing boundaries for the job holders. Good procedures actually allow managers to control events in advance and prevent the organization (and employees) from making costly mistakes. You can think of a procedure as a road map where the trip details are highlighted in order to prevent a person from getting lost or "wandering" off an acceptable path identified by the company's management team.*

Policies & procedures are required when there is a need for consistency in your day-to-day operational activities. Policies and procedures also provide clarity to the reader when dealing with accountability issues or activities that are of critical importance to the company, such as, health & safety, legal liabilities, regulatory requirements or issues that have serious consequences."

Well, at least there are some metaphors in there. I don't think I'm trying to be cynical. After all, I have written and circulated enough policies of my own in my time for the greater benefit of mankind. I suspect that 'my' policy is 'your' tissue paper but, rightly or wrongly, policies are here to stay and they are the first documents School Inspectors want to see. Obviously, (although not always fully appreciated by 'stakeholders'), the gap between the theory and the practice should be minimal or non-existent; sadly, this is not always the case. Perhaps the best Curriculum Policy, after all, is the one that says 'we teach them to read and write'.

All of this just goes to show that Ian had some serious reading to plough through before he could take on the mantle. Gone were the days when one extremely successful Headmaster in a certain Benedictine community not very far away from All Hallows suggested that successful headmastering consisted of *"wearing a ball gown, talking of monastic vows, demanding champagne, smoking a cigar in all 'no-smoking' areas and being vulgar and razzmattazing on establishment occasions."* I'm not sure, however, if I passed on to Ian any of these selected and genuine children's observations about Headship presented to me as I 'stepped aside': *"Before you become a Head you have to be normal"*; *"You have to live in a house in the school so that you can escape parents"*; *"Heads try to grow a beard to look more important"*; *"Head of the school = King of the World"*; *"Heads have to be twenty years old"*. And the best – and truest – of them all: *"Heads have to really, really, really, really, really like children"* – a brilliant insight from former pupil Ellie Porter.

Thus did the transition, then, became effectively as seamless as possible. If it fell to Chris Dick, as Chairman, to manage one aspect of the handover of Headmasters, it fell to his successor, Patrick Nixon, to make sure that everything worked out. Given Patrick's c.v. below and his consummate skills in managing people and situations, it is no surprise to learn that the school continued in good shape.

Once again, however, no amount of training really prepares one for the reality; one has to live it. If my first professional experience as Headmaster was dealing with an absconding pupil, Ian Murphy's early dealings were no less momentous. Matron had brought to his attention that the rather large female guinea-pig that had seemed unusually interested in the other female guinea-pigs was, in fact, an alpha male with guinea-pig domination on his mind. Apparently, the guinea-pig – let's call him Don Juan – had heard somewhere that guinea-pigs were in danger of dying out unless he did something to propagate the species. Ian reached for those training manuals to which we have referred but the indexes could not help so he called into play his training in biology and realised he would have to authorise the payment for the animal operation commonly known as castration. Ever the money-conscious entrepreneur – taking his obligations seriously regarding the need to manage school finances prudently – he considered conducting the operation himself, without the need of engaging a professional, reckoning that he could deliver a hefty blow with a cricket bat on the unsuspecting parts of the guinea-pig by creeping up behind Don Juan as he munched on a lettuce leaf. On more considered reflection, however, Ian decided to call in the Castrator General and hide the costs under 'Repairs and Renewals' (which, incidentally, is possibly the best joke in this book). The whole process was handled very sensitively, away from the Pet Room, and all was quiet thereafter (quiet, that is, apart, from Don

PATRICK NIXON, CMG OBE
(Former Pupil & Chairman of Governors)

Patrick was a pupil at All Hallows from 1952-1958 who gained an exhibition to Downside and, thereafter, an exhibition to Magdalen College, Cambridge, reading Latin, Greek and History. He still fondly recalls Francis Dix and Dom Wilfrid Passmore (then Headmaster of Downside) as demanding drivers of his academic studies, as well as remembering the inspiration provided by classics teacher Kevin Newman at Downside. Perhaps because he had been so well stretched at school, he switched from Latin and Greek, at Cambridge, to major in History because he felt the classics ground had already been covered at his schools. Whilst at Cambridge he became President of the Fisher Society, the Catholic Chaplaincy under Monsignor Gilbey. Together with Francis Dix, Mario (Mr Dix's adopted son) and fellow pupil Philip Channer (another classics scholar), Patrick was invited to undertake a Hellenic Cruise in the Easter vacation and developed his taste for travel and for languages. At All Hallows he was Pack Leader of the Lions, a member of the 1st XV, gaining his Colours, and took part in several school plays. Patrick joined the Foreign Office in 1965 moving around the world to places like Nepal,

Beirut, Lima, Tripoli, New York and the UAE amongst other regions. In the course of that time he held the posts of Executive Director of the British Information Services in New York, HM Ambassador to the State of Qatar, High Commissioner to Zambia, Director of the Foreign and Commonwealth Office, Ambassador to the United Arab Emirates and Regional Co-ordinator in Iraq. Patrick was required to learn Arabic at the Middle East Centre for Arab Studies and whilst engaged in the diplomatic service he met and married Elizabeth who was working at the Beirut Embassy. He worked in Cairo just after the six-day war, helped negotiate the mine clearance of the Suez Canal in the 1970s, was an influential figure in New York in presenting the British government's position on various world issues including Northern Ireland and the Falklands, established Kurdish safe havens in the aftermath of the Gulf War which started in 1991, participated in talks with the Cuban government, negotiated with the Taliban, promoted British trade abroad and met Allied troops in Basra with Prince Charles – amongst other things! He was declared an enemy of the state in the Zambian parliament and endured angry protests outside his office in New York from those opposed to Britain's policy in Northern Ireland; and was awarded the OBE for his services in America and the CMG as Ambassador to the state of Qatar. Becoming a Governor at Downside and Chairman of Governors at All Hallows was therefore straightforward…or so he thought! Patrick was Chairman of Governors from 2005 until 2012 thus becoming another former pupil of the school who could claim a sixty-year connection with the school even if it was broken up by the odd fifty years in-between 'doing other things'. Patrick saw through the change of Headmastership between Chris Bird and Ian Murphy and was, not surprisingly, a diplomatic source of strength, wisdom and experience in handling various issues that required at times sensitive leadership.

Juan who felt that such invasive surgery was probably worth a whimper or two). And like all good humorous stories, it is true.

In 2006, the Choir repeated their earlier triumphs by visiting and performing again in Rome. Paul Dowbekin's Tour Diary records the following:

Tuesday 28th March	*The day of our departure. An exciting email from The Vatican confirming that Mr Mercer[110] has been officially accredited as a papal photographer on the day that we are singing in St Peter's so we will get some fabulous photos and we can always exaggerate how brilliant we sounded....We are a strange bunch as we arrive at the EasyJet check-in.*
Wednesday 29th March	*We finally all meet up at 5.00pm in the fabulous (and huge) Basilica of Santa Maria Maggiore. There is a rehearsal in the sacristy (which is about twice the size of our school chapel) and we meet His Excellency the Bishop, an imposing figure. Mass goes well, the choir sounds fabulous, we are asked to sing an extra piece at the end and receive tumultuous and tearful applause. His Excellency's verdict?.... 'Magnifico!'*
Thursday 30th March	*Nicky Moulton notices that there is a convention of Italian firemen, all in uniform, staying at the same Centre; breakfast takes longer than usual. Another day of sightseeing...starting at the fourth century church of Santa Sabina....before heading back to Frascati... and preparation for the concert in the town's cathedral. Again, a stunning performance from everyone which is received with great enthusiasm by the audience.*
Friday 31st March	*Today The Vatican and St Peter's.....we pour out of the coach and he drives away. We do a head count, one missing; Henry Stonehouse is still on the coach. It seems he was asleep. 'Didn't you wake him?' I ask. 'Well, we hit him on the head' they reply. In an astonishingly calm manner and all within about ten minutes, I manage to trace the coach company, get the driver's mobile number, ring him, arrange for Henry to be woken and brought back to us...and I age about five years. There are long queues to get into St Peter's so I explain to some of the guards that I need to let someone know that we have arrived...two of them simply pick me up and carry me over the barriers with the alarms going off left, right and centre, triggered*

---

[110] Tim Mercer has achieved many outstanding things in his own chosen fields but on being reminded of this procedure he has now decided to style himself 'Photographer to the Pope'.

by their machine guns. As the time for Mass approached, I find the organist, Signor Capone. There is to be no rehearsal (not allowed) and he checks the music that we will sing (already approved by them in November)...some changes have to be made...I have to translate the English anthems for him (I make it up) and he mentions vaguely that we should sing the Kyrie and Agnus Dei (unprepared) and the Responses (totally unknown to anyone under the age of fifty)... no pressure, then! Capone and three of his minders in black frock coats stand by watching our every move...there is a difference of opinion about the speed of the Sanctus. As I conduct the Choir, Capone and his henchmen sing loudly at the speed they use; we sing louder. Capone starts to conduct as well. Poor Mark Wood now has to contend with two conductors, one on his left and one on his right and he thinks the Church of England has problems with women bishops! But we all get there somehow and the experience is strangely moving..and had a profound effect.

Saturday 1st April　　*The usual April Fool jokes...shopping in Frascati and then home. Five very busy but very special days. Many thanks to Mark Wood, Trevor Richards, David Ellery, Nicky Moulton and Cathy Cardozo and to all the many parents and friends. Most of all I am grateful to the children: Great fun to be with, they sound like I have never heard them before and they were a brilliant advert for All Hallows... well done to everyone!*

Travelling anywhere, particularly abroad, adds to one's experience, forces one to draw on unknown resources and changes perspective almost always with positive results.

Changing perspective is an illuminating process and it can be done anywhere. In writing this book, I spent four happy hours, one day in late April, in 2013, in the anticipated quiet of Mrs Renouf's eyrie in the Learning Support Department, trying to research and write, but actually watching the All Hallows world go by beneath my gaze. How Mrs Renouf ever gets any work done I shall never know. Forty years ago, I would have been sitting in a former stable block, firing air rifles down the range and watching Mr Dix's boys roller-skating across the quad; eighty years ago, I would have been in live stable lofts looking down on Hammer and Tongs, the two Paget horses, chomping on the hay strewn over the cobble-stoned yard. In 2013, I sat in a splendid heated office (it had been a relentlessly cold April) watching staff criss-cross the dozen entrances and exits to that proscenium, meeting and greeting each other with papers, bundles of lost property, cricket bats, or coffees in hand, or perhaps the latest offerings from the dining room, and prospective parents touring with Registrar and Headmaster, as the sun shone down on the spring cherry blossom, and children ran (they always run) with wellies, musical instruments, bags, balls, books and biscuits, hither and thither. Not one cross word, not one sign of anger – just busy, happy people going about the business of the day. Three members of staff were explaining to a group of seated, interested pupils from the junior department what they were about to do that afternoon in Scouts' Wood when, all of a sudden, a violent hailstorm swept across the courtyard forcing them under the cover of the red archway. It wouldn't be All Hallows, after all, if, even in sunshine, we didn't experience the madness of a storm. And I pause to look around me in the office, whilst the young children cannot contain their excitement any longer and go wheeling round the courtyard in the driving white hailstones, to read the various notices on the walls entitled '*You Matter! So Look After Yourself!*' and '*The All Hallows Children's Charter*' and '*Worries and Complaints – A Pupil's Guide*' and '*Are You Worried? Who Can I Talk To?*' and the sun returns and I hear a child laugh and the world really doesn't seem such a bad place at all.

Back to 2006....Brian Walton, the gentleman Carpentry Master, following in the tradition of Carpentry teachers like Mr Trotman from 1946, retired after twenty-seven years of unobtrusive service to the school, having seen through generations of pupils in their burgeoning woodwork skills creating items ranging from table-mats to full-sized canoes, thus adding considerably to the logistical headaches at Heathrow, as proud boys arrived through customs with their various wooden edifices; Rose Keene, one of our splendid 'Lady Cooks', retired after thirty-one years dispensing victuals, vegetables and Victoria sandwiches to an ever-hungry clientele; personnel of a more recent vintage joined the school as former pupils Oliver Mellotte, Dominic Walker and James Lombard[111] became 'Gap' students for a while; Father Jim Williams added his charismatic everyday spirituality to proceedings; and Richard Arnold-Jones' play 'The Air Hostess' was produced at school in homage to his long association with All Hallows which seemed destined to remain undiminished as he celebrated his eighty-fourth birthday.

And one must not forget the literary contributions of the modern pupil. It is easy to wade nostalgically in the past and marvel at the achievements of those who have gone before but, in education, and in life, such examples are only there to inspire, and ultimately, to surpass. Records are made in order to be broken; think 'Dr Roger Bannister and the first four-minute mile'. He came from a humble background. He felt he was up against others from a Public School education. *"I came from such a simple origin, without any great privilege, and I would say I also wanted to make a mark. It wasn't until I was about 15 that I appeared in a race...I enjoy singing, and the instruments which truly move me are the horn, the trumpet and the 'cello. I think that.... a universal adolescent feeling* (is) *trying to find your place. The adolescent who is perfectly adjusted to his environment, I've yet to meet.....I wanted to be a neurologist"*; such pronouncements provide much food for thought. In 1954, the stadium announcer for the staged attempt on the 'four-minute mile record race' was Norris McWhirter, who went on to co-publish and co-edit the *Guinness Book of Records*. He excited the crowd by delaying the announcement of the time Bannister ran for as long as possible: *"Ladies and gentlemen, here is the result of event 9, the one mile: 1st, No. 41, R.G. Bannister, Amateur Athletic Association and formerly of Exeter and Merton Colleges, Oxford, with a time which is a new meeting and track record, and which—subject to ratification—will be a new English Native, British National, All-Comers, European, British Empire and World Record. The time was 3..."* The roar of the crowd drowned out the rest of the announcement. Bannister's time was 3 min 59.4 sec. The point about the Bannister story is not that he was an old boy of All Hallows (although he was educated in nearby Bath) but that world-shattering achievements in various fields can often, usually, occasionally, ironically, be effected through modesty, accident, devotion, determination and skill which reminds us all of the notion that we need an encouraging measure of 99% perspiration to

[111] We'll give **James** Lombard a little footnote of his own (so that he buys the book) because he lingers in the memory for two reasons: (1) he was a key player in the uncoordinated choreography of a group of unintentionally comic characters in a Renouf production of '*Bugsy Malone*' as one of the boxers who '*could 'ave been anything that they wanted to be*' and (2) he carried, almost single-handedly, the gradually cheese-rotting, garlic-packed lunches in giant cardboard boxes through the Paris Metro when we were all racing ahead down The Champs-Élysées, in order to catch the last train home, with variously encouraging shouts behind us like 'Come on, James, keep up!'
Ok, Ok....I'd better keep sibling rivalry in mind....**Oliver** Lombard was a seriously good sportsman and we still present the 'Lombard Shield' in his honour to commemorate batting exploits (winners have included Oliver, himself, Toby Owen, Archie Pearson, Tom Doe, Hugh Jennings, Sam Harris, Wilf Neville, Max Dellwhite, Rory Cadbury, Ben Whitemore and Tom Channer) and ***Charlotte*** Lombard won a scholarship to St Mary's, Shaftesbury, but, sorry boys, she was the most fragrant of you all.

The choir at Westminster Cathedral

1% inspiration. Wasn't it Newton[112] who said he was simply throwing pebbles from the shore and that he was only 'standing on the shoulders of giants'??

And so, we pick up a literary connection through the inspiration of that different medium of achievement by showing how the pupils' writing of the present-day can match and perhaps surpass that of the past (Auberon Waugh, et al, take note).

Lucy Howlett, former pupil, entered the following unedited entry to 'The Headmaster's Essay Competition' in 2007....

The Eyes of Janus

Our name is Janus, hers and mine.

One body, one heart, one name and two faces. Hers is complete and pretty, apart from one area, a little to the back of her scalp, where there is mine - a growth, a carbuncle, a protuberance. One body, one heart and, they told us, one brain. So – one brain, one name, one person, one disfigured deformity. But they are wrong. I am here.

[Conjoined twins (noun, plural): Identical twins whose bodies are joined together in utero. Occasionally one of the twins will fail to develop properly, effectively acting as a parasite upon the normally developed twin: this condition is known as parasitic twinning or heteropagus twins.]

This is my story, though I cannot tell it to you. Seven years ago, I woke from my soft, wet cocoon of ignorance and equality into a world of shocked faces, cameras, and pointing fingers, taken from the struggle in the dark to the exposure of a blinding light. I was not alone – never alone, but my life of loneliness began that first day. You see, I am a parasitic twin, a limbless and doughy shape growing from the head of my sister.

[Parasite (noun, singular): a being living on another, drawing nutriment from its host often to the detriment of the host.]

I never saw her. I could not turn and look. She looked onto life, I looked away, held from the sights and sounds of life, always looking, but not able to seek out my view. I am the dark side of the moon.

And so we lived, she and I. Here are the realities of my life. We were breast-fed by our fearful, tearful mother, and the perfect nutrition flowed through us both, feeding our growing structure,

---

[111] *"I do not know what I may appear to the world, but to myself I seem to have been only like a boy playing on the sea-shore, and diverting myself in now and then finding a smoother pebble or a prettier shell than ordinary, whilst the great ocean of truth lay all undiscovered before me."*

vessels, skin, hair, eyelashes. But only her mouth tasted the sweet, tender milk, and only her face nuzzled against the warm breast. Mine remained cold. My lips lead nowhere, I have no oesophagus. We breathed in the smells but only through her nostrils. I have no airways, no trachea, no lungs. We heard. The world was not silent to me, but full of sounds to delight, or to chill a child's blood. The sound of the birds belonged to us both, but the words of love belonged only to her. We moved our mouths, she and I, but only hers made the sounds so loved by our mother, and then the words. The words I longed to say too. The words I understood so much more deeply. I have no vocal cords. We thought, we longed, we wished and this we could both do.

*[**Consciousness** (noun, abstract): awareness, person's conscious thoughts and feelings as a whole.]*

Oh yes, we both thought and felt. Sometimes I was sure for a moment that she knew I understood the world, that I had my own thoughts, but if she did, she was alone in this. If I could talk, they would have known. But as it was, I was a lump. The spasms of life from my eyes, that might have been interpreted as an attempt at communication, were not seen. Thought was, for me, impossible. The doctors said it, so of course it must be true, mustn't it?

*[**Communication** (noun): imparting or exchange of information etc, social dealings or connection.]*

She grew. We grew. She sat and crawled, while I slowed her movements and pulled her always to one side, an ugly millstone. Then, late and with difficulty, she walked. And so, of course, I followed, gazing at where we had been, never at where we were going. We had to go to school. We had no choice – she was, though slow, capable of some education. Together we suffered staring, teasing, and I felt a new shame and guilt. I was the reason that she had no friends; I was the reason that she had no one to talk to, I was the reason, I was always the reason. Teachers would turn the other cheek, unsure whether I really existed at all. After a while they found it easier to ignore us.

The lack of body for me to control left my mind with nothing to do but to contemplate, and listen to other people. I developed a secret intellect beyond my years, and far, far beyond hers. I am sure that if she was in the same position, she would have done the same. But she wasn't. She was treated as a person by our parents, given toys and things to amuse her. She had moments of excitement. She had choices to make.

*[**Choice** (noun abstract): The power to choose between alternatives. Freedom to determine a course of action]*

She had choices to make, and there were choices to be made for her. As she grew, and as my unacknowledged brain demanded blood to feed its curiosity and its anger, she began to fail and sicken. She cried, and pulled and poked at my skin, my eyes. As I sapped her mind and strength, she begged for release. Surgeons have murmured, difficult sentences have been carefully said. The parasite is taking a dreadful toll upon its host, its supporter. If I live, we both die, if I die, she might, possibly, live. A knife is needed.

*[**Death** is the permanent end of the life of a biological organism. Death may refer to the end of life as either an event or condition.]*

The inevitable has happened. Seven years and five months after I entered this world, I have become a killer, and so I will be killed. I cannot ask, I cannot choose, and I cannot let them know. I can only submit. If I could summon my powers of thought into some physical expression, I would scream my anger, my rage. I would tear her head open and creep inside to inhabit it, to use her flesh to live and to choose. I would stop my sacrifice. I would tell my story.

But I am the past, and she is the future. The new Janus.

*[**life** (noun singular): A state of existence as a living individual; in philosophy, the essence of the manifestation and the foundation of the being; in Christianity, the essence of God, its own revelation; the world in general; existence; the span of time during which an object operates; (colloquial) A term of imprisonment of a convict until his or her death. More formally called a life sentence; **a worthwhile existence.**]*

Mention has been made earlier of the charitable work undertaken by the pupils under the direction of various members of staff over the years and the year 2007 seems to have been particularly busy. Almost £10000 was raised through mufti days, the 'world's biggest coffee morning', wearing pink, sponsored spellings, the Craft Fair, Christmas shoeboxes, cycling trips, knitting, cake sales, vegetable sales, concerts, workouts, tea parties, making jewellery, walks to the quarry, mountain climbing, a domino run in the gym, a sponsored silence amongst many other activities. The principal charities to gain benefit from all these initiatives included Jeans for Genes, MacMillan nurses, Breast Cancer, NSPCC, the Poppy Day Appeal, the children in Serbia, a Nepalese Orphanage, LEPRA, The Meningitis Trust, The RNIB, Bristol Hospital, Cancer Research, hospices for the terminally ill, homes for the deaf and blind, and many more. In this year, initially through the contact established by parent Julia Parker, and later taken on by Sarah Temple-Pederson, who coordinated the collection of unwanted school uniform items, our first charitable connections were made with 'our' school in Sang'a, at the foot of the Mount Kenya, and not only did we receive photos of smiling African children wearing the All Hallows uniform but some of the monies raised went towards the building of new latrines for them.

In 2007, Miss Adams retired from All Hallows…

HILARY ADAMS
(Head of History 1986-2007)

"I came to Somerset from a prestigious Girls' Grammar school in Yorkshire, teaching 11-18 years olds, and having enjoyed the enthusiasm of the 11-13 age group in particular, as I ran the Junior Drama Society, and loved the practical aspects of History, a move into the energy-filled world of the Prep School seemed a viable step in my career. Twenty-one years later sees that career ending with, inevitably, many regrets, as I shall miss the children, my colleagues, this beautiful setting and sharing History. There are so many memories! Snapshots over the years: being grateful for my long hair up in a bun as I moved at speed past the beams in the first History Room; line-ups along the Cran Wall; as Head of Discipline teaching a new group of prefects the locking up procedure and doing it holding a small hedgehog we rescued en route; taking photos of everything and everyone, including two prospectuses; my blue roan Cocker spaniel, Megan, asleep in the corner of the classroom with children's hands just 'happening' to hang down at stroking level when she woke up and wandered round the desks; taking year groups to the Young National Trust Theatre 'Living History' events at Buckland Abbey, Stourhead, Dunster and escorting children and myself in full Tudor costume up the M5 to Baddesley Clinton, getting some very odd looks in the Service Station; combing charity shops for clothes that could be converted into costumes; the 16th and 17th century Dance Display on the Library Lawn for Cardinal Hume's visit; begging for an interactive whiteboard; moving boxes and boxes of books and costumes, plus two wardrobes, into The Crane Wing and wondering if I could take over The Foyer as well; researching, writing and rewriting notes; teaching the children how to highlight; sharing moments of excitement when we discovered something new about the Middle Ages or the Tudors or the Victorians; but, most of all, memories of the children, every one unique.

History is an integral part of life and we are all living our own part of the human story. As I retire, I hope that a few hearts as well as minds have been touched by this fascinating subject which it has been my great privilege to share with young people for over thirty years."

Every now and then one encounters a teacher who will be long remembered. Hilary Adams was one such teacher. One hears time and again of former pupils whose first memories mention Miss Adams' teaching, perhaps the highlighting (as mentioned above), and her energy and enthusiasm. Hilary became very involved with the production of drama at the school often in connection with the lighting and one can remember her plaintive cry for 'More Nine!' on many an occasion as she coordinated the overall effect of the various spotlights with a practised eye. The gardens and birds around the school were also dear to her heart as she helped the boarders plant various offerings or weave the Willow House, help plan, dig and plant the wildlife pond, and run the Bird-watching Club (which I never found intrusive). Hilary, of course, also organised so many History Trips to The Big Pit, Chepstow Castle, Coldharbour Mill, Montacute House and so many other destinations, near and far, with customary flair and administrative efficiency to make a Cromwell jealous. I remember also being bullied by Hilary into dressing up into what can only be described as a pair of green silk curtains and then being forced to dance some madrigal or other in St Bede's to prove I could enter into the spirit of things. Hilary had survived three Headmasters and four room-changes in her twenty-one years at All Hallows and she left an indelible mark on the school.

Hilary possessed such energy it was never likely that she would retire to a sedentary life; she was last seen acting as an official Tour Guide at Wells Cathedral and it was noted that her group was often the largest – and best disciplined – as they entered into the world of history as explained by Miss Adams.

In 2007, visiting artist Penny Somerville worked closely with the children in making the stained glass window panels still to be seen in the Foyer of The Crane Wing. Hilary Adams would have approved since Penny wanted to bring in the light, colour and energy of the natural world to inspire the day's activities by focusing on the drawing workshops she set up in Scouts' Wood. The old walnut tree became a central source of inspiration which led on to the symbolism of trees throughout time and different cultures, as well as considering how important trees are as we respond to the environmental issues of our own time. The vertical borders of the windows contain the ten qualities of life celebrated in the Hebrew Tree of Life: The Crown/Glory, understanding our intelligence, wisdom, strength, mercy and love, splendour, firmness, foundations, beauty and The Kingdom of God. Many sacred trees are engraved into the top borders and various quotes about the importance of trees are included at the base of the window. Mr Jody Wells and Miss Charlotte Knowles took a small touring party to Barcelona for two Boys' hockey matches and returned with one victory (against a team that decided at half-time that they had to leave in order to catch a bus) and one defeat against one of the best club teams in Spain when Sam Harris, in goal, and Jack Cadbury, on the pitch, distinguished themselves with excellent performances. The Tennis Academy, under Ian Murphy's developing vision for this significant feature of the school, and directed by Dean Cornish, continued to flourish in 2007 and was beginning to gain wider notice from the LTA. Finian Orme and Yasmeen al Rumaithi won 'The Road to Wimbledon' Tournament and went on to the County finals with Yasmeen also gaining the chance to train with the Australian National Coach, Pete McGraw, who was the ex-coach of Anna Sharapova. A young Peter Islip and Erika Cotton (of whom we shall hear more later) were also beginning to emerge as players of real promise on the courts.

In 2008, Mark Wood, who had joined the school in 1991 as Director of Music and who had relinquished that role subsequently to care for his daughter whilst his wife continued teaching had decided to bring to an end his career at All Hallows, for he had carried on as a peripatetic music teacher in the interim, and left the school in order to take on the prestigious post of Vicar of Wilton. Mark's brilliance on the organ and his quiet sense of humour became hallmarks of his time. Wendy Hunt, Head of Latin, was also leaving, this time in order to retire, having spent a lifetime in teaching and we were fortunate that she chose to end her career at All Hallows where her enthusiasm for her subject and her bountiful pastoral care with the boarders, particularly, in her capacity as a residential Houseparent, were much appreciated by all. She even taught Latin to the parents on occasions and her natural warmth and empathy reached out to all; no wonder it was recorded in the 2008 Chronicle that Wendy deserved the adult version of the Paget Cup for her 'integrity, enterprise and sensitivity to the needs of others'. The School Council came into being for the first time[113], which

[113] In 2008, we thought that the idea of a 'School Council' was quite symptomatic of our innovative thinking. Here we were, taking into account the views of the pupils! Yet, one learns of 'The Right Honourable, the Lord Tebbit, CH, PC, former Secretary of State, former Chairman of the Conservative Party', joining his own School Council in Enfield, as long ago as 1947, as "probably the best extempore speaker in the school". Perhaps we were just catching up.

was the pupils' representative and elected body to recognise that they had a voice in the school and they had a right to express their opinions! Megan Stride was its first Chairperson. The Council set about leading assemblies on sustainability, influenced menu-planning, decided the activities for the House Charity Day and met twice a term to consider wider school issues. The Council produced ideas for development which the Headmaster picked up and drove through, including the 'hitting wall' on the south of the Crane Wing, the wooden benches in front of the Crane Wing, the central tree and round-seat in the Stable Courtyard, and new additions to The Adventure Playground. One hopes that the views of pupils were always considered but, in reality, the concept was rather alien to the mores of earlier times. To imagine that Francis Dix would wake up in the morning and wonder what the day would bring subject to the wishes of the pupils or that Matron might say "Well, Bron, what time would you like to go to bed tonight?" or Paul Ketterer, for that matter, would call a line-up to ask the children what they wanted to be taught that day are all examples of 'things that didn't happen' (and, to be fair, they don't actually happen today either) but the formalisation and recognition of children as having some input into affairs, which then has a genuine influence on events, is a modern, important and worthwhile step forward. Anya Boulton and Wilf Neville were splendid appointments as Head Girl and Head Boy respectively and got on very well together which is not surprising since they were, in fact, cousins. Wilf distinguished himself on the sports field playing an important role as a member of a successful rugby 1st XV which won ten of its thirteen matches and, later in the year, knocked off four innings of over fifty, top-scoring with a fine 77 with the bat. In the same cricket team, Captain Hamish Pearson topped the bowling averages with thirty wickets and scored a cultured 105 n.o. against Warminster, the first All Hallows century for eleven years, although I'm racking my memory to come up with the name of the boy who scored the century in 1997. I am delighted to record in this book, before it goes to print, the fact that Josh Whitemore has just hit 100 not out in June 2013 against Sherborne (having scored 97 against the same school when playing for the Colts a few years earlier). Head Girl Anya, not to be outdone by her Head Boy cousin, represented the school in the National Athletics Championships in the Discus and won an academic scholarship to Prior Park College. One has been aware of the impact All Hallows has had on the lives of many of our British pupils but one is reminded of the determining influence the school has also been able to exert further afield as we read in the Chronicle of 2008 the farewell words of Monica Urquijo: "*All Hallows has been part of my life since I was born. My earliest memory of it was seeing my big brother, Jaime, getting ready to go to boarding school. I remember he 'stole' my sister's slippers to take with him – she was so mad! When I was four, I visited All Hallows for the first time with my mum. We had tea in the Old Library and it seemed massive to me but I really wanted to come. Paloma, my older sister, came when I was five and I really missed her and couldn't wait to join her. Now I am about to leave! I can't believe the time has gone so fast. I will miss it LOADS – my friends, the atmosphere, the intimacy of everyone and the amazing life of boarding. It's been part of my life for so long – one of my uncles (aged 32) also came to the school and when we are together we have so many*

things to remember about All Hallows. After five schools, this has definitely been the best." In 2008, under the inimitable style of Sophie Ball, the Reception class was inspected by Ofsted on the penultimate day of the academic year and came through with 'outstanding' in every category with no recommendations to follow up.

The 2009 Chronicle looked back on celebrations that marked the school's seventieth birthday and the Prize Giver in the summer was former pupil Bernard Trafford (F.P. 1963-1969) who had gone on to become the Headmaster of The Royal Grammar School, Newcastle on Tyne, as well as Chairman of HMC 2007-2009. It was also noted in the June 1969 Chronicle that, as a boy, he was The Headmaster's Librarian and had gained the distinction of winning 110 stars (merits) for The Panthers. In the absence of any other knowledge to the contrary he might just be the first old boy who went on to become a Headmaster, although a more recent former pupil, Kit Thompson, a grade eight 'cellist, chorister, distance runner and sportsman, also became Headmaster of Unicorn School, Kew Gardens, Richmond, in September 2013. Kit Thompson's bad memories of All Hallows consist of picking up leaves and clearing snow, like many a former pupil of Paul Ketterer's time, as well as the urgent injunction to *"Mind the Paintwork!"* as squads of boys carried various items of furniture around the school, since there were never enough rooms dressed up with the right equipment often enough. Incidentally, no matter how many classrooms one builds or subject-specific areas one creates, there is never enough room to house, semi-permanently, all the multifarious activities in a school, without the major shifting of 'stuff' in this manner. Nowadays, it is true, there appear to be rather more members of an adult work-force to undertake these physical tasks but one likes to think that the slaves, i.e. the pupils, should still be made to work, occasionally, for their living for the good of their souls, you understand. It is always somewhat ironic that the pupils usually end up being the press-ganged labour force who move the classroom desks into examination halls, thus adding, when 'assessments' come upon us each new season, a rather 'nice' twist to the image of soon-to-be-hanged-prisoners who habitually have built their own scaffolds. But, in the matter of exams, it's not all 'poor children', you know, for set against the slightly gentler few days when teachers invigilate, there follows a period at least twice as long when the teachers have to mark the blessed scripts, realise there is still a huge way to go and find a way of explaining to parents what is to be done. Exam howlers are rightly celebrated the world over but a particular favourite is the genuine script handed in with odd-looking red marks all over the page with a scribble down the side of the paper saying *"Miss – sorry about the blood"*; no doubt, a particularly challenging paper. Another child was convinced that God made a *"convent"* with Abraham – presumably to keep the nuns happy – and, in answer to the question that raised the matter of behaving appropriately in church, there came the reply *"we should not mess about in chapel because the priest might spill the wine when he's drinking"*. In fact it is often the Religious Education paper that throws up the best 'interpretations' which the reader might find interesting in a Catholic school. Two more examples of children interpreting, in unanticipated ways, tasks asked of them; the first example was in a science exam: "How would you go about separating two solutions in a science experiment?" - Answer: "*Well, first of all, I'd sit down and make a nice cup of tea.*" The second you may recall from notes on Cardinal Hume's visit but it is worth repeating: "Make up a prayer about your parents which we can send the Cardinal" - Response: "*Let us pray for our parents, especially our mothers and fathers.*"

Back to Bernard Trafford, our Guest Speaker on Prize Day, who looked back on the school's 25th birthday on All Saints Day and the Fancy Dress Competition, as well as the reciting of the School Alphabet by Francis Dix, whom he recalls had the nickname 'Smacks' (no prizes, however, for guessing why) ..."*In my older brothers' time they remember he was indeed a terror. By my day, he was getting old and certainly less fiery.....it's good to see it this year in such fantastically good shape and lay a few ghosts*". Children, the advice is clear, only join a school with a Headmaster who is already old. Fortunately for them perhaps, all children consider all their teachers to be about fifty years of age – even the youngest ones – and, as for those who really are over fifty, we are all rushing headlong to our 100th birthday.

Not that Libby Doe-Wansey was reaching 100 in 2009 but she did retire, earlier than she might have anticipated, in order to look after her mother, but Libby was another member of staff who had given twenty years or more of unfailing service to the school.

In 2009, we had a special Mass at Clifton Cathedral and many former pupils and friends joined us in various musical celebrations through the year including a number of celebratory recitals with our friends from Frascati, as well as a charity concert to raise funds for the church roof at Nunney, the St Cecilia Gala Concert in which former pupils George Howlett, Jasmine Wood, Harriet Sasada and Freddie Mercer all played significant parts, and the summer term finale of 'Cranstock' when George Howlett, again, the Year Seven pupils in 'Bombshell', Dominic Greensmith, Thumb Wars, The Phoenix Fall and Rocketeer (a well-established band containing three of Roger Bevan's grandchildren) all provided a fitting warm-up to Glastonbury! '*Glastonbury*' or the Pilton Pop Festival, as it used to be called, has been referenced a few times and it has been said by some Common Room wag that "*90% of our prospective parents arrive at the front doors of the school because of existing parents' recommendations whilst the other 10% see the mud and the rain and the fields and think they've found the Pilton Pop Festival.*" One set of parents who didn't think they had arrived at the Pilton Pop Festival were the parents of Timothy and Lucy Brooksbank because Michael Eavis was the children's grandfather and he was an honoured guest, one year, at the school's Prize Giving, probably in a fallow year of the Glastonbury Festival.

Much has been mentioned already about the charitable work undertaken by the school and, in May 2010, two intrepid 'Dads', Mike Burns and Andrew Jolliffe, generated huge interest and funds by raising money for 'Blood Bikes' a subsidiary of Freewheelers EVS, a registered charity, providing voluntary 'out-of-hours' emergency courier services in transporting blood supplies, medical documents and other essential items between hospitals in the region. Mike

LIBBY DOE-WANSEY

(Head of French 1989-2009)

"Teaching French at All Hallows has been a real privilege and I am grateful that the opportunities to take children to France have been encouraged by three Headmasters during my time here. It makes such a difference in the classroom to be able to enthuse about going to France soon to speak French 'sur place'. When I first arrived there was a very good Exchange system in place with Château-Gontier which is the twin town of Frome. The brave Year Eight pupils (or Form Six as it was then called) spent a fortnight with a previously-unknown French family. They attended the correspondent's school for a week and then spent a week on holiday with the French family. They learnt so much French – they had no choice! In those days we drove the mini-buses to France with all the luggage on the roof wrapped in black bin-liners. On one occasion, Madame Moore and I found that in a violent storm all the bags split and we left a trail of black plastic flying behind us. The next Exchange we set up was with a school in the centre of Le Havre which was situated next to a prison. There were very high walls around the school, a grey courtyard and no grass. When those French pupils returned to England and saw the rolling fields of Somerset and the country setting of All Hallows they were amazed. All the annual Normandy trips for the younger children have been memorable when we have been able to take in the experiences and sights of the Normandy war-time beaches, the war cemeteries, Pegasus Bridge, Mont St Michel, Bayeux and, perhaps the highlight, Paris. Travels on the Metro were sometimes fraught – we once had to run virtually the length of the Champs-Élysées to catch the last train back – and Mr Bird remembers a less than happy time stuck in the Eiffel Tower lift with all the children for forty minutes or so. I shall miss those trips and all the children and colleagues at All Hallows very much".

Libby was another member of staff who had to move around the school a little as one Headmaster after another had a better location for the language teaching and she moved very quickly with the times – even ahead of the times – as various new technologies were introduced in order to help the children hear and speak French in an everyday fashion. One thinks of the French satellite TV arrangement, for example, alluded to earlier in this book.

Libby might be interested to read the following words written by the French Department of 1967 long before she ever arrived at the school....

"French – the audio-visual way"

"In recent years much research has been carried out into the teaching of Modern Languages. The organisations which have backed these researches have had widely differing aims: the Nuffield Trust researching into the teaching of foreign languages in schools; the French Government intent on spreading French as a commercial language throughout the world; the United Nations interested in raising the educational standards of backward nations as quickly as possible; the Army researching into the quickest method of preparing officers and men for service in non-English speaking countries....At All Hallows we are now using an audio-visual course called 'Bonjour-Line' which consists of a series of film strips and tapes dealing with the adventures of a group of children.... we are installing a Language Laboratory at All Hallows which consists of a series of six booths each with its own tape-recorder, headphones and microphone...in addition the classroom has been fitted with a projection unit with loudspeakers and we have notice-boards to carry additional visual material. It has now become known as 'The French Room' rather than IVB".

I still remember, however, teaching Common Entrance French myself in the 1980s and relying heavily on text books, writing, grammar, etc, with very little need to speak the language at all – but perhaps that says more about my French-speaking ability than the technology or teaching approaches of the time. Fortunately, some of these concerns do not now apply since the French Department is led by Madame Emmanuel Kerboul, a native French speaker, whose perfect accent and wide vocabulary have already produced outstanding results in the oral examinations.

Libby spent some years towards the end of her career as a residential Houseparent giving even more of her time in the evenings and weekends to the children in the dormitories after having taught them all day in the classroom. Libby retained an excellent sense of humour throughout her time and maintained a fragrant sense of grace and gentility through it all.

and Andrew got into their saddles on their bicycles and completed a gruelling 1170 mile cycle ride from John O'Groats to Land's End, over five hundred hours, during the month of May. Throughout their adventure, Mike and Andrew ran an excellent blog – in between bouts of drinking copious amounts of Red Bull - which allowed the school to follow their progress, ask questions, interact with map reading skills, learn co-ordinates, study habits and lifestyles of wildlife at key points on the journey, design a tartan and plan their own bike ride back at school. On their return, Mike and Andrew 'challenged' the pupils to cover that same distance of over one thousand miles by running, cycling, swimming and walking round the school grounds on a number of circuits which the children duly did on House Charities Day. Through all such activity and sponsorship, over £11000 was raised which went towards the purchase of a new BMW R1200RT motorcycle. Senior pupil Luke Holland won the competition to name the bike *The Flying Crane* and the bike is now in active service across the south-west.

The year 2010 saw two highly complimentary Inspections of the school, one by the ISI which highlighted the excellence of the teaching and the depth and breadth of opportunities available to the children, whilst the separate Boarding Inspection pronounced the school's pastoral provision as 'outstanding'. Three members of staff retired in 2010 whose influence was also outstanding, although not in the classrooms, but in their own fields of endeavour: Ginny Major retired after 23 years' service in the catering department where her specialities, perhaps, started with breakfasts – and porridge in particular – in the morning; Liz Davis retired after 18 years as Head Matron and Harry Godden, Head Groundsman, also left the school after over twenty years.

William Rees-Mogg had been an interesting and distinctive pupil during his years at the school and with his literary and family connections it was no surprise, perhaps, to learn that he excelled, particularly, in English. I had every reason, during an inspection of the school, to be glad of his presence in my English class one day when, with the severe-looking inspector settled

LIZ DAVIS
(School Matron 1992-2010)

Liz Davis represents that crucially important figure in any boarding school: The Matron. All Hallows had been lucky through the years to have engaged the services of ladies like those listed in Appendix E, all of whom added their own unique contributions to the story and Liz was no exception. She was a highly qualified, experienced and professional nursing sister who administered to the medical needs and general good health of pupils and staff first and foremost. It was a great comfort to parents and a great reassurance to the Headmasters she worked with to know that the children's physical well-being was in such capable hands. Liz worked tirelessly in the interests of the school and never fully understood the concept of 'time-off'. The Matron, of course, is always on duty even when she is 'off-duty' but Liz took this dedication to a new art form altogether. Liz lived on the premises, literally 'above the shop', for her flat was situated one floor above the Sickbay. She kept an open-house surgery refusing to establish set hours for the children and in this way she became readily available and ever-vigilant. Liz attended to pastoral duties in the mornings and nights and the children swore that she knew the sound of every creaking floorboard and never slept so that any midnight raids they might have been planning were nipped in the bud before they had started.

Liz knew all the secret hiding-places for tuck, she knew where all the lost underwear could be found and she knew what the children were thinking before they had dreamed up those thoughts. Liz possessed a measure of extreme efficiency which impressed even that most exacting of administrative task-masters, Paul Ketterer, and kindly nurtured the callow Heads that followed in their early years thereafter. She ran 'The All Hallows Hotel', as it became known, with calm and welcoming assurance as more and more day pupils arrived in the mornings with their pyjamas and slippers ready to sleep over for the night. Liz was a strong presence over the weekends when many parents and visitors were in need of contact points and she happily joined touring groups like the French Excursions so that her medical and pastoral skills could be utilised across the Channel. We never had any trouble getting through Customs when Liz Davies was with us. If ever an unusual problem developed, one would always go first to Liz who, invariably, had the solution in one form or another. It was Liz Davis I had in mind when I was writing of the general virtues of the 'School Matron' on page 105. Children remember her fondly, or with fear, though all had reason at some or another to thank her for her medical dispensations.

unobtrusively in the back of the room, behind the door, before the pupils entered, I began to prepare myself, somewhat apprehensively, for my opening remarks. I was spared that task by William's bursting enthusiasm as he barged into the room.

"Sir, Sir, I've just finished Paradise Lost, as you suggested, and it's brilliant!"
"Ah, Good morning, William," I beamed. *"And what did you think of Milton's Satan?"*
"Didn't like him, Sir!"

HARRY GODDEN
(Head Groundsman 1990-2010)

Harry also belonged to that fine tradition mentioned earlier that had included the likes of 'Nash', the Metcalfes, Jim Dredge, Oliver Gibbs and Mike Cook, to name but a few, and his claim to fame, or at least longevity, perhaps, surpasses them all since he was actually born in Cranmore Hall when the house was used as a maternity home during the war years between the time of the Pagets and the arrival of Mr Dix with his growing school. Harry's association, therefore, goes back sixty-five years! Harry tended to the gardens and grounds as if they were his own. He arrived early in the morning, before the boarders had woken up, and worked non-stop outdoors in all weathers to make sure that the playing surfaces were of a sufficient standard to withstand all kinds of sports and any number of muddy feet whilst also developing and maintaining the beautiful appearance of the estate. His summer-blooming hanging baskets around the school were stunning and the grounds were always in immaculate condition. Like many exacting men with high standards, one had to tread carefully when requesting certain requirements but Harry's smile and hearty laugh was a joy to behold once one had negotiated the accidentally-cultivated exterior. Cricket masters would always consider their strategy when asking for a certain kind of wicket and, despite taking all the plaudits from the children when the hot-air balloon came down out of the skies one September evening onto the front field, I made sure I approached Harry the next morning, as we inspected the huge dent in his beautifully kept grass, with a large bottle of whisky. Harry became famous locally for his incredible Christmas Lights which spring up each year all over the front of his house and also for his national success with chrysanthemums and vegetables which he still proudly shows today.

JOYCE GODDEN
('Lady Cook' 1984-2012)

Joyce Godden merits her own special mention not because she is the wife of Harry, nor because she threatened to end my writing career before it has truly started if I didn't highlight her contributions, but because she is a legend in her own right. Joyce was another of those fine women found in the kitchens whom we shall call 'The Lady Cooks'. Joyce made it her business to know every child (and every member of staff for that matter) who came past her gaze and her dispensing ladles at every meal time. There was a practical point behind this practice for she could then alert Matron or a member of staff if certain pupils, particularly boarders, were not taking sufficient amounts of food or were perhaps taking unbalanced diets. Fortunately, in her experience, Joyce tells me, most children needed no encouragement to take enough food. But the broader and more important point was that, by knowing the children, Joyce could gauge their moods and their happiness and, in so doing, she was able to provide the right portions of humour and kindness where it was needed most. Sometimes I pretended to be sad just to be able to reach the end of the day knowing that at least one person had smiled at me along the way. Joyce was a formidable Lady Cook!

There then followed a few minutes of detailed banter between us on the depiction of literary heroes and villains with a good helping of views on Christian imagery, stylistic devices and the way writers can manipulate readers' responses before I began the lesson proper on Japanese Haiku. The Inspector's mouth had dropped open sufficiently wide to indicate to me that she was already impressed and the rest of the lesson was a doddle. Good for William, I say! William won the Headmaster's Essay Competition[114] in 2010 (for reasons unconnected to the favour I owed him that day of the lesson inspection) with his entry for the title 'First Light'.

FIRST LIGHT by William Rees-Mogg

The desperate first light fell, a ragged, wounded beast on the hard unforgiving ground. It snaked its way amongst broken rock into ancient, decayed buildings. Shadows prowled and slid, cooling tiny insects and feeding bright fungi. Terrible, fearful things worried away in the rubble spree, dark holes concealing terrifying secrets remaining dank and ruthless. Floating on water lay the remains of mottled bones yellowed on cracked tarmac roads. Occasionally seen gripping stones, scorch marks decorating what would have been buildings and ruined trolleys were blown hither and thither. The skies thundered and the purple clouds split. Acidic rain poured down leaving pocks and scars wherever it touched and water flooded in carrying detritus and pollution in a decadent wash that destroyed all in its wake. Thunder continued to roll lethargically, pushed on by dry desert winds, coming from the barren wastelands surrounding the city. Great waves crashed across buildings smashing concrete aside as a cow would have swatted a fly. Paper was picked up and whirled, so soaked that no words were any longer visible on the aged sheets. Broken mobile phones cracked and hissed as water landed on their overprotected circuits, miraculously still active after an eternity of damage. From the centre of the city poisonous clouds fumbled gracelessly over rubble, bright green and viscous they came from an unspeakable crater that watched the city as a god. Massive numbers of skeletons were seen here as if in a form of worship, their black skulls not betraying the unimaginable pain in which they died. Here and there the kings of the city were seen, strange half-starved creatures clad all in rags that dropped down and feasted on the ants and insects beneath them. Like exotic monkeys they leapt fearlessly from window to window, never making a sound, never breaking the sanctified silence. Ever aware, lay bodies in green and brown khaki fatigues, clustered

---

[114] The Headmaster's Essay Competition had been running formally since 1995 although it appears that entries for something similar had appeared in 1957 and perhaps earlier but, in its modern format, it presents the leaving pupils with a three-week task of writing 'their best ever essay' after considerable research, thought and planning. Titles are deliberately chosen to be stimulating and thought-provoking and have included: *The Heart of Darkness, Carpe Diem, Mr Bojangles, Metamorphosis, Honi Soit Qui Mal Y Pense, Horses of the Camargue, The Sekani, Hong Kong Days, Flannan Isle, The Mirror Crack'd from Side to Side, Eldorado, Sennacherib, It was the Best of Times, it was the Worst of Times, The Chelsea Hotel, The Merchant of Venice* and many more.

around tanks or transporters with black metal weapons clutched in bony hands covered with papery skin. Bunkers lay open, maps and clothes swirled within, tiny skeletons of children crouched in corners as if in hiding or escape from some bogeyman, from some nightmare. Night came as a blessed relief. The dark, red clouds had cleared and stars shone dully through the weak, powerless remains of the atmosphere. Those stars did not twinkle; they flared and beeped, scanning the landscape. Far above in space, the sight was utterly depressing: colossal amounts of water washed across what had been continents, purple and red clouds hid monstrous volcanoes, whilst dense, dead jungles were clearing to reveal more gigantic skeletons. Solar flares traversed the dangerous distances of space, alternately roasting and frying the planet leaving charred ash far into the ether like a slug's trail. Blood curdled in the streets like orange milk, baked hard and cold it crunched underfoot, spilt and homeless, lying ready for the ants and cockroaches to feed freely. Termite mounds lay on the last suburban lawns and great green creepers sneaked amongst the broken windows now fallen into cracked silver puddles on the ground. Sharp-leaved blades of grass spread amongst the hulks of cars. Reptiles slithered around corrupted concrete and over garish lines. Ancient computers clicked and tried to reboot after millennia of abuse and overuse. The remains of an Orwellian society were plain to see. Campaign posters glared out from once-great apartment blocks eternally watching over the dead city. Television screens were still mounted in every plaza and square. First light rose, desperately from the calm expanse, a ragged wounded beast on the hard unforgiving rocks as, pathetically, it snaked its way from the broken ground.

The 2011 Chronicle highlights the introduction of the International Primary Curriculum (IPC) in the Junior classes from January 2011 and opens with the teacher's rationale as follows: "*The principle of the IPC is to focus on a combination of academic, personal and international learning platforms for children combined with innovative, exciting, engaging and real ways to learn. Fundamental to the IPC approach to learning is a clear progression in skill development. This even applies to the personal learning goals which emphasise adaptability, resilience, thoughtfulness, cooperation and respect, which, as a result of progressive skill development, help children to become able and inspired learners. The IPC is the first curriculum in the world to have international-mindedness explicitly built into the learning. Internationalism is embedded throughout, helping children to develop a coherent international-mindedness through all subjects; approaching their learning from their own local perspective as well as from the perspective of others around the globe. This global consciousness is fundamental to Catholic education. The IPC is founded on recent brain research on how children learn best. It helps to engage and inspire children of all abilities as a result of stimulating, child-centred, thematic, cross-curricular units of work which encourage collaborative learning and address learning styles and multiple intelligences. The*

IPC is an international, comprehensive and future-orientated curriculum aimed at children growing up in the 21st century. It is a curriculum which nurtures a love of learning and encourages children to develop the necessary key skills and personal qualities."

Now it is just possible that, having read all that, Mr Dix, Mr Trappes-Lomax, Mr Blunt, Mr Bevan, Mr Scotland, Mr Ketterer and perhaps, Mr Bird, and others, are shifting a little uncomfortably in their various seats asking what ever happened to the 'Bible, Kennedy's Latin Primer and the Cane?' but then that was then and this is now. It is heartening, however, to note that some of that rationale was instantly appropriated by the pupils in Form One who interpreted their early IPC as studying *'different food groups, making pizzas and fruit kebabs dipped in chocolate which they thoroughly enjoyed eating. They followed this up by setting up a restaurant and an ice cream parlour in the classroom after visiting two ice cream parlours as an important part of their research.'* There are no flies on children. To 'flesh out', however, the theory and to extrapolate meaning from the jargon, the IPC is an interesting and worthwhile curriculum development which is already paying great dividends. For example, it genuinely orientates towards a child-centred approach with none of the indulgence such a phrase commonly invokes. Pupils are part of the planning process and, importantly, the assessment procedures. Topics are devised with innovation by staff and greater collaboration follows across the academic disciplines. It is an engaging and inter-related way of capturing interest whilst also encouraging pupils to experiment with and develop their research skills. More and more schools in the independent sector – and across the world – are taking on the principles of the IPC and adapting them to their own programmes. It would appear to have a real impact and relevance in the junior and middle years even if the Key Stage Three teaching still needs to follow rather more traditional syllabuses in preparation for Common Entrance and Scholarship routes, as well as the existing National Curriculum schemes. Not that I am necessarily instantly engaged and persuaded when a syllabus promotes itself as *'future-orientated'* but then I would say that, wouldn't I? Nevertheless, I am genuinely excited by the possibilities of writing one's own cross-curricular topic-themes and I would love to write a suitable text book. Now there's a thought! Helen Mewburn, in particular, a key teacher in the middle school, is quickly becoming something of an expert in the IPC and has the drive, passion and conviction to motivate others.

Drama continues to flourish in these modern years, both in the Speech and Drama lessons which lead to various grades being awarded under the auspices of LAMDA in verse speaking, solo and group acting and so on, as well as in the major productions undertaken by the different year groups. In recent years around this time (i.e. the summer term), Naomi Holland, in particular, aided by other key members of staff like Sophie Ball, Paul Dowbekin, John-Paul Renouf, James Callow and Matthew Redman, had presented such productions as *Charlie and the Chocolate Factory, Alice in Wonderland, Bugsy Malone, Carrots, Rock Toyz, The Wizard of Oz* and *Fame*, some of which were now so demanding of space and special effects that they needed external sites such as the Merlin Theatre in Frome, the King's

Bruton Theatre and the Amulet in Shepton Mallet in order to be staged. In 2011, Sport also continued to thrive in the number of teams competing at different age groups and different ability levels on a regular basis, thus allowing 'sport for all' to remain a living reality rather than one of those grand aspirational statements that look good in prospectuses. The Boys' Hockey 1st team had an unbeaten season, won the County Championships, reached the semi-finals of the IAPS regional tournament and were runners-up in the West of England competition with Jack Cadbury, Miles Hackett, Will Stoyle, Ben Whitemore and Mike Stride outstanding even up to County representation. Will Brand-Lyons, Miles Hackett and Howie Phillips also all gained selection for the South West Barbarians Under 13 Rugby Squad. The Under 12 Girls became West of England Champions in hockey and the Under 10 Girls won the Millfield Tournament. And Lucy Baldwin, after featuring strongly in previous years with her cross-country running and athletic performances, enjoyed her annus mirabilis in 2011 by becoming the South West Champion Cross-Country Runner and the Under 13 National Champion for the 1500 metres.

A focus on Michael Stride will serve as an example of the excellence of some of these team and individual performances as well as providing inspiration for others to follow...

MIKE STRIDE
(F.P. 2006-2011)

Mike...when did you start to play hockey?
I was about eight years old. I went with a friend and just loved it. For a long time my dream had been to play for England one day.

Have you had to work hard?
Most of the time I train or play about three times a week but during the Lent Term with school commitments too I probably play every day. I drive Mum mad when I practise some of my stick skills in the house though.

Where were you and how did you feel when you knew you had been selected for the England Lions?
I was in Nottingham playing in the National Under-13 Championships with the West Panthers.... The team had won the tournament – the first time the West team had won in the sixteen years the tournament had been running – and we were very excited and rather loud. After the presentations, our Head Coach asked to see a few of us and handed us all an envelope – that was the 'congratulations – you have been selected..' letter. Words can hardly express my excitement – I was ecstatic! Four of my team mates were also selected and we had pizzas to celebrate!

Mike has continued his sporting prowess since moving onto King's School, Bruton, on a sporting scholarship. Some of his achievements are as follows:

2011/12
* Selected for UK Lions U14 squad. Captained the squad and selected as 'Player of the Year' after final tour. Tours included: Lille, Glasgow and Ireland.
* Captained a very successful Bath Buccs U14 team.
* U14 Hockey captain and 'Sportsman of the Year' at King's School, Bruton.

2012/13
* Selected for England Hockey U16 Futures Cup Squad.
* 1st team for King's School, Bruton (several years 'young').
* Captain of Bath Buccs U16 teams, including indoor.
* Qualified for U16 Indoor National Finals.
* Selected for a four month, unaccompanied, visit to New Zealand to play hockey at school, club and regional level.

Good luck to you, Mike, in all your future endeavours! We shall watch your progress with interest - and just in case there are some up-and-coming 'stars' of the future who think that in order to succeed you need arrogance and other related characteristics, think of Mike who is one of the most modest and unassuming young men one could hope to meet. What he does possess, however, is dedication and determination (and talent, of course).

Lucy and Jody Wells also moved on from All Hallows in 2011 and, in a decade, made a considerably positive impact on school life. Lucy started first in November 2001 as a class teacher in the Junior Department and Jody, like all dutiful husbands, followed her in September 2002. Jody and Lucy threw themselves wholeheartedly into school life and quickly became resident houseparents with Jody rising to Senior Housemaster responsible for driving through a hugely successful Boarding School Inspection process when the school emerged with 'outstanding' in all categories. Jody moved on to become Deputy Headmaster at Forres Sandle Manor in Hampshire. Lucy's constantly sunny disposition and – 'likewise' - Jody's boundless energy made them an ideal couple to oversee the academic, sporting and personal development of many All Hallows pupils.

Art has long been almost one of the 'best-kept secrets' at All Hallows partly because Nick Somerville has directed all connected matters with characteristic modesty but he has huge flair and has presented any number of exciting opportunities for the children over recent years dating back to 1989. For many years, Nick was one of the few members of staff who taught every child in the school, as even the youngest pupils came up to the Art and Pottery Rooms, although other specialists have since added their skills to the department. Nick had always liaised carefully with subject and form teachers to ensure that a range of innovative ideas and projects can continue to inspire the children and he has shown a keen

PAUL DOWBEKIN
(Director of Music 1999-2011)

Paul became Director of Music in 1999 and he has been referenced in various places throughout this book in conjunction with the musical contributions he made to the life of the school. He followed on from the fine traditions and expertise shown by Jamie Bradley, Roger Bevan, and Mark Wood – a tradition which has now been picked up by Matthew Redman, the current Director of Music. All such post-holders bring to the job a love of music, great personal accomplishment, the power to enthuse and inspire and the highest standards of expectation and performance. Paul also brought odd-coloured socks and a distinctive flair. He was popular with pupils and engendered devotion in some. Since leaving All Hallows he has almost become busier in establishing his own musical company, for want of a better description, called

Salutemus, which provides musical entertainers of various hues for a whole range of events, as well as continuing private tuition and public examining. He has also 'retired' to the village of Nunney where he insists he is one of the least eccentric characters there. Paul – and other Directors of Music – would be the first to commend the highly-qualified band (there is no other more suitable word) of peripatetic music teachers who provide one-to-one tuition in as broad a range of musical instruments, including voice, that one could imagine. These men and women are extremely proficient in their own right, often professional performers, hugely demanding of their pupils and yet suitably patient in all things, including trudging round the school to find the pupil who has not turned up for a lesson. 'Salutemus', indeed!

interest in collaborating with other colleagues so that the work has some wider meaning; for these reasons, he has welcomed the introduction of the International Primary Curriculum (IPC) – see comments above – because the project-led basis of much of the work leans readily towards extended artistic endeavours as well as other possibilities. The art rooms, themselves, of course, become dynamic living spaces in which the excellence of the work produced by Nick and the children is clearly evident but such work has spilt out down the staircase and into the corridors around the school, as well as in designated galleries for a wider audience. It is inevitable that most of the work produced, of course, goes home eventually, to adorn bookshelves and walls in parents' and grandparents' homes but it is a rewarding thought that so much stunning art work is being given a lasting life of its own outside of school. There are so many pupils who have excelled over the years but in the 2012 Chronicle we read of two girls; Isabelle Weir and Lily Piper, who both achieved art scholarships to Millfield and Bruton School for Girls respectively. Isabelle liked especially drawing and painting with watercolours and oil pastels and found that her interest in drama inspired much of her work whilst Lily always put art down as her favourite subject and enjoyed producing landscapes, experimenting with new mediums, still life, Fauvism, Pop art, working in 3-D, manipulating wire, painting silk and making sculptures. They are two names to watch.

In 2012, two more stalwarts of the school retired in the persons of Jan Buck and Viv Pemberton, and one other, Pip Davies, changed schools after an association that went back forty years.

JAN BUCK
(Teacher 1994-2012)

Jan was a much valued member of the teaching staff in the Junior Department for almost eighteen years providing secure, experienced classroom delivery to our youngest pupils – many of whom will now be engaged in adult careers of their own, having passed through her capable hands. Jan always maintained a warm and remarkable sense of humour and equilibrium, especially during the time of a worrying illness, and was a sociable and friendly member of the Common Room. She provided solid, fundamental grounding in literacy and numeracy in the classroom and coped admirably with the many changes in organisation, personnel and systems that she encountered at All Hallows, as well as mastering and accommodating the various changes that occurred in the wider educational world. She had bundles of energy and a firm but kindly manner with the children.

VIV PEMBERTON
(School Secretary 1992-2012)

Viv worked tirelessly and loyally in the School Office, first for Paul Ketterer, then Chris Bird and, more recently, for Ian Murphy. Quite what Viv thought of them is perhaps best left unrecorded but each Headmaster came to appreciate Viv's quiet, concentrated efficiency, sorry, perfection, in performing faultlessly on various letters, texts and other school documents whilst also attending to countless administrative tasks. Viv was renowned for her unflappability and her perfect attention to detail. She mastered new school systems, new technology, new offices (and new Headmasters, of course), keeping impeccable records and also retaining almost irreplaceable records in her head when her memories and instincts have provided cool, calm responses to the countless mini-crises that occur almost every day. She worked happily alongside many different colleagues and was happy to become involved in the Common Room and even school trips whenever required. Her professional approach and her ability to manage sensitive and confidential information was exemplary. Viv has continued to work for the school on a consultative basis even since her retirement, especially in proof-reading.

PIP DAVIES
(F.P. 1978-1986; Staff 2000-2012)

As pupil Philippa Goodson, in the late 1970s and early 1980s, Pip was a loyal friend and an excellent sportswoman and she later replicated those virtues throughout the time of her teaching career when she worked alongside Jayne Knowles and Ann Lydon before becoming Head of the PE Department herself. Pip's firm and fair approach to the girls on the Games field ensured appropriately disciplined responses from the girls and there are countless examples of successful teams achieving beyond expectations because of Pip's expert coaching and tuition. For many years as a pupil and long after, Pip held the school High Jump record but nobody was more pleased than Pip herself when Florence Kerr broke that record in only relatively recent times when she was a pupil (Florence, like many other former pupils, is now a key member of the sporting and pastoral teams as a 'grown-up').

Pip was modest, full of common-sense and, like many modest people, somewhat uncertain of her own achievements and the part she played in the achievements of others, but she had a steely determination and a non-nonsense attitude, linked to a genuinely caring instinct for young people. Pip willingly gave of her time and happily took on additional duties that were asked of her such as providing excellent support on skiing trips, taking on academic lessons in the Geography Department and playing a superb pastoral and mentoring role as an empathetic Form Tutor. Her mother was Chair of Governors, her brothers and sister all attended All Hallows as fellow pupils and her own children, Emma and Lucy, were also educated at the school. Pip left All Hallows to undertake further educational challenges by accepting the post of Head of Games at Bruton School for Girls in 2012.

Girls Games has been extraordinarily well-served at All Hallows in its Heads of Department, first with staff like Moira Thompson, then through the excellent dedication of Jayne Knowles and Ann Lydon. Each has brought particular flair but each has maintained the highest standards both on and off the pitch. These years have been characterised by unbeaten seasons, tournaments championships, county selection and even national recognition in hockey, netball, rounders and athletics. Moira has been highlighted elsewhere; Jayne brought a refreshing zest and loveliness to all proceedings; Ann has provided coaching expertise, motivational skills and pastoral guidance in equal measure.

In 2012, Sam Graham, winner of the 'Unsung Hero Award' wrote these farewell words for the School Chronicle... *"You know when a school is very good when you can notice an improvement in yourself. Undoubtedly, this school has helped me to improve academically and it has also helped me to improve socially. I love the way All Hallows lets students have their own opinions and express themselves as individuals. When I first came here I was warmly welcomed by everyone. The welcoming letters were so kind and I was really eager to join. I never thought the day would come when I really wanted to go to school. All Hallows is a school that really helps you get through your studies and thrive in subjects which you are*

unsure about. I love the way All Hallows has worked hard for us after Common Entrance to make sure we enjoy our last few weeks. I will honestly miss this school enormously. I very much doubt I could have enjoyed another school as much. Thank you All Hallows!"

Pupils, staff and governors still feature in the unfolding story under Ian Murphy's Headship years....

COLONEL MIKE RUSSELL
(Chairman of Governors 2012--)

Mike Russell took over the Chair from Patrick Nixon, having been a Governor during the latter years of Chris Bird's Headship, and now leads the school story forward into its next chapter. Mike recently retired from the Army and is currently writing a biography. He is the father of Jamie, Kirsty and Sarah who all attended All Hallows as pupils. His approachable style and good-humoured demeanour has enabled him to act as a 'hands-on' Chairman with whom teaching staff feel able to communicate freely and he has also seen through a significant overhaul of the Governing Body in a process that ensures all members are fully aware and appropriately qualified to meet the ever-more demanding and accountable requirements of that role today. No doubt his story – and that of the school – remains part of the future...

In thinking of 'unsung heroes', if Chairmen of Governors and Headmasters and pupils have played their part in the story of the school, there are, of course, dozens and dozens of others who have contributed in countless everyday ways which are, perhaps, more difficult to trace. I am thinking of the domestic/catering/maintenance staff who have 'come and gone', or have remained for many years, providing the same reliable and dedicated service. In many cases these personnel have maintained great good humour, loyalty, consistency, and, probably patience, in their personal demeanour. Whilst fulfilling the prosaic nature of their jobs they have also, through their personalities and interest in people, supplied a rich source of everyday comfort to the pupils in particular and their interventions have often ensured that individuals are recognised and equilibrium restored. The following names spring to mind: Mrs Ford – still living in the village of Cranmore and moving towards her one hundredth birthday (it is believed she was also a member of the domestic staff during the time of the Pagets); Mrs Hurle who for many years lived next door to Mrs Ford; Mrs Greenaway and Mrs Baker, other names from the past; Wendy Banfield, so popular with the children; Maureen Gibbs, daughter of groundsman, maintenance man and occasional cricketer, Oliver Gibbs; Mary Wiltshire, an Irish character larger than life who liked to live and smoke with enthusiasm; Eileen Treanor, another Irishwoman who worked in the Linen Room and knew the whereabouts of every last sock and whose bark was worse than her bite; Terry Young, a worker through and through; Joyce and Harry Godden – see details elsewhere; Ginny Major, breakfast queen; Diane Fear, forever happy; Pauline Cook, who somehow managed the laundry needs of pupils and games staff with a smile; Mike Cook – a meticulous, gentle, willing carpenter and craftsman; Allan Howe, genial giant of the Carpentry Shop, Scouts' Wood and, more recently, Sang'a school; and, in the year 2013, we say farewell to Maria Keirl, Jenny Colbourne and Jenny Herridge who, between them, have clocked up over ninety years' service to the school. It is said that Maria can remember past pupils simply by their linen numbers (test her and see if it's true…44 – Jamie Hart & Jaime Urquijo; 10 – Mark Bassett, 101 – Jamie Bird, and so on). Jenny Colbourne liked to keep out of the limelight but exerted a benign and caring influence, principally as seamstress (a dying art these days) but also possessed an intelligent warmth and humour that was appreciated. Jenny Herridge dispensed food in the dining-room with equal grace and gentle kindness and had enough faith in the school to enrol her daughter as a pupil. I present apologies for inevitably leaving out others but, as with similar name-checks throughout the book, these splendid people stand as representatives of so many more; of whom it could be said 'these also stand who only serve and wait'.

As I write on this beautifully sunny day in early May 2013 (there have not been many so far this year), not long after I have just escorted round the school another septuagenarian old boy who had returned to re-visit some memories from the past, I am happy to reflect warmly on the observations and sentiments of Sam Graham and think of many others like him who retain positive memories of the school, whilst recognising that there were many old boys from the 1930s and 1940s who also had similarly happy memories (and, no doubt, some former pupils throughout the history of the school - even from the second millennium and beyond - who might regard things less favourably). The point of all such rumination is that, like all schools, we might not have been able to please everybody all of the time but the collective and historical intentions have been, by and large, well-meaning and our aspirations for the children genuinely life-enhancing. I am reflecting also on another day of celebration not so long ago when almost three hundred friends attended Paul Ketterer's Thanksgiving Service in the School Chapel of All Saints on 20th April 2013. Sue Hiller[115] brought all her abundant secretarial skills to bear in contacting former pupils, teachers, parents and friends. Felicity Finlayson, the first Head Girl, had come over from Australia, and many former parents, teachers, governors and pupils – even from Paul's time at The Oratory - were in attendance

---

[115] See box details on page 294

"

The individuals of All Hallows...
must always provide stories for people to tell...
more children and more parents need to
hear the All Hallows' story

"

in what became a splendid ceremony and reunion. 'Flick' Finlayson remembers Paul as *"kind, stern, focused and passionate"*. James Down recognises that *"he was a great Headmaster but he scared the life out of me"*. Greg McDonald is sure PFJK introduced shoe-cleaning as a regular routine into the life of the school because of his own filthy schoolboy shoes when once being presented to a prospective parent as a typical All Hallows' pupil (Greg freely admits that he is obsessed with clean shoes to this day). Another pupil remembers Paul shooting rabbits with a shotgun at 6.00am (I think it was an air-rifle and I believe Paul never actually hit his intended target although a few treetops received a nasty surprise). And former pupil Thomas Taylor had parents who attended the Service registering the fact that *"Thomas' life was transformed, his potential released and all our lives miraculously made whole"* as a result of Paul Ketterer's insights and direction.

Dom Alexander[116] conducted the service and gave the eulogy and Chris Bird and John Jackson both delivered readings or prayers. Many others had sent their apologies for being unable to attend but wanted to record their warm wishes and memories of Paul whose kindnesses and strong stewardship of the school had become life-changing experiences for so many. Former pupil Kapumpe-Valentine Musakanya wrote on behalf of his family and twin sister, Chana, from Zambia to say that Paul Ketterer *"was a great man, headmaster and parental figure to my twin sister and I during our time at All Hallows. During our time at All Hallows, my father was in prison, accused of being part of a coup, as were most of Zambia's economic or intellectual elite. Paul had the misfortune of having to call my twin sister and me into his office one day and explain that the trial in Zambia of my father had been concluded and that my father had been sentenced to death. Paul could hardly hold back the tears from his eyes as he took off his glasses and wiped his eyes and tried to put on a brave soul for me and my sister. He then told us to take as much time as we wanted by taking a walk. We went outside and sat on the wall looking down at the stream and cried till we couldn't cry anymore. The world felt very large. Paul, his family and the school throughout our time tried to ensure that life was as normal as possible and All Hallows became our world. The pain, though never really discussed, remained between us."* There is a happier ending, however. Kapumpe continues… *"My father was released some two years after this event and then passed on in 1994….we have a debt to the community of All Hallows"*. Chana and Kapumpe went on to Woldingham and Stonyhurst, respectively, and have many happy memories of Sacha and Sonia with whom they were very close. Ms Adebimpe Shonekan, mother of former pupils Tolu and Yemi Sawyerr, couldn't attend the Memorial Service either but wrote saying *"I was saddened to know that Paul Ketterer had died. My children are today confident and well-educated and have impeccable manners because of this lovely man. My condolences go to the family especially his wife who was such a loving and understanding teacher to my son. May his gentle soul rest in perfect peace."*

Felicity Finlayson, the first Head Girl, puts it this way: *'The core value that Paul imparted was that of trusting others, sometimes at our own cost. He gave me, and others, the opportunity to grow*

---

[116] Dom Alexander and other Chaplains – see box details overleaf.

because of the trust he had in us to be (or develop into) co-operative people capable of assuming responsibility and exercising authority with the good of others, either individually or collectively, in mind. I am eternally grateful for having attended All Hallows' under Paul (and Jean's) leadership'.

There were many other similar messages. Deep though his personal faith was, Paul was not, however, always saintly. His daughter Sonia recalls the time when he gave her a detention for being back late one day from an appointment with the orthodontist. Insult was added to injury when Sonia protested saying it was the driver's fault, only to be admonished by the Headmaster who told her she would have to make sure in future that the driver kept better time. The identity of the driver?... none other than Paul himself.

It seems, somehow, appropriate to drop in here references to secretarial and sacred support...

SUE HILLER
(School Secretary 1975-2011)

Sue joined the staff in 1975 and, after two days of working in the catering department was whisked off by the Headmaster (because he heard that she could type!) to the role of School Secretary which she maintained under three Headmasters and, today, thirty-eight years later, continues to work on a consultative, part-time basis for the school. Sue ended up taking on numerous tasks like designing and drawing the Car Park area around the Chapel, mapping the school, making up policy booklets, teaching maths to the junior children for a term, helping the Headmaster plan the timetable, and even found herself delivering Latin lessons that had been left for her when Paul Ketterer was unavoidably detained on other school business - although Sue might be the first to admit that her Latin skills were not her strongest suit! Sue has shown her secretarial skills, however, to be of the highest order and she has brought to the role an unflappable efficiency and discretion. Sue's particular characteristic was the high-speed manner with which she approached and completed tasks. Despite being advised in various Headmasters' Training Books 'never to touch the same piece of paper twice', I struggled for an hour or so through the morning post in my early years as I religiously read every letter in case I missed

something important. Sue took on that task for me and presented me, ten minutes later, with the letters I needed to do something about; inevitably that pile was significantly smaller than the one I was used to handling (what Sue did with the other letters I never asked – John-Paul Renouf will now be saying 'she gave them to the Deputy Headmaster'). Sue has coped admirably with the technological and systems changes that have occurred and embraced willingly the various training courses needed to manage the administrative machinery. Sue has always given off a good-humoured charm and has shown remarkable adaptability in coping with the working idiosyncrasies of three Headmasters, all rather different in style and method; fortunately for us, she has kept her observations to herself. Sue has worked tirelessly out of school on behalf of various charities, including *The Red Cross* and has accompanied school trips to France where her medical training has been put to good use. Her most recent addition to her Job Description has been that of External Common Entrance Exam Invigilator which requires rather more than simply saying "Silence!" to the assembled candidates. Despite the fact that she is officially retired, we see her most weeks, it seems – long may that continue!

CHAPLAINS & PRIESTS

A fairly accurate recording of All Hallows 'priests through the ages' comes up with the number of fully sixty ordained priests who have established long or fleeting associations with the school, which includes at least eleven principal Chaplains, four Abbots, four Bishops and one Cardinal. In this plethora of religious indulgence, I highlight below, three Chaplains of relatively recent vintage, although I could have focused on others of different vintages, so, please draw no conclusions, as well as add the names of the following former pupils and staff who went on to become ordained....

Thomas Atthill, Paul Dewe Matthews, Robin de Guingand, Michael Corbould, William Bellasis, Dennis O'Regan, Michael Mullin, Anthony Mitchell, Nicholas White, Brian Butler, David Corbould, Gabriel Cave, Francis Cochrane, Anselm Hurt, Mr Adams, Mr Douglas and Mr Taylor.

See Appendix E for a fairly comprehensive list of other priests who have led the school in prayer, conducted memorial and thanksgiving services, said Mass, heard Confessions, christened babies, officiated at weddings and provided religious instruction or pastoral support for the school. The list – and those names above – represent a broad range of humanity which was mostly well-meaning, even saintly in a few cases, but, inevitably, includes a small number of others with eccentricities, human frailties and defects not consistent with a proper execution of responsibility towards the young. As Oscar Wilde said: "Every Saint has a past and every Sinner a future" which is reassuring for all of us.

DOM ALEXANDER GEORGE OSB

Father Alexander was Chaplain and teacher of Religious Education at All Hallows from 1982-1995 – which took into account the final dozen or so years of Paul Ketterer's time as Headmaster - and, together with Roger Bevan, that 'holy trinity' provided rigorous Catholic instruction and example to generations of pupils. Father Alexander was initially engaged to act as visiting Chaplain but was delighted when the opportunity arose for him to be crucially involved in the delivery of academic instruction in Religious Education right up to Common Entrance and Scholarship levels. Such a development afforded him the chance to become more fully involved in the excellent Common Room of the time – which saw many Head Teachers and Heads of Department emerging on their own professional routes – whilst also getting to know the children who were "*lovely*". Father Alexander loved the old chapel, which had a charm of its own, especially at liturgical events like Corpus Christi and Candlemas but it was clearly recognised as being "*too small*", hence the need for the beautifully conceived new Chapel of All Saints "*which was devoted entirely to religious and sacramental occasions in those years*" (I have mixed views on that particular observation). Father Alexander maintains that his experiences at All Hallows "*taught me how to preach*". His sermons were memorable for their simple and mercifully short expositions of important and thought-provoking truths. Father Alexander remembers two important journeys on the road between Downside and All Hallows (not Damascus) – a route he took many times. The first involved a 'near-death' experience when two fast-moving quarry lorries were occupying at least half of the road he was expecting to use when driving along the notoriously dangerous switch-back road by *The Waggon and Horses*. As he lay in the ditch, having been forced off the road, with wheels and thoughts spinning of first and last things, one of the concerned quarry lorry drivers leant over him, spotting his monastic robes, and said "*Your Boss was looking after you, all right*". Father Alexander – who knew the owner of the local quarry – replied "*Rather more, I fear, than the way your boss will be looking after you*". They could have gone down as 'famous last words' couldn't they? Fortunately, Father Alexander recovered. The sign on that stretch of the road which was subsequently erected proclaiming: 'Blind Summit' is entirely down to Father Alexander. The second incident concerned the seemingly never-ending spillage of water and ice in winter months by the junction at Waterlip. Father Alexander suggested to the local council that a sunken culvert would reduce or eliminate the problem and – lo and behold! – it was done. Just to show the power of his effect on the local environment, he also very quickly saw the injustice and inconvenience of having cows and schoolboys crossing awkwardly over the country lanes of Cranmore and suggested that the farmer and the Headmaster simply swap fields, which action was duly effected. Sometimes, recreational and agricultural needs are determined by simple monastic wisdom. Governor Diana McNulty should have consulted him, not the local Council, about the directional sign to 'All Hallows'. Father Alexander has been forty years a monk and has, in that time, fulfilled the functions of teacher, Housemaster, Infirmarian, Guest Master, Sacristan to the Abbey Chruch, Parish Priest, the Bishop's 'Vicar for Religious', i/c Oblates and Retreats, as well as running clubs for debating, cookery and, what looks like in my scribbled handwriting as, "windsocks", although I suspect that this was some other society that went under a different name (but if there are any OGs out there who remember the Windsocks Society please get in touch). To Father Alexander, the school of All Hallows owes a debt of gratitude for such clear spiritual direction, replicated, almost entirely, by all other Chaplains and Priests.

THE VERY REVEREND DOM DANIEL REES
(1931-2007 RIP)

Daniel Rees was ordained a priest in 1961, having joined the monastic community at Downside one year earlier. He became a qualified teacher and was for many years the principal Librarian at Downside, custodian of the largest library in the West of England, surpassed only by that at Longleat. He remained a "*genial Benedictine*" and was renowned for his gentle good humour which reached out to younger children as well as those with more erudite tastes. He once described the pupils at All Hallows as having such wide-eyed innocence that it "*made one want to doubt the concept of Original Sin*". Perhaps because he lived much of his life amongst the ancient tomes of the Library which housed over 150000 books including 50 well-preserved medieval manuscripts, over 200 pamphlets from the fifteenth-century and a collection of rare seventeenth-century recusant literature, he was a self-confessed and slightly mocking technophobe who never learnt to drive and once told a modern visitor "*Computers? I believe there are some somewhere in the school*". He wrote occasionally for various publications and edited two collections of essays on Monastic life. He was a former President of the Theological Commission of the English Benedictine Congregation and he also lectured in ancient Hebrew and church history at Bristol University. At his best, his preaching had enormous power and depth with scholarly and razor-sharp logic, even if the younger pupils at All Hallows found their powers of sitting still tested to the limit and even if the present writer is supposed to have once nodded off (according to the pupils) – I like to think I was merely closing my eyes to cogitate on a particularly subtle point. He was Novice Master, Prior, Housemaster, local parish priest and Cathedral prior at Gloucester. And a much-loved Chaplain and Governor at All Hallows.

FATHER ROGER BARRALET

Father Roger is a Fransciscan Brother who became a Headmaster in his own right of Barrow Hills School, in Surrey, and then Chairman of Governors at that school. He became connected to All Hallows through a personal contact with Paul Dowbekin, following our choral association with St Ignatius Loyala School in Essex and was appointed Chaplain at All Hallows thereafter. He threw himself into the wider responsibilities of Chaplaincy by visiting the pupils and staff in the classrooms and offering wise educational and pastoral support but was probably chiefly remembered by the children for the memorably witty, warm and accessible homilies during the weekly Mass. It is easier to quote the children's own words about him…

"He spreads the Word of God…it's as if God tells him something and he passes it on to us…at his first Mass he told us we were allowed to smile…I remember his homily about the green people and the blue people because really we're all the same…I like his story about the geese all flying together…he tells very funny stories and makes us laugh…he takes over our lessons which is good when it is maths…he joins in our card games…he thinks his Toyota is cool…he acts way younger than he really is…he shows an interest in us and knows my name…he's a man you can speak to…he comforts us when we're sad or lonely".

Some people are just good at leaving powerful impressions – perhaps he really was passing on messages from God.

Celebrations of a different kind often take place when writing historical accounts, for one remembers key dates and occasions, inevitably, and it is only right and proper that we should highlight certain dates in order to record reflections of the time, as well as provide some perspectives for future interest. One recalls, therefore, in 2012, as we celebrated Queen Elizabeth II's Diamond Jubilee to commemorate her sixty years on the throne, the school also welcomed her arrival on the throne sixty years before, at that very time. The slight anomaly was that although the Queen ascended to the throne in February 1952, the Coronation celebrations did not actually take place until June 1953, so that our All Hallows participation, such as it was, didn't quite occur fully sixty years ago from the time indicated. You might remember that the All Hallows community watched episodes from the Coronation celebrations in 1953 on a television in the corner of St Bede's, not very far away from where the modern mobile phones are stored and from where Wednesday Night Tuck is dispensed. In 2012, despite the odd republican and uninterested murmurings from some quarters, Jan Bird ensured that we would embrace with gusto, conviction and fervour 'the moment'. *"We wanted to celebrate this very special event in style! The day before the nation embarked on a long weekend of festivities, with their own street parties, watching the flotilla sailing down The Thames…All Hallows held its own tribute to Her Majesty Queen Elizabeth II. Our children understand that they are part of 'living history'. In addition to us recognising sixty years on the throne, it is highly likely (we hope) that Her Majesty will still be on the throne in 2016 and beyond – thus breaking the record set by her great, great grandmother Queen Victoria. One of the personal highlights of this period for Queen Elizabeth has been the work done by the Commonwealth in promoting its shared ideals. It was very fitting, therefore, that we spent much of the day raising money for our linked school, Sang'a, in Kenya. All the children wrote their own individual messages tied to helium balloons – red, white and blue, of course.* (Ed's note: I know because I spent a long while blowing all the balloons up early that morning). *With military precision worthy of a major logistics event, 300 children carefully carried their own balloons onto the Library Lawn, in the shadow of the colonnade, all gathered in their specially designated areas – and clutched steadfastly to their balloons until the countdown moment of release. It was a magical moment when all the balloons floated off together, ever upwards, even towards Windsor, we felt, and the look on the children's faces was priceless. Afterwards, of course, we celebrated with food, and somehow it seemed appropriate to go with fish and chips served in Union Jack boxes. The afternoon ushered in a carousel and carnival of sponsored House Charity activities with egg-and-spoon races, three-legged assault course, a Bouncy Castle and a treasure hunt in Scouts Wood, a lively fun-dance session in the Courtyard and ice creams to boot. Alongside these specific celebrations went hand-in-hand the wider project of creating our own Jubilee Swan, under the expert direction of visiting artist Fiona Campbell, who had been commissioned to produce one of the sixty swans that were to be placed in and around the city of Wells. Fiona used items of decoration brought in by the children to weave an emblematic and striking-looking swan that was subsequently named 'Candela' to sit proudly outside The Bishop's Palace in Wells until we had the chance to re-purchase it and re-site the swan in the school grounds".*

From the pages of recent Chronicles and from personal experience, one can discern a pattern of consolidation and change, innovation and progress, under Ian Murphy's Headship. Record pupil numbers were again recorded in June 2013 when the school roll stood at 321 thus emulating every previous Headmaster in achieving one measure of obvious success in their own times. Ian was also keen to develop and maintain a reputation for creating the 'wider curriculum' so previous traditions in the school were picked up and given a modern twist; I am thinking of the use of Scouts' Wood into Forest School (see box below); the growth in the Tennis provision under the auspices of the Tennis Academy (which achieved official LTA clubmark status, as well as reaching out to the local community and schools, under the refreshing direction of the resilient and charming Mary Brown); the increased range of sporting opportunities for pupils through team encounters as well as golf, trampolining, judo, riding (which may have begun many years before on those Dartmoor spaces but not in such a competitive fashion) and fencing[117]; and the greater

---

[117] I remember watching the first fencing session in the School Gym when the instructor could hardly contain the wide-eyed excitement of approximately fifteen boys whose eager hands clutched greedily their rapiers as they tried to plunge and thrust into the chests, stomachs and other body parts of their would-be-opponents despite the instructor's best efforts to talk about safety and etiquette. Ivanhoe did not feature that day as a guiding mentor.

emphasis on whole-school and year-group drama productions. Furthermore, a major shift in the timetable occurred which included a new Saturday Morning Enhancement programme, instead of academic lessons for the senior years, which has proved to be very popular with day pupils, boarders and some parents alike, with its varied programme of life skills and creative pursuits. Mandy Ley-Morgan, facilitator, co-ordinator and P.A. extraordinaire to the Headmaster, has had her work cut out in managing all initiatives and in maintaining a sweet smile as her role as Minister without Portfolio has gathered pace. And Sammi Stride, who arranges the weekly extra-curricular timetable, might be the only person on site who really knows what day of the week it is. Ian quickly developed an incredibly hard-working and rapid management style. Ian sent his first report to the Governors, as Headmaster Designate, saying that *"a good deal of my time has been spent meeting with staff, children and parents. This has enabled me to build up a clearer picture of the school's current progress and educational provision. This has been invaluable in my planning for the future development of the school as well as providing a good insight into the basics of our day-to-day running. Additional meetings with the SMT have laid foundations for re-modelling in certain areas....there is considerable interest in the lower end of the school (Key Stage One) and one of my proposals will reflect a desire to capitalise on this with a view to maintaining it on an annual basis. I have spent time with senior school Heads and it has been valuable to glean an understanding of those Head Teachers' views of the All Hallows' 'product', which they have summarised in these terms 'relaxed self-confidence without arrogance; well-rounded academically; good at sport; thoughtful; happy and popular with peers; extraordinarily proud of their Prep School!' My focus on Catholic school leadership – within its modern context and our contemporary educational and social climate – has been particularly enjoyable.....the individuals of All Hallows and our community must always provide stories for people to tell... more children and more parents need to hear the All Hallows story..."*

That story is continuing to be told by people like James Callow and Trevor Richards who now occupy senior positions in the management of the school.

James Callow joined the school over a decade ago and has brought a vitality and personal charm to proceedings. He has grown professionally throughout that time, delivering on the games field, in the classroom and on the pastoral front where he now occupies a key role in the boarding house and in the broader welfare of the children as Child Protection Officer. Trevor Richards, similarly, has become a key academic leader in the school in his current role as Director of Learning. He has espoused the concept of education being a lifelong learning process and he has lived out that philosophy in his own professional formation as he gained qualified teacher status many years ago from within the environs of All Hallows and now moves towards his doctorate in educational psychology. His breadth of experience and length of service to the school are important aspects in maintaining traditions whilst breaking in new initiatives. Together, these two still relatively young men can play their parts in propelling the school forward.

Back to that 'All Hallows Story'.....Ian had wanted to re-shift the focus onto the learning process rather than limit his approaches simply to the more traditional emphasis on teaching. He

The choir at Clifton Cathedral

SCOUTS' WOOD

"Scouts Wood", as it is known, is part of the larger 'Hiltyning Wood' and our portion of that ancient woodland is situated opposite the 'back' or 'side' entrance to the school alongside the old Chapel of St James. The wood runs for a few acres in a linear fashion which broadens out in its middle portion and then runs at a right angle thereafter into the Wild Wood which leads up to the main A361 road, with Shepton Mallet away to the west and Frome, past Tor Quarry, to the east. As its name implies, it was used principally by the Scouts (and later cubs and brownies) when the school first moved to the site of Cranmore Hall and, when those groups were disbanded, it offered two strands of almost opposite ends of the pleasure spectrum: tree-climbing, den-building and mucking-about at weekends for the boarders, and, through the week, during Games time, part of a gruelling Cross-Country Course for all. As a teaching resource, its specific use began to develop more purposefully in the late 1990s when Chris Bird and Nick Somerville started to manage the pathways in a more ordered fashion and created outdoor teaching centres, with the expert assistance of woodsman and Environmental Education Consultant Raymond Wheeler, who helped develop other spaces that could be utilised. If you want to 'read' a wood and become inspired, ask to spend ten minutes with Raymond Wheeler above the floorgrowth, amongst the bushes and beneath the trees. As a result, successive Year Seven pupils began to use the resources around them to produce thoughtful and expressive poetry (see the lyrics of Will Todd's school song)[118] and the

---

[118] In October 2007, composer Will Todd visited the school in order to collaborate with the pupils in creating a new school song, as he had done some ten years before, in another place, when working with young people in Durham Cathedral in producing *Lighting the Way*. Will spoke to the All Hallows' children in Year Seven particularly about the task ahead and how their ideas could be incorporated into the song that they would compose together. He told the pupils that there are only two types of music: music that is good and music that is bad. He spoke of the importance of music in his life and he related his own school-time memory of always trying to arrange music lessons in violin, organ, guitar, clarinet and saxophone in order to avoid going to maths lessons (which might just have given a few of them some unnecessary encouragement, perhaps, to do likewise). Will re-visited the school in January 2008 to follow up the interest he had generated and referred to the many examples of haiku poems that we had provided for him which had been written by the Year Seven pupils. He loved the expressions of personal emotion in these poems capturing different moods. He enthused about the spiritual imagery, the links with the natural world and the connections of the past with the present. The rain fell heavily as he spoke, dripping relentlessly on the colonnade outside the Music Room in which we sat, until his rousing enthusiasm, and the words of the pupils and his inspirational playing of the piano mingled together in that collaboration he had sought. The rain-clouds dispersed and ushered in sunbeams and shadows to fall across the room and onto the sparkling faces of the children; truly, a small moment of epiphany as the rising music and the streaming sun illuminated the stained glass windows bordering the door and other gateways to other worlds.

There's a secret hidden in the swaying trees/ A melody in the soaring wind, Moonlight pouring on my face / A gateway to another place. Loneliness has left me now in this other world / In this other world.

On the winding pathway I am lost and cold / But the whispering trees hold me close. Where seas of flowers wave like hands / Where wishing, weeping willow stands Gentle breeze embracing me in this other world / In this other world.

There's a message written in the glistening leaves/ That will always be the heart of me, The gath'ring dusk and morning light /The colours of the birds in flight, Gateway to the hope that's true in this other world / In this other world.

Art Department produced individually carved paganesque icons to form a complete totem pole. The stone statue of Saint Francis was moved into the wood to mark the edges where the Wild Wood began and that saint has exerted his benign and watchful influence over all living things ever since. We have even, in Father Roger's company, indulged ourselves in a mini-pilgrimage to the statue of Saint Francis to intone our Night Prayers even if he might have raised an eyebrow at the outdoor fish-and-chips supper that followed our incantations; (Saint Francis, that is. Father Roger was tucking in to his fish-and-chips like there was an impending embargo on consuming anything connected to water or potatoes and looking to see if any boarders couldn't finish their own portions.)

The concept of Forest School took all such initiatives onto another plane altogether.

An Ian Murphy Newsletter of 2012 describes Forest School thus: "*Having pioneered the fresh approach to learning that Forest School status brings, All Hallows' innovative and inspiring outdoor environs are now an integral part of the curriculum and enjoyed by children (and adults) of all ages. In a recent inspection by an experienced ISI (Independent Schools Inspectorate) team, the Forest School at All Hallows was described as "excellent" and recognised as "making a major contribution in enabling pupils to achieve the educational standards that they do." The Forest School concept encourages and inspires children through positive experiences and participation in motivating and engaging achievable activities in a woodland environment. The activities help the children to develop personal, social, problem-solving and emotional skills, whilst continuously learning about their natural environment and the world around them. Children thrive when their learning experiences are fuelled by a spirit of adventure. It is with genuine conviction that we believe a child's creative experiences must be encouraged and nurtured throughout the entire curriculum. Creativity is the miraculous fusion of the uninhibited energy of a child with the talent and guidance of experience, and it can be the key to unlocking potential, wherever it may lie. Forest School and Outdoor Education is a wonderful vehicle to enhance and enrich this philosophy - it helps to foster the skills and wider perspective that truly encourage innovation, risk-judging and positive risk-taking, self-belief, ambition and a genuine sense of optimism.*
At All Hallows, the spacious and picturesque outdoor areas (an onsite wood and an additional woodland away from the school site) house two outdoor classrooms, pizza ovens and outdoor food preparation areas, fire-pits, den-making equipment and a roundhouse, plus vegetable garden, which are all used to teach curriculum-related, child-led topics outdoors. The learning activities are carefully considered and there is a cross-curricular focus as part of the whole school curriculum planning. Driven by the belief that learning is enhanced when fuelled by a spirit of adventure, All Hallows pioneered the Forest School concept becoming the first prep school in the UK to be awarded Forest School status eight years ago. Our wonderful outdoor environs offer a fantastic base for training. Facilities include open air classrooms, pizza ovens, outdoor kitchens, fire-pits, water pumps and a Saxon Roundhouse. All of our courses are approved and recognised by 'Archimedes' – the regulatory body for Forest Schools. Courses are led by Charlotte Lucas, who is a passionate enthusiast for all things outdoors and who is a fully qualified Primary Years teacher and Forest School practitioner. She oversees a fully integrated Forest School curriculum and has recently opened 'Welton Freerangers' – a Forest School Nursery. We also run taster opportunities for local pre-schools and primary schools as well as holiday courses for children."

Nici Castell is another fully qualified, key teacher in the delivery of Forest School programmes and other staff have taken on similar qualifications, like Allan Howe, as well as being supported by mainstream teachers like David Ellery and others in the Junior Department. Nici, particularly, has made Forest School in Scouts' Wood something of a specialism and deserves immense credit for instilling in the children such a knowledgeable and empathetic core-belief in the value of protecting and learning from our natural surroundings.

Chris Bird remarks: "*If I had any residual influence over the powers-that-be I would build a writers'/artists'/photographers' shed in the wood with overnight accommodation, a few subtle torches and a decent wine cellar buried nearby in the leaves. It is a resource that needs developing still further.*

(Oh, and I was Acting Head of Scouts' Wood/Forest School for a while, too)."

was keen to introduce opportunities for the children to discover new interests and passions. Ian brought into school currency the terms 'resilience' and 'risk-taking' and was pleased to express a vision synthesising learning opportunities with a relevance to children in the twenty-first century. (Personally, I never missed an opportunity to tell children towards the end of my career that I spent most of my growing up and teaching in the last century which, effectively, underlined my Methuselah credentials, along with my whitening beard and my lack of a mobile telephone). Ian believes that his interest and support for the development of the arts in drama, design technology and creative performance have impacted on him to the greatest extent since becoming Headmaster because such avenues of exploration and expression were rather more unfamiliar to him as a boy. He likes to think of the school as being peopled by children and adults with 'warm hearts, bright eyes and muddy knees'. At the time of writing, exciting plans are in place to extend the school's provision downwards towards a pre-school/nursery class, whilst also establishing a fully-fitted Creative Centre to enhance those areas of the arts and technology already mentioned.

As I near the end of this story, it seems fitting to include a section on Headmasters' Wives, if only to let them have the last words, which were characteristic traits for which none of them, allegedly, needed any special training.

I cannot find another, or perhaps better, place to insert just a few thoughts on boarding. It is one of those alien concepts to most of the civilised world. It is alien to most of Great Britain too. Commonly, we are told that only 7% of the nation's children have 'come through' (perhaps the operative phrase) a boarding education. Today, in 2013, 'the old school tie' connections reverberate in the corridors of power with more overtly critical observations from media and the public than ever before. I was not educated myself through a boarding school environment (although there were some strange pupils called 'boarders' and some even more strange Christian Brothers in my school – but that is another story) and, philosophically, emotionally, morally, even, the arguments against 'sending one's child away' to board are easily made by any right-thinking person of any political or social persuasion. And yet. And yet. Hold your horses and stay your prejudices or reservations. If we concede that Evelyn Waugh's assertion - that he sent son Auberon to board at

HEADMASTERS' WIVES

The feminists out there, and the wives themselves, might bristle a little at the nomenclature of this section of the book as well as by the fact that the wives of the Headmasters are gathered up like some homogenous ball of wool and awarded a collective space of their own (yet only a cramped space) as if receiving condescending blessing from a generous god. And, also, ladies, Evelyn Dix gets a box of her own *as well* elsewhere! Apologies have no place here, except for the apology I'll make on behalf of all the Headmasters for dragging our wives into our worlds in the first place. If I have conveyed successfully the idea that a Headmaster's lot is rewarding and frustrating by turns – difficult to define – let us turn to the Job Description of 'The Headmaster's Wife', for, of course, there is none. From the moment one attended the initial interview, it was clear that the Headmaster's wife would be expected to 'take a turn' for inspection by the appointing body. Again, few jobs demanded such a subtle condition. I am struggling to avoid sentimentality or cliché in this description but the role of the wife can influence hugely the way the Headmaster carries out his tasks. In one case, I believe accurately in my observation, (not highlighted in this box, by the way), the 'Headmaster's wife' played a large part in an aspiring Head *not* being appointed and I feel sure this factor has exerted a similar influence in other circumstances when Governors meet to appoint their next Head Teacher. One wonders whether Headmistress' Husbands are equally important.

Evelyn Dix gets her own highlighted box (see earlier pages) because she effectively started the school herself, whilst her husband carried on teaching for a while at Avisford, and because she found the premises at Scorhill, with a few random gas-masked boys in tow, and because she exerted a restraining presence, eventually, when the Headmaster in his study rage slippered the boys, and because she brought flowers and the smell of woman into the lives of that male-orientated world of the 1940s, 1950s and 1960s.

Of Mrs Mortimer, little is known by this commentator except that she played an active part in the business of the school and received this accolade from Colonel Yule, who had also written a eulogy on her husband, at the time of their departure in 1971: "*Many of these responsibilities he shares with – or maybe palms off on to – Mrs Mortimer. Running a Prep school is a family affair and those of us who have had occasion to visit the school during the holidays for consultation with the management have some idea of the hard work the family have put in during their holidays to prepare the way for us for next term. Mrs Mortimer's part is the most exacting and unobtrusive and the most taken for granted. We are all grateful to her, not only for the provision of excellent messing and comfortable quarters, and thoughtfulness for our individual needs – my Horlicks, for instance! – but also for her unfailing cheerfulness, directness and equanimity on the occasions when our paths cross.*" These words may have been written by an ex-army officer with military expectations in a male-orientated style redolent of the 1930s but they are also written by a man who recognises, respectfully, the role played behind-the-scenes by Mrs Mortimer with just a hint that she could be formidable in her own right when occasion demanded. It is known from reliable sources that Mrs Mortimer was extremely kind to the boys and brought a touch of feminine charm, even compensatory homeliness, to the harsher edges of school life so prevalent at the time. She was welcomed back to the school by Paul Ketterer in later years.

No less formidable, and with a refreshing youthful fragrance, was the benign arrival of Jean Ketterer, a young lady, really, still in her twenties, with a nursing background and a remarkably firm way of managing her husband. When others stepped back or skirted judiciously around the intimidating ripples that could emerge from encounters with PFJK, Jean would dive straight in and provide an impassioned bucket-full of common-sense. Jean took on the management of the daily catering needs, as well as supervising the workforce in their medical, laundry and domestic chores. She reassured prospective parents, particularly of boarders, who were posted or living overseas and who were encouraged by the fact of her presence and the manner of her bearing in their children's lives. Jean had an excellent sense of humour, great personal warmth and kept Paul grounded. She became a conduit for staff and perhaps the best thing she did was cook Paul breakfast at 10.00 am every morning, after he had whirl-winded through the start of the day, so we could all get on with teaching. Jean, of course, was a superbly-welcoming and attentive hostess who charmed governors and parents, when charm was needed, whilst providing stern efficiency when practical order demanded. On one occasion she removed all the labels off the tins in the kitchens in order to collect vouchers for a portable television set leaving the lady cooks with the challenge of guessing over several weeks which foodstuff was contained within which tins. The spontaneity of her engaging and spirited outbursts was a perfect foil to the occasionally labyrinthine irrationalities of her husband's clock-worked bureaucracies and it was a secret joy to behold her in full flow, in the confines of the Headmaster's Study, when Paul was striving to retain his authority.

Jan Bird brought to her interpretation of the role a similar passion, engaging charm and fount of common-sense practicality wrapped up with boldness, decisiveness and a winning smile. Jan had a background in education and catering, and swiftly set about teaching and overseeing aspects of the domestic arrangements with a stylish eye. She also co-ordinated the grand occasions like a golden galleon in its pomp, leaving others bubbling in her wake. She assumed the role of 'Headmaster's Wife' with ex cathedra authority and hovered somewhere between Assistant Head, Principal Private Secretary and Archangel. She always said that her job was to make me look good whilst, at the same time, taking care to prick my pomposity. Jan, like Jean, also brought up a busy family throughout it all, and set aside her own aspirations, finding stimulation and fulfilment in adapting to the role thrust upon her. In supporting her husband she forged a professional identity for herself as an excellent classroom practitioner and, as she emerged more independently in her own right, she also assumed the role of Registrar to become, often single-handedly, responsible for recruiting many pupils and parents through the warmth and force of her convictions and presentation. As the pressures of school life eased, following my decision to step aside from Headship, Jan retained her own professional roles but was also able to pursue personal interests such as becoming a Magistrate and acquiring a right royal reputation in the city of Bath on the Bridge circuit. When pressed as to what she would have done in life otherwise, Jan always says she wanted to be a midwife. Bizarre and amusing anecdotes follow her career in the way her spectacles don't, and a favourite remains the time in Normandy when she was charged with administering cream to a pupil's bottom - which needs to be told aloud rather than written about, so, if you're intrigued, you'll have to ask us to relate the story. For all her ministerings, lightest of touches and freely-given kindnesses, I thanked her privately and publicly on many occasions and made it absolutely clear that I could not have done the job without her. And so we come to the present incumbent of Headmaster's Wife who is, perhaps, the most self-effacing of all, never entirely comfortable with the trappings such a 'title' brings.

Rachel Murphy is a teacher par excellence and she is never happier than when delivering lessons in the classroom and attending to her pupils' pastoral needs. Her attention to detail and her mastery of modern teaching approaches is second to none, all befitting the self-confessed perfectionist. Ian Murphy has not, it seems to me, made as much of this trait as he might, since a man who is married to a perfectionist must possess fairly special qualities himself in order to pass whatever rigorous tests Rachel had devised when they were courting. Rachel prefers a less projected role in the public execution of her wider duties, through natural modesty and personal inclination, and yet exerts a background influence on school matters and, like Ian, attends every function, every concert, every production, with unfailing good humour, grace and duty. Rachel was more embarrassed than most, when taking to her bedroom one morning with a migraine - for she had sent young daughter Megan to let Ian know that she was feeling poorly - only to learn subsequently that Megan had burst in on a Governors' Meeting, at which her husband was present, to announce "Daddy! Daddy! Mum's lying on the bed with no clothes on and she says she needs you quickly!" And like all the Headmasters' Wives before her, she keeps, for the benefit of all, the Headmaster in check lest delusions take hold.

Perhaps as a reflection on the difficulty of the role of the Headmaster's Wife, this has been the most difficult section of the book to write. It remains to be seen whether or not I have written successfully thereof.

All Hallows 'as a reward' for good behaviour one holiday - is possibly tinged with the flippant asperity of the times, there is, actually, something wholesome, character-forming, liberating and ultimately positive about the experience of boarding, at least in my contention. Ironically, of course, a boarding school experience in 2013 – when independent schools are struggling for numbers against a falling trend – is undoubtedly an extremely 'good thing' in comparison with previous years and regimes. But, one cannot help thinking that independent schools have got it the wrong way round today. They should be offering boarding at lower fees than day fees. If I was a Headmaster today, I would break the mould, buck the trend, and offer boarding at cut-price rates. I'd wager the 'take-up' would still balance the books and offer a much better experience for all concerned. And all that from a position of pre-determined conviction rather than that of 'knee-jerking' to market forces. There isn't an independent school in the country that sets its fees level in that way. It's a risk, of course, but perhaps one worth considering. If the modern day-parent of independent schools wants independent day-education, then choose an independent day-school. If what is wanted is a boarding-school ethos – as a Day Pupil – then pay appropriately for it. Boarding parents who provide the underlying provisions should be rewarded with lower fees. Without them the boarding schools would not be the same. It's not about the money; it's about the regime and the conviction. And it is certainly not about 'class' (whatever that is today). Perhaps that's why I'm not a Headmaster today.

Recent surveys show that boarders like *'friends, activities, facilities, free time, learning independence and food'. They dislike 'homesickness, rules and school food'*. The homesickness passes (and it is better experienced at age ten than age eighteen). The rules are actually good for them (they just don't know it yet). And whenever have you heard of a child who likes school food?

But, don't take my word for it.

I offer you not 'Onemey', but Toomeys. Gabriel Toomey is son of Benedict, both of whom boarded at All Hallows, the former from 2008-2013, and the latter from 1975-1981. Son Gabriel remembers *being away from home and family is never easy* but even 'the worst of times' would offer up contrasting consolations such as midnight Fire Alarms when the dark, disorientated winter nights would be offset by dark, disorientated winter nights with *"a duvet wrapped over my whole body walking through the snow!"* which conjures up images and realities of magic and memory not easily forgotten. Gabriel realised that by focusing *"on those parts of your character that make you happy you receive recognition for this and can then be placed in a much better and responsible position within the school and become a role model for younger pupils. This 'wisdom' is really only the person you already are"* but might not know it yet. Gabriel once hoped that the school *"would shut down for a whole year"* when he was *"always in trouble"* but *"shortly after this period I realised that I actually loved All Hallows"*. Perhaps he was one of those Communion-wine secret guzzlers! You have to live it. Gabriel (no doubt inspired by Dickens) finished by saying that *"if asked to give advice to the junior pupils I would use the line 'we had everything before us, we had nothing before us' as a way of getting my point across"*. He also says that his *"real despair has always been not being chosen to play for the 'A's in hockey when I thought I should have been"*. Games Masters and pupils please note: Gabriel went on to become Captain of the Hockey 1st XI. Mind you, he thought that his appointment as Head Sacristan was *"probably my biggest opportunity"*. If a 'roughtie-toughtie', poetic, games-playing, boarder can assert in the year 2013 that his 'biggest opportunity' was his appointment as Head Sacristan, it is possible one can say that there is not much wrong with All Hallows or boarding or Gabriel Toomey.

Step forward Toomey Père. Benedict has been employed as a Games Coach and Boarding School Master at All Hallows in recent years and has brought to both roles the stamp of his own boarding experiences and that of his military career. He loved his time at All Hallows, as a boy, and actually agrees with his son that one is responsible, oneself, for making something out of life's experiences. Benedict remembers bare wooden floorboards, the red-lipsticked, Chanel smell of matron, detentions in the Library, being gated, being thrown out of the Scouts for misuse of a catapult, and sleeping regularly in St Ignatius dormitory which was reserved for naughty boys. He remembers fondly Paul and Jean Ketterer for their homely attentions, and, Paul, in particular, for his prowess in throwing and catching balls via the slip cradle on the Library Lawn. Teachers like Eve Jackson feature strongly in his memory for her use of the abacus and smelling of peppermint and dispensing smarties (once they had been counted) and he puts down his love of mathematics to her interventions and guidance. Similarly, Greg Jones, the science teacher, impressed with his skills in drawing and labelling and Benedict took those skills himself into his Biology A-Level exams. Benedict recalls PFJK saying on more than one occasion: *'You Boy! Buck up and pipe down!'* (he has tried to follow that advice ever since). He does not ever recall being bullied (apart from the odd games master or two) and remains through and through an All

Hallows and Downside boy. Experiences can be very different, even in the same school, at the same time, but there is something very fundamental and persuasive in the Toomey belief – father and son – that if it is true '*we had everything before us, we had nothing before us*', it largely depends on oneself what is gained and lost.

Some Conclusions

As one draws towards conclusions, one thinks that this book probably needs an Index but publication deadlines loom and that may be a task for a later time or never. For those former pupils and teachers looking for a name-check, and for any educationalists, social historians, poets or priests wanting to consider - and possibly challenge - any assertions, the references you would otherwise have looked for in an Index can be found between page 1 and page 315; in other words, you'll have to read the book (and you might just appear in one of the Appendices!)

And so the dance goes on because life goes on. And there will always be a need for education and for schools; one cannot 'dis-invent' something. But times and circumstances change. That much is certain just from a casual reading of this story. And those charged with the responsibility of managing All Hallows Preparatory School today – and all those whose vested interests remain linked to its continued success – should remember, that, actually, nothing remains for ever and that "the lone and level sands stretch far away". Looking back, from a perspective in a fast-moving world where 'change' is a currency perhaps stronger than ever before, it is easy to reflect nostalgically and in a somewhat superior fashion on the ministrations of those who have gone before. I have fallen into this trap myself, I fear. But permanence is a chimera. Education, or more precisely the right to education for all, is a relatively recent phenomenon in this country and it was only in the spirit of the great Reform Bills of the nineteenth-century and the development of a governmental mind-set that gradually, almost reluctantly, took on responsibility for its citizens' health, welfare, working conditions and rights – including education – that schools began to flourish. One of our local villages, Downhead, with its own interesting history well-documented in a fascinating and enticing booklet entitled '*Downhead – Landscape of Distinction*', edited by Penny Stokes and produced in collaboration with Mendip District Council, has some useful anecdotal stories that link in with the point I am making about growth and change and permanency. And there are further connections in the persons of Fran and Steve Britten (who contributed significantly to the research for the material contained within the book by Penny Stokes through their Shute Farm studios offering such inspiration to so many) since they are parents of former pupils at All Hallows. The Downhead Village School, alas, is a school no more but its building survives as a private dwelling on a bend in the road admired by all who drive past. It was built as a school in 1859 as an endowment from the 1st Viscount Portman who, like many other benefactors of the time, felt a duty to educate voluntarily the masses, even if it was left to the religious institutions – in this case the Anglicans and the Non-Conformists between them – to equip, maintain and appoint the teachers. In order to manage these tasks such organisations needed to gift grants on application from local vicars which actually increased pressure on the schools since this introduced, by degrees, an element of accountability. One presumes it is at this developing point that Truant Officers became the vogue since schools were granted financial aid on the basis of the number of pupils attending, so pressure was created to entice the working community to send its children to school when they might otherwise be working in the fields or at home. In the case of Downhead School, it is reported that puddles filled the playground, windows were cracked, lavatories dirty, drains blocked and heating inadequate, and yet, even right up until its closure in 1921, the Inspectors were recording favourable comments about its identity as a centre of learning. The point of the anecdote is to underline the transitory nature of things despite the efforts of good people, committed in a common cause. Sometimes, 'events, dear boy, events' just take their course. The Church, similarly, (interestingly, from our point of view, began life as St Nicholas' but was re-named 'All Saints' after significant restoration towards the end of the nineteenth century) went through hesitant and unpromising times when the buildings were neglected and the resident population dwindled or attended other churches in the locality. It, too, eventually lost its status as a parish church - as recently as 1981. And, just to complete the story of three Downhead buildings, the Methodist Chapel, most recently de-commissioned and used as a studio base for Mercer Design (whose consultant and professional support of All Hallows has made the production of this book possible) had enjoyed a successful life-story of its own from about 1865 with, initially, thriving numbers, then a diminishing and aging group of members, until its closure in 1973, notwithstanding a final flourish of interest and increased income towards its demise. I draw these strands together in an attempt to show how circumstances, institutions and people are inter-connected in surprisingly familiar ways, with shared difficulties, similar stories and variously different fortunes, although the reality of risk and the certainty of change are never far from people's minds.

Education, education, education...the rule of three...seven multiple intelligences...seven characteristics of a catholic school...Facts! Facts! Facts!... Reading, Writing, 'Rithmetic...bible, latin and the cane...we all fall into this trap – looking for the wisdoms of an age articulated in the memorable phrase, that often drops simply into a platitude, at once unforgettable and fatuous. Sound-bites that neither sound not bite, purporting to offer insight but merely straining the horizons, bringing no comfort save that of immediacy, no legacies, no convictions, no direction, no inspiration. We have to be comfortable with our own dispensations and with the way we articulate our convictions. Too many educationalists have a kind of vision but they cannot see. *"Too many Headmasters talk to their pupils about God when they should talk to God about their pupils"* said Dr Giles Mercer, Headmaster of Prior Park College, when he was Chairman of the Catholic Independent Schools Conference. They articulate without clarity. They attempt to persuade without conviction and they lead without leadership. Convictions come from the heart not the mind. And what lies at the heart of education? You and me. If All Hallows has a wider story, and a future, it lies not in the word 'hallows' but in the word 'all'; as in for *all* the 'saints'.

But it is easy to become seduced by the ideals and the soundbites. Easy to be unreasonably inspired – possibly in INSETs (but I doubt it) – into subscribing superficially into a mission statement. I prefer to return to an earlier theme of forgiveness. Schools, like life, should embrace forgiveness and accept, even welcome, the 'Angels with Dirty Faces'.[119] The wholesomeness of aspiration must be married to the flawed nature of humanity; mavericks, martyrs, saints and sinners make up our human story and, from the mix, arises prevailing goodness. As Oscar Wilde once said: '*All Saints have a past and all Sinners have a future*'.

I have referenced before in this book that some monastic views at Downside might well assert that educationalists there are preparing the pupils for death – and whilst I know what they mean - I prefer the more immediate and possibly more comforting notion, at least in the short-term, that we are preparing our pupils for life. Perhaps it is all one in the end but the manner in which our vocation is expressed is important even if the message is actually the same. One of the characteristics of living and working in a boarding school is the peripheral and core manifestation of life. Children are everywhere: working, playing, breathing, running, living. Flying balls regularly winging past one's windows – and sometimes through them (perhaps those are the ones PFJK always told me to keep my eyes on); crying, laughing and shouting heard more often, one imagines, than in your average workplace; encountering at every turn an incessant noise that is background, middle-ground and foreground (apart, that is, from those brief times of examinations and prayer - two silent pursuits, perhaps, not altogether unrelated, at least in the hearts and minds of schoolchildren); to-ing and fro-ing constantly pounding the walkways to equal the footfalls of any busy city; flashing colours shimmering and shining; the donning of different clothes several times a day to accommodate the changing needs and moods of the moment; the lowing of patient cows; the cawing of irritable rooks; the smelling of country aromas; falling rain - just falling and falling; sparkling moments of genuine epiphany streaming like departing trains; darkening moments of despair; large-looming doubts and convictions on the colouring canvas; wavering resolutions and the vying of broken promises, steadfast faith and honest endeavour; reverberating successes and fortifying failures applying in almost equal

---

[119] For those of a certain age, when you read the phrase '*Angels with Dirty Faces*' you will think of the film starring James Cagney and Humphrey Bogart, directed by Michael Curtiz, who went on to direct both stars, independently, in '*Yankee Doodle Dandy*' and '*Casablanca*' – that's some c.v. already! It's a bit like hearing the answer given by James Joyce to the question "What did you do in the War?" which was "Oh, I wrote '*Ulysses*'". By some serendipitous neatness, the film was made in 1938, the year All Hallows was founded, and although its synopsis as "*a priest tries to stop a gangster corrupting a group of street kids*" is **not** a metaphor for our school story, and even though the film is set in New York rather than England, characters like Soapy and Swing and Bim and Pasty and Crab could well have featured, under different names, in different times, with similar fates, in the history of All Hallows. Perhaps sentimentally, perhaps with a touch of deliberate heroic pathos, the film ends predictably unpredictable but watch it if you haven't!

measure; the ringing of school-bells like relentless watchmen (approximately eleven thousand in the course of the year); pulsing rhythms and the sun also rising out of the woods and sinking over West Cranmore beyond St Bartholomew's Church.

And Gerard Manley Hopkins' lines permeate through the memory.... *"The world is charged with the grandeur of God / it will flame out, like shining from shook foil / it gathers to a greatness"* - and despite our habitual forgetfulness – *"There lives the dearest freshness deep down things / and though the last lights off the black West went / oh, morning, at the brown brink eastwards, springs / because the Holy Ghost over the bent / world broods with warm breast and ah! Bright wings!"* This is inscape. This is the 'thingness' that makes things what they are. This is the uniqueness of the individuals who make up the All Hallows Story.

I cannot think of a nobler profession since all others develop from the parent that is education and we are all teachers - aren't we? – and we have all, certainly, been children and *"of such is the kingdom of heaven."* Teachers are lucky. Confucius[120] said *"Choose a job you love, and you will never have to work a day in your life"* and he knew a thing or two.

It has been said recently in a reputable Sunday newspaper's Books section that 'historians are dependent on their sources'. One refutes this statement, of course. Such a glib dismissal of other valid, contributory influences like bias, fairness, insight, reflection, style, interpretation, perspective, humanity, and, dare one say it, wisdom, is contrary to the evidence of experience. Many 'history books' come alive, and provide fresh meaning to events, without necessarily becoming solely reliant on their sources; this process goes well beyond revisionism. It is my hope that this book offers much more than the evidence of its sources. There are wants and there are needs and there are musts in every walk of life...and there are might-have-beens... but all one can hope is that life really is unfolding as it should and that one has played one's part with sufficient integrity and service to others.

William Bellasis, the former pupil mentioned earlier, believes that All Hallows fostered and nourished, as life-lessons in the 1940s, *"Independence, interdependence, leadership, concern for others, generosity, orderliness, hard work, prayerfulness and liturgical sense"*. We'd be happy to think that those virtues remain in place today even if the modern youth's grasp of orderliness and liturgical sense are not as strong, perhaps, as they once were. Abbot Aidan Bellinger of Downside believes that the Benedictine philosophy has been translated into Downside education through *welcome, reverence and humility, listening, teaching and learning, personal discipline, stewardship of gifts, concern for the individual and building communion;* I repeat here that an All Hallows' interpretation of our mission offers the following identification of Catholic characteristics in schools: *a recognition of uniqueness, a culture of forgiveness, a pattern of service, a sense of sacramentality, a place of prayer, a beacon of Christian witness, a world of community.*

---

[120] Confucius, (551-479 BC), Chinese teacher and philosopher, championed ancestor worship, family loyalty and respect of elders by children! His *Golden Rule* has Christian echoes: *"Treat others as one would like others to treat oneself"*

The final words fall, of course, to Francis Hunter Rawdon Dix, born in 1899, who asserted in the 1988 Jubilee Appeal Brochure, that *"Life is about growth through change with the essential spirit persisting.... so that in the future pupils in their thousands may experience those blessings which previous generations have enjoyed"*.

Enough. (For now).

Appendices

Appendix A – Hymn: *For All The Saints*

Words: Francis Dix 1899-1983
Music: Roger Bevan 1918-1998

Omnes Sancti obsecramus
Liberi qui vos amamus
 ut pro nobis nunc oretis
Et amalis liberates

Omnes Sanctos salutemus
Omnibus candelam demus
Per vos melius vivamus
Laboremus et ludamus;
Simus omnibus benigni
Tandem caelo simus digni

Et vos liberi eratis
Qui in caelo habitatis;
Similes ut simus vobis
Sancti subvenite nobis.

Appendix B – Chair of Governors

The full Governing Body and the Finance Committee, as well as the occasional sub-group like the Development Committee and the Appeals Committee, have all been fully supportive of the Headmasters and the school in plotting the way forward. The Governors have also been grateful for the wisdom and advice offered by educational consultants, who have sat on the Board, in the persons of external Head Teachers like Abbot Passmore, Sister Campion, Pat Cartwright, Jeremy Goulding, Giles Mercer, Dom Anthony Sutch, and Dom Leo Maidlow Davis, as well as being extraordinarily well-served by another former Headmaster, Richard Arnold-Jones, who had maintained the role of Vice Chairman for so many years, filling in, on occasions, as Chairman from time to time.

Lord Howard of Penrith	1962-1968
George Simey	1968-1977
John Jackson	1977-1982
Tom Barrington	1982-1989
Sue Goodson	1989-1996
Chris Dick	1996-2005
Patrick Nixon	2005-2012
Mike Russell	2012-

Appendix C – Head Prefects

1938	--	1976	John Maher & Alexander Dick
1939	Peter White	1977	Sebastian Watkins & James Jenkins
1940	John Halfhide	1978	Siobhan Walsh
1941	Robin.Couchman	1979	Dominic O'Hagan
1942	Maurice Coreth	1980	Mark Wood
1943	NO APPOINTMENT	1981	Andrew Bidgood
1944	John Arbuthnott	1982	Charles Inness
1945	John Ford	1983	Niamh O'Connor
1946	Alexander Craig-Mooney & Patrick Mullin	1984	Keri Glenday
1947	Francis Cochrane / Peter Keily / Martin Reynolds	1985	Alexander Clothier
1948	John Lavery / Larry O'Callaghan	1986	Rachel Kerr
1949	Hugh Arbuthnott	1987	James Hooper
1950	Christopher Amery	1988	NO APPOINTMENT*
1951	Timothy Melhuish	1989	Margaret Lang
1952	John Hickman	1990	Neil Heffernan
1953	AnthonyAddison / Jonathan Green-Armytage	1991	Bernard Franklin
1954	Erik Pearse	1992	Meriel Buxton
1955	Christopher Barrington / Nigel Hollis	1993	Stuart Thompson
1956	John de Fontblanque	1994	Julia Brown
1957	Philip Channer	1995	Victoria Thompson
1958	John Hooley	1996	Eleanor McNulty
1959	Anthony de Lestang / Tom Barrington	1997	Polly Reeve
1960	Nicholas Carver	1998	Laura Renouf
1961	Peter Prout/Christopher Martin	1999	Ian Mollison
1962	Michael Ralli	2000	Stephanie Newmarch
1963	Martin Heddy	2001	Oliver Lombard
1964	Martin O'Leary / Paul Goalen	2002	Rosie MacKean
1965	Christopher Fenton / William Fricker	2003	Peter Januszewski
1966	Martin Beach / Anthony O'Reilly	2004	Freddie Mercer & Katherine Haggett
1967	David Coffey / Hugh Ostocke	2005	George Ellwood & Megan Opie
1968	Christopher Mortimer / David Walker	2006	Sam Harris & Gigi Isola
1969	Geoffrey Hamilton-Jones / Joe Raad	2007	Wilfed Neville & Anya Boulton
1970	Peter Griffiths	2008	George Stonehouse & Victoria Keeling
1971	Mark Pettitt / Dominic Wilson / Simon Pringle	2009	Charles Channer & Tilly Compton-Welstead
1972	Benedict Burke	2010	Luke Holland & Justina Alexandroff
1973	Guy Barker & John Cierach	2011	Joshua Bex & Isabelle Weir
1974	Felicity Finalyson & Justin O'Hagan	2012	Luke Freely & Xanthe Gash
1975	Charles Rickards	2013	George Williams & Lucy Pughe-Morgan

* In the year 1988, suggested by the Staff, it was decided to make no appointment and 'spread out' the responsibilities throughout the year group on the grounds that all pupils should aspire to leadership and the status of role model; 1989 saw a return to the previous tradition which has remained in place subsequently with the pattern, since 2004, of a Head Boy and a Head Girl

Appendix D – Awards

* = Internal Award in first-term of senior school
**= Double Award
***= Triple Award

1942
Robin Couchman — Beaumont

1943 - 1944
No Scholarships Awarded

1945
Adrian Pettitt — Dartmouth
John Arbuthnott — Dartmouth

1946
Antony Reavell — Malvern
John Ford — Dartmouth
Alexander Craig-Mooney — Downside
Michael Corbould — Ampleforth

1947
Francis Cochrane — Ampleforth

1948
John Lavery — Downside
Henry Bodenham — Beaumont
Martin Allen — Downside
Geoffrey Shaw — Dartmouth
Peter Brittan — Dartmouth

1949
Larry V O'Callaghan — Downside

1950
Brian P Kelly — Downside
Mark Lavery — Downside
Hugh Arbuthnott — Ampleforth
Brian P Butler — Downside
Christopher Amery — Marlborough
Richard George — Downside

1951
Timothy Melhuish — Downside

1952
Nicholas O'Farrell — Downside
Auberon Waugh — Downside
Christopher Cochrane — Ampleforth
Paul Green-Armytage — Downside
James Young — Ampleforth
Patrick Durnford — Douai

1953
Martin Powys-Lybbe — Downside

1954
Jocelyn Feilding — Downside
Jonathan Green-Armytage — Downside
David Corbould — Downside
Thomas Atthill — Downside
Timothy Coffey — Ampleforth
Anthony Pearson — Downside
Robin Grant — Ampleforth

1955
Anthony Gilroy — Downside
John Gilbert — Ampleforth
Erik Pearse — Ampleforth
Richard Cuthbertson** — Ampleforth

1956
Martin Dillon — Downside
John Jackson — Downside
Christopher Barrington — Downside
Julian Mathias — Downside

1957
Peter Feint — Downside
Peter Young — Ampleforth
Duncan Mara — Downside
Nicholas Fitzgerald — Downside
John De Fonblanque — Ampleforth

1958

Philip Channer	Downside
Hon Philip Howard	Ampleforth
Nicholas Bourke	Downside
Paul Burden	Beaumont
Patrick Nixon	Downside

1959

Marek Gawel	Downside
Anthony De Lestang	Downside
Andrew Crocker	Downside
Peter Mackenzie-Smith	Downside
Anthony Trafford	Downside
John Hooley	Downside

1960

Simon Burt	Downside
James Fitzgerald	Downside
Peter Stone	Downside

1961

Peter Prout	Downside
James Blunt	Downside
Gervase Clarence-Smith	Ampleforth
Jocelyn Crocker	Downside
James Fitzgerald	Downside
Alistair Crombie	Downside
Robert Leonard	Downside
Guy Otten	Downside

1962

Timothy Davidson	Downside
Leonard Egan	Downside
Christopher Martin	Downside
John O'Dowd-Booth	Downside
Hon David Howard	Ampleforth

1963

Peter Woodford	Downside
Martin Heddy	Ampleforth
Robert Colledge	Downside

1964

Martin O'Leary	Downside
Stephen Bankes	Eton
Damian Trafford	Downside

1965

Thomas Dunn	Ampleforth

1966

Julian Birkett	Downside
Hon William Howard**	Ampleforth

1967

Nicholas Iddon	Aldenham
Patrick Nixon	Downside

1968

Edward Clarence-Smith	Ampleforth
George Roffe-Silvester	Downside
Barnaby Woodham	Downside

1969

Bernard Trafford**	Downside
Peter Curling	Millfield

1970

(No Scholarships awarded)

1971

Peter Hyde	Millfield

1972

Simon Pringle	Worth

1973

Nicholas Britten	Downside

1974

John Cierach	Downside
Brian Pote-Hunt	Downside
William Farquharson	Harrow
Jonathon Whatley	Douai

1975

Kevin Ceurvorst	Downside
Justin O'Hagan	Belmont

1976

Liam Davies	Downside
John Maher	Downside
Jonathan Schütz	Downside

1977

Liam Davies*	Downside
Dominic Fitzpatrick	Downside
Sarah Maher	Cheltenham

1978

Guy Barry	Westminster
Paul Thompson	Downside
Gavin Ruddy*	Marlborough

The Cherry Jumpers

1979	
James Gotto	Ampleforth
Henry Camilleri	Downside
Kate Watson-Smyth	Christ's Hospital
Christopher Mackenzie	Christ's Hospital
Mary Kingston	Sherborne
Richard Rawlins	Christ's Hospital

1980	
Richard Neill	Clifton
Jamie Thompson	Downside
Iain Heath	Downside
Oliver Wingrove	St. Edmund's Ware
Mark Norman	Downside
Andrew Mackenzie	Oratory

1981	
David Monaghan	Christ's Hospital
Charles Jackson	Downside
Jane Seaward	Bryanston
Stephen Harrow	Douai
Jennifer Browne	Millfield
Redmond Walsh	Douai
Mark Down	Sherborne

1982	
Benjamin Monaghan	Christ's Hospital
Joanna Horgan	Millfield
Spencer Jeffery	King's Bruton
Andrew Jackson	Millfield
Andrew Bidgood	Ampleforth
Clare Jackson	Millfield

1983	
Christopher Thompson**	Downside
Christopher Ludlam	Marlborough
Anna-Maria Garcia	St. Antony's-Leweston
Thomas Ellis	Millfield
Simon Goodson	Douai
Kate England*	The Royal, Bath

1984	
Timothy Millard	Bryanston
Oliver Steele-Perkins	Millfield
Mark Reckless	Marlborough
Julian Wastie	Millfield

1985	
Juliet Hall	St. Leonards-Mayfield
Edward Moorhouse	Sherborne
Hugo Jelly	Downside
James De Vivenot	Sherborne
Richard Kenyon	Downside

1986	
Emily Johnson-Jones	Millfield
David Pryce	Oratory
Hugo Robinson	Sherborne

1987	
Franz Ketterer	Downside
Vanessa Walker	Clifton
Claire Greenrod**	Millfield

1988	
Thomas Pryce	Oratory
Andrew Batt*	Downside
Kathryn Johnson-Jones	Millfield
Joanna Tench	Mayfield

1989	
Victoria Kenyon	St. Antony's-Leweston
George Allardice	St. Leonards, Oxford
Eleanor Llewellyn	St. Antony's-Leweston
Jessica Halliday-Waddell	Kingswood
Hugh Parkinson	Wells Cathedral School
Michael Greenrod	Millfield
Francis Molony*	Downside

1990	
Jeremy Kenyon	Downside
Mark Elliott	Dauntsey's
George Allardice*	St. Edward's, Oxford
Paul Gadsden	Millfield
Frith Chamberlain	Millfield
Zoe House	Millfield
Richard Dalgety	Millfield

1991	
Robert Bruce	Oratory
Neil Heffernan	Clifton
Tamasin Cline*	St. Antony's-Leweston
Thomas Fysh**	Downside
Claire Brown	Mayfield

1992	
Gawain Lagnado	Downside
James Greenrod	Millfield
Nichola Brown	Millfield
Victoria Lomas	Millfield
Toby Chamberlain	Millfield
Thomas Blathwayt	Prior Park

Appendices

1993

Anna Boyd	Bruton School for Girls
Anna Grundy	The Royal Bath
Daniel Britten	King's Bruton
Seamus McNulty	Downside
Duncan Brown	Stonyhurst
Felix Moreno	Ampleforth
Meriel Buxton	Sherborne
Miranda Pountney	St. Mary's Shaftesbury
Honour Conroy	Prior Park
James Gay	King's Bruton

1994

Hugh Carter	Downside
David Holiday	Sherborne
Giles Dawnay	Downside
Jonathan Lambe	Ampleforth
Oliver Freeman	Downside
Stuart Thompson	King's Bruton

1995

Julia Brown	Millfield
Zoe Parkinson	St. Mary's Shaftesbury
Luke Fenton	King's Bruton
Sarah Price	Canford
Peter Grant*	Winchester
Sarah Roberts	Canford
Peter Moxey	Royal Hospital School

1996

Benedict Carter	Downside
Simon Marks*	Prior Park
Michael Davis	Sidcot
Sarah Melvin	Dauntsey's
Katie Edwards	Kingswood
Patricia Moxey**	Royal Hospital School
Katy Holiday	St. Antony's-Leweston
Victoria Thompson	Prior Park
Sarah King	Millfield

1997

Meg Barne	Rendcombe College
Charles Hare	Prior Park
Jim Barne	St George's, Windsor
Rosemary Henderson	Wells Cathedral School
Carrie Bird*	Prior Park
Genevieve Huntley	St Leonard's Mayfield
Clare Blathwayt	Prior Park
Sarah Jenkins	Prior Park
Jordan Evans	King's College, Taunton
Eleanor McNulty	Badminton
Joseph Fenton	King's, Bruton
James Nicholson	Downside
Jamie Habershon	
Millfield	

1998

Matthew Cross	Downside
Kate Moxey**	Royal Hospital School
Andrew Edwards	Prior Park
Olivia Silk	St. Mary's, Shaftesbury
Emma Habershon	Millfield
Aaron White	Blundell's

1999

Timothy Ball	Downside
Katherine Roberts	Canford
Rachel Daniels	Royal Hospital School
Rosalyn Shephard	King Edward's, Bath
Charlotte Lombard	St. Mary's, Shaftesbury
Anna Walker	Dauntsey's
Vicki Patel	King's, Bruton

2000

Harry Agius	Downside
Ian Mollison	Downside
Amy Chan	Prior Park
William Rawlins	Warminster
Eve Harvey	Taunton School
Anna Scott	Bruton School for Girls
James Humphries	Prior Park
Sebastian Sorapure	King's School, Bruton
Lucy Loughlin	St. Antony's-Leweston
Caroline Veitch	Red Maids
Oliver Mellotte	Downside

2001

Hannah Forshaw	Prior Park
Belen Tejada	Prior Park
Sophie Keefe	Prior Park
Celia Asquith	St. Mary's Shaftesbury
Isobel Neville	Prior Park
Josh Scouller	Downside
Stephanie Newmarch	Prior Park
Adam Sealey	Wells Cathedral Schooll
Grainne Sweeney	Prior Park

2002

Amy Bishop	Prior Park
Alistair Mills**	King's School, Bruton
Nicholas Hampson	Wells Cathedral School
Bob Morgan-Jones	Oratory
Jack Harrington	Downside
Harry Smith**	Prior Park
Michael Jones	Prior Park
Charles Willis	King's School, Bruton
William Leigh	Downside
Edward Johnstone	Downside
Oliver Lombard	Downside

2003

Gus Allen	Millfield
Jack Rawlins	Prior Park
Matthew Budd	Prior Park
Kit Scouller	Downside
Henry Davis	Ampleforth
Jamie Sharp	King's, Bruton
Olivia Eadie	Sherborne Girls
Henry Spencer	Sherborne Boys
Daniel Forshaw	Prior Park
Thomas Veitch	Queen Elizabeth Hospital, Bristol
Hettie Hobbs	Prior Park
Dominic Watson	Downside
Barty Isola	Downside
Charles Willis	King's, Bruton
Rosie MacKean**	Prior Park
Thomas Yardley	Prior Park
Jack Opie	Prior Park

2004

Isabel Asquith	St. Mary's, Shaftesbury
Johnny Neville	Sherborne
George Howlett	Prior Park
Zoe Strickland	Prior Park
Peter Januszewski	Prior Park
Tomas Ukleja	Prior Park
Eduardo Miñon	Sherborne
Tom Wilkinson	Prior Park

2005

Isabella Alexandroff**	Downside
Oliver Nias	Downside
Oliver Aplin	Downside
William Ormerod	Downside
Michael Berridge	Downside
Sophie Parker	Godolphin
Thomas Doe	Downside
Luke Pickthall**	King's, Bruton
Katherine Haggett	Badminton
Katherine Rogers	King's, Bruton
Emily Haggett	Badminton
Harriet Sasada	Downside
Dominic Huntley	Downside
Annabel Staib	St Anthony's
Emily Jennings	Downside
Saul Thompson	Wells Cathedral School
Matthew McRae	Downside
Harriet Veitch	Red Maids'
Freddie Mercer**	Downside
Serafina Vick**	Prior Park
William Morrison***	Clifton College

2006

Lily Bennett	Downside
Hugo Morris Adams	Wells Cathedral School
Emma Burgess**	King's Bruton
Camilla Munro	St. Mary's Shaftesbury
Helena Constable Maxwell**	Prior Park
MeganOpie***	Truro School
George Ellwood	Sherborne Boys
Claudia Temple-Pedersen	St. Mary's Shaftesbury
Katherine Eyles**	Prior Park
Rebecca Turner	Bruton School for Girls
Clara Hughes	Prior Park
Briony Venn	St. Mary's Shaftesbury
Hugh Jennings**	Downside
Kirstie Wombwell	Malvern College
Philippa Loakes***	Downside
Madeleine Kelly	Prior Park

Appendices

2007

Robert Berridge**	Downside
Charlie Morris-Adams	Wells Cathedral School
William Botsford**	Downside
Florence Munro	St. Antony's-Leweston
Jack Cadbury	King's School, Bruton
Finian Orme	Wells Cathedral School
Lily Fattorini**	Canford School
Charlie Ormerod	Downside
Sasha Gracie***	Prior Park
Henry Stonehouse	King's School, Bruton
Samuel Harris	Downside
Rosanna Temple-Pedersen	St. Mary's, Shaftesbury
Lucy Howlett**	Prior Park
Gabrielle Tomlinson	Roedean School
Jessica Hubner	Wells Cathedral School
Joel Thompson	Wells Cathedral School

2008

Anya Boulton**	Prior Park
Henry Bruce-Jones**	Downside
Laura Eyles	Prior Park
Honor Gilbertson	Downside
Mollie Hunt	Prior Park
George Robson	Canford School
Wilfred Neville	Prior Park
Elliot Rutter	King's, Bruton
Hamish Pearson	Prior Park
Theresa Constable Maxwell**	Prior Park
Edward Horler	Millfield
Philippa Jalland	Ampleforth
Meg Stride	Bruton School for Girls
Edward Botsford	Downside
Poppy Weir**	Downside
Nico Alexandroff	Wells Cathedral School
Isobel Johnstone	Downside
Amelia Parker	Marlborough
Ellie White	Downside

2009

Isabel Munro	St. Mary's, Shaftesbury
Miles Ryall	Downside
Yasmeen Al Rumaithi	Millfield
Nicholas Gracie	Downside
Jessica Brown	Bruton School for Girls
Thomas Hughes	Downside
Lucy Slade	Redland High School for Girls
Thomas Ormerod	Downside
Max Dellwhite**	King's Bruton
Kirsten Russell	Downside
William White	Downside
Hugo Morgan	Downside

2010

Carla Kerslake	Warminster School
Amelia Burns	Downside
Tilly Compton-Welstead	St. Mary's Shaftesbury
Edward Henderson***	Dauntsey's School
Charlotte Rickards	St. Mary's Shaftesbury
Lucy Parker	Marlborough College
Cecilia Jennings	St. Mary's Shaftesbury
Tasie Morgan	Downside
Isabella Nunes Da Costa	St. Mary's Shaftesbury
Joe Morris-Adams	Wells Cathedral School
Anna Fohlmann	Prior Park
Cecilia Jennings	Downside
Lucy Boulton	Prior Park
Olivia Bruce-Jones	Downside
Alexander Fisken	Prior Park

2011

Justina Alexandroff	Wells Cathedral School
Milo McCloud	King's Bruton
William Brand-Lyons	Downside
Howie Phillips**	Prior Park
Rory Cadbury	King's School, Bruton
Sophie Sage	King's Bruton
Jack Ferguson Ray	Prior Park
Millie Smith	Prior Park
Joseph Fone	Wells Cathedral School
William Stoyle	Monkton
Guy Green	Downside
Michael Stride	King's Bruton
Miles Hackett	Clifton College
George Thackray	Downside
Luke Holland	Bryanston
Harry Travers	Downside
Freya Logan	Leweston
Lucinda Tucker	Prior Park

2012

Emily Ake	Wells Cathedral School
Edward McCabe**	Downside
Lucy Baldwin	Millfield
Heather O'Keefe	Downside
Joshua Bex	Radley College
Lily Piper	Bruton School for Girls
Fin Brown	King Edward's, Bath
Amelia Pughe-Morgan	Downside
Joe Cahill	Prior Park
Fiona Rundle	Kingswood School
Tom Channer	Ampleforth College
Cordelia Sheridan	Downside
Laura Hodges	The Royal School, Bath
Isabelle Weir**	Millfield
Isabel Jolliffe	Downside
Tom Williams	Wells Cathedral School
Daisy Mant**	King's Bruton

2013

Sam Abel	Dauntsey's
Daisy Holland***	Clifton College
Rupert Bayliss	Kingswood
Tom Hunt***	Marlborough
Joe Blain	Prior Park
Julia Jolliffe**	Prior Park
Arabella Burns	Downside
Kitty Mant	King's Bruton
Caitlin Cahill**	Prior Park
Poppy Marsh	Downside
Natalie Crowe	King's Bruton
Hugo Morgan	Kingwood
Olli B Eke	Clifton College
Oliver Nielson**	Downside
Tom Fone	Wells Cathedral School
Lindsay Pickett	Prior Park
Luke Freely	Downside
Abigail Rees-Jones	Clifton College
Xanthe Gash**	Downside
Eli Richards	Wells Cathedral School
Harry Gillingham	Downside
Leila Richards	Wells Cathedral School
Thomas Godwin	Downside
Harriet Wakelin	King's Bruton
Charlotte Gould	King's Bruton
Dulcie Spindler	Dauntsey's School
Elliot Gould**	Downside
Jack White	Downside
Georgia Heath	King's Bruton
Annie Wooler**	Clifton College

Appendix E – Priests

The following priests have provided important spiritual direction, pastoral support and/or religious education from Bognor Regis, Buckfast Abbey, the parish of Totnes, other Devon locations, the Downside Community, local Somerset parishes, Prior Park College, as well as from other places such as Ampleforth. Some have established a contact over many years and acted as principal Chaplains, others have visited just occasionally; all have contributed hugely to the character, ethos and identity of the school. Many are mentioned in the main body of the text. Many apologies for any omissions.

Father Hagan*
Father John Pedrick*
Father Laurence
Father Albert
Father Lawrence
Father Winfrid
Father Russell
Father John
Father Aelred
Father O'Leary
Father Cahill
Father Metcalfe*
Father Simon van Zeller
Father Alban Brooke
Father Mark Pontifix*
Father Edward Cruise
Father Willie Sharp S.J.
Father Benet Innes
Father Edwards
Father Thomas
Father Edmond

Father Arthur
Father Francis Little
Father Everard Faulkner
Father Wulfstan
Father Tomlinson
Father Aldhelm Dean
Father Nicholas Holman
Father Buckley
Father Hubert van Zeller
Father Denis Agius*
Father Carroll
Father Creech
Father Lavery*
Father Thomas Atthill
Father Edward Corbould
Father Langford
Father Luke Bell
Father Peter Cornwall
Father Barnaby Dowling
Father Philip Jebb
Father Raphael Appleby*

Father Anthony Sutch
Father Leo Maidlaw-Davis
Father Alexander George*
Father Daniel Rees*
Father Anselm
Father Boniface Hill
Father Roger Barralet*
Father Philip Thomas*
Monsignor Leyden
Abbot Wilfred Passmore
Abbot Charles Lombard
Abbot Richard Yeo
Abbot Aidan Bellinger
Bishop John of Plymouth
Bishop of Clifton Joseph Rudderham
Bishop of Clifton Mervyn
Bishop of Clifton Declan Lang
Cardinal Basil Hume

* Principal Chaplains

Appendix F – Matrons

Matrons receive an appendix of their own because there are few, if any, roles in a boarding school that command the same dubious honour accorded to them by staff floundering in a sea of indecision who, when encountering a problem they would rather not deal with, simply say "Go and see Matron". The list below includes 'Assistant Matrons' who might not have been fully qualified nursing sisters but, nevertheless, applied tourniquets and bedside manners when the need arose. *There's a medical problem – send for Matron; a discipline problem – send for Matron; a pastoral issue – send for Matron; a hamster has died – send for Matron; a Fire Alarm has gone off – send for Matron; the food is revolting – send for Matron; the children are revolting – send for Matron; the staff are revolting – send for Matron; a difficult parent has arrived – send for Matron; an unexpected visitor has arrived – send for Matron; there's an unexploded bomb on the front field – send for Matron; The Queen is in the Lobby – send for Matron.....*you get the picture.....we mere mortals salute you all.

Mrs Tivey
Miss Wilson
Miss Courtney
Miss Britt-Compton
Miss Badger
Miss Petre
Miss Godfrey
Miss Hunt
Miss Shoosmith
Mrs Young
Miss Russell
Miss Jones
Miss Phillips
Miss Britton
Miss Griffin
Miss Broad

Mrs Key
Miss Norman
Miss Sweetland
Mrs Watson-Smyth
Mrs March
Mrs Page
Miss Moule
Miss Murray
Miss Fooks
Mrs Tearle
Mrs Cambridge
Miss Creer
Miss Furnival
Miss Poffley
Miss Price
Miss Whitemore

Mrs Moxey
Mrs Davis
Miss Blakeley
Mrs Ellwood
Mrs O'Donnell
Mrs Loughlin
Mrs Duckworth
Mrs Mitchell
Mrs Cordon-Lloyd

(By the way, just as it's about time we had a female Head, it's about time, chaps, we had a male Matron)

Appendix G – Projects that didn't happen

All Hallows could have gone off in different directions at various times and could have developed systems, structures and facilities not currently in use. Some have been long discarded, some may yet come to fruition. It has been an education in itself to be reminded, or to learn for the first time, of such possible projects as I have researched and written this book. They include in no particular order:

- Extend the age range and academic provision upwards to GCSE
- Buy St James' Chapel and convert it into Changing Rooms
- Move the school to Bristol
- Build a new Swimming Pool
- Buy Home Farm adjacent to the Headmaster's House
- Build a new Dining Room
- Set up a Caravan Park around the Front Field
- Build Changing Rooms in the Old Spinney
- Turn the Old Chapel into Changing Rooms
- Convert the Junior Common Room opposite the Headmaster's House into a small Oratory in which the Blessed Sacrament could be reserved
- Convert Saints T-More, Andrew, Richard and David dormitories into Changing Rooms
- Create additional dormitory space and staff accommodation above the Old Carpentry Shop and Billiard Room
- Dispense the weekly Eucharist from the Gymnasium during the building of the Chapel
- Build a new free-standing Boarding Wing between the Cran and the Pet Room
- Put a Pets' Graveyard in The Spinney behind The Chapel
- Purchase more land on the other side of the Swimming Pool
- Move The Front Drive
- Build a two-storey extension to The Science Wing to house Design & Technology facilities
- Buy, or rent, a property in France
- Turn The Ketterer Wing into two laboratories to house Technical Drawing, CDT, Computing and Graphic Design Studios
- Enclose the Colonnade to expand the Art facilities (the Art Room was formerly in The Orangery)

- Build a Cricket Pavilion
- Build a Squash Court and Viewing Gallery on the back of the Sports Hall
- Sell off Scouts' Wood
- Appoint Two Headmasters to serve at the same time and share the job
- Turn the House and Grounds into a Theme Park (only this last one, I think, has been made up)

In the same vein, the title of this book could easily have ended up as any of the following: *Musing on an Exeter Platform; Saints Alive! ; Hallowed Grounds; School For Saints; School Tales; Tales From School; Telling Tales from School; School Days and Ways; Happiest Days of Our Lives; Class Acts; Growing Pains; Candle Days; Sainted Memories; Magic Tricks; Conjuring Rabbits; The Little Saints; Communion of Saints; Somebody Saints; Hallowed Be Thy Names; Songs of Innocence and Experience; Suffer Little Children; Children of the Future Age; Seen and (Not) Heard; Voices of Children; Schools of Thought; Original Sins; The Dancing Crane; Hallowed Halls; All Saints Days; Holy Ghosts; The Countless Host; Cherry Jerseys; The Red Jumpers.*

(I thank the Eke family who came up with the eventual title 'The Cherry Jumpers' during a car journey).

Appendix H – For All The Saints lyrics

"For All the Saints Who from Their Labours Rest"
by Bishop William Walsham How, 1823-1897

1.
For all the saints who from their labours rest,
Who Thee by faith before the world confess,
Thy name, O Jesus, be forever blest,
Alleluia! Alleluia!

2.
Thou wast their Rock, their Fortress, and their Might;
Thou, Lord, their Captain in the well-fought fight;
Thou, in the darkness drear, their one true Light.
Alleluia! Alleluia!

3.
Oh, may Thy soldiers, faithful, true and bold,
Fight as the saints who nobly fought of old
And win with them the victor's crown of gold.
Alleluia! Alleluia!

4.
O blest communion, fellowship divine,
We feebly struggle, they in glory shine;
Yet all are one in Thee, for all are Thine.
Alleluia! Alleluia!

5.
And when the strife is fierce, the warfare long,
Steals on the ear the distant triumph song,
And hearts are brave again, and arms are strong.
Alleluia! Alleluia!

6.
But, lo, there breaks a yet more glorious day;
The saints triumphant rise in bright array;
The King of Glory passes on His way.
Alleluia! Alleluia!

7.
From earth's wide bounds, from ocean's farthest coast,
Through gates of pearl streams in the countless host,
Singing to Father, Son, and Holy Ghost,
Alleluia! Alleluia!

8.
The golden evening brightens in the west;
Soon, soon, to faithful warriors cometh rest.
Sweet is the calm of Paradise the blest.
Alleluia! Alleluia!

Appendix I – The future

This page, of course, is blank and just waiting to be written....

Appendices